PSYCHOANALYTIC PSYCHOTHERAPY

The EFPP Book Series

Editor-in-Chief: Anne-Marie Schloesser

OTHER TITLES IN THE SERIES

Chief Editor: John Tsiantis

- *Countertransference in Psychoanalytic Psychotherapy with Children and Adolescents*
- *Supervision and its Vicissitudes*
- *Psychoanalytic Psychotherapy in Institutional Settings*
- *Psychoanalytic Psychotherapy of the Severely Disturbed Adolescent*
- *Work with Parents: Psychoanalytic Psychotherapy with Children and Adolescents*
- *Psychoanalysis and Psychotherapy: The Controversies and the Future*
- *Research on Psychoanalytic Psychotherapy with Adults*

Series Editors: Monica Lanyado and Didier Houzel

- *The Therapist at Work: Personal Factors Affecting the Analytic Process*
- *Invisible Boundaries. Psychosis and Autism in Children and Adolescents*
- *The Development of Consciousness: Psychoanalysis, Neuroscience and Child Development*
- *The Analytic Field: A Clinical Concept*
- *Play and Power*
- *Crossing Borders—Integrating Differences: Psychoanalytic Psychotherapy in Transition*
- *Assessing Change in Psychoanalytic Psychotherapy of Children and Adolescents*
- *Bearing Witness: Psychoanalytic Work with People Traumatized by Torture and State Violence*

PSYCHOANALYTIC PSYCHOTHERAPY

A Handbook

Edited by

Matthias Elzer and Alf Gerlach

Routledge
Taylor & Francis Group
LONDON AND NEW YORK

First published 2014 by
Karnac Books Ltd.

Published 2018 by Routledge
2 Park Square, Milton Park, Abingdon, Oxon OX14 4RN
711 Third Avenue, New York, NY 10017, USA

Routledge is an imprint of the Taylor & Francis Group, an informa business

British Library Cataloguing in Publication Data

A C.I.P. for this book is available from the British Library

ISBN: 9781780491196 (pbk)

Edited, designed and produced by The Studio Publishing Services Ltd
www.publishingservicesuk.co.uk
e-mail: studio@publishingservicesuk.co.uk

CONTENTS

ACKNOWLEDGEMENTS

The editors want to thank the colleagues who reworked their lectures: Irmgard Dettbarn (Berlin, Beijing), Ulrich Ertel (Frankfurt), Christine Gerstenfeld (Berlin), Stephan Hau (Stockholm), Klaus Kocher (Frankfurt), Wolfgang Merkle (Frankfurt), Hanni Scheid-Gerlach (Saarbrücken), Anne-Marie Schloesser (Göttingen), Joachim Rothhaupt (Darmstadt), Hermann Schultz (Frankfurt, Shanghai), and Michael Wolf (Frankfurt). We also express our thanks to the following organisations, which supported the publication with proof-reading: the German Psychoanalytic Association (DPV); the German Society for Psychoanalysis, Psychotherapy, Psychosomatics and Depth Psychology (DGPT), Breuninger Foundation.

Many thanks also to Gisela Sippel (Germany, Botswana), who read proofs of the English papers of the German lecturers, and to Oliver Rathbone and Rod Tweedy from Karnac for their friendly co-operation.

ABOUT THE EDITORS AND CONTRIBUTORS

Irmgard Dettbarn, PhD, is an academically qualified psychologist who studied psychology in Berlin and did her psychoanalytical training in Zürich and Berlin. She works in private practice in Berlin, and from 2007 to 2010 worked as an IPA training analyst in Beijing. She is a member of the German and of the International Psychoanalytic Association, and is a lecturer at the Karl Abraham Institute in Berlin.

Matthias Elzer, Prof. MD, is a specialist in psychiatry, psychotherapeutic medicine, psychotherapy, psychoanalysis, a group analyst, and a supervisor of Balint Groups and psychotherapy. He is a member of the German Psychoanalytic Association (DPV) and the International Psychoanalytic Association (IPA), Vice-president of the Frankfurter Psychoanalytisches Institut (FPI), professor of psychiatry, psychotherapy, and counselling at the University of Applied Sciences in Fulda, and a psychoanalyst in private practice. He has published in the field of psychoanalysis, psychotherapy, and health communication.

Ulrich Ertel is an academically qualified psychologist who studied psychology in Brussels and Marburg. From 1979 to 1993, he worked as a clinical psychologist and psychotherapist in different university hospital departments of psychiatry and psychotherapy, and since then has been in private psychoanalytic practice. He is a member of the German and International Psychoanalytic Association, a teacher at the Munich Institute for training in psychoanalytic treatment of psychosis, and has published in the field of supervision in psychiatric institutions, and psychotherapeutic treatment of psychosis.

Alf Gerlach, MD, is an academically qualified sociologist who studied sociology and medicine at the Universities Saarbruecken and Frankfurt am Main. From 1974 to 1986 he worked at the Department for Psychotherapy and Psychosomatics in the University Hospital of Frankfurt. Since 1986, he has worked in private practice; since 1992 in Saarbruecken. He has carried out research work in the field of mass hysteria in South China since 1983. He has been a lecturer in psychoanalytically orientated psychotherapy for the programme of the German–Chinese Academy for Psychotherapy since 1997. His scientific publications are on the subjects of clinical psychoanalysis and ethnopsychoanalysis. He is a member of the German Psychoanalytic Association and of the International Psychoanalytic Association, and a training analyst at the Psychoanalytic Institutes in Mainz and Saarbruecken. From 2001 until 2003, he was Chair of the German Society for Psychoanalysis, Psychotherapy, Psychosomatics and Depth Psychology (DGPT). He is a member of the China Committee of the International Psychoanalytic Association.

Christine Gerstenfeld, MD, studied medicine in Cologne, London, and New York, specialising in psychiatry, psychotherapy, and psychoanalysis. She is a training analyst of the German Psychoanalytic Society and of the International Psychoanalytic Association. She has publications about forensic psychiatry, Freud's work, and psychoanalysis and film to her name.

Stephan Hau, Professor, PhD, is an academically qualified psychologist who studied psychology at the universities in Giessen and Frankfurt. From 1991 to 2005, he was a research scholar at the Sigmund Freud Institute in Frankfurt (Research Institute for Psychoanalysis and its Applications) while working part-time in private practice. His scientific work is in the fields of (experimental) dream research and psychotherapy research. A member of the Swedish Psychoanalytical Association and of the International Psychoanalytical Association, from 2005 to 2009 he was an associate professor at the University of Linköping, Sweden, and since 2010 has been Professor of Clinical Psychology at the Department of Psychology, Stockholm University.

Klaus Kocher, MD, studied medicine at the university in Frankfurt, specialising in psychosomatic medicine and psychoanalysis. From 1990 to 1995, he was a clinical psychotherapist at the University Hospital for Psychiatry and Psychotherapy in Frankfurt. He is a member of the German and International Psychoanalytic Association, and has worked in private practice since 1990. He specialises in the field of clinical supervision and couple psychotherapy.

Wolfgang Merkle, MD, has been the Director of the Psychosomatic Clinic, Hospital zum heiligen Geist, Teaching Hospital of the University of Frankfurt (thirty inpatients, fifty day-clinic patients, eight pain complex therapy patients, outpatient clinic) since 1996. He is a psychoanalyst (IPA), a specialist in psychosomatic medicine and psychotherapy, and in psychiatry. He is also a specialist in pain therapy. He studied medicine in Ulm, and did his internship in the Psychiatry department, University of Ulm, and his dissertation in 1982 was on the subject of therapy in chronic cancer pain patients. He trained in psychoanalysis in Ulm and Stuttgart-Tübingen, and is senior physician in the psychosomatic department in Esslingen. He has publications about psychosomatic treatment of psychogenic pain, and family therapy of patients with psychogenic pain to his name.

Joachim Rothhaupt, MD, studied medicine in Frankfurt. From 1979 to 1986, he worked at the Department for Psychotherapy and Psychosomatics in the University Hospital of Frankfurt. Since 1986, he has worked in private practice in Frankfurt and Darmstadt as a specialist in psychotherapeutic medicine, psychoanalysis, and psychotherapy. He is a member of the German and International Psychoanalytic Association, and has publications in the field of theory and therapy of psychosomatic diseases and psychosis.

Hanni Scheid-Gerlach studied at Frankfurt University. She is an academically qualified psychologist and psychoanalyst in private practice in Frankfurt and, since 1992, in Saarbrücken. She is experienced in counselling for families and couples, in supervision for kindergarten staff, and counselling for women with breast cancer. She is a member of the German Psychoanalytic Society (DPG), and a lecturer at Saarländisches Institut für Psychoanalyse und Psychotherapie, Saarbrücken.

Anne-Marie Schloesser is an academically qualified psychologist, psychoanalyst, psychodrama therapist, and client-centred therapist. From 1975 to 1993, she worked at the Department for Medical Psychology at the University of Göttingen, and since then has been in private practice as psychoanalyst. She is a training and supervising analyst of the German Psychoanalytic Society (DPG) at the Lou Andreas Salome Institute, Goettingen, and of the IPA. From 1997 until 2001, she was Chair of the German Society for Psychoanalysis, Psychotherapy, Psychosomatics and Depth Psychology (DGPT), and is President of the European Federation for Psychoanalytic Psychotherapy (EFPP). She has scientific publications on psychology in the medical field and supervision in the field of forensic psychiatry to her credit, and is co-editor of several books on psychoanalytic topics. She is Editor-in-chief of Karnac's EFPP book series.

Hermann Schultz, MD, is a specialist in psychiatry, psychotherapy, psychosomatic medicine, and psychoanalysis, is a full member of the German and International Psychoanalytic Association, and an IPA interim training analyst. He worked for more than twenty-five years as a teacher and trainer in psychoanalytic and psychotherapeutic training, and also in child and adolescent psychotherapy (theory seminars, case supervision, psychoanalytic self-experience). From 1985 to 1994, he was head physician of a psychosomatic hospital. At present, he mainly works as a training analyst in IPA psychoanalytic training in Shanghai, as a teacher in the Chinese–German Training Courses for Psychoanalytic Psychotherapy, and in private practice as a psychoanalyst, psychotherapist, and supervisor. His publications are mainly in translations (Redlich & Freedman, *Theory and Practice of Psychiatry*; Kernberg, *Borderline Conditions and Pathological Narcissism*; Bellak & Small, *Short-Term Psychotherapy and Emergency Psychotherapy*; Zhang Tianbu, *Zhuxiang and Resistance*). He is studying Chinese language and culture (basic level).

Michael Wolf, Prof., PhD is an academically qualified psychologist. He worked for ten years at the Psychiatric Clinic, Offenbach and at the Department for Psychotherapy and Psychosomatics of the Centre for Psychiatry at the University Clinic, Frankfurt. He has been in private practice as a psychoanalyst, psychotherapist, and supervisor since 1993, and at the same time has been Professor of Psychology, Counselling and Health Promotion at the University of Applied Sciences in Fulda. He has published in the field of psychoanalytic concepts, psychoanalytical social psychology, and applied psychoanalysis, particularly on the subjects of supervision, organisation, and leadership. He is a Member of the Frankfurt Psychoanalytic Institute, the German Psychoanalytical Association, the International Psychoanalytical Association, and the International Society for the Psychoanalytic Study of Organizations.

SERIES EDITOR'S PREFACE

Within the EFPP book series, this handbook, with its, at first sight, sober subject matter, is something very special.

Starting from their work as co-ordinators of the ongoing training courses in Shanghai, the editors, Matthias Elzer and Alf Gerlach, have brought together fundamental papers on the theory and practice of psychodynamic psychotherapy that were generated and discussed there and then reworked for this volume.

The book provides the reader with a presentation of the state of the art and is best suited to all who are interested in understanding what psychodynamic psychotherapy is about. This concerns both the obvious and the hidden forces and dynamics which are meant to facilitate, but might also hinder, a process that has to be installed and maintained in order to help patients to regain their psychic health, thus engendering the capacity to cope with their conflicts at a mature level and to lead an autonomous life.

Anne-Marie Schloesser

PREFACE

This handbook, *Psychoanalytic Psychotherapy*, is an introductory textbook for psychiatrists and psychologists who are starting to use psychoanalytic psychotherapy in their daily professional work with patients.

It tries to give a complete and fundamental overview, from a psychoanalytical point of view, on theoretical and clinical aspects of psychodynamic or psychoanalytic psychotherapy. This includes the theory of the human mind, psychic development, psychic conflicts, trauma, symptom formation, and dreams (Chapters One to Four). Important aspects of technique and treatment are discussed: the therapeutic relationship, the setting, the diagnosis, and the process of treatment (Chapters Five to Seven). Chapters Seven to Ten deal with the psychoanalytic understanding of specific clinical disorders, including neuroses, personality disorders, psychosomatic disorders, psychosis, addiction, and suicide.

The idea of the basic book was developed from a group of German psychoanalysts, who worked together as experts in different training courses in China from 1997 until today. The chapters of the book are a compilation of central lectures for beginners on the training programme at Shanghai Mental Health Centre. They were reworked for this edition. The experiences of teaching, presentation, and discussing the different topics are flowed into the papers. The authors used different styles of teaching and writing. Therefore, the book is not homogeneous, as it would be if written by one author. Some topics are mentioned more than once, but in different contexts.

Matthias Elzer (Hofheim am Taunus)
Alf Gerlach (Saarbrücken)

CHAPTER ONE

PSYCHOANALYTIC THEORY OF THE HUMAN MIND

Hermann Schultz, Joachim Rothhaupt, and Michael Wolf

Psychoanalytic models of the mind

Hermann Schultz

What is psychodynamic psychotherapy; what does the term "psychodynamic" mean? For an answer to this question, let us look at the origins of psychodynamic science, rooted in psychoanalysis and developed by Freud from 1893 onwards. Psychiatric diagnosis in Freud's time was no more than classifying people into different diagnostic categories, for instance, the so-called "psychopathic personalities" with hysteric, perverse, criminal, or addictive traits, the psychoses (schizophrenia, manic–depressive illness), neurasthenia, etc. Today, our diagnostic systems in psychiatry are much more refined, operationalised, and validated than they were at the turn of the twentieth century: we have ICD-10 or DSM-IV guide us. Nevertheless, the content of these diagnostic systems, too, is restricted to descriptive symptom diagnoses and does not tell us anything about the psychodynamics of the patient's psychic disease. Therefore, for our psychotherapeutic purposes, the symptom diagnosis has to be supplemented by a psychodynamic diagnosis (see "Operationalised psychodynamic diagnosis" in Chapter Seven).

Psychiatric therapy in Freud's time was mainly somatic treatment, operating on the body through hospitalisation, psychopharmacological medication (e.g., sedatives and stimulants—Freud also experimented with cocaine), electrotherapy, etc. However, for neurotic disorders these somatic therapy forms proved ineffective. Freud found out that in order to help these patients, it was not enough to explore their symptoms, formulate a descriptive symptom diagnosis, and prescribe some somatic treatment. What these patients needed was a therapist who would explore why patients became ill and developed their symptoms at a particular moment or in a specific situation of their life; the reason for their becoming ill (the function and the meaning of their symptoms); in other words, try to understand understand the patient's symptoms as an expression of some inner "power struggle" between conflicting forces, especially emotional conflicts between specific wishes, needs, and fears of the patient.

Freud discovered that often the deepest longings and fears are unknown to the patient himself (they are unconscious), so you cannot simply ask the patient and get an answer. The therapist must, rather, learn the non-verbal, symbolic, and highly emotional "language of the unconscious mind", which is expressed not in words but in the patient's behaviour, his relationships towards other people, his emotional signals, phantasies, and dreams. By understanding not only words but also these non-verbal expressions of the patient's deepest motives and hidden emotions, we can help the patient to better understand himself and others and to master his problems without becoming ill as a result of them.

This approach—not just exploring symptoms as such, but wanting to understand their function and meaning in terms of the underlying emotional forces—is Freud's most important discovery, and this is what he called the psychodynamic point of view. The old Greek word *dynamis* means power, or force. Of course, here we are dealing not with physical forces, but psychological forces, which we describe in terms of

- drives (e.g., the sexual drive, aggressive impulses of competition or revenge);
- needs (the need for safety, for closeness, for affirmation and self-assertion, for autonomy and independence, the need to feel great sometimes, the need to have someone you can admire and take as a model, etc.);
- emotions (love and hate, anxiety and fear, shame, guilt, envy, jealousy, pride, arrogance, admiration, contempt, etc.).

What Freud and later psychoanalysts discovered is that often

- these manifold dynamic forces are not in harmony but in conflict with each other;
- one important reason for conflict is that some of the deepest needs, emotions, and impulses are rather immature, persisting from childhood and in conflict with adult self-concepts and values; in short, with the adult part of the patient's personality;
- our patients' deepest emotional conflicts, which made them become ill, are often unknown to them because these are mostly unconscious;
- such unconscious conflicts are often expressed indirectly, non-verbally, in the patient's symptoms, interpersonal relations, emotional and behavioural signals, which we must understand in order to help the patient in therapy;
- in clinical practice, symptom diagnosis alone is mostly insufficient and has to be supplemented by a psychodynamic diagnosis in terms of emotional conflicts and the way a patient deals with them (defence mechanisms), developmental deficits, personality structure, etc.;
- psychoanalytical psychotherapy aims to help the patient to better understand and accept himself, to realise his emotional conflicts and to develop more adequate solutions for them. Since many of our patients have been hampered in their personality development, resulting in developmental deficits, an additional aim of psychodynamic psychotherapy should be to help them to face reality and resume their personality development in those areas where they are still clinging to childish or juvenile forms of behaviour and experience—in other words, help them to grow up to be a mature adult person.

On the basis of his clinical observations, Freud tried to order his findings systematically and develop a psychological model of mental functioning. Since the neuro-scientific knowledge of the brain and its functions was still very limited in his time, Freud had to give up his first attempt, in 1895, at constructing a neuropsychological model of mental functioning in health and mental disease. So, from that time on, he tried to outline a psychological theory of mental functioning. I want to be brief and concentrate upon the essentials.

In the development of psychoanalysis, we may distinguish first Freud's three models of the mind. After Freud's death in 1939, the development did not stop, but as the clinical spectrum changed, psychotherapists were confronted with new kinds of patients (for instance, patients with narcissistic and borderline personality disorder), necessitating new psychodynamic models to understand and treat them. From our clinical practice today, we see that the earlier models were not completely wrong and they still have their value, albeit limited, but they had to be supplemented by new models as soon as new kinds of patients appeared whose mental disorder could not be explained by way of the old model. So, all these models have to do with the kind of patients whom psychoanalytic therapists had to treat.

The first model—the model of "blocked affect—therapeutic abreaction"—was developed by Freud and his colleague Breuer when they treated hysterical patients with dissociative symptoms and found that many of these patients suffered from some early trauma, such as sexual abuse, early loss of a beloved parent, etc. In the beginning, Freud used hypnosis in order to facilitate remembering, later (in the 1890s) he replaced this with the technique of free association—psychoanalysis. In the course of treatment, when the patients remembered the trauma that had been repressed, they often enacted the traumatic event in dramatic form in the therapy situation, and afterwards, they often felt much better or even lost their symptoms.

The second topographic model was suitable for a wider spectrum of neurotic disorders: anxiety hysteria and phobic neurosis, conversion hysteria, and obsessive–compulsive disorder.

The third, structural model had to be developed to account not only for the symptom neuroses, but also for depression, and narcissistic, masochistic self-defeating, and paranoid personality disorders.

Later models of the mind developed after Freud's death (e.g., object relations theory, self psychology) are still more apt to account for the less integrated forms of severe personality disorders, for example, borderline, narcissistic, schizoid, and antisocial personalities.

Freud's first model to explain what he observed in his—mostly female—hysterical patients was a model of blocked affect and therapeutic abreaction. We find a good description, together with very vivid case presentations, in his book (with Breuer) *Studies on Hysteria*, published in 1895. Using hypnosis, or his early forced association method, Freud often found that at the centre of the patient's suffering there was some repressed memory (of sexual abuse, for example, or early loss of a beloved parent), or some secret passion, forbidden love, or hidden death wish against a close relative, etc. When therapy succeeded in recovering this personal secret, thus helping the patient to remember and admit what had happened and to re-experience vividly in the therapy situation the traumatic event, together with the painful emotions associated with it, the neurotic symptoms (such as hysterical paralysis, functional pain, anxiety attacks) disappeared—at least for some time. So, Freud (1895d, p. 7) discovered "Hysterics suffer mainly from reminiscences". The typical sequence of events, according to this model, is as follows.

1. The patient had been overwhelmed by her emotions in connection with a psychic trauma or unbearable passionate experience (secret passion, forbidden love, or hidden death wish against a close relative, etc.).
2. The traumatic experience was repressed from consciousness, because it was too painful, so it could not be remembered (amnesia for the trauma). The traumatic affects (death anxiety, excitement, helpless rage, shame, and guilt) were blocked from feeling and "converted" (conversion) into functional somatic symptoms—so-called neurotic (hysterical) symptoms.
3. In therapy, the patient feels safe enough to lift the "repression barrier" and re-experience the traumatic events, together with the painful affects, because, under the protection of therapy, the traumatic affects are no longer blocked, but can be expressed, that is, "abreacted". By way of abreaction of the formerly blocked affect, the patient is relieved from pressure and the symptoms are dissolved.

Limitations of this model are: relief from symptoms usually was only temporary; often the symptoms reappeared later (no working through); psychodynamic understanding was limited; there was insufficient appreciation of inner conflict.

The unconscious (topographic model, 1900)

Freud's first model of the mind was a model of the traumatised psyche, a model of the post trauma mind. When Freud realised that at least some of the traumatic events which he reconstructed from the fantasies, dreams, and associations of his hysterical patients probably had never really happened, but had been a fantasy construction of the patients, he arrived at a crisis. In the end, he recognised that on the unconscious level, our minds are not able to distinguish between fantasy and reality, so, in the unconscious mind, fantasy is treated as if it were real—not factual reality, but psychic reality. This finding was very important. Freud had discovered the enormous psychodynamic role of unconscious wishful fantasies and of negative unconscious convictions. For example, Anna O, the famous female hysterical patient of Freud's colleague Breuer, towards the end of her treatment with Breuer, developed the unconscious wishful fantasy that she was pregnant by her therapist, so that he would leave his wife and live with her. Although this was not real, the patient behaved as if it were real. What she presented was a false pregnancy, but with the typical appearance of a real pregnancy.

In the seventh chapter of his book *The Interpretation of Dreams* (1900a) Freud described his new topographic model of the mind. According to this model, the mind is an organ (a "psychic apparatus", as he called it) for the processing of stimuli—perceptual information from outside, drive impulses and emotions from inside. These stimuli are stored in memory systems, that is, associative networks of emotionally charged ideas. Parts of these memories are preconscious, which means they are accessible to consciousness, which is kind of an inner sense organ. Other memories or ideas are unconscious: they are kept out of consciousness by repression or some other defence mechanism, because awareness of these memories or wishful fantasies would cause painful feelings of fear, or shame, or guilt. So, Freud's new model was like a topography of the human mind, with an unconscious, a preconscious, and a conscious area (Figure 1.1).

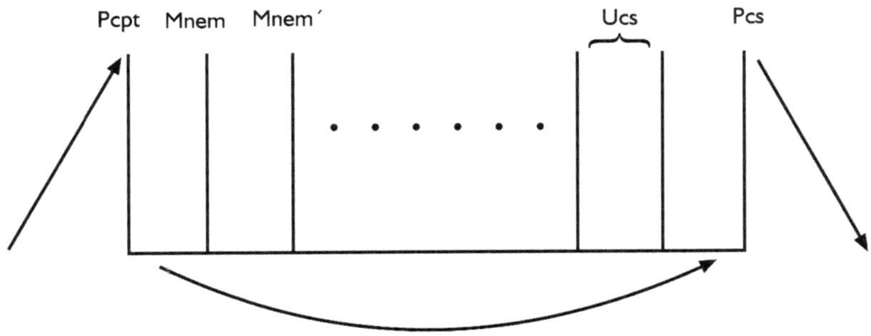

Figure 1.1. Freud's "topographical model" of the "psychic apparatus" (1900a, p. 541). Excitement of the "psychic apparatus" starts from the perceptual organs (Pcpt), turned towards the body and the external world. Sensations are stored and filtered through a series of mnemic systems of growing complexity (Mnem, Mnem′, Mnem″ . . .), up to the system Unconscious (Ucs) and Preconscious (Pcs), until the impulse—now in a psychic (mentalised) form—reaches conscious awareness or is executed in motor action.

Unconscious fantasies, wishes, or fears can be very powerful when they are triggered by certain life circumstances. Because these fantasies, wishes, or fears are unconscious and often associated with strong anxiety, we cannot deal with them in the normal way, for instance by thinking about these ideas, trying to find out if they are realistic or not, and what you will decide to do. Instead, in the case of our neurotic patients, these unconscious fantasies and impulses are blocked from consciousness and transformed by the preconscious system into some form of neurotic symptoms: for instance, functional disorders in hysterical neurosis (inability to speak, to walk, to write without organic causes), obsessive–compulsive hand washing, and controlling, phobic avoiding, etc.

Dreams offer an excellent opportunity to see the unconscious system at work, since in dreams the unconscious memories, fantasies, and wishes gain more influence upon our thinking. So, Freud found that unconscious thought processes are organised differently or follow a different logic when compared to preconscious thinking: unconscious thinking is organised according to what Freud calls the primary process (e.g., in dreams), characterised by features such as condensation, displacement, symbolisation, and weakening of reality constraints such as space, time, and causality. Unconscious thinking, for Freud, follows the pleasure–unpleasure principle: wishful thinking and clinging to pleasurable ideas, while unpleasurable and painful thoughts are avoided. Most of the time, conscious and preconscious thinking is organised on a higher level, according to what Freud calls the secondary process, characterised by the laws of verbal logic, rational problem-solving, and a realistic frame of reference. Hence, Freud called the principle that guides our normal, everyday life thinking the reality principle.

During this period of his theory development, Freud's conceptions increased in complexity. Besides repression, he now described several varieties of defence strategies (or "defence mechanisms"), characteristic of different forms of neurosis: conversion; dramatic enactments in hysteria; displacement and isolation of affect in obsessive–compulsive neurosis; avoidance and affectualisation in phobic and anxiety neurosis. He developed a form of systemic thinking (in describing the different organisations of the unconscious system and preconscious system) and he refined his theory of the instinctual drives (sexual drives *vs.* ego drives, including aggression, later also narcissism); he outlined a psychodynamic theory of dreaming and dared to extend his research into the complexities of psychosis (the "Schreber case", 1911c). Compared with Freud's first model, the topographic model encompassed a much broader clinical spectrum.

However, there were certain shortcomings with it, the most important being that Freud's topographic model describes psychological processes, structures, functions, ideas, emotions, etc., abstractly, like component parts of a "psychic apparatus". This was a very fruitful point of view, leading to many important discoveries about mental functioning. But the human person and the relationships between self and other persons (the ego and object-relationships), so important in clinical work, were lost from sight in theory.

The psychic apparatus (structural model, 1923)

So, beginning with his articles "On narcissism: an introduction" (1914c), "Mourning and melancholia" (1917e) and other papers from the time of the First World War, Freud began to formulate a new model, summarised well in his essay *The Ego and the Id* (1923b) (Figure 1.2).

This so-called structural model incorporated all the important findings mentioned before, but organised these data within a new frame of reference: the intrapsychic structure of the individual was sketched according to a model of interpersonal relationships. The concept of an inner world of inner object relationships between more or less personalised agencies (id, ego, and superego/ego ideal) was born. This makes sense because:

- The person is not unitary, but often experiences him- or herself as divided between "I" as the subject and "me" or "myself" as the object of self-observation, self-esteem, self-love, self-hate, self-identity. We may understand "narcissism" as an encompassing term for the whole range of a person's relationships with himself or herself. I can have an internal dialogue between different parts of myself, or between different personifications in my inner world, with whom I more or less identify myself. To explain this more in detail:

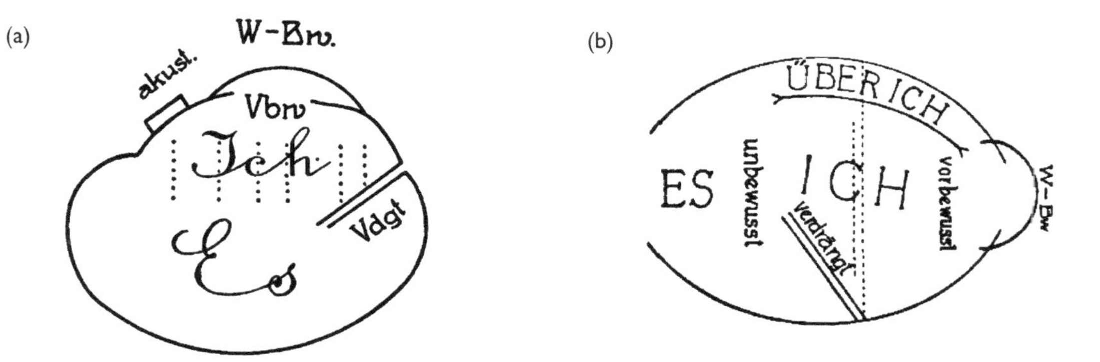

Figure 1.2. The psychic apparatus. Two original graphics by Freud: (a) Ego and id (Freud 1923b, p. 24), (b) Ego, superego, and id (Freud 1933a, 22, p.78).

- Sometimes we feel under the powerful influence of (more or less personified) inner forces who push or pull us in different directions: There might be an inner conflict between the "id" part of ourselves, that is, our wishing, demanding, pleasure-seeking instinctual-drive nature within us, and our conscience, the "Superego" part, reminding us of moral standards and "what people would think of me", or our "ego ideal" part, which is our ideal model of how we ought to be or wish to be. It is the task of the ego to mediate these different and often conflicting tendencies, not only within the person, that is, in the inner world, but also in external reality, especially in the interpersonal reality of emotional relationships, what we call object relations.
- Not only clinical experience, but also the psychology of child development shows us the major importance of identifications in the forming of the person, and the role of conflicts between contrary identifications (partly conscious, mostly unconscious) in the development of neuroses and personality disorders. The ego and the superego/ego-ideal system derive from internalised object relationships, which might show realistic features of the persons we identified with, or often strongly idealised or demonised features, according to our emotional imagination. The experience of relationship patterns with important persons of our childhood (e.g., loving care and appreciation, or emotional coldness, neglect, strictness, or cruelty) will be internalised and influences the way we treat ourselves and others. This point of view can really help us to understand individuals in the context of their experiences and relationships during the formative years.

As already mentioned, within this new frame of the structural model the earlier, topographical model of the mind, with its concepts of conscious, preconscious, and unconscious processes, of drive impulse and defence, of primary and secondary processes, etc., still remained valid. So, Freud tried to combine both models and allocate certain mental functions and processes to the three agencies: id, ego, and superego/ego ideal.

The id is the deep unconscious instinctual part of ourselves, the part that connects mind with body; it is the area from where instinctual drive impulses and bodily needs come. Besides the drive aspect, other authors emphasise the "unconscious wisdom" aspect (Freud's "primal fantasies", Jung's "archetypes", Langs' "unconscious wisdom system") and the existence of a deep, unconscious, instinctual "fear/guilt system" (Langs, 1999).

The ego developed from out of the id, with the dawn of conscious awareness. Freud describes the ego as performing a broad array of functions, e.g., cognitive functions (perception, thinking, memory), defence functions or mechanisms (repression, denial, affect isolation, projection, introjection, splitting, etc.), executive functions (action planning), and, on a deeper level, symbol formation and mentalization.

Parts of these ego functions are working unconsciously, automatically, not with a sense of sense of "self-as-agent": I do it, I perceive this object, I think this thought, etc. Nevertheless, in psychoanalysis we call them "ego functions", even if we are often not consciously aware of the workings of our minds. So, we have to admit that part of our ego is unconscious, functioning outside of our awareness.

The superego/ego-ideal system is described by Freud as "a gradation within the Ego" (this means a subsystem within the ego system), which is formed by taking over other people's point of view and identifying with how others might see one. In this way, the reflective functions of self-consciousness, self-observation, self-evaluation, self-criticism, and self-esteem will gradually develop. These are the functions that Freud ascribes to the ego–superego/ego-ideal system: he sees neutral self-observation mostly as an ego function, self-criticism as a superego function, self-approval and positive self-esteem as a function of the ego ideal (Figure 1.3).

According to the structural model, human beings live in two worlds: in our inner world of internalised object relationships and in external reality with relationships to other people. There is a permanent exchange between inner and outer worlds, and between the inner worlds of different people (through language and other informational and emotional exchange). Our inner world is very much shaped and modified by our experiences with persons in the external world. For example, the young boy introjects his image of his father as a representative of moral rules and forms his superego accordingly to become an inner authority. On the other hand, when he experiences his father as being an admirable person, a model he wants to emulate, he introjects this idealised and admired image of his father as his ego ideal.

The reverse is also true: our relationships in the external world are very much shaped and modified by our inner objects and object relationships. This is what we call transference: For example, we may be very sensitive to the critical remarks of someone whom we experience as like our own superego. Another example: a mother sees her daughter as embodying mother's ideal self (or ego ideal), so the daughter is expected to accomplish what mother had wanted to accomplish herself but was not able to.

Yet another example: a patient experiences her female psychotherapist as like her mother, so she is not willing to exert herself but expects that mother will solve all problems for her. Another patient is very suspicious of his male doctor and authority figures in general; even if he does not recognise why he feels this, we are not surprised to hear that his father often beat him. We may also say the patients project their father or mother image upon the therapist, experiencing her or him similarly.

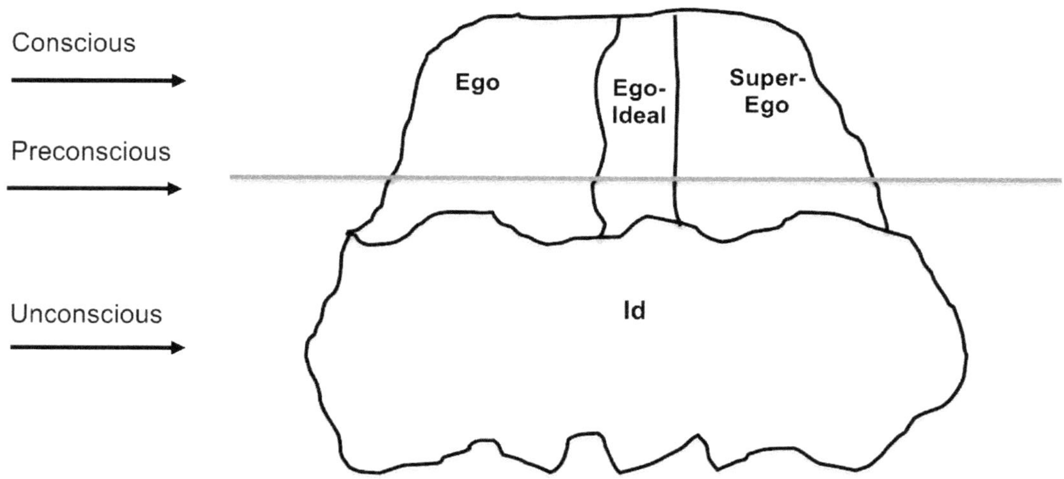

Figure 1.3. The psychic apparatus (structural model) as an iceberg.

Transference is everywhere in our daily life, but only in psychodynamic psychotherapy will transference be analysed, understood, and used for the aims of therapy. In later chapters, this concept, which is important in both its practical and theoretical aspects, will be described in detail.

Freud always emphasised that his theories are only provisional models, to be corrected by further research if new data cannot be explained within the frame of current theory. Indeed, such corrections turned out to be necessary when new types of patients and new kinds of mental disorders appeared in psychotherapeutic practice.

Patients with borderline personality disorder, for instance, have not reached the degree of structural stability and integration which is presupposed in the tripartite structural model of three distinctly delimited agencies: ego, superego/ego ideal, and id. Their internalised object relationships have not developed into an integrated personality structure. Instead of an ego with solid identity and object constancy, they have contradictory self-representations. Without having a stable and holding superego/ego-ideal system, they suffer from primitive persecuting guilt feelings, annihilating shame, and fear of dissolution. Because they do not have an integrated and object-related structure of their id drives, they are driven by chaotic impulses of polymorphic perverse sexuality and undifferentiated aggression.

Schizoid and narcissistic patients, on the other hand, have managed a superficial adaptation to their environment, but it is a sort of role-playing adaptation; they enact their functioning false selves, but inside they feel empty, meaningless, and fundamentally isolated, because their true selves remain hidden and unable to express their real needs for human contact. For this type of patient, too, a new model of the mind was needed to account for structural deficits in certain areas of the ego and superego/ego ideal, as well as for ego splitting and related phenomena.

Within this chapter, the emphasis is on Freud's models of the human mind. We have seen how Freud started with his first theory of the origin of neurosis in psychic conflict, specifically an emotional conflict or drive conflict. Later, this theory of unconscious drive conflict (topographic theory) proved to be insufficient for new types of patients, so Freud developed the structural theory of ego–superego/ego ideal, in short: ego psychology. Later authors, expanding Freud's ideas about narcissism and object relations, developed object relations theory and self psychology. These important additions to our psychoanalytic "models of the mind"—the ego and its defence mechanisms, object relations theory and self psychology—will be introduced in detail in later chapters.

Contemporary models of the human mind

In clinical practice, we need to know all these models, or, at least, their basic characteristics. What model we use depends on the type of patient we are treating in psychodynamic therapy, and also depends on the contemporary clinical situation.

Today, mainly four psychologies of psychoanalysis (Pine, 1988) are employed in the psychodynamic understanding of our patients. These are as follows.

1. *The theory of drives and emotional conflicts*. Here we ask: which are the predominant emotional conflicts of the patient, how does he deal with his emotions (is he able to feel his emotions and express them, or does he need to act them out or to somatise them)?

2. *The theory of ego, superego, and ego ideal functions.* Here, the focus is on ego functions, for example, the functional level of coping and defence mechanisms, the capacity to organise one's own life, profession, relationships, etc.
3. *The theory of narcissism and self-psychology.* The focus here is on the healthy or pathological narcissism of the patient; the level of self-esteem, its development and regulation is especially important.
4. *Object relations theory.* Here we ask about not only the quality of the patient's relationships with other people, but also the emotional relationships in the patient's inner world, his images and concepts of himself and other important people in his life.

These four theories, or "models of the mind", belong together; each of them emphasises a specific point of view or perspective. Sometimes, it may be most helpful to see the main problem of the patient in terms of his conflicts with sexuality or aggression; at other times, developmental deficits in the ego functions of the patient are in the foreground. In other cases, the central problem might belong to the area of narcissism (low self-esteem and narcissistic vulnerability of a patient or his arrogant attitude towards others), and very often, a formulation in terms of object relations may be most helpful to understand the patient's inner world and the problems in his relationships with others.

A note on symbolisation and mentalization

A section on "models of the mind" should not be closed without introducing two important concepts, symbolisation and mentalization, which are often discussed today, because in clinical practice, we frequently have to deal with patients whose main problems or deficits seem to be located in just this area. These are patients who seem unable to feel their emotions and talk about them: for example, the therapist recognises the patient's anger, whereas the patient does not feel anger, but suffers from headaches and muscular tension. Their perception of what other persons feel is equally limited. They are lacking an awareness of any "inner" "mental" problems or conflicts; what they describe are only somatic complaints or factual problems in the external world. It seems as if these patients did not develop a "mental space" or "inner world" and awareness of what they feel, or an inner dialogue of thinking about themselves and others. Their phantasy life is extremely restricted; most of them will tell you they never dream.

Many of our psychosomatic patients, among others, belong in this category, but also some apparently "normal" people who emphasise that they are normal, "not crazy", although they might have grown up in an extremely traumatising family atmosphere that they think is "normal". These are patients with severe deficits in their capacity for symbolisation and mentalization, so that certain areas of their mental life are underdeveloped. They might be good at dealing with facts, technical problems, etc., but in the area of subjective experience (feelings, phantasies, hopes, and fears) they feel helpless.

Symbolisation concerns the transformation of "raw experience" into mental signs at different levels in an increasing level of organisation (Lecours & Bouchard, 1997). These "mental signs" may be feeling states, phantasies, dreams or daydreams, ideas, or verbalised thoughts, etc., which can be communicated in inner dialogue with oneself or shared with other people.

Mentalization concerns self-object differentiation, the ability to see things from the other's perspective, and the ability to conceptualise and understand mental states in general, both one's own and those of others (Fonagy, Gergely, Jurist, & Target, 2002). Symbolising and mentalising are meaning-making processes through the whole of life.

Clinical experience shows that the main causes of disorders of symbolisation and mentalization are twofold.

1. Psychic trauma, necessitating global defence against any strong emotions: not repression proper, but total refusal of symbolic representation (in images or words), what Freud (1894a, p. 58, 1914c, p. 85) calls "foreclosure" (*Verwerfung* in German); we may also say: de-symbolisation or de-mentalization—pushing the traumatic experience out of the mental system.
2. Developmental deficit: in terms of mentalization of emotions and socio-emotional development (often, but not exclusively, in families of low socio-economic status). It makes a big difference whether a child grows up in a family where emotions, hopes, fears, fantasies, opinions, and conflicts are shared and discussed among each other, or whether in the child's family there is no talking with each other, no awareness of, and communication about, personal feelings, no thinking and discussion about emotional problems, but only direct acting out of emotions, for instance in interpersonal pressure and open violence, alcohol and drug abuse, and intrusions into each other's personal sphere. Such a family atmosphere does not stimulate the development of symbolising and mentalising capacities: although there might be children who develop a secret phantasy life as a refuge from their terrible family reality, others will prefer not to feel, not to imagine, or think about their situation.

Later, under more favourable circumstances in their life or in psychotherapy, they may get the chance (or overcome their reluctance) to develop new symbolising and mentalising capacities.

Drives and psychosexuality

Joachim Rothhaupt

Psychoanalytic therapy is the only therapeutic method based on developmental theories. In other words, it is based on theories of individual development from birth. When a patient comes to us with a symptom, we cannot isolate the symptom from the patient. We have to understand the whole person, his history as well as his psychic development with the inherent development of the symptom. As most symptoms have their painful origin during early development, we should relate to our patients as empathically as possible.

No psychological theory can exist without a concept of motivation. Freud's drive theory is such an example. Sooner or later, we have to explain why a human being is acting or behaving in a particular way.

For Freud, drives were the central cause of any activity or creative power, forcing the psychic apparatus to become active, originating from organs of the body, expressing central bodily needs.

Freud conceptualised different dualistic drive theories, that is to say, the dualism of sexuality *vs.* ego (instinct for self-preservation), sexual drives *vs.* aggressive drives, and life drives *vs.* death drives. He differentiated the aspects of drives between the urge, the source, the aim, and the object.

The urge is understood as the dynamic and motor moment, the source is linked to the body, namely the erogenous zones (oral, anal, and infantile genital), which he conceptualised in his sexual theory (libido theory). The aim of a drive is always satisfaction, a satisfactory body experience with or without another object. Thus, the aim has priority, the object aspect is secondary.

The topic of my section of this chapter refers to Freud's psychoanalytic theory of psychosexual development, which he conceptualised on the basis of analysis of adult patients.

Originally, Freud thought of a traumatic genesis of neuroses. He thought that neuroses are the result of the psychic incapability to compensate for overwhelming affects which develop during a traumatic situation. If a person is not able to abreact the affects resulting from a traumatic situation (weeping, avenging, or talking successfully about), he would have no choice but to repress the affects, the thoughts, and the pictures belonging to the traumatic experience. In future, associations could reawaken these repressed elements and the encapsulated affects, so that new and more powerful repressions would be necessary to repress the painful experiences all over again.

As the content of the traumatic experiences often focuses on sexual abuse in childhood, Freud started having doubts about traumatic experiences as the only source of neurotic development, and became more and more convinced that intrapsychic conflicts were the main pathogenic factors in the development of neuroses.

During further theoretical developments, Freud did not renounce the trauma theory, but modified, completed, and finally conceptualised it in the structural model as the ego, the id, and the superego. Trauma was understood not as a singular event, but as a repetition of frustrating (intrapsychic and traumatic) experiences, which, in their threatening dimension, were not psychically tolerable.

The clinical work with neurotic and perverse patients increasingly led Freud to the conviction that the central needs and experiences of frustration, leading to neurotic conflicts and symptoms, centred on sexuality in a much wider sense than mature genital sexuality.

Bi-phasic psychosexual development

Freud conceptualised the development of a psychic structure (structural model) and an ontogenetic developmental theory based on the development of the sexual drive.

The central theses of his developmental theory focus on two stages of psychosexual development. The first period of childhood development, characterised by a specific organisation of the libido of the dominance of the erogenous zones (oral, anal, and genital), ending in the solution of the oedipal conflict. This period stretches from the age of one to five or six years.

Between the first and second period of sexual development, Freud places a phase of latency in which the infantile sexual fantasies and experiences become repressed and sublimated. They become unconscious.

The second period of sexual development, starting with hormonal influences during adolescence, leads to a mature adult sexuality with conscious needs for satisfaction. Freud understood this bi-phasic development as unique to humans.

Before a person becomes genitally mature, he or she has to pass through several phases of pre-genital and psychic development:

- the oral phase (first year);
- the anal phase (second and third year);
- the phallic (infantile genital) phase with the Oedipus complex (fourth to fifth or sixth year);
- latency phase (fifth or sixth to tenth or eleventh year).

These four premature phases (pre-genital stage of psychosexual development) then flow into the

- genital phase (tenth or eleventh to eighteenth year). This stage is called puberty (maturation of the body) or adolescence (psychosocial development) (Figure 1.4).

Drives and erogenous body zones

From the point of motivation, Freud centres his developmental theory on the development of libido. He conceptualises the libido as a permanent floating energy underlying the transformations of sexual instinct (sexual drive).

He defines libido as a non-specific sensual drive for bodily gratification, which, at different stages, becomes predominantly focused on particular bodily zones (erogenous zones). He postulates that the preoccupation with the more infantile zones never disappears completely, but persists in normal adult sexuality as well as in perverse sexuality.

Milton, Polmear, and Fabricius (2004, p. 28) give a good description of the developmental phases, as follows.

1. During the oral stage, infant libido is centred on the mouth (erogenous zone) and pleasure derived by sucking. Freud thought infants are mostly autoerotic. Living by the pleasure

Psychosexual phases						
Oral	Anal	Infantile-genital/oedipal	Latency		Genital	
Early	Childhood			Pre-	Puberty/Adolescence	Adult age
1	2. – 3.	4. – 5./6.	6. – 10.	11.	12. – 18./20.	20. – Death

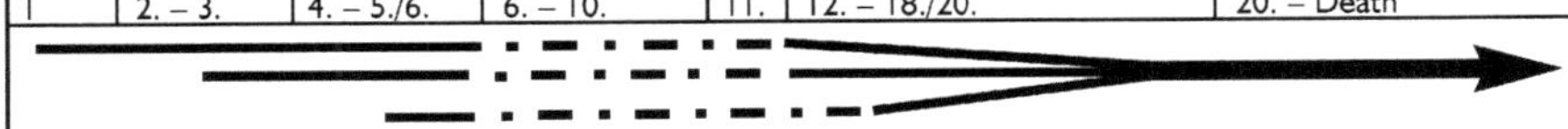

Figure 1.4. Psychosexual phases and partial drives becoming mature sexuality at the beginning of adulthood (Henseler, 1973, modified by Elzer, 2009a).

principle, the infant is able to achieve hallucinatory gratification, for example, by sucking his own finger. However, such a mechanism will not work indefinitely and even the most attentive mother is not always able to satisfy her baby at once. In this way, the infant becomes aware of reality. The non-occurrence of wished-for satisfaction is needed (according to Freud) for the development of the capacity for thought, which in turn is necessary to bring about action in the real world, and is an important step in the development of a mature ego. A well-tempered frustration of oral infantile needs is the pre-condition for the development of the capacity to mourn for unrealistic wished-for ideals. This is related to the development of the capacity to contain emotion and deal with reality in a realistic, rather than idealistic, way.

2. During the anal stage, while a small child is learning bowel control, he may often find anal (erogenous zone) activities pleasurable and absorbing. This stage also involves the negotiation of retaining and letting go of faeces and other things. Control issues can include much besides the sphincter, for example, battles over eating and dressing. Problems here may mark the beginning of persistent difficulties with "give and take" within a relationship.
3. From about the age of three years, children become increasingly aware of their genitals, finding them pleasurable to touch (erogenous zone). They start to show off their bodies, and become curious about other children's, especially those of the opposite gender. Freud calls this the phallic stage, as he thought that the penis was the central organ of interest for both sexes (Freud's thinking is obviously linked to the patriarchal times in which he lived and worked). In respect of our knowledge of female development, we speak of the infantile genital stage.

The Oedipus complex is the centrepiece of the psychoanalytic theory of development. While psychoanalysts since Freud may have disagreed on the timing or exact nature of the Oedipus complex, all have thought of it as being of fundamental importance to development. Freud named this complex after the Greek mythological hero. The oracle of Delphi predicted that Oedipus would kill his father and marry his mother and, due to an unfortunate set of circumstances, this prediction came true.

Freud found that all adults he studied, including himself, show evidence of a more or less deeply buried attachment to the parent of the opposite sex and concomitant hostility to the parent of the same sex. He thought this originates between the age of three and five and speculated that the theme had become embedded in the Greek myth because it struck a universal human chord.

Freud thought that oedipal wishes are renounced as a result of fear (castration fear). For example, a boy fears that his father may punish him by castration, a belief that may be stimulated by the observation that a girl does not have a penis.

Because of this fear, according to Freud, a little boy gives up his ambition to take his father's place beside his mother. In so doing, he internalises his father as both an external and an internal authority. In this way, the superego is formed. Thereafter, incestuous desires are forbidden and the whole affair is repressed and lost from conscious memory.

Not only fear, but also mourning—the coming to terms with what cannot be had—plays a part in resolving the Oedipus complex and this aspect has been more strongly emphasised by theorists following Freud. Love for the parent goes alongside fear and rivalry (Milton, Polmear, & Fabricius, 2004).

During the phallic, infantile genital phase there is an important change in the somatic–sexual development. Increasing excitability is now focused on the genital regions (clitoris and penis) and children display sexual activities such as masturbation or exhibitionism, or have voyeuristic tendencies, which are normal developmental phenomena. Concerning object relations, there is an important shift from dyadic to triadic relations.

After the fears and passions of the phallic, the infantile genital, or the oedipal phase, Freud saw children of school age entering a latency phase in which there is a de-sexualisation of the child's interests, and libidinal energy is directed to social, intellectual, and other skills through the mechanism of sublimation. In this phase, the Oedipus complex is solved by the child's identification with the parent of the same sex. This is the precondition for the development of a final male or female identity. However, for sound biological reasons, actual sex within the family has to be taboo and the erotic aspect of this childhood love has to be forgotten or obscured.

Puberty brings about an upsurge in sexual and aggressive feelings, which demand that a young person should develop feelings and fantasies in relationships with peers.

One of the vital tasks of adolescence is to shift erotic attachment to the outside world, so that sexual development can finally progress to the genital stage.

When we speak of the two phases of human sexual development, we refer to the infantile genital phase as the first phase and the genital phase in adolescence as the second phase.

Object relations

Michael Wolf and Hermann Schultz

Psychoanalysis means analysis and treatment of the psyche. The psyche is the inner world of the person. What is an inner world, by which principles and structures does it work, and how is it built up or how does it emerge? How does it relate to the self and the external world, what we call reality, and which kind of dynamics are involved in it?

The inner world of a human being does not exist right after birth. Although from recent research we know a great deal about the capacities of a baby to act (rather than only react) from birth on, and although even embryos already show rather differentiated competences, the inner word will emerge and develop only during the first months and years of life. This development is embedded in relation to, and interactions with, the child's parents or other relevant persons. Thus, we come to a first psychoanalytic insight: the inner world emerges by internalisation of experiences of these interactions.

They are usually called object relations, seen from the point of view of the infant as subject, as well as seen later by the adult—for us, by the patient—in psychotherapeutic treatment.

Object relations theory

The term "object relations theory" refers to the idea that the ego, or self, exists only in relation to other objects, which may be external or internal. The internal objects are internalised versions of external objects, primarily formed from early interactions with parents. Some cornerstones of this theory will be mentioned, despite the fact of their validity being questioned in the light of some recent research.

According to Freud's instinct theory, an instinctual drive has a source and an aim, both of which are genetically determined and, hence, little influenced by environmental variations, and also an object, the means through which the aim of the drive is achieved; the object can be variable and depends on the given environment. Freud specified that the child's first love object is the mother's breast, and he refers to the early suckling relationship with mother as the prototype of all later love relations. Even in this first statement, however, he broadens the basis of this earliest of relations beyond orality. The mother, in stroking, kissing, and rocking her baby, is fulfilling her task "in teaching him to love".

The ego psychologists (e.g., Hartmann, Mahler, Spitz), while accepting Freud's theory of psychosexual development, emphasise the development of object relations in the context of the development of ego functions.

There is general agreement that the newborn is a rather undifferentiated organism, undifferentiated under structural, topographic, and dynamic aspects. Neither id nor ego have yet emerged from their common undifferentiated core, and distinctions between conscious and preconscious processes are irrelevant or do not yet exist. The baby is unable to discriminate objectively among things in his environment or between persons and things. Indeed, he cannot even distinguish clearly between himself and his environment, which implies that he cannot discriminate between sensory input from his own body and sensory input from the external world. Therefore, the newborn is described as experiencing everything as part of himself, or, in terms of developmental theory, all of his libidinal energy is contained within himself—a self which might include the not yet differentiated environment. Since the baby cannot even distinguish his mother from himself, he cannot relate to her as an external "object"—that is, a love object. This first period of life is characterised by what Freud called "primary narcissism"; others label this first period as "undifferentiated" or "objectless".

In general, the development of object relations is viewed here as proceeding through three main stages:

1. An undifferentiated or objectless stage.
2. A transitional stage.
3. A stage of object relations.

So-called undifferentiated narcissistic, or objectless, stage

In emphasising the (relatively) undifferentiated nature of the newborn, the ego psychologists do not claim total lack of differentiation. They all acknowledge constitutional "givens" or inherited potentials (German: *Anlagen*), which are genetically determined beginnings of more complex processes, which will mature later. However, they view the newborn's responses, even the most complex reactions, as tied to inborn visceral, autonomic, or emotional organisations within the baby rather than based on perceptual discrimination of the environment.

Transitional stage

This is a period between the undifferentiated first stage and the stage in which clear-cut object relations are finally established. During this transitional period, certain ego functions develop, and one can speak of a primitive "body ego". Distance receptors become more important. Memory traces of former experiences are consolidated. Certain kinds of goal-directed behaviour emerge. A distinction can be made between self and non-self, although this is by no means complete, and the infant is still viewed as being incapable of cathecting a true object.

True object relations

Anna Freud (1937) defined this stage as the stage of object constancy, which enables a positive inner image of the object to be maintained, irrespective of either satisfactions or dissatisfactions. The baby now clearly perceives his mother as a person separate from himself. No longer do libidinal cathexes come and go in accordance with his need state. Now he is capable of maintaining his tie to her, irrespective of his need state, and regardless of whether she is currently gratifying or frustrating his needs and wishes, and whether she is present or absent. Although the object cathexis is still too fragile to be sustained during very long absences of the mother or primary carer, the child has some internalised representation of her that will persist, if the separation is not too long. When the mother leaves, she is not forgotten. Even though the child's bodily needs may be gratified by other persons while mother is absent, he misses her and is distressed.

Part-objects and whole objects

The central thesis in Klein's object-relations theory was that objects (in the external world as well as internal objects in the child's fantasy) play a decisive role in the development of a subject. Klein distinguishes between part objects and whole objects, depending on how the object is perceived: only as serving a certain function (e.g., for a baby, mother's breast, the feeding function) or recognised as a whole person (a mother). Consequently, both the mother as a person, or just the mother's breast or feeding function, can be the locus of satisfaction for a drive. Another use of the terms part object *vs.* whole object has to do with the inability of young children to conceive of an object which can be both "good" and "bad" (e.g., a loving yet sometimes frustrating mother). Because of this inability, infants view objects as either all good or all bad, thus seeing only a part of that object instead of the object's whole good–bad reality. Infants are too young to understand that objects can be both good and bad; they see only one part of the spectrum.

This way of keeping separate good and bad relationship experiences is what we call the splitting defence mechanism. For the very young infant or child, there are only part objects that are either good or bad, corresponding to the child's own feelings. If a baby is given milk, mother's breast will be a good object. If the baby is hungry and mother is not there, she will not just be a good but absent mother, but, in the baby's experience, she is a bad mother. If things go well enough, an infant/child will gradually learn that his objects are not only either good or bad (part objects), but there is a broad range of qualities between the extremes, from good to bad. In this way, part objects will come together and be integrated to form whole objects. Mature persons are able to perceive and acknowledge others as persons in their own right (whole persons, "whole objects"), not only as a means for satisfaction of one's drives and needs (part objects). The inability to do so is an indication of a more or less deep regression.

Recent decades in developmental psychological research have shown that the formation of a mental world is based upon, and enabled by, the infant–parent interpersonal interaction which was the main thesis of the so-called British object-relations tradition (e.g., Fairbairn, Guntrip). These thoughts are linked to attachment theory, which was developed by Bowlby and Ainsworth, and which differentiates four different types of attachment styles (secure, ambivalent, insecure–avoidant, disturbed) related to four different levels of defence organisation in the adult personality. Children who grow up in dysfunctional families are at risk of having poor quality attachments to their parents and, as adults, are at risk of treating their children in the same way.

The different schools of psychoanalytic theory have different concepts how psychic development works: by projection, projective identification, retrojection, symbolisation, mentalization, and others. In the end, however, they all agree on the fact that psychic development primarily evolves by internalisation of structures and relationships with and within the environment, which is also valid for cognitive development (Piaget) and moral development (Kohlberg). Internalisation is the motor by which experience is transformed into inner regulations of drives, affects, and behaviour, as well as intrapsychic dynamics in general.

We should imagine this internalisation not as a one to one transformation from the outside to the inner world. Rather, it is the way that Piaget (1952) describes: cognitive development via accommodation and assimilation, the reactive and the active mode of integrating new experiences, and building up new stages of cognitive functioning.

The development and differentiation of object relations will be shown later in comparison with the development of drives and of the self.

Narcissism and self-system

The term "narcissism" is derived from the Greek myth of Narcissus, which can be summarised as follows.

In a valley lived a beautiful nymph named Echo, who loved to chatter all day long. Once upon a time, a sad "spell" fell on her. As a consequence, Echo was no longer able to speak independently; she could only repeat, very faintly, the last few words of a sentence spoken by someone else. In the same valley lived a good-looking youth named Narcissus, who was so charming that every maiden who saw him fell in love with him. Narcissus, however, was totally absorbed with himself and did not love anybody else. He rejected all his admirers. One day, Narcissus was wandering with a group of friends but became separated from them and suddenly found himself alone. By chance, Echo observed him and immediately fell in love with him. Secretly, she followed him. She would have liked to talk to him, but because she was under the spell, she was not able to do so. While Narcissus was parting some branches to look for his friends, he exclaimed, "Is anybody here?" "Here!" Echo answered faintly. Narcissus looked around, not knowing to whom the voice belonged, and said, "Where are you? Come here!" whereupon Echo responded, "Here!" Narcissus couldn't see anyone, but he knew that there was someone close by, so he continued questioning and calling. Finally, Echo decided to come out of her hiding place. She appeared in front of Narcissus and attempted to embrace him. However, Narcissus rejected her and fled from her into the deepest part of the forest. Poor Echo was deeply hurt; her heart was broken, she stopped eating and died. Nemesis, the goddess of revenge, felt compassion for her and punished Narcissus for his vanity and coldness by making him unable to love anyone but himself. One day Narcissus was thirsty and went to a pool to take a drink. Just as he was about to sip from the pool, he saw the reflection of his own face in the water, without realising it was only a mirror image. He was fascinated by this image of a perfectly beautiful youth, which, however, was inaccessible, on the other side of the mirror. Desperate, he stopped eating and finally died. Afterwards, his body was transformed into a beautiful flower that was named after him, Narcissus (Picture 1.1).

In this myth of Narcissus, we find some typical characteristics of what we call a "narcissistic personality": his extreme vanity, his need to be loved and admired by others, and, at the same time, a deep fear of losing himself in a close and intimate relationship with another person who might become too important to him. There is still another important and often neglected part of the myth of Narcissus: the nymph Echo and his relationship with her. She

Picture 1.1. *Narcissus*, by Caravaggio (1594–1596), in the Galleria Nazionale d'Arte Antica, Rome.

mirrors him, without being able to contribute something of her own to the communication (always repeating the last words, as an echo does); she is his complementary counterpart, unable, or not allowed, to develop a mature relationship with him which would give him the chance to get out of the jail of his selfishness. Finally, both will die, she from not being recognised and loved, he from being unable to love anyone but himself. So, both were trapped in the narcissistic mirror relationship with each other, unable to meet each other as individual persons in a real object relationship of intimacy and otherness.

Narcissism and the self

According to the German psychoanalyst, Mentzos (1982), we should recognise that the term narcissism is used in at least two different contexts and meanings.

1. Narcissism, in the first sense, is a protective device, a defensive strategy, implying withdrawal from the object and turning towards the self. From this point of view, all those tendencies or fantasies that we call "narcissistic" are characterised by turning away from the object towards the self, resulting in increased libidinal cathexis of the self (or, in Freud's terms, the ego) as a defence strategy against object-directed tendencies, mainly because of self-centred fears such as fear of losing oneself, or losing one's independence, or losing the other's admiration by turning out not to be the perfect person others had thought him to be. So, behind the "narcissistic" attitude, there is a deep insecurity about oneself and one's own worth in the eyes of others.
2. On the other hand, narcissism in the second sense, as synonymous to the self system, includes all needs, satisfactions, affects, mechanisms, etc. involved in the constitution and differentiation of the self and the regulation of the self-esteem (Kohut, 1966). In this second meaning, the term "narcissistic" may be used, for instance, to characterize object relations which contribute to the increase of self esteem or self-identity, as well as experiences shattering self-esteem (so-called narcissistic injuries). Anger, grudge or rage as a result of hurt narcissism (humiliation, shame) is called "narcissistic rage" (Kohut, 1972).

In the first sense, the narcissistic attitude stands in opposition to object-relatedness; in the second sense, the narcissistic function, for example of a certain behaviour or object relationship, is opposed to its drive-related function.

This differentiation is important, since "narcissistic" in the second sense can often be object related, too: the narcissistic homoeostasis—the regulation of the self-esteem—depends heavily on the narcissistic supply (affirmation, appreciation) and, therefore, on the objects. This is valid not only for some of our patients but also for healthy adults: we all need recognition and appreciation—"mirroring of the self by self-objects (to be precise: the self-object-aspects of one's love-objects)", as Kohut calls it.

Historical review

As early as 1914, Freud (in his paper "On narcissism: an introduction", 1914c) realised that the aim of the human psyche—as of any living organism—is not only to seek drive satisfaction and avoid painful experiences (pleasure–unpleasure principle), which necessitates adaptation to external reality (reality principle), but in addition to these important principles there is another aim of all our psychic regulations: the maintenance of a feeling-state of well-being. Freud and others call this balanced state "narcissistic homeostasis". Reich (1960) stressed the aspect of self-esteem regulation, and Sandler (1960) worked out a "security principle", which is very important also in psychotherapy, where the patient should feel safe: ("the background of safety"). People can be in a conflict between their striving for pleasure and the need for safety; and there are situations in which self-realisation, living up to one's potential or one's personal truth and values, may be more important than avoiding the unpleasure of conflicts or hard work. So, there is a qualitative difference between drive tendencies and self-needs. The sense of well-being provided by sufficient self-esteem and identity is totally different from relaxing after drive discharge.

Hence, we are able to understand better that sometimes conflicts arise between drive needs and narcissistic self-needs, even though they normally agree with each other (e.g., the feeling of narcissistic grandiosity experience by people in love).

We can also understand how drive satisfaction may be substituted by narcissistic satisfaction and vice versa. A child renounces certain drive satisfactions in order to receive his mother's appreciation. Conversely, children—and also adults—comfort themselves for shameful narcissistic injuries by using sweets or thumb-sucking, or increased eating or drinking as a substitutive oral drive satisfaction.

Today, then, we distinguish between a drive development on the one hand and a narcissistic development on the other. The development of self and object relations mediates between them and they are based on it (Table 1.1).

Regulation of self-esteem

One of the most important functions of the self-system is the maintenance of the narcissistic homoeostasis, the maintenance of an optimal level of self-esteem. Our self-esteem is endangered by narcissistic injuries, withdrawal of usual narcissistic supply, failures, defeats, and other bad experiences. What options are available in order to avoid or compensate for a threatened or already existing disturbance of one's self-esteem?

Table 1.1. Psychic development: drives, object relations, and self.

	Age (about)			
	0–1	2	3	4–5
Drive development	Oral stage	Anal stage	Phallic–narcissistic stage	Infantile genital stage
Object relations	"Symbiosis" or dual relationship	"Separation"/ individuation	Self-centredness	Triangulation
Self-system Self- and object representations Processes and principles	Emerging differentiation Part objects Grandiose self	Part objects Secondary process Reality principle Primary process	Whole objects Idealised objects Ideal self	Real self Real objects Superego Ego ideal

1. Regressive withdrawal and fusion with primary elements (e.g., nature): such regression is often experienced as a kind of fusion with a primary object, such as "Mother Nature", mountains, oceans, etc., providing a feeling of participation in the greatness and strength of nature, beyond interpersonal relationships with the associated risk of being hurt.
2. Denial of painful reality by means of grandiose fantasies: this way of compensation for disturbances of the narcissistic equilibrium is a normal stage for the infant, described by Kohut (1966) as the "grandiose self". Parents support this development by confirming the infant to be lovely, beautiful, good, and great. The "gleam in mother's eyes", the "mirror-function" of the parents, is, according to Kohut, a necessary precondition for the fulfilment of narcissistic needs and progress in the building of a stable self.
3. Compensation through idealisation: the experience of his limited power and skills gradually forces the child to question his former grandiose self-image (Kohut, 1972). Instead, the child will idealise or identify with seemingly almighty and all-knowing objects (his parents) to save his self-esteem. This is a normal stage in the child's development at the age of three and later. The idealised image of the parents will be corrected step by step and become more realistic.

Regarding the object relations of children (and adults), the relevant persons in early childhood are not only necessary for drive satisfaction, that is to say, in their function as drive objects. They are also very important for the constitution and development of the self. In this sense, Kohut refers to them as self-objects. The child needs these self-objects first for mirroring (being praised, encouraged, admired), second as persons to idealise and to identify with. How important these idealised self-objects will remain in later life is evident from the relevance of heroes for the narcissistic equilibrium of the masses.

The ideal self

The over-valuation of one's own self and the over-idealisation of the parents is overcome by gradual decline of the grandiose self and the idealised object(s). A more realistic self-ideal emerges, which Sandler (1960) described as a buffering structure against narcissistic injuries, allowing one to say, "Although I am not perfect, basically I am good and all right." The healthy ideal self gives the person relative independence from praise and reproach by others, enabling inner security, self-consciousness, and calm self-confidence.

The self-system: "three pillar model" by Mentzos

We can demonstrate and explain the self-system in its relation with significant self-objects needed for recognition or mirroring, following Mentzos' conceptualisation (after Kohut and others) in a model of three "pillars" of narcissistic homoeostasis on different levels of intrapsychic and object-relation maturity (Mentzos, 1995) (Figure 1.5). According to Mentzos, three pillars build up the basis of narcissistic self-esteem:

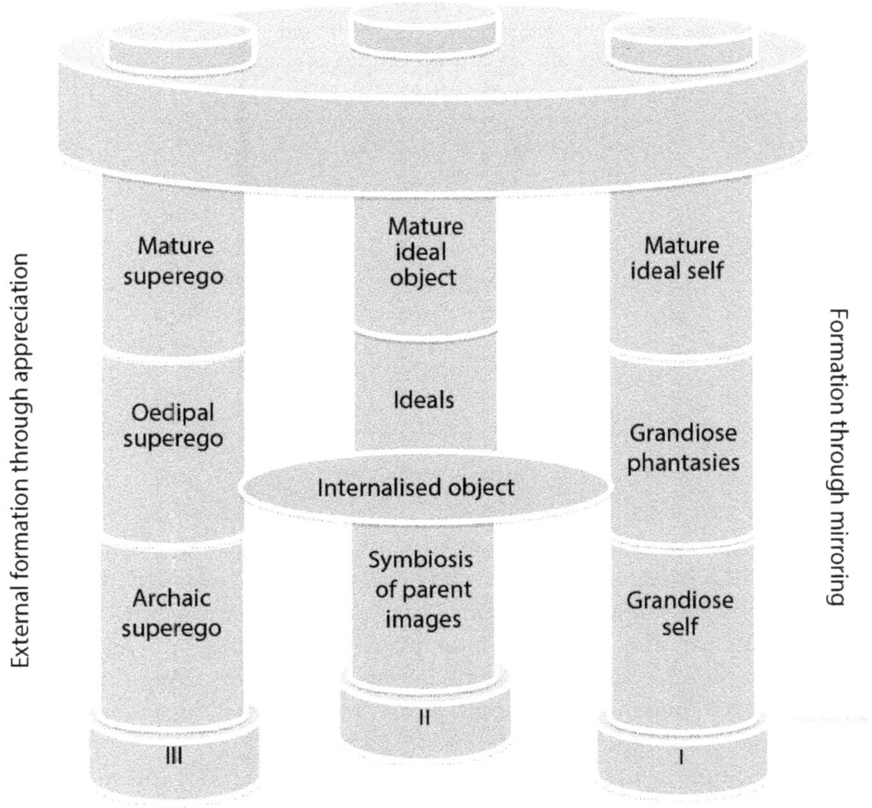

Figure 1.5. The self-system: "three pillar model" (Mentzos, 1995, modified).

(i) grandiose self, fantasies of oneself being perfect → "ideal self";
(ii) ideal object, admired others, they become models → "ideal object";
(iii) pride in self-restraint, self-discipline, submitting to the law → "superego" (Table 1.2).

The pillars have been designated I, II and III from right to left. The platform at the top of the illustration represents adequate self-esteem and a relatively balanced narcissistic homeostasis, as long as this platform remains stable in a horizontal position. It stands on these three pillars.

The first pillar, on the right side, represents at its base the "grandiose self"; in the middle part, our more or less lifelong present, half-conscious "grandiose fantasies", and last, towards the top, the mature ideal self (the realistically corrected, positive image of oneself), which, despite inevitable mistakes, failures, negative criticism, etc., guarantees a certain degree of consistent self-confidence as a "buffer" against narcissistic injuries (disappointments, defeats, humiliations).

However, such a favourable development (good stable composition and adequate functioning, particularly in situations of crisis) will depend decisively upon certain prerequisites,

Table 1.2. The self-system: "three pillar model" (Mentzos, 1995).

Developmental level	Self			Related self-objects
	Pillar III	Pillar II	Pillar I	
Mature level (more or less independent self-esteem regulation by internal structures)	Mature superego	Mature ideal object	Mature ideal self	Normal adult narcissistic supplies through recognition and mirroring
Intermediate level	Oedipal superego	Ideals	Grandiose phantasies	Internalised self-objects
Primitive level (narcissism strongly dependent on self-objects)	Archaic superego	Early parent-images	Grandiose self	Early self-objects

such as the physical and mental "capital stock" (health, completeness, satiety, physical well-being, talents, etc.), and also depend on good-enough mothering, affirmation and positive mirroring of the child's existence and personal value, that is, consistent narcissistic supplies coming from the primary object (the "gleam" in mother's eyes (Kohut, 1972)). To a certain extent, these supplies are also available later from relevant others. This positive admiring mirroring, not recognition for good achievements—as in the third pillar—but gratuitous acceptance, is a guarantee for the emergence of a healthy, realistic and durable ideal self ("Even if I botch things up sometimes, basically I am a good chap").

The second pillar, that is, the middle pillar, represents at its base the early dependency on one's parents, and later also the participation through identification in the idealised parental imagoes. Its middle section represents the identification with other role models. The upper section represents the mature (assimilated rather than merely introjected) ideal object. Here it is not the developing self who feels admirable, as in the context of the dynamics of the first pillar, but the individual has developed his own ideals and values, by taking admired other persons—first his idealised parents and later others—as his role models.

The stabilising effect, bolstering self-esteem regulation, does not come about through physical or mental vitality of the self, and not by mirroring from the outside (as in pillar I) or through the recognition of good achievements (as in pillar III, further below), but through closeness and warmth and, later, through identification with the ideal object and participation in the greatness and strength of the ideal object.

Finally, the third pillar corresponds with the archaic immature superego at its base, in the middle section the oedipal superego, and, in the upper section, the now mature conscience. It embraces the sum of the adopted parental prohibitions and commands, later transformed into self-discipline and moral conscience. The pillar's strength and quality and other characteristics correspond to the specific features of the adopted superego. Its stability is built on recognition for accomplished achievements. The function of the pillar is orientated towards achievement and action, guaranteeing the fulfilment of duties and the observing of prohibitions regarding the satisfaction of instincts and/or the rights and well-being of others. On its highest level, representing mature conscience, it is one of the most powerful and most successful regulators of social interaction, beyond individual psychology. The internalised standards, securely anchored in the personality structure, will contribute considerably to the development of a sense of justice.

Primary process and secondary process, pleasure–unpleasure principle, and reality principle

Internalisation and psychic development towards maturity influence the general modes in which the psyche or inner world is functioning. We distinguish between the primary process, following the pleasure principle, and the secondary process, following the reality principle.

Freud's terms "primary process" and "secondary process" designate two opposed, yet, nevertheless, complementary modes of functioning within the psychic apparatus. The primary process is typical for mental processes which are dominated by drives (e.g., sexual or aggressive) and operate according to the pleasure principle, aiming at immediate tension release and free flow of psychic energy. Secondary processes, which presuppose the binding of this energy, intervene as a system of control and regulation in the service of the reality principle. Psychic life is entirely regulated by the equilibrium between these two types of processes, which varies between subjects and at different points in time (waking consciousness *vs.* fantasies and dreams, influence of drugs, and other regressed mental states, such as hallucinating in psychoses, etc.).

Freud raises the prospect of this fundamental duality as early as his "Project for a Scientific Psychology" (1950[1895]). Briefly put, a desire or drive wish will trigger a process of discharge. As we know, drives always need an object for satisfaction. As soon as a drive wish arises, a memory of the drive-related object will be activated. If the object is not really available, the subject, on the level of primary process functioning, will not be able to imagine the object as being absent; instead the object will be hallucinated as if it were present. But, to take an example, a hallucination of food will not really satisfy the hunger drive. As Freud (1911c) says, an organism functioning exclusively on primary process level and according to the pleasure–unpleasure principle (blind seeking for pleasure, avoiding unpleasure), disregarding the reality of the external world, would not be able to survive. This is the reason why, besides the earlier drive system of primary process, a second system is necessary that is able to renounce wishful thinking and recognise reality as it is, without avoiding unpleasant facts. This kind of functioning according to the reality principle we call secondary process functioning. It includes an ability to inhibit primary process tendencies, to imagine an absent object in order to search for it in the external world (instead of hallucinating its presence), and to develop strategies for recognising and mastering real situations according to the so-called reality principle.

In the beginning, a human baby is dominated by drives and bodily needs and functions almost exclusively according to the primary process. How is the baby able to survive? Freud's answer, as early as 1895 in his "Project for a Scientific Psychology", was to constitute the keystone of the contemporary development of theories of psychogenesis, by bringing the mother–child relationship into consideration: the mother must complement her baby's deficiencies by her care, her availability as an object as the baby needs her, and by her own realistic (secondary process) ego functioning.

In his topographic model of the psyche—the so-called "mental apparatus"—Freud (1900a, 1915e) discerns:

1. Areas outside of conscious awareness: "Ucs", the "unconscious system", dominated by the primary-process mode of functioning, as can be recognised in the "primary process logic" of dreams, characterised by displacement, condensation, symbolic and imaginary thinking, etc.
2. Areas available to conscious awareness: "Pcs", the "preconscious system", dominated by the secondary-process mode of functioning: logically structured, realistic, and verbalised thinking. In his article on "The unconscious" (1915e) Freud describes the preconscious as the locus of the secondary processes and their regulating function over the primary processes characteristic of the unconscious. It is this regulation that binds the cathectic energy used for representations, and, therefore, enables the development of cognition. Indeed the work of thought ("thinking as a kind of trial action") requires that the representations upon which it is based remain stable and distinct. This would not be possible if the free flow of energy, and the condensations and displacements characteristic of the primary processes, prevailed.

According to Holt (1989a,b) and other psychoanalytic thinkers after Freud, there is not an absolute contrast but, rather, a continuum between primary and secondary process thinking. In specific situations—for instance, in dreaming, in daydreams, erotic intimacy, creative and intuitive acts, and in neurotic symptoms—we find a certain degree of regression to primary-process thinking, imagery, and symbolism, which is not totally unconscious but can also be available to conscious awareness.

Kernberg (1995) explicated the object-relational aspect of primary and secondary process thinking: both are connected with object relations, either more "primitive" or "archaic" ones (with primary process) or more elaborated and differentiated ones (with secondary process). This means, in both forms of thinking, we find specific self-representations, object-representations, and emotional relations between self and object.

This view is in agreement with infant research (Stern, Lichtenberg) and attachment theory (Bowlby, Ainsworth): the development of the person or the self is deeply embedded in, and dependent on, object-relations. This is also valid for a person's relationship with him- or herself—what we call narcissism. As we shall see, narcissism, with its aspects of self-esteem, self-identity, self-presentation, etc., is dependent on appreciation and affirmation, mirroring and recognition by others who serve as so-called self-objects. These aspects have been elaborated in Kohut's psychology of the self (Kohut 1966, 1972), as we have described in our section of this chapter, on "Narcissm and self-system".

CHAPTER TWO

PSYCHOANALYTIC THEORY OF PSYCHIC DEVELOPMENT THROUGH THE LIFE SPAN

Hanni Scheid-Gerlach, Klaus Kocher, Christine Gerstenfeld, and Wolfgang Merkle

Methodology of psychological theory of development

Hanni Scheid-Gerlach

The psychoanalytic theory of human development is founded on different scientific methods: reconstruction, observation, and baby-watching.

Reconstruction

The contribution of psychoanalysis to human understanding is its explanation of neurotic mental disorders in terms of fixation or regression of the libido. Libido, a term that means desire, is defined as the instinctual sexual energy underlying all mental activity. The development of human beings goes through different stages, which Freud called the oral, anal, and genital (oedipal) phases. Since the development of this theory, conflicts in adults can usually be reconstructed through their experience in childhood and how they developed from birth until puberty. To understand mental disorders, it is necessary to reconstruct the childhood of patients, during which they developed special defences that are responsible for their present suffering.

Observation

Anna Freud could draw on her experiences as a teacher when pursuing her interest in psychoanalysis in the field of early adolescence. She had ample opportunities to observe children's development in daily life and recorded her experience in writing, transforming her observations into theory in *The Ego and the Mechanisms of Defence* (A. Freud, 1937). She established courses in child analysis and later founded the Hampstead Child Therapy Clinic. Dorothy Burlingham and Melanie Klein also observed children. These observations were very helpful in increasing our knowledge about development and provided many impulses for the advancement of psychoanalytic theory.

Baby-watchers

Spitz is one of the best known researchers on infant development. He carried out research in various settings: for example, in foundling homes or penal nurseries. Spitz developed special designs for observation, by utilising methods commonly used in experimental psychology. Through direct observation, he developed the diagnosis of hospitalism. Other baby-watchers worked in laboratories, where they stayed with babies and observed them in different states, such as while awake, or in an acute state of hunger. Later baby-watchers who followed include Mahler, Emde and Stern. Since 1970, there has been special research on the interpersonal interaction between mother and infant. Video technology has made it possible to show the nonverbal effects of mimicry and gesture that form the interaction between mother and baby.

These results significantly influenced further theories of development and new constructions of development theories. The baby is no longer understood to be a closed system who only responds to the mother or the nurse. He actively searches for contact and social interaction, and the character of object relations is highly significant for development. The interaction between mother and child, which is internalised, can be seen later in the interaction with the therapist. The emotional dialogue between the two interacting partners is of great importance. The baby, therefore, is a very competent subject, who has to go through different stages of development. How he achieves his development stages depends on emotional interactions with his environment, that is, the mother, father, and other important people around him.

In psychoanalysis, human development is a lifelong process with certain tasks associated with it.

Special imprints of the character of an adult arise during the early phases of development. In the way the infant is handled and how his basic drives are satisfied by the objects around him we find the determinants of the growing structure (ego and superego; ego ideal) of the inner world. The mother, or primary carer, and subsequent significant others (father, siblings, teachers, etc.) have a great influence on the early childhood. Early disturbances by the caretaking objects (mainly the parents, but also all other environmental elements such as money, life style, and political convictions) might interfere with the process of development.

Overview of the fundamental theories on psychic development

In the following section, I refer to the *International Dictionary of Psychoanalysis* (De Mijolla, 2005).

Sigmund Freud (1856–1939)

Freud's theory is one of the most fundamental for psychoanalysis. He held sway over the domain of psychology and psychoanalysis for more than fifty years, working on the theory of dreams, free association, structure of the personality, psychosexual stages of development, the concept of id, ego, and superego, the concept of conscious, subconscious, and preconscious mind, and ego-defence mechanisms, which are still an integral part of psychology today. His productivity remained high almost until the end of his life. Even during his last twenty years, when he was suffering from cancer and had to undergo thirty-three operations, he continued to work. He produced twenty-four volumes of work expounding his theories and documenting his valuable experiences. Freud is known for his theory and practice of psychoanalysis, and for developing the first psychological therapy ever designed to solve people's mental problems. He analysed his own dreams and developed an insight into the dynamics of his personality development. He explored the memories of his childhood and formulated the stages of psychosexual development that will be presented in the next chapters of this textbook.

Freud's understanding of the child's mental development was centred on the oedipal (infantile-genital or phallic) stage. The method of reconstruction to obtain valid material is limited, because the child has to "forget", or has to repress, the largest part of his first years' memory (infantile amnesia). Observation of the baby's and the child's behaviour, both in his natural environment and under experimental conditions, became more important.

René A. Spitz (1887–1974)

Spitz, an Austro-Hungarian psychiatrist and psychoanalyst, was born in Vienna and died in Denver, Colorado. He examined the development of object relations, focusing mainly on the non-verbal dialogue between mother (or caring others) and baby.

He carried out medical examinations in nurseries, where infants were medically taken care of and fed, but nevertheless suffered from mysterious psychosomatic diseases. Many babies died. Spitz discovered that not being in contact with sufficiently nurturing people caused infants to suffer from social deprivation. Spitz described this phenomenon as anaclitic depression and hospitalism by emotional neglect.

According to Spitz, infants pass through three stages that correspond to categorised developmental stages in object relations (Table 2.1)

Table 2 1. Three organisers of psychic development (Spitz, 1965).

Age	Developmental stage
0–3 months	The objectless stage, characterised by "non-differentiation" between baby and mother
Approx. 3 months	Smiling at everybody
3–8 months	The stage of "the precursor of the object", in which the smiling indicates the beginning of object relations
Approx. 8 months	Fear of the stranger
8–15 months	The stage of the libidinal object, by which time the mother is recognised as a real partner and the infant can distinguish her face from a stranger`s face. In the beginning of the second year the child enters into semantic communication with gesture and the use of "no", indicating the emergence of the autonomous ego
Approx. 12 months	The child expresses "no" by facial play, gestures, and words

John Bowlby (1907–1990)

Bowlby, psychiatrist and psychoanalyst, was born in London and died on the Isle of Skye. After the war, he worked in the Tavistock Clinic, and was Winnicott's secretary in the British Psychoanalytical Society. In contrast to Melanie Klein, he paid more attention to the role of the environment of children. Bowlby worked with handicapped children and, therefore, he was highly sensitive to the function of the mother–child bond and the environment.

Influenced by scientists in the field of ethology (such as Harlow), Bowlby emphasised a biological species-specific genetic bias to become attached; he developed the position, that the instinct for preservation and security is as important as that of sexuality; he also postulated that the mother–child bond is independent of infantile sexuality. Attachment is the name for an emotionally close relationship. The newborn develops a special attachment with his parents and other relevant people. The attachment is important for an infant, for it shelters him from real, external danger and inner threats (anxieties, pain, etc.).

Attachment behaviour can be observed by watching how a baby laughs or screams, how it holds a person, and how it crawls to the mother. Differences in the parent–child interactions form different "inner working models". These models develops in the first year of life and are stable throughout life. The different "inner working models" depend on the quality of the relationship. To be empathic and emotional and to understand the babies' needs is most important. For the first six weeks of a baby's life, different people may deal with the child, but after that the baby will react to a new person, for it has already built up an object constancy.

The early mother–child interaction is inclined to lead to generalisations. Other researchers discovered that the attachment patterns have a transgenerative aspect: when insecurely attached children become parents, they, in turn, mostly have insecurely attached children. If we have enough information about the attachment patterns of mothers, it is possible to predict, with high degree of confidence, the future attachment patterns of still unborn children.

Melanie Klein (1882–1960)

Melanie Klein was a psychoanalyst who was born in Vienna, but moved to Britain to work. She died in London.

She was interested in psychoanalysis because of her own traumatic history. She underwent treatment with Sandor Ferenczi. Learning from Freud's "Little Hans", she began investigations of her own children. Later, she was often in disagreement with Anna Freud and her theoretical opinion. Two analytical schools developed out of this conflict.

Klein formulated two main positions: each infant has to go through the stages of the paranoid–schizoid position and the depressive position.

Within this concept, Klein proposed an early phase of oral sadism of the newborn child, in which the infant tries to suck out the body of the mother and wants to steal all her contents. With this process of introjection, in which the child projects his hate to the mother, she becomes a dangerous, persecuting object. This part of Klein's theory has its basis in Freud's death drive.

In her thinking, the infant divides the mother object into part-objects. The integration of the two positions of a "good mother" and a "persecuting mother" would lead to an emotional state that she defines as the "depressive position". In this state, the infant has to mourn all he has lost, because the mother can never provide everything that the infant hallucinates. The infant develops guilt feelings for being too hungry and also for being full of fantasies of destroying the mother object.

To offer protection against the pain and the guilt feelings, defence operations must emerge. This is the so-called paranoid–schizoid position. The problem is that the depressive position by itself is a difficult state of feeling. If the infant is able to work through the depressive position, it might not remain in a state of melancholy. Therefore, it is important that an infant can internalise the good part of the mother (good breast), which represents inner stability, security, and trust. Also, a child must develop the capability for reparation. This means that a child develops the confidence to believe that the damage that was done can be repaired or overcome.

The paranoid–schizoid position is the state where the bad parts of the mother object are overwhelming, meaning that the child has to bear a lot of anxieties which, according to Klein, belong to the death drive. This overflow of negative affects destroys the inner structure of the "ego" with the result that it might fall apart.

To prevent this possibility, the inner life must evolve another defence mechanism: "projection". This means that the negative feelings have to be projected into the environment (people, things, dolls, animals, etc.). In this case, the infant (later the patient) feels pursued by everything from outside. Projection and introjection are the basic processes with which the ego shields itself. Bad parts are expelled from the inner life and are projected to useful objects on the outside; this state Klein called "projective identification".

The central construct in Klein's theory is the concept of "splitting": she points out that we should be aware of the double movement: on the one hand the "bad breast" itself is split into many parts, on the other, there is a splitting between the "good" and the "bad" breast. The good part of the breast may lead to an idealised fantasy of a "good" breast, where no disappointment is possible.

Margaret Mahler (1897–1985)

Mahler, a physician and psychoanalyst, was born in Hungary and died in New York. Her interest in psychiatry and psychoanalysis developed as she turned away from the rarely empathic, sterile practice of paediatrics. She met Aichhorn and Abraham, and attended Anna Freud's child analysis seminar.

Because of the Second World War—her mother died in a concentration camp—she first moved briefly to Britain, and then to the USA.

Her theory of the beginning of life is published in the book authored with Pine and Bergman (1975), *The Psychological Birth of the Human Infant*. They point out the process from the close mother–child relationship (dyad) to individualisation through separation. The phases are set out in Table 2.2.

As shown, Phase 1 is the week of birth, the period of psychic gestation. In Phase 1.1, the normal autistic phase, the baby is centred on proprioceptive and enteroceptive sensations that represent a "model of a closed monadic system", self-sufficient in its hallucinatory wish fulfilment. Phase 1.2 is the symbiotic phase, where infant and mother form a "dual unity within one common boundary".

Table 2.2. The phases of separation and individuation (Mahler, Pine, & Bergman, 1975).

Phases of separation and individuation	Age
1. Precursor of the process of separation and individuation	
1.1. Normal autistic phase	First few weeks
1.2 Normal symbiotic phase	Up to 5 months
2. Phases of separation and individuation: differentiation and development of body pattern	
2.1 Hatching	5–12 months
2.2 Practising	12–18 months
2.3 Rapprochement	18–24 months
2.4 Consolidation of individuality and the beginning of emotional object constancy	24–36 months

Phase 2 takes place from four to five months and marks the beginning of the separation–individuation process. In Phase 2.1, from five months old, the infant is able to differentiate: Mahler calls this period the "hatching" of a primitive self from the earlier symbiotic attachment to the mother. From10–12 months until 16–18 months, the infant enters Phase 2.2, becoming a toddler with growing motor and cognitive skills with which to enjoy a "love affair with the world".

From 16–24 months up to thirty months, in Phase 2.3, the toddler experiences both separateness and associated crisis of dependency, while Phase 2.4, a final, open-ended sub-phase that Mahler characterises as "toward object constancy", occurs as the child achieves an individual and variable measure of autonomy and emotional balance associated with a relatively stable and differentiated intrapsychic representation of the mother. Mahler's concept of "separation–individuation" is still of great importance today.

Donald W. Winnicott (1896–1971)

Winnicott, a paediatrician and psychoanalyst, was born in Plymouth and died in London. He is close to Mahler's theory, for their main view is focused on the dependent relationship between mother and child. They both point out the development from the mother object to more autonomy.

Winnicott had a great deal of experience as a physician and as a paediatrician, where he could collect much information about child development and mother–child relationships. His theory is positioned between that of Melanie Klein and that of Anna Freud. He concentrated his attention on the effects of the environment on an infant.

He states that in the first months the baby is symbiotic with the mother; the infant is aware of the mother as a part of himself. In Winnicott's thinking there is not an "ideal mother", who is "damaging" her child by not fulfilling his ideal. He is speaking of a "good enough mother", by which he means the mother is able to see and feel the needs of the baby. The mother object should try not to leave the baby alone emotionally. During his development, the infant separates himself more and more from the mother object as he begins to crawl, walk, speak, etc.). In this process the child realises that he is not a part of the mother object. In the process of separation, Winnicott postulated the so-called "transitional object". This is an object chosen by the child that helps to fill the gap when the baby is without the mother. The transitional object represents the early mother–child relationship. It might be a teddy bear, a piece of blanket, a doll, etc. This stage takes place between the age of four and twelve months. The transitional object will be given up as the infant becomes older. So, this object is a connection between the inner and the outer world; this means that when the mother object is bad or absent, the baby can use the transitional object, so that he does not feel alone in his inner world. The baby becomes disturbed when lacking a "good enough" environment, for instance, when a mother is physically or emotionally absent, disturbed, or intrusive, or when the baby has needs that cannot be fulfilled.

Erik H. Erikson (1902–1994)

Erikson, a teacher of arts, was born in Frankfurt in 1902 and died in Massachusetts in 1994. Erikson worked together with Eva Rosenfeld and Dorothy Burlingham, both close friends of Anna Freud, as a psychoanalyst.

He used his concept of ego identity to move psychoanalytic theory away from Freud's libido approach. Erikson saw society as a constructive source for the ego to grow. He expanded on Freud's thoughts and divided the development of a human into eight stages, from birth to old age.

As you can see from Table 2.3, each stage may be resolved for good or for ill. The first five stages roughly correspond with Freud's stages, while the last three rather follow Jung's ideas about humans in their more mature age.

Heinz Kohut (1913–1981)

Kohut had different professions that provided him with inspirational inputs. He was a medical doctor, a psychiatrist, a neurologist, and a psychoanalyst. He devised new theories when there was a lack of patients with hysteria or compulsive neurosis. He had to deal with patients who suffered from working disorders, perverse actions, or with feelings of being empty, meaningless, or depressed.

He recognised that these patients could not recuperate during therapy when working with their drive conflicts. These patients suffered from disorders of their self and narcissism.

Table 2.3. Erikson's life stages of development (1950).

Age	S. Freud	E. H. Erikson
0–1	Oral	Trust *vs.* mistrust
2–3	Anal	Autonomy *vs.* shame and doubt
4–5	Infantile-genital (oedipal)	Initiative *vs.* guilt
6–10	Latency	Industry *vs.* inferiority
11–18	Puberty, genital	Identity *vs.* identity diffusion
Early adulthood	Genital	Intimacy *vs.* isolation
Middle adulthood	Genital	Genital generativity *vs.* self-absorption
Later adulthood	Genital	Integrity *vs.* despair

Kohut states that a healthy narcissism, which expresses a strong, viable "self", is able to increase its abilities and to satisfy its own needs. A pathological narcissism of a weak "self" presents itself by playing roles with grandiosity. If this pattern fails, the object will become depressed. Kohut extended the spectrum of treatment with psychoanalytical methods. He added thoughts to the Freudian drive theory and the ego-orientated theory. In his theory, he states that the baby is in a symbiotic state where the inner balance of total shelter will be changed by the limitations of the mother object, but the child keeps an inner representation of "total", an ideal which Kohut calls "grandiose self". This structure might come into conflict with the real parents, who are not fulfilling the inner ideal. During the time immediately following birth, the parents may mirror the "grandiose self" of the baby and present themselves as ideal parents. Then, according to Kohut, a "mainself" is installed, and a kind of realisation movement will happen simultaneously with the child separating (Mahler) from the mother object. In the early stage of development, it is very important that the mother object is empathic, can calm the baby, and tries to understand the body language of the newborn. Missing or negative reactions to the baby will increase the likelihood of a growing-up structure being weak and unable to withstand strong regressive affects. Kohut later rejected Freud's structural theory of the id, ego, and superego. He then developed his ideas around what he called the tripartite (three-part) self.

According to Kohut, this "three-part self" can only develop when the needs of one's "self states", including one's sense of worth and well-being, are met in relationships with others. In contrast to traditional psychoanalysis, which focuses on drives (instinctual motivations of sex and aggression), internal conflicts, and fantasies; "self psychology", as Kohut termed it, thus placed a great deal of emphasis on the vicissitudes of relationships.

Kohut further explored the implications of Freud's perception of narcissism. He maintained that a child tends to fantasise a grandiose self and ideal parents. He claimed that, deep down, all people retain a belief in their own perfection and the perfection of anything of which they are a part. As a person matures, grandiosity gives way to self-esteem and the idealisation of the parent becomes the framework for core values. When psychological trauma disrupts this process, the primitive and narcissistic version of the self remains unchanged. Kohut defined this condition as "narcissistic personality disorder".

Joseph Lichtenberg (1925–)

Lichtenberg, an American psychiatrist and psychoanalyst, integrated the research on infants and children, among others, into psychoanalysis. From the point of view of self psychology, he constructed a system of motivational systems which were to replace Freud's theory of drives (libido and death drive).

Lichtenberg suggests five different systems, which are connected with each other. These systems apply from birth throughout life.

1. *The necessity to satisfy physiological needs*. This system regulates hunger, thirst, breathing, warmth, excreta, tactile stimulation, sleep, etc. The regulation of the physiological needs is not only a biological substructure for sexuality and object relations, it is a system on its own.

2. *The need for bonding and later attachment.* Actions by the baby, such as searching, touching, clinging, and snuggling, as well as communicating and wishing to be understood without words, being close, and feeling empathic resonance.
3. *The need for assertion and exploration.* This means that a tendency in each child to be competent and effective should be increased. The objects should be happy about the things that someone does successfully.
4. *The need to react aversively by protest or withdrawal.* This means to have the capability to overcome aggressive emotions. This system helps to regulate the self-esteem.
5. *The need for sensual enjoyment and sexual excitement.*

The last point is of great interest in Freud's theory. Lichtenberg points out that these needs are only specific experiences, with specific rhythmic body feelings, which are connected with the affects of interest, joy, happiness, and relaxation. Several parts of the body could be the source of this experience: lips, mouth, anus, penis, genitals, and skin.

Lichtenberg points out that for each of these motivational systems the meaning of affects is most important, for they represent the essential emotional communication between children and their objects. Disturbances during early childhood should be differentiated, depending on which system was disturbed.

Conclusional remark

The history of theories on psychic development shows that different analysts put particular aspects at the centre of their understanding and neglected other aspects (see Freud *vs.* Winnicott *vs.* Lichtenberg). Some aspects, such as the understanding of the first weeks of life (i.e., autistic stage of the baby), are not up to date scientifically, but the main concepts of the theories are still valid and helpful in understanding psychic development generally, and patients with special conflicts and trauma in their early life history.

Perinatal stage and the first year of life: the oral stage

Psychic development starts during pregnancy, synchronised with the development of the sensory nervous system (i.e., the foetus can perceive painful stimuli by the twenty-fourth week, can see and recognise different structures and can hear different voices by the thirty-third week of pregnancy).

In the final weeks of pregnancy, the foetus can communicate with the world outside the mother's body.

The Swiss biologist, A. Portmann described the human baby as a "premature birth": compared with other mammals, the newborn baby is not ready or sufficiently developed to exist independently and needs the "social uterus of the family" for bodily maturation and psychosocial development. This aspect of seeming developmental deficit is understood by the neuropsychological sciences as an advantage: the "uterus of the mother–child and family relationship" has an important influence on the process of cognitive, emotional, and social development and bodily maturation. After the mother's pregnancy and baby's birth, the baby is dependent on the family, in particular the mother.

Many psychoanalysts contributed different aspects and theories about the first year of life: theory of drives (Freud, Klein, Spitz), of object-relationship (Spitz, Bowlby, Mahler, Winnicott), and of self and narcissism (Kohut, Lichtenberg). Not only the psychoanalytical theories, but also the non-psychoanalytical neurosciences of today stress the importance of the first year of life for a healthy somatic, mental, and social development.

Here, we want to emphasise most of all Freud's understanding of the first year. The oral stage is the first stage, where satisfaction is derived by the infant via the mouth through sucking a nipple or a thumb, which appears to be independent from nutritional needs. The mouth is the dominant erogenous zone of the body to satisfy these needs (food and communication and interaction with the mother and care-givers).

The feelings that arise when a baby is fed are realised by the infant through the pleasure (desire for good feelings) and the non-pleasure principle (aversive feelings). Freud said that the psychic apparatus wants nothing except the satisfaction of desires. So, if a baby is confronted with a high quantity of non-pleasurable feelings, his inner world will react with a defence. This happens because non-pleasurable feelings are very difficult to contain at such an early stage of development. The baby, at this age, has a very primitive psychic apparatus (bodily feelings, but no cognitive structures as yet) and does not yet understand what is happening to him. Thus, the baby depends totally on others in order to derive sufficient pleasure satisfaction. Sucking the mother's breast or his fingers gives the baby a feeling of satisfaction (he is not hungry any more), which can be felt all over the body, including the skin. Through the skin, the baby feels the mother, and it might have the impression that it is still inside the mother's body. Also important at this stage is how a mother carries her baby or tries to stop his crying, which is caused by unbearable non-pleasurable feelings of the baby. Feeding, as an oral pleasurable event, is, therefore, not only the giving of food, but also an interaction with the mother. The modus of interaction is oral. Thus, something is put into the mouth that gives pleasurable feelings inside the body. By means of this pattern, the baby incorporates the mother's behaviour.

The baby depends totally on the mother or care-giver. He lives in a dyad (Mahler), in unity with his mother. Feeding, bodily care, playing, talking, and moving are important stimuli for mental and bodily maturation. Crying and laughing are the most important methods of communication, but exploring his external environment through the use of eyes, ears, and hands becomes more important. Spitz, Mahler, Winnicott, and Bowlby pointed out different aspects of the mother–child relationship: basic trust and attachment.

At the age of six months, the baby cuts his first teeth. As a result of this, the oral satisfaction of the drives and the interaction with the mother or other care-givers can give rise to an aggressive approach by biting. The baby begins to turn his body and tries to move by crawling on his stomach to reach interesting things. After the close and satisfied relationship of the first year, the baby also begins to develop the first moments of independence from the mother object.

We all know this kind of pattern. When we are grown up, most of us still like to kiss our lover; we also like to be caressed by our lover. Deep bodily sensations can occur and, if they are formed by the pleasure principle, these good enough feelings with the care-taking objects can be internalised. This means that the baby depends totally on the objects to provide enough satisfaction to activate the pleasure principle.

The second and third year: the anal stage

Klaus Kocher

I should like briefly to describe the inner world of the child during the second and third year. We shall take a look at the anal stage, and I shall present a characterisation of the second and third year from a psychoanalytic viewpoint of development.

This is certainly a challenging period of life, during which enormous growth happens in all kinds of different fields, including physical and mental development.

When we look at Freud's statement, "the ego is above all a physical ego", we have indeed to emphasise the impact of physical development and its influence on the conscious and unconscious level of perception of the self. Freud's perspective on human development focused mainly on the unfolding of drives, which he thought were the predominant motivating force of human nature.

Consequently, he formulated a line of succession of the development of drives, starting with the oral stage, followed by the anal stage, which is the subject of my lecture today, and, later, the oedipal phase, which gives way to the genital stage in mature adults.

It is important to understand the anal stage from the viewpoint of drive development, taking into account the unfolding of object relations as well as the impact of attachment between the young child and his care-givers.

In my opinion, a contemporary psychoanalytic viewpoint on development should integrate these different perspectives, which enable us to perceive the psychic growth of the infant in all its fields that are interdependent. Development means the interaction of congenital and inborn aspects, such as the unfolding of drives, which is connected with physical growth, and their inner representation in the unconscious, as well as the interaction with surrounding objects the child meets in his environment and that are crucially important for promoting favourable conditions.

During the anal stage, the centre of pleasure and attention shifts from oral sensations connected with the area of the mouth, which is predominant and characteristic for the oral stage, to the anus.

Following the maturing of physical development, the child becomes more able to control bodily functions such as excreting or retaining faeces and urine. This capacity of being able to control becomes an important source of sexual pleasure.

These bodily sensations become linked with erotic feelings of self-stimulation resulting from excreting or holding back faeces, as well as being touched by care-givers during bodily care.

As the child develops physically, he will be able to move around more actively and explore his surroundings as well as his own body. Freud emphasised the enormous narcissistic and libidinal pleasure which results from the child realising that he is able to produce something by himself, and faeces, therefore, are enriched with unconscious meanings of different kinds. They might, for example, be unconsciously perceived as a present that is offered to, or refused by, the parents.

It becomes obvious that what happens during this stage in the child is the interacting with the activities of the parents and other care-givers who influence his inner world. During the time when Freud conceptualised his theories about the development of sexual drives, and we are speaking of a period which is now about 100 years ago (his *Three Essays on the Theory of Sexuality* was published in 1905), parents used to force their children in a rather strict way to become able to use the toilet as soon as possible. So, the question of controlling bodily functions became an important issue, and the education designed to lead to cleanliness frequently resulted in a power struggle between parents and their children, often leading to personalities which later suffered from various compulsive symptoms that were rooted in the way they were treated during this stage. The so-called "anal character", a personality who is extremely compulsive and controlling in his behaviour and who is characterised by strong rigidity of mind, can be considered a result of the use of such a controlling manner to achieve cleanliness at all costs and to suppress everything which could be considered dirty and unacceptable to society.

During the anal stage, the organisation of the libido shifts from the oral to the anal area, and the anal zone becomes the main source of erotic pleasure and corresponding fantasies which deal with issues of sexuality and the ubiquitous question of where little children come from, a topic that young children are enormously interested in and which represents a question of enormous fascination. Children at this age love to play with dirty things, such as mud, and their anal products are examined with great interest. During this period, the feeling of revulsion is not yet known to them; it appears later and can be considered a result of internalisation of parental education designed to lead to cleanliness.

At the same time, the child gradually achieves the capacity for symbolisation, which means that bodily functions are underlined with unconscious meaning; faeces then represents something which attains significance in the relationship with parental figures, such as a present or a method of manipulating the object. Under the influence of unconscious sexual fantasies, faeces might even represent a baby, which is given to the parents as a present that the child is extremely proud of because it shows his productiveness and power.

During the second and third year, the child is exposed to a multitude of different aspects of development. He realises his growing capacity to do things actively and independently of the support of his care-givers, and sometimes he is overwhelmed with feelings of his own grandiosity. Along with the maturing of cognitive and muscular functions, he becomes able to discover his world and, at the same time, he is still deeply dependent on the caring presence of others looking after him. The child realises that he is separate from his mother and, little by little, he leaves the symbiotic stage he shared with her during the oral stage. At the same time, he becomes aware that mother and father share a relationship that he is excluded from—a topic which will dominate the following oedipal stage.

He can start to communicate more actively, and acquires the capability to speak. An important hallmark of this development of speaking is the ability to say "no", which implies that the child now attains the capacity to distinguish himself from others and their wishes. This becomes an important nucleus of a growing sense of the self, and defiance is an important part of this process because the child becomes progressively more conscious of his own wishes, which might conflict with the wishes of others.

For the first time, he is able to imagine an absent object, which marks the beginning of the ability to symbolise.

Sometimes, the enormous growth of different capacities may be irritating for the child, as it makes him realise how deeply dependent he still is.

All in all, the intensive processes the child goes through during this period of life depend on the interaction of his internal libidinal development with his parental objects, which constitute his external conditions of life.

One important aspect of the anal stage is the curiosity of little children during this developmental period. They are immensely interested in everything around them, including their own body and its functions, and anything and everything is able to become a potential object of attention, ready to be investigated. Freud described this drive for empowerment as an important part of the development of aggressive drives, which dominates the pre-genital libidinal organisation of children during this time.

During the anal stage, the child has attained the capacity for intensive bodily perceptions followed by increased control of body movements. Now, he wants to conquer his surroundings, and he starts to investigate everything within reach. If his attempts at empowerment risk breaking down, the result will be an enormous object-directed rage of frustration. We have all witnessed the cruelty of small children towards objects of their curiosity: they may dismantle toys to find out how they function, they destroy dolls to see what is inside, and they kill little creatures such as insects, just because of the lust for functioning and to observe what happens.

Enduring the concurrence of these hostile and aggressive feelings with loving emotions towards care-giving objects, such as the mother, in the sense of acquisition of ambivalence, tolerance becomes one of the central tasks of the anal stage.

The child might sometimes be troubled by these diverging emotional states of mind, which create a feeling of disharmony, and he will go into a state of regression to the former oral stage in order to feel safe and protected, just as if he were a little baby. During more active moments, he quickly reaches over-stimulation and a feeling of being overwhelmed, and then reacts with rage and frustration towards himself and others. So, the little child is in a state of moving back and forth in order to find a new internal balance, and clinging to the mother and then rejecting her shortly afterwards demonstrates the stirred up emotional stages he is living through.

These characteristic object-related hostile and aggressive feelings that show up during the anal stage caused Freud to call this developmental step the anal–sadistic phase. Typical examples are: biting, scratching, boxing and fighting to conquer the other, often together with identification with the aggressor. To quote Freud:

> The cruel component of the sexual instinct develops in childhood even more independently of the sexual activities that are attached to erotogenic zones. Cruelty in general comes easily to the childish nature, since the obstacle that brings the instinct for mastery to a halt at another person's pain—namely a capacity for pity—is developed relatively late. (Freud, 1905d, pp. 191–192)

These feelings of rage and hostility that sometimes irritate the child during this stage of development represent an enormous challenge for his still immature ego. The mixture of an aggressive breakthrough with sexual arousal may lead to the feeling of being overwhelmed and cause intense feelings of anxiety and fear. If the object is then perceived as not being protective enough, or reacts with rage himself, the ambivalence which is already hard to bear and contain will be reinforced. Then, the unconscious sadistic and masochistic conflicts the parents bring into interaction with the child could damage the ego development of the child and cause later psychic disturbances.

It is, therefore, very important for the young child to be contained in a securely framed relational context where it can experience trust and the feeling of being held in a loving and reliable atmosphere. In recent years, attachment theory has drawn more and more attention to this aspect of the development of young children. The importance of a securely framed environment in which the child can experience trust cannot be overestimated.

Along with the unfolding of drives during the different stages the child is going through during his development, attachment theory has focused on the very basic congenital instinct for a strong relationship with the mother. We can consider this basic environment of trust as an assumption for any further development of the child. Only when the very basic need for a secure relationship with primal objects is satisfied can the child find an atmosphere of favourable conditions in which to grow and unfold. Much empirical research has been undertaken to gather evidence that secure relationships are, indeed, the cornerstone for any further development of the child.

The second and third year can be considered as vitally important for the whole developmental process of the unfolding personality of the child. During this period, particularly, the acquisition of language and the conflicts which occur during the phase of re-approaching the mother are important for the development of the core sexual identity and the beginning of gender identity. During the anal stage, children find out whether they are boys or a girls. The psycho-sexual phenomena linked with this important discovery justify the naming of this period as an early genital stage. Concerning early education about cleanliness, girls may be forced more than boys to become clean as soon as possible, and this may cause early conflicts with regard to acting out aggressive and sexual impulses. According to average expectations of society, the development of motor functions of girls is often less acknowledged narcissistically, which might explain why they concentrate on the development of cognition and mental functions earlier.

For both sexes, it becomes important to identify with mother or father as role models in order to consolidate their sexual identity, giving way to the further development of the subsequent oedipal stage.

In the third year, children who have been raised relatively safely and who have experienced good enough relations with their parents or other care-givers normally overcome their crisis of re-approaching, which leads to more and more stable inner-object representations and the capacity to stay alone for some time without being completely overwhelmed by fears of abandonment. This growing inner capacity becomes an important precondition for further processes of learning and development, and the tasks the child has to face during this period can be described as further consolidation of individuality.

In his third year, the child has to master his fears of abandonment, which have sometimes threatened during his second year. His capacity of basic trust and a feeling of security become more stabilised. Feelings of omnipotence, which have been predominant during the early anal stage, diminish, slowly giving way to a more realistic self-image that allows the child to cope with developmental tasks in a more realistic and adequate way.

Progressively, he gains more capacity of affect control and can control feelings of disappointment and frustration better without having constantly to fly into a rage.

He can slowly give up splitting good and bad object representations, which leads to a more mature representation of the object as a whole.

All these aspects continue to add to a more consolidated image of the self-representation of the child.

I have tried to describe the most important aspects of the development of young children during the second and third year. According to the unfolding of drives, this period is dominated by the anal stage. We have also seen how object relations and the development of physical and mental functions strongly interfere during this period to form a more consolidated feeling of an own unfolding self with a growing sexual identity as a boy or a girl.

The importance of attachment has been emphasised in order to internalise stable object relations as a secure base for developmental processes.

During one of the forthcoming evening lectures, we shall watch a film which illustrates in an impressive way how children can be deeply disturbed by brief separations from their parents.

Joyce and James Robertson (1976, 1989), a couple doing attachment research together with John Bowlby, an English psychoanalyst who conducted a great deal of research concerning attachment theory during the 1960s, observed young boys and girls during periods of separation from their parents to explore how this disruption of the relationship to the parents affects the children. It is very moving to observe how sensitive young children react to such a separation and how this affects their attachment system.

Fourth to sixth year: the infantile-genital (oedipal) stage

Christine Gerstenfeld

Among the developmental concepts put forth by psychoanalysis, those related to the oedipal stage belong to the most intriguing and most discussed by anthropology, ethnology, and other branches of the cultural sciences. This might be due to the fact that these concepts offer an explanation as to why, in the everyday affective yearnings of children and their parents at this age, one encounters the conflictual dynamics of love, desire, jealousy, aggression, and murderous wishes that have so often inspired mythology and art in many cultures. Depending on the analytical school, the concepts tend to emphasise more the side of sexual development (the "genital" aspect) or the side of psychic maturation inherent in the conflicts of this stage (the "triadic" or "triangulation" aspect).

It is important not to look at any psychosexual "stage" in isolation. We should always keep in mind that the previous developmental steps (especially the quality of the emotional attachments in early infancy) greatly influence the intensity and the outcome of the developments that we will be discussing below.

We should start by remembering the physical, cognitive, and emotional development of the child at this age of 4–6 years: we see a little boy or girl who has mastered the sensory–motor development of the previous years, achieving control over his or her body functions. The child has acquired language and symbolic function, sometimes even being able to decipher letters and to count. He or she has acquired a core gender identity as male or female (around age 2–3), and is able to make a more stable distinction between reality and fantasy. The child has internalised a range of objects and has some experience of tolerating separations from them. Hence, the child is entering a phase in which he or she feels distinctly as an individual, developing a sense of his or her own personality and exerting a strong autonomy. One could say that the child almost feels a kind of imaginary "maturity". Therefore, the new conflicts arising at this age hit especially hard and inflict painful narcissistic injuries.

As we read Freud's description of the oedipal conflict in a boy. we can immerse ourselves in his feelings (and in those of a girl experiencing them the other way around):

> In its simplified form the case of a male child may be described as follows. At a very early age the little boy develops an object-cathexis for his mother [object-cathexis = investing libido into an object], which originally related to the mother's breast and is the prototype of an object-choice on the anaclitic model [anaclitic = love of an object because it gives security and one is dependent on it]; the boy deals with his father by identifying himself with him. For a time these two relationships proceed side by side, until the boy's sexual wishes in regard to his mother become more intense and his father is perceived as an obstacle to them; from this the Oedipus complex originates. His identification with his father then takes on a hostile colouring and changes into a wish to get rid of his father in order to take his place with his mother. Henceforward his relation to his father is ambivalent; it seems as if the ambivalence inherent in the identification from the beginning had become manifest. An ambivalent attitude to his father and an object-relation of a solely affectionate kind to his mother make up the content of the simple positive Oedipus complex in a boy. (Freud 1923b, pp. 30–31)

Freud discovered these emotions in his own self-analysis in 1897. They reminded him of the tragedy of Oedipus (Picture 2.1), written by the Greek poet Sophocles and first performed around 425 BC, and so he named the conflict the "Oedipus complex".[1] This story, whose material is based on much older folk legends, has become something of a "master-tragedy" in European culture. Psychoanalysis has often been criticised for its ethnocentric views and it might, indeed, seem arrogant for Freud to assert the universality of a psychic conflict based on the similarity between infantile phantasy and a 2500-year-old Greek drama. However, a survey of early "cultural fossils", the myths of humankind in various cultures, reveals that the topic of incest and murderous rivalry in triadic familial constellations is quite prevalent and sometimes only slightly altered. Ming Dong Gu, for example, explores the oedipal topic in Chinese literature and suggests that it has undergone a cultural transformation into a "filial piety complex". He concludes, "oedipal themes in Chinese literature are restructured according to Confucian morality, taking the disguised form of parental demands for filial piety and children's fulfilment of filial duties" (Gu, 2006).

How can we understand Freud's phrase that the "boy's sexual wishes in regard to his mother become more intense"? Does the boy really unconsciously want to have full sexual intercourse with his mother? Can we assume that this is what is unconsciously meant by the frequently uttered sentence "I want to marry mother/father"? Obviously, this cannot be entirely correct, since the child most often does not know even the rudiments of sexual performance. Some individuals do remember explicit genital sexual wishes in relation to their

Picture 2.1. Oedipus and the Sphinx.

parents, but usually they occur at an older age. We could infer the child's sexual wishes from what it slowly begins to know: the parents have a relationship to each other of their own and they are doing something, which can lead to additional children, from which the child is excluded because he or she is too small ("primal scene"). According to the developmental level of the child, its phantasies about what the parents actually do at night in their bedroom can assume quite absurd forms ("primal scene phantasies").

Here are some examples of phantasies about parental sexuality. A patient remembers playing "cowboys and Indians" with his father and older brother around the age of five and finding the idea of being tied and harnessed like a horse sexually very arousing. He thinks that he might have previously seen intercourse between horses in the countryside. He remembers having wished that both mother and father "rode" him and being jealous because usually the older brother was selected to be the "horse". He used this phantasy for masturbation until around the age of nine. The "riding activity" was not linked with any conscious phantasy of penetrating or being penetrated.

Another, more disturbing, example is that of a woman who remembers that as a girl of four she felt strong clitoridal excitation while watching a brutal scene on television, after which she masturbated for a few years with the phantasy that she was being beaten or even killed.

In these phantasies, we recognise that while children may develop the wrong ideas about the actual content of sexuality, which is coloured by their developmental level and by the coincidences of observation, they generally have an accurate idea that there exists some privileged sexual activity between adults from which they are excluded. Unless we assume that there exist in the mind unconscious and accurate preconceptions about sexuality that are genetically inherited, we could, more prudently, describe the "sexual wishes" of children as being handled in the same way as how the children imagine that the parents handle each other during adult sexuality.

Additionally, we note that in example A, the boy's sexual wishes were related to both parents simultaneously. This clinical finding would fit well with the psychoanalytic concept of psychic bisexuality of humans. For Freud, the "complete" oedipal complex consists of two different triadic configurations (1923b, pp. 32–33): possessive sexual wishes in relation to the opposite-sex parent with rivalry to the same-sex parent ("positive oedipal configuration", or "positive Oedipus complex", and vice versa ("negative or inverse oedipal configuration").

So, both girls and boys want somehow to sexually possess one parent and develop a rivalry with the other parent, but in the child's psyche the "rival parent" is already a tremendously important inner object, and so the child really suffers because of his antagonism towards an actually beloved parent. What could be the reason for these dramatic emotions to arise in our psyche? For this, we must look at some of the tasks that the genital phase is supposed to prepare, and as we do so, we will realise how difficult these tasks are and why they are never fully accomplished.

Drive maturation

The main sexual developmental task of the genital stage is thought to be the integration of the partial sexual drives of the pregenital stages (polymorph-perverse sexuality of the infant: autoerotism, orality, anality, voyeurism, exhibitionism, sadism) into an adult form of sexuality that will eventually allow the procreation of the species. Thus, these pregenital desires must be placed under the primacy of the genital organs, so that, from now on, sexual satisfaction will be pursued mainly by means of the genitals. In this stage, the sensitive outer genital organs—the clitoris and the penis—become the origin of strong sensations in the child (the main erogenous zone). This can be easily observed in the frequent masturbation that is characteristic of these years, as well as in the pleasure that children show in exhibiting their genital organs. This age is also marked by an unbounded curiosity about sex and procreation and by the emergence of elaborate phantasies about it. All these are aspects of a normal and healthy sexual development. (In primates, one can observe a phase of "mock sexual play", in which juvenile apes assume between each other or with adult apes—including their parents—the typical sexual postures of intercourse. Upon further maturation, the parents become more reticent and, finally, they refuse to "play sex" with them any longer.)

Developmentally, this stage is divided into two parts: the early "infantile" genital phase between the ages of four and six years, which prepares for the genital primacy, but in which the child is not yet sexually mature. Then comes the period of latency, which was previously assumed to be a phase of decreased sexual drive and interest, but in reality the "sexual life" of the child continues and very often masturbation or sexual games with other children occur in this phase. Both sexes experience orgasm while masturbating, some precocious boys even experiencing the first ejaculation of fluid at around age nine. The second part is then the hormonally activated genital stage of puberty with the onset of spermarche (ejaculation of fluid containing sperm) and menarche (onset of menstruation). At the end of puberty, sexuality becomes mainly geared towards pleasure in intercourse. However, all the former pregenital polymorph-perverse libidinal pleasures remain an inseparable part of human sexuality and are integrated in foreplay and arousal (e.g., kissing, fondling, exhibiting, voyeuristic and aggressive aspects) and, of course, also in adult sexual phantasy and masturbation.

Formerly, this phase was called "phallic phase" (phallus: Greek for penis), but today this term is used very seldom. The term originally derived from Freud's belief that in the infantile imagination, only the penis "counted" as a genital organ. Thus, for Freud, children do not see two sexes. They see just one sex, the male, and the female sex has "nothing", is, thus, like a "castrated male", and envies the male (so-called "penis envy") (Freud, 1905d, p. 194). This theory reflects Freud's embeddedness in the cultural errors about gender prevailing at his time and could itself be considered a sign of a masculine narcissistic defence against the boy's obvious awareness of the sexual attributes and capabilities of the female/maternal body and the painful realisation that he is different. Developmental observation of children shows that initially both sexes identify with the mother and try to emulate her mothering: wishes to nurse a baby are among the first to be expressed and by far precede the genital phase (see Lax, 2003). However, this masculine inner-psychic "phallocentric" defence seems to have been enforced on the totality of many cultures because of their usually patriarchal social structure. It is most obvious in the absence of adequate names for the clitoris in the upbringing of little girls and also in the desire of some extreme patriarchal cultures to destroy the sexual pleasure of women (e.g., clitoridectomy). It is, therefore, preferable to reserve the expression "phallic" for the description of attitudes typical of male gender cultural norms (e.g., a boy or a girl wanting to drive a racing car would be pursuing a "phallic" activity, because generally this activity is culturally ascribed to the male gender. In contrast, a little girl's clitoridal masturbation is not "phallic", it is "genital".)

Object choice

Simultaneously, the genital drive must become situated in the affective yearning of the individual so that he or she will be actively seeking a new object which is suitable for procreation: an object of the opposite sex. From the very beginning of his psychic development, the child has always been part of triadic configurations ("triadic" is defined as a relationship of the pattern "myself, X, and Y", whereby X and Y can be parents, siblings, or other relatives). Nevertheless, the libidinal wishes and demands of the child on his parents are usually framed in "exclusive dyadic" patterns ("I want mother to love only me" and "I want father to love only me"), thus not "gendered" along heterosexual lines. The very young child often actively tries to separate kissing parents, thereby expressing its wish for dyadic exclusivity with one of the parents and its dislike at being excluded from their adult relationship.

However, due to the biological drive development in the oedipal phase, there arises now a tendency to a more manifestly heterosexually gendered triadic conflict: boys develop a rivalry with father around the possession of the mother, girls develop a rivalry with their mothers. This heterosexual preference (see Freud, 1905d, p. 226) leads the way to the heterosexual object choice in adulthood. Late childhood is thought to be a period of sensitivity for the choice of the gender of the erotically desired object.

In this perspective, the problem of inserting the human sexual drive into preceding, already existing triadic configurations of emotional attachments with different-sex parents offers one additional possibility that might explain why the outcome of the sexual object-choice in the human species is so much more of a "gamble" than in animals: preferential homosexuality is a stable trait of human sexuality in all cultures (1-4%). Again, as we have seen with other remnants of infantile sexuality, even in heterosexual individuals there remains evidence of the possibility of the "other erotic choice", as manifested in the homosexual sexual fantasies of adults.

We must bear in mind that there is yet no comprehensive explanation for the extraordinary variation and plasticity of human sexuality and gender orientation. We know that sex hormones prenatally influence both the development of the genital organs in the embryo as well as the building of the embryonic brain. Thus, constitutional gender differences in behaviour between boys and girls exist right after birth (Friedman & Downey, 2008). One reliable finding is that prenatal androgens influence the toy preference (early androgen exposure in girls has a masculinising effect on sex-typed toy preferences). Another reliable finding is that boys prefer "rough and tumble play". Physically aggressive play and competition with other males is a more prominent feature of their development than with girls, as well as their need for "all male peer groups". However, these constitutional gender differences cannot explain the variety in gender roles that we see in the development of individual boys and girls, and "social learning" is now acknowledged to play a major part. Social processes influence the gender development not only via learning and identification, but also psycho-biologically, as sex hormone excretion in humans (and other mammals) is also modulated in reaction to the social environment.

If we simplify a little, we can work out two patterns of "regular" gender identification and sexual object-choice of children in late childhood:

- the girl has the same female gender as her mother and so she can keep the earlier primary gender identification, but she has to give up the mother as the initial love object and shift her genital desire to the father's male sex (shift in object-choice);
- the boy had also been identified with the mother, but he had dis-identified with her feminine gender much earlier and identified with his father's male gender (shift in identification), but he can keep the mother's female sex as the object of genital desire.

Incest avoidance

Third, it is not enough that the new object be a genitally desired object of the opposite sex, it must also be different from the next of kin. This is why some anthropologists regard this phase as a "transmission link" between our individual psychic development, the biological roots of the species, and the cultural inheritance of the previous generations.

The avoidance of incestuous sexuality with first-grade relatives (parents, siblings) is a universal behavioural tendency in mammals ("biological incest taboo"). In animals, it seems to be enforced by the avoidance of sexual relations with those animals with whom one has been closely associated in infancy ("familiarity theory"), but the precise mechanisms by which this is achieved are not yet understood. In human societies, however, the incest prohibitions might go even further and prohibit mating with more distant relatives. For example, some societies prohibit mating with parallel cousins (offspring of the parent's siblings of the same gender: the children of the father's brother and the mother's sister) but, at the same time, allow marriage with cross cousins (offspring of the parent's siblings of different gender). Note that this does not make any sense biologically, since all these cousins have the same genetic distance. Thus, in human societies, incest taboos can be more accurately defined as prohibitions against committing certain acts of sexual intimacy (variations exist specific to culture) between certain persons of a certain kinship grade (this also varies between cultures). One could say, therefore, that humans have both the "biological" incest prohibitions and additional "cultural" ones. The anthropologist Lévi-Strauss, whose ground-breaking work offers an explanation for these cultural prohibitions, showed that this is a fundamental step by which a society achieves an increasingly complex and more differentiated social kinship order. In anthropological terms, the task of the genital phase might be to firmly establish both the biological and the specific "cultural" incest taboo of one particular ethnic group in the child's psyche and to make him abandon the "forbidden" objects.

If this were true, how would this work intrapsychically? What would make us abandon parents and other kin as incestuous objects of desire? Biology offers the above mentioned "familiarity theory" as an answer. Psychoanalysis offers several answers to these questions, which, of course, do not have to be mutually exclusive (Blass, 2001). Note that these explanations are also thought to be the reason why the oedipal conflict and the childhood years preceding it are repressed from conscious memory ("infantile amnesia").

Futility: the first reason, one could say the simplest, is that the oedipal desire has to vanish because of its futility, given the physical inability of the child to actually perform a genital sexual act. In contrast to more general triadic conflicts between siblings, where the rivalry of the children concern "goods" which can be attained and divided (love, attention, time, or money of the parents), the triadic oedipal conflict with a parent concerns "goods" which are physically impossible to attain at this stage. This points to the painful narcissistic blow inherent in the oedipal conflict.

Ambivalence conflict: another explanation is the inner conflict between love and hate that the child feels in relation to the "rival".

To give an example, a parental couple slept in separate bedrooms and the boy was allowed by his mother to sleep in her bed. Thus, he felt that he had actually "won" over the father and was arrogantly ignoring his father, who felt hurt and started beating the boy for trifling reasons. However, in analysis as an adult, he remembered that during this same period he used to wait full of longing at the window for the father to return home from work. He said, "I still have the typical sound of his car engine in my ears when he drove into the alleyway . . . I missed father so much . . . but I did not dare to show it . . . how could I love him when he was beating me? . . . and besides, it would have angered my mother."

We see that the rival parent is not only a hated "obstacle". If the child were able to remove the "obstacle", the child would lose a beloved parent, an inner object and an identification figure. In this version, the resolution of the oedipal conflict comes about by an inner ambivalence conflict in the child and his or her wish not to hurt the beloved rival (Blass, 2001).

Additionally, it is very important to realise that the oedipal conflict is always linked with painful feelings of loss and narcissistic hurt with regard to both parents. The child may feel intense rage with both parents for the fact that they still "prefer" each other and may feel betrayed by both when they produce a new sibling.[2] Both inner representations of mother and father are threatened by the child's inner ambivalence and hostility if it clings to its desire for exclusive possession of one parent.

Fear of damage: a third explanation, which was seemingly preferred by Freud, is that the child's hostility towards the rival creates an anxiety that the jealous rival parent will retaliate and damage the child physically: the so-called "castration anxiety". Since the child's wishes would have painful consequences for the child's body, the sexual nature of the desire is surrendered.

The fear of corporal damage is frequently observed in children (and also in dreams of adults) and expresses itself differently in boys and girls: boys have a much more obvious castration fear centred on the penis, especially if the parents have used this threat to prohibit masturbation. It is quite probable that this masculine fear has some ethological background: in fights about dominance in primates, it is very common to actually bite off the rival male's testicles and penis. Additionally, remember that boys tend to constitutionally display much more physically aggressive rivalry patterns. In girls, the fear is expressed as a fear of being penetrated and destroyed in the inside, of being robbed of the possibility of giving birth, or of losing physical attractiveness.

This fear of damage extends, of course, to fears of being emotionally damaged or hurt. We must assume that part of these anxieties is real (as opposed to merely being a projection of the child's hostility) and reflects the fact that the child is correctly sensing the hostility of the rival parent (note also the very frequent topic of infanticide or infanticidal wishes in mythology and early art). The intense aggression of parents against a possessive oedipal child can be readily observed and often leads to lifelong estrangement in mother–daughter or father–son relationships. In this phase, the oedipal feelings of the parents themselves are reactivated, and if they have not acquired sufficient capacity for "triadic" love in their childhood, they fail to give their child continuing support during its inner turmoil and attack it instead.

In all these explanations, the surrender of incestuous desires derives from the fact that the presence of the "third", the jealous rival, places the child "in a conflict over its own well-being" (Blass, 2001). It is either the narcissistic pain of realising that he or she is much too immature to actually fulfil the sexual needs of the adult, or the loss of a beloved inner object, or the fear of being physically or emotionally hurt by the rival.

Structural changes emerging from the resolution of the oedipal conflict

In psychoanalytic theory, there exists a basic principle of psychic maturation, which is that mastery of an inner conflict brings about gains in structural change. Therefore, resolving the oedipal conflict is thought to bring about new psychic capabilities.

In order to solve the conflict, the individual actually has to face a painful loss and a narcissistic injury at the same time: the surrender of possessive erotic wishes and of feelings of entitlement to an exclusive relationship. Freud explains that the loss of an object can be overcome by identification with the object (1923b, p. 28). It is equally correct to use the term internalisation of the object, or introjection of the object. The concepts of "internalisation", "introjection", and "identification" are often used interchangeably by Freud and by later authors. Although numerous authors have tried to clarify the confusion in the use of these terms, they did not quite succeed. Essentially, there seems to be the following difference between them: while internalisation/introjection stress the taking of an object into one's inner world (without necessarily identifying oneself with it), identification stresses more the activity of trying to become like the internalised/introjected object. Of course, internalisation and identification are continuous from birth, but the resolution of the oedipal conflict is thought to be a special maturational step.

Because the oedipal conflict includes both the "positive" and the "negative" configuration and, in consequence, both "inner parental objects" are threatened by loss, both are "saved" by identification. The outcome of the oedipal conflict is, therefore, an identification with both parents. Freud describes that, for example, a boy may identify with his father and thus enhance his masculinity, but also with his mother, and this would form his "feminine side", and vice versa for a girl (1923b, p. 31).[3] The internalisation of the parents is thought to be an important aspect of character formation. By identifying with the parents, the child acquires an ego ideal. Their love or their punishment become an aspect of his own conscience, which approves or disapproves of him or her (consolidation of earlier superego structures and acquisition of moral norms of the group). The child then utilises the internalised parents as an "inner source of strength for repressing its desires" (Blass, 2001). By postponing the fulfilment of sexual wishes until adolescence, he or she acquires the capacity for sublimation.

The child also internalises the parental relationship. This is thought to be an important step in the acquisition of the "triadic capacity" of mature love. What is meant by this? Essentially, it means that the individual tolerates loving someone, who, in turn, has an important and independent relationship to another person (the "third"). Thus, the individual realises that any kind of exclusive love is not possible, because in any relationship there is always a third who demands his part of affection. The child learns to love both parents at the same time and to have his own independent relationship with them, as well as allowing the parents to have an independent relationship of their own. As a consequence, triadic capacity naturally includes tolerating the feeling of being excluded from a meaningful relationship of the loved person (for further reading see Britton, Feldman, & O'Shaughnessy, 1989; Feldman, 2008).

Unsurprisingly, the ability to tolerate a "third" tends to remain severely limited in case of sexual relationships, since this is the biological bedrock of evolution. This makes it even more remarkable that the triadic inner-psychic maturity is often able to override powerful biological or cultural constraints, as one can observe in situations in which a partner in a loving adult relationship is able to tolerate to some extent that the partner fell in love, or had a sexual relationship, with someone else, without losing the feelings of love for the partner and without breaking off the relationship.

The parents can help the child at this age by tolerating his or her feelings without retaliating, shaming, or belittling the child. It is very important that the parents protect their own relationship against intrusions of the child. In this way, parents who have acquired a "good enough" triadic capacity in their own childhood will not seduce the child into an overtly exclusive relationship and into illusionary fantasies of oedipal victory, even if they are bringing the child up on their own. Generally, psychoanalytic theory places a much greater importance on the father as being the parent who introduces the triadic dimension and "protects" from incest, leading the boy away from a potentially too close incestuous relationship with the mother or the girl from a potentially too close symbiotic identification with her. (In view of both sexes' primary identification with the mother, this seems to be valid, but it might not take into account that paedophilia as a psychic disposition, as well as sexual abuse of children, is perpetrated chiefly by men.)

The ability of the both parents to allow the child to develop an intense relationship to the other parent or to other people from birth onwards ("early triangulation") is essential for a successful outcome of the oedipal phase. Triadic capacity is, essentially, an inner psychic ability to keep the "Third" as a presence in the mind, as an element (person, object, idea) that institutes the prohibition of "exclusivity" (= incest) in the relationship. In the therapeutic relationship, it is often the frame of the treatment that carries this function in the therapist's mind.

On the other hand, the parents can greatly intensify oedipal conflicts and endanger their resolution. Intense jealousy between the parents might arise now, and the feelings of the children are modulated by the corresponding feelings of the parents. Laplanche goes as far as to say that the oedipal desires and anxieties of the child are actually instigated by the parents (Laplanche, 1997). The presence of infanticidal and paedophilic tendencies in adults could be seen as a corroboration of his thesis. His theory has the advantage of making us aware that the child receives constant unspoken messages of the parent's desire—such as the message the boy received from his mother by being allowed to sleep in her bed in the example given a little earlier. This mother seemed not to be able to become the father's lover and partner at night, rather than the boy's.

Notes

1. Complex = an organised assembly of unconscious impulses, ideas, and feelings that influence the behaviour. The use of "complex" in psychoanalysis is very similar to its use in medicine: an organised assembly of parts that work together, for example, "enzyme complex".
2. A child might not forgive the desired parent's unfaithfulness. As a defensive result, a boy may split the inner representation of his mother (and, thus, of future women in his life) into a desexualised woman of "unimpeachable moral purity" and a sexualised "promiscuous woman", the latter being sexually desired. Conversely, a girl would split the representation of the father into an image of a desired "promiscuous man" and a genuinely devoted, but desexualised, man in whom there is no sexual interest (Josephs, 2006).
3. Boys who show "feminine" characteristics are attacked culturally more severely than girls who show "masculine" traits. Psychoanalytically, this could be explained by the need of boys to dis-identify with the female maternal sex. Therefore, the masculine gender identity is more vulnerable and has to be more strongly defended against femininity throughout the life cycle.

Sixth to tenth year: latency

Wolfgang Merkle

According to Erikson, we have a group of feelings and conflicts that dominate each period of life as a task of mental development, often according to the development of the body. (See Table 2.3, p. 33, above.)

The stages of early childhood (first to fifth or sixth year) were mentioned above. We call this "childhood" (sixth to tenth year). According to Erikson, we have the problem of performance *vs.* feelings of inferiority during the latency phase, in puberty, identity and role confusion, in early adulthood, the problem of intimacy *vs.* isolation (this means that in this stage we have to manage the task of being sexually intimate and to determine sexual preference), and in adulthood the possibility of being creative or to stagnate. Finally, there is the period of being old, where we have the dialectic between ego-integrity and despair.

Stage of latency

This is the stage of consolidation of the primacy of the genital organisation, finding identity, consolidation of the social role and organisation of future perspectives. Erikson describes the main conflict of latency to be performance *vs.* a feeling of inferiority.

According to psychoanalytic views, from the age of six or seven until puberty, the sexual interest of the child moves into the background. Sexuality rests during the latency stage. The part-drives are suppressed or partially sublimated; this means they lead to non-sexual purposes. All this can be observed, for instance, in the way children come together almost self-evidently in groups of male or female. The children disassociate from the other sex. From the boys' point of view, the girls are silly, and from the girls' point of view, the boys are stupid (or similar).

Both are improving their cognitive skills. Thinking becomes more technical and social contacts are made at school and around the home. The boy or girl wants to do something right together with others.

The child wants to look and learn, wants to observe and participate, and he has learnt to complete a job.

If the child often fails there is a possibility that his basic confidence and self-confidence are damaged. In this case, the child needs the protection of the parents.

In psychosomatic patients who are at this stage, we can often detect a disturbance of maturation if these children are forced to take responsibility too early or are forced into parentification (this means that children are forced to take care of their parents or siblings) so that they develop too fast into a stage of adulthood, without enough mental maturation. For example, in China, where the country's development is so fast, there is the danger that parents cannot cope with the rate of change and force their children to help them in the new world.

During this stage, there are not many changes in the drives; however, there are in the ego and in the superego formation as well as in the influence the superego has on the ego.

Therefore, damage at this stage, for example, through sexual attacks or contempt for incest taboos, leads to deep ego distortions. The shift of the cathexis from outer to inner object is very important in this stage and the child becomes more stable in his moods. The child is able to express himself more in words than with body language.

Disconnection from tradition, mainly due to the Cultural Revolution, caused enormous stress and loss of confidence for the Chinese people. The stress extended throughout Chinese society, affecting families, parents, and even children. For example, children, say aged five to ten, are expected by their parents to learn many skills, such as dancing, playing the piano, playing chess, learning a foreign language, or doing difficult mathematics, so that the children have little free time at this stage.

In this way, China has developed very fast, because parents force their children to take on more duties and to play less than is adequate at this stage.

Due to the one-child policy, children can be overloaded with their parents' own dreams and expectations.

Eleventh to twenty-first year: puberty or adolescence

Wolfgang Merkle

For this second decade of life, we use the terms "puberty" for the aspect of biological maturation and "adolescence" for aspects of psychosocial development.

The challenges for young boys and girls during adolescents are shown in Table 2.4.

The development of drives at this stage of development should be considered from a psychoanalytical point of view.

Erikson (1950) and Blos (1962) worked intensively on this stage. Freud himself talked about the two steps of sexual development of human beings: the first step of drive is accomplished after the oedipal stage. The second starts with puberty.

During adolescence, the acquired psychic structure is destablised by the maturation of the sexual body. Regressive processes occur and oedipal topics, oral, anal, and unsolved conflicts are revived.

The id is partially advanced compared to the development of the superego; now the sexual arousal of the body is such a strong force, but the ego and the object relations lag behind. These dynamics are very important concerning temporary disturbances and crises, which are very normal during adolescence and young adulthood (Figure 2.1).

Eissler (1966) talkes about "liquefaction" of the psychic structure of adolescents.

Table 2.4. Five important challenges of adolescence (Elzer, 2009a).

1. Maturation of the body, in particular sexual function.
2. Commitment to their own sexual identity and personal identity.
3. Psychosocial detachment and autonomy from the primary objects of the family; connecting intimate relationships outside the family during persistence of economic and psychic dependency on the family.
4. Developing of the cognitive and intellectual function (peaking at age sixteen).
5. Socialisation (enculturation) of the individual into the cultural and normative system of society.

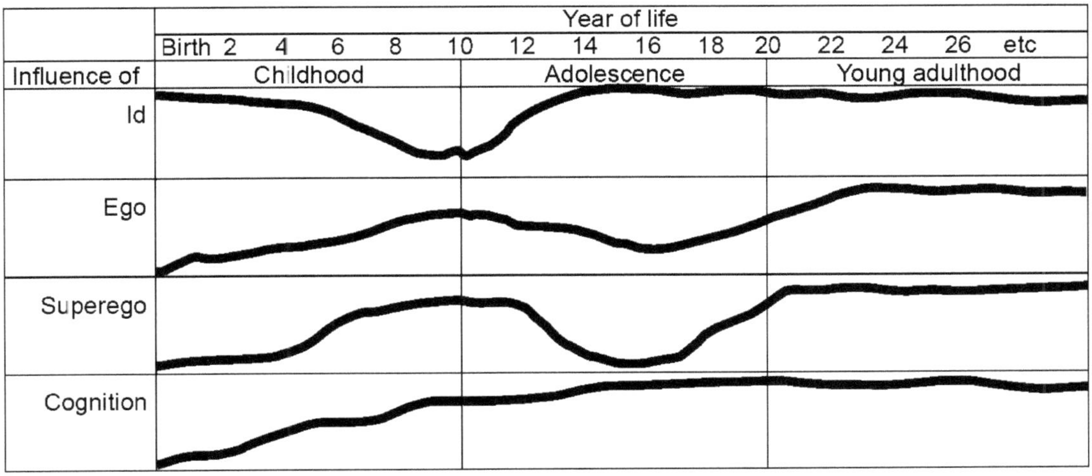

Figure. 2.1. Schematic illustration of the influence of the psychic apparatus (id, ego, superego) and cognition during the first two decades of life, especially during adolescence (Elzer, 2009a).

Puberty is a critical time and a kind of predetermined breaking point for unsolved conflicts of early childhood on the oral, anal, or infantile genital level. However, it is also a new chance to master these unsolved conflicts. Most mental disturbances (psychosis, neurosis, and psychosomatic disorders) show some prodromal symptoms at the end of adolescence and are manifest during young adulthood.

Intercultural aspects: Erdheim (1984) emphasises the creative and innovative function of adolescence in society, culture, science, and technology. Many mental and technical innovations were and still are developed by adolescents. Erdheim could show, in his ethno-psychoanalytical investigations, that a society that cannot understand the social criticism and rebellious behaviour of young people, and suppresses them instead of adequately grappling with them, will perish (cold and hot societies). Social dissatisfaction and criticism, which lead to trouble, demonstrations, and violent confrontation with the police and the military, as well as to reforms or revolution, are normally inaugurated by teenagers. They possess a more radical, independent, and sometimes also unrealistic position and are able to raise the painful subject of society, more so than adults.

The following considerations about adolescence are valuable for the development of youth in Western industrialised civilisations. In more archaic traditional authoritarian cultures, there are similar challenges in a psychosocial way, but they cannot be recognised in detail. For example, in Islamic cultures, adolescents, especially those who are female, have to accept the authority of the patriarchal family. Social political rules are less repressive than familial or religious rules.

Protest against the family, or leaving the family clan, is very often impossible and can cause a rupture in the cultural identity (compare families of migrants).

Adolescence (about ten years in duration) can be subdivided into the following sections according to Blos (1962), as described in the following sections.

Eleventh to twelfth year: preadolescence

During this stage, there is an increase of pressure on the drives. This leads to an indiscriminate cathexis of all libidinal and aggressive kinds of satisfaction. Each event can be sexually stimulating, even thoughts, fantasies, and acts that usually have no sexual meaning. Boys make use of their genitalia as an unspecific organ for a discharge of tension. There is a differentiation in the subjects of play and characteristics of boys and girls at this stage:

Boys look for heights to fall down from, and movement, and how the movement can be channelled and controlled.

Girls open and close, or block, inner rooms and find ways to invade them. The change of body shape is a great problem, especially for girls, to integrate with the body-self. This change causes a great deal of disturbance and alienation. The menarche develops both the detachment from maternal dependency and the identification with the mother as the prototype of reproduction.

Not all defence mechanisms are able to face these attacks of the drives, so there are often temporary symptoms of fear, phobia, and nervous habits: headaches, stomach aches, nail-biting, drawing in of the lips, stuttering, muttering, hand-to-mouth behaviour, hair-twirling, fiddling with things, or thumb-sucking, among others.

Boys behave in a hostile fashion towards girls, belittle them, and try to avoid them; in their company, boys brag, boast, and tease, show off and exaggerate. In essence, they deny their anxiety rather than to attempt to establish a relationship. The castration anxiety, which brought the oedipal phase to its close, reappears and forces boys into the exclusive company of their own sex.

In girls, this phase is characterised by a

> thrust of activity, during which playacting and tomboyishness reach their height. In this demonstrative denial of femininity may be discerned, the unresolved childhood conflict of penis envy, the central conflict of preadolescent girls, a conflict which finds a dramatic temporary suspension while phallic fantasies have their last fling before femininity asserts itself. (Blos, 1962, p. 60)

Boys arrive at the genital orientation by way of detours (pregenital drive cathexis). Girls turn to the other gender much faster.

Castration fear concerning the phallic mother is a central subject of preadolescence.

Twelfth to about twentieth year: adolescence

We can summarise the main problems in adolescence, according to Laufer and Laufer (2002):

- reaction to the genital primate;
- change of the relationship to the primary objects;
- finding of new love-objects;
- integration of pre-oedipal and oedipal identifications and present attitudes of expectations.

Twelfth to about fourteenth year: early adolescence

The maturation of the body causes the menarche in girls and the "pollution" in boys. Both are very confusing and irritating: childhood is suddenly over. In industrialised countries, the menarche occurs for first time between the ages of ten and twelve, the onset of sexual maturity of young boys slightly later, between fourteen and sixteen.

During early adolescence, there is the greatest difference between the sexual body and the psychic constellation. Demonstration of autonomy and playing with limits, prohibitions, and rules lead to a lot of conflicts. We call this the narcissistic withdrawal from the primary objects to the self and to one's own developing body. Genital masturbation still remains autoerotic, but is more like a trial.

Fourteenth to about sixteenth year: middle adolescence

One rule becomes important: you are only adult if you can appreciate something that is also appreciated by your parents!

At this stage, the following becomes significant: you can feel that you are not only someone who can feel pain and lust directed at you by others, but you can also feel that you yourself can be the source of pain or lust for someone else, and can be hated or loved for that.

A crucial detachment from the parents is necessary before there is the possibility of a non-incestuous choice of object. There are often instances of defiance and revenge in order to hurt parents and to punish them for not being their satisfying objects any more. To look for a good-for-nothing love object is an ideal choice for revenge.

In middle adolescence, the heterosexual position gains clarity and irreversibility. Object libido is turned outwards again. The realm of the reality principle increases.

According to Erikson, the main conflict can be described as "identity vs. confusion of roles". During this stage, we have a number of difficulties with object cathexis.

The need of the child to be loved must be fused with the need to give love. The need to get something joins slowly with the need to give. The need to get something done is changed gradually into the wish to do something for someone else.

The rebellion against the superego in male adolescence is often an active opposition against passive–feminine tendencies.

During this stage, the young adult turns to heterosexual love and definitely leaves the infantile love-objects. Emotional life is much more intense, deeper, and is given more room.

There is a search for ideals, idols, and admiration of artists, athletes, heroes, ideas, etc.

The withdrawal of cathexis from the parents—in other words, from the object-representation of them in the ego—is managed by transferring some of the energy of cathexis into the self.

During this stage, boys and girls turn away from their parents, from the family origins, to join a peer group. The values of the parents seem to be exchanged for those of the peer group ("subculture": own language, dress, behaviour, music, and literature, among others). The peer group is like a transitional object or space between the primary objects of the family and a loved object outside the family.

In both genders, we can observe an increase in narcissism. It is very easy to observe that adolescents can easily give up self-sufficiency and autoerotism as soon as there are tender feelings for the other gender. A boy commented, "As soon as I think of a girl, it is not necessary to eat like a pig or to masturbate all the time" (Blos, 1962).

Narcissistic defence, which is so characteristic of adolescence, is caused by incapacity to give up the satisfying parents (where the child was accustomed to their omnipotence) and to rely on the development of one's own possibilities. The adolescent seems to be quite incapable of facing his disappointment concerning his really limited capacities.

The decathexis of object representations takes them away as a source of satisfaction, so a huge hunger for the object emerges, a greedy wish that leads to permanent changes, superficial bonds, and identification. This might demonstrate the economic function of being ravenous. Hunger and the tendency to fill themselves with food are only partially caused by adolescents' physical need for growth. It can be observed that the need for food decreases as soon as a satisfying object enters their life. The important role of orality in this separation process may explain the frequency of depressed moods in the adolescence as a transitory regression to the oral-incorporating stage of development. Furthermore, here we have the very beginning of eating disorders.

Parents, who are initially overestimated, are seen to fall precipitously in this separation process. There is a regression in the service of the ego to narcissism. This process is quite normal during this stage.

Inner processes are now experienced as perceptions from the outer world. They are almost like hallucinations. So, we often have a pseudo-psychotic characteristic of adolescence. The ego-integrity is very stressed at this stage of life.

The diary that is written at this stage (more by girls than by boys) has the characteristic of an object.

Before new objects of love are able to reconstitute the place of primary objects, there is a period in which the ego is impoverished by the withdrawal of the parents and the alienation of the superego.

Exceptionally tender feelings of love are part of adolescence. This precedes heterosexual experiments. The noisy capture of girls is, in fact, at its height during this stage, but sooner or later these rough games are interrupted by erotic feelings that are simultaneously enchanting and limiting to young men. Homosexual episodes are quite common during this stage.

Sixteenth to about eighteenth year: late adolescence

During this stage, there is the obligation of physical intimacy. There is commitment to competitive behaviour, and the establishment of the aim of a profession. During this phase, there is the structuring of psychosocial self-definition. An identity crisis with temporary anxiety, depression, and confusion can be normal during this phase, because there is a psychosocial moratorium at this stage, often welcomed, since this is the time of studying.

According to Seiffge-Krenke (1994), this is the time with the highest accident frequency (double the rate than in the time of latency). The rate of suicides grows (one third of the causes of death). A third of delinquents are less than twenty-one years old and over 40% of drug consumers are younger than eighteen. These are European statistics.

The characteristics of late adolescence (Adatto, 1990) are:

- similar to the narcissistic personality disorders of Kernberg, vague feelings of emptiness and depression;
- feelings of grandiosity and hunger for objects;
- intellectualisation as a frequent defence, especially in study (retardation of conflict resolving);
- caution in assigning diagnosis (psychic changing of structure);
- reduction of superego: masochistic symptoms, intensification of guilt.

It is the task of late adolescence to arrive at a point where "this is my way of life" can be expressed and felt more confidently. There should now be more clarity of purpose and awareness of the self.

The studies of Vaillant (1995) show that success or failure in intimacy during this period is an important factor in mastering the next stage of adulthood.

Eighteenth to twentieth year: post-adolescence

The subject of late adolescence continues to be dominant during this stage; in particular, the consolidation of sexual and social identity is as important as the topic of love relationships outside the family. Perhaps the young adults are leaving home and unresolved problems from earlier development (first and second decade) now become clearer.

Twenty-first year to the end of life: adulthood and old age

Wolfgang Merkle

The theoretical system of adulthood is not as structured as that of childhood and adolescence. Adulthood is the stepchild of development psychology. Different authors focus on different aspects of this period.

Twenty-first to about thirty-fifth year: early adulthood

Erikson described the main conflict of this significant period as "generation *vs.* stagnation". During this stage, the new formulation of our lifestyle takes place. We try to dissolve our infantile dependency to become truly adult. Sometimes, there is a stagnation of this process, or even a regression in a collusion in the partnership. In the case of collusion, we find partners who are complementary in their characteristics. For example, we have one partner with a tendency for dependence and the other is in defence of his tendency of dependence. Hence, we have the possibility that one develops a dependency on alcohol and the other becomes co-alcoholic.

Living together without children

During this phase, the couple looks for common ideas in the relationship and stability in the partnership. They must regulate closeness and distance. At this stage, wishes and threats exert great influence.

The person is now dealing with loss and separation. Perhaps there are problems connected with patchwork families, children from different partners. There is, perhaps, the necessity of dealing with single parenting. This is extreme in the West, where the incidence of divorce is very high. At this stage, internalised experiences of relationships exert a strong influence on development. The role of the relationship with the original families becomes very important. Changes to the ties among the extended family take place. There is a challenge between tradition and changing tradition.

Financial affairs become more and more important. The couple has to find a way of regulating these affairs.

Living together with children: triangulation

A child often connects, but also separates, the couple. There are now revitalisations of internalised object relationships. The couple is forced to distribute roles and tasks. There are often battles about traditional roles and a search for new distribution, and the couple has to deal with disappointed expectations. Quite often there is a change in sexual experience, especially after the birth of the first child. Perhaps the mother is exhausted and she has fewer libidinal wishes. Perhaps the husband feels excluded from the symbiosis between mother and child. Perhaps the mother is so involved in the relationship with the child that she is not able to care for both the baby and the husband. Sometimes, the experience around the birth leaves some wounds and repelling feelings in the man's inner world.

There are also possible conflicts between generations that emerge. Traditionally, there is conflict between the wife and her mother-in-law. This conflict is dealt with in many fairy-tales and myths.

There is often a conflict about child-care during the first years. The grandmother has a more important role and helps the family, but this help can cause other problems and disturbances.

The child changes the behaviour and social contacts of the family; there is often more contact with other families.

Living together with a child changes the partnership. The mother has a big influence on the relationship between father and child. Usually a light dominance of the father is good for the development of the child. This dominance can help to facilitate the separation process between mother and child. The father can easily become an important third. Of course, there is also the possibility that the father can be benevolent to the mother–child symbiosis. Therefore, the father needs some possibility for sublimation.

There should now be a possibility for the parents to construct a stable border between generations; for example, it is very important that both parents say "no" to the child and do not enable the child to split them. Every child tries to situate itself between the parents. Sometimes this is very concrete, such as the child who sleeps in the parent's bed for a long time. Perhaps this problem is even more important in a one-child family, where the child has greater power to get between the parents.

There is also the necessity to set borders for the original families. This point of view is very important in China, as the bonds in the extended family are very deep.

A battle for power can erupt between the parents about the child. This battle can be open or hidden.

At this stage, there can be the arrival of a second child. The second child changes the family atmosphere. Now all the family's resources are needed and often both parents are forced beyond their capabilities.

Living as a single

Living as a single has different possibilities and difficulties: the greatest problem may be loneliness. Even in modern societies we can see little change in humans' wish to be in a stable partnership. Investigations of changes in living situations and wishes have shown that, even in the past few decades, there was the persistent wish for a stable partnership.

Research in the West has shown that a late decision to form a long-lasting partnership is better than one taken too early (that is, under twenty-three years).

Thirty-fifth year to about sixty-fifth year: middle adulthood

During this stage of life, there is the separation of the children, when parents perhaps have to deal with empty nest syndrome, which involves mourning for the dissolution of the family and the loss of their task and of their being needed.

During this stage, we could have some existential crises and doubts related to self-esteem. Perhaps we might recognise that we failed to achieve our aims.

There are many difficulties in maintaining a stable relationship during this time. In the West, this is the time when many relationships end in divorce, sometimes resulting in patchwork families with special dynamics.

Now, too, people are sometimes sandwiched between having to care for their children and also for their parents. Or perhaps parents have already died and they are faced with the fact that they are now the next generation to die. The denial of death becomes more difficult.

There is the possibility that one could become redundant at work, and functions, performance, and power decrease as one becomes older. Besides psychic illnesses, there are somatic diseases and handicaps. Generally, losses and separations increase. The result is that there are more depressive disturbances in the second half of life.

Over sixty-five years: late adulthood, old age, and death

Erikson described this period as the conflict of "ego-integrity *vs.* despair".

Perhaps most differences can be seen at this stage of life if we compare the West with China, even though things are changing in China.

During this stage, we have to face the symptoms of old age. This means the reduction of power, of health, and of speed, even if we can compensate for that for a certain time through wisdom and experience. We have to face our limits and the loss of our position in the workplace through retirement. Sometimes the wife has problems with the retirement of her husband. Suddenly he is at home all day. Perhaps he tries to reorganise the household in a masculine way. The loss of tasks has effects on self-esteem. Boredom can become the source of stress.

In different cultures and countries, it varies as to how the elderly are allowed to participate in the daily lives of their families. In China, for instance, there is a great difference between urban and rural regions.

During this stage we often have a problem with sexuality. At this age, sexuality for joy and satisfaction is used too rarely. There are moral inhibitions, too. Sometimes this interest is neglected and there might be a taboo in society against sexuality among the elderly. Men and women have difficulties with physical barriers to deal with. These can be caused by low oestrogen levels and dry mucosa in women, or by prostate hypertrophy and cancer in men, with the consequent loss of erection and ejaculation.

This stage is also dominated by the question of whether the elderly are able to deal with dependency. Many people have great problems with receiving something from others, to admit to needing something and to be grateful. They have to change their attitude.

It is very difficult to go back into second file and listen to younger people while staying curious enough to participate in their life.

This phase can be difficult because of the new togetherness with the partner, when one might realise that one has forgotten how to live together day by day.

Sometimes there is the problem of desynchronised aging. One partner might become older sooner and possibly become handicapped, whereas the other is still healthy and sporty. One of the partners might suffer from dementia.

During this stage, we can perhaps look back to integrate life events with reconciliation. Alternatively, we might feel despair at having failed the core of the self, regretting decisions taken and failure to make use of chances.

A great opportunity at this age comes from having grandchildren. One is now allowed to forget the superego of education, and enjoy them without the feeling of responsibility one had with one's own children. One is aware of the continuum of life and it is possible to learn to play and enjoy during this stage more so than with one's own children.

Needless to say, we should not forget that this is the age of dying, and we might have to face the death of our partner. New problems arise: how to deal with the death of one's partner, how to mourn, or, after mourning, considering the possibility of a new partner. What reaction does a new partner evoke within the family? Are they understanding or malevolent?

Finally, there is the task of dying oneself. This task is difficult to describe and is very dependent on one's own view of life and death and whether one believes in life after death.

CHAPTER THREE

CONFLICT, TRAUMA, DEFENCE MECHANISMS, AND SYMPTOM FORMATION

Michael Wolf, Alf Gerlach, and Wolfgang Merkle

Primary and secondary process

Michael Wolf

The main topic of psychoanalysis is reality, and not, as is often asserted, the irrational. This concept of reality (defined by the reality principle posited by Freud) addresses the cognitive perception of reality (rather than delusion, thinking disorders, and other distortions investigated through psychiatric exploration). Furthermore, it addresses social perception and the recognition of reality. This is the main meaning of the "Oedipus complex", referring to the fundamental acceptance of the differences between the sexes and the generations and the position of the person in this biological as well as social order.

The pleasure principle (defined by Freud as the universal tendency to avoid reluctance and to provide pleasure by discharging of tension) relates exclusively to the tensions and the satisfactions of drives. The reality principle is a modification of the pleasure principle that takes into account that it is sometimes necessary for the satisfaction of drives and, therefore, the achievement of pleasure to be deferred because of the prevailing conditions.

The question then arises of whether all psychic contents and processes are covered by these two principles. In particular, can all affective states be understood as directly emanating from drives that follow the same principle of relaxing through discharging?

> We would reiterate that the apparatuses which the ego constructs during the course of its maturation and development are prompted in their development ultimately by the need to control feelings and their principle role is to widen the tolerable range of conscious or unconscious experiences without unduly disrupting the basic feeling tone of safety, wellbeing or security. (Joffe & Sandler, 1968, p. 453)

Argelander (1971) highlighted the security principle as the opposite of the pleasure principle and Kohut (1971) developed an independent psychology of the self. I feel obliged to emphasise a qualitative difference between id tendencies and self-needs. The sense of well-being engendered by sufficient self-esteem and an awareness of one's identity is totally different from the relaxation achieved as a result of drive satisfaction. Hence, we are able to better understand the rivalry and conflict that sometimes occurs between drive needs and narcissistic self-needs, even though they normally agree with each other (e.g., the feeling of narcissistic grandiosity that is common with people who have fallen in love). This differentiation enables us to better describe the possibility of substituting narcissistic satisfaction for drive satisfaction and vice versa. Thus, a child renounces certain drive satisfactions to obtain its mother's approval.

So, here, I distinguish between a drive development on the one hand and a narcissistic development on the other. The development of object relations is based on this differentiation, and mediates between the two. Table 3.1 illustrates the processes and principles involved in psychic development from birth to 5–6 years old.

We can see, at different stages of development, how the primary process involves the pleasure principle and the secondary process involves the reality principle. Freud's terms "primary process" and "secondary process" designate two opposed, yet complementary, modes of functioning within the psychic apparatus. The primary processes, directly animated by the drives, serve the pleasure principle and work to implement a free flow of psychic energy. Secondary processes, which presuppose the limiting of this energy, intervene as a system of control and regulation in the service of the reality principle. Psychical life is entirely regulated by the equilibrium between these two types of process, which varies between subjects and at different points in time (awareness and consciousness *vs.* fantasies and dreams, the influence of drugs, and regressed mental states such as hallucinatory wishful thinking in psychoses, etc.).

Freud posits this fundamental duality as early as his "Project for a scientific psychology" (1950[1895]). Briefly put, desire, or the wish for something, unleashes a process that leads to discharge. However, since in this "precocious phase" the psychic apparatus is not capable of distinguishing between the representation of a missing object and its perception in reality, the fulfilling of the wish is, therefore, hallucinatory and "requires a criterion from elsewhere in order to distinguish between perception and idea".

Table 3.1. Processes and principles related to psychic development.

Approx. age	Processes	Principles	Drive development	Object relations	Self-system: self- and object-representations
0–1	Primary process	Pleasure principle	Oral	Symbiosis or dual relationship	Emerging differentiation Partial objects Grandiose self
2–3	Primary–secondary processes	Pleasure–reality principles	Anal	Separation–individuation	Partial objects
3–4	Secondary process	Reality principle	Phallic–narcissistic	Self-centred	Whole objects, idealised objects, ideal self
4–5/6	Secondary process	Reality principle	Infantile–genital	Triangulation	Real self, real objects, superego, ideal ego

Whereas the activity of the first system, that of the primary processes, is "directed towards securing the free discharge of the quantities of excitation, the second system, that of secondary processes, succeeds in inhibiting this discharge".

Specifying the opposition between the pleasure principle and the reality principle, whereby he posits the pleasure principle as temporally primary, Freud would later write, "It will be rightly objected that an organization which was a slave to the pleasure principle and neglected the reality of the external world could not maintain itself alive for the shortest time, so that it could not have come into existence at all" (Freud, 1911b, p. 219).

His answer was to constitute the keystone of the contemporary development of theories of psychogenesis in their entirety, by bringing the mother–child relationship into consideration.

The opposition or complementarity of the primary and secondary processes was described first by Freud in economic terms. However, he also accords it a topological dimension. In "The unconscious" (1915e), he specifies that the preconscious is the locus of the secondary processes and their regulating function over the primary processes, characteristic of the unconscious. It is this regulation that creates boundaries for the cathectic energy used for representations, and, thus, enables the development of cognitions, which occurs via the passage from thing-representations to word-representations. Indeed, the work of thought, which functions via the "displacement of small quantities of energy", requires that the representations upon which it is based remain stable and distinct. This would not be possible if the free flow of energy, and the condensations and displacements characteristic of the primary processes, prevailed.

So, as Kernberg assumes, both modes of psychic functioning, or, rather, both poles of this continuum of psychic functioning, are based upon and related to object relations, either those which are more "primitive" or "archaic" (in primary process) or those which are more elaborated and differentiated (in secondary process).

The reality principle itself, and the psychic functioning that is allied with the secondary process, is not established by taking one step upwards on the ladder of development. It is a longer process that ends with the resolution of the Oedipus complex through renunciation of grandiose (primary process) drive wishes ("killing father, marrying mother") and successful internalisation of one's specific position in the order of sexual and generational differentiation via the "incest taboo" (reality principle).

The way it functions best is not only by "inhibiting" discharges of energy connected with early drive wishes, but also by supporting narcissistic gratification of these inhibitions through transforming them into renunciations that are rewarded by other gratifications, such as, for example, recognition of achievement and success at school, in sports, or in other fields of mind–body activities that lie beyond the confines of the core family.

Conflict

During the whole life span from birth to death, psychic development has to deal with and resolve many conflicts. Conflict is part of normal development. The word "conflict" comes from the Latin word *confligere*, which means "clash": A clashes with B due to a confliction of each individual's wishes. Solved conflicts lead to progress in development, whereas unsolved conflict can halt normal development. The individual tries to repress the conflict to continue his or her psychosocial development, but when the conflict cannot be suppressed by the defence mechanisms any longer, it produces symptoms of suffering.

We can understand psychoanalysis as a psychology of intrapsychic conflicts and their solutions through treatment. First, we have to differentiate external conflicts (with other persons or norms, or objects, animals, etc.) from internal (intrapsychic) conflicts (between different parts or subsystems of the psyche, such as, for example, ego and superego), as shown in Table 3.2.

What is known as regression of libido, etc., implies the regression to former stages of psychic development and stages of conflicts in the life-cycle. The best-known and differentiated model of these conflicts is that of Erikson (1959). The conflicts identified in Table 3.3 have to be solved at their particular stage or they will persist and hinder the free development—and conflict solving—at the next stage of development.

We use Erikson's typology in considering other topics (see Chapters Two and Seven). Another contemporary typology of conflicts presents the "operationalised psychodynamic diagnostics" (OPD) model. OPD proposes the typology of conflicts set out in Table 3.4, arranged in a continuum of life-cycle development that is comparable with Erikson's model.

Another concept of conflict is that of "psychosocial arrangements and collusions". Because psychic development is always related to other persons (care-givers), all these conflicts can be understood also as intertwined with human relations and their typical conflicts. A psychodynamic perspective adds something specific: the fact that both (or more) participants in

Table 3.2. External and internal conflict (Mertens, 1981, p. 130, modified by Wolf).

External conflict	Internal conflict
Can be followed by: Alloplastic action: – modification of environment; – successful conflict solution; – active reality adaption or: – autoplastic action; – modification of self; – deferred satisfaction; – with temporary satisfaction of fantasies	Can be treated intrapsychically, with or without success, or followed by: – regression of libido, ego, and object relationships; – re-emergence of the infantile instinctual aim at the point of fixation; – mortification of the ego ideal; – superego disapproval; – resolution via symptom formation

Table 3.3. Typology of conflicts in the life cycle (Erikson 1959).

Stage and age	Type of conflict
Oral–sensory, baby	Basic trust *vs.* distrust
Muscular–anal, toddler	Autonomy *vs.* shame and doubt
Locomotor–genital, play	Initiative *vs.* guilt feelings
Latency, primary school	Industry *vs.* feeling of inferiority
Puberty, adolescence	Identity *vs.* identity diffusion
Early adult	Intimacy *vs.* isolation
Adulthood	Generativity *vs.* selfishness
Maturity, ripe adulthood	Integrity *vs.* disgust for life

Table 3.4. OPD axes III: repetitive–functional conflicts.

1. Dependency *vs.* autonomy.
2. Submission *vs.* control.
3. Care for *vs.* self-caring (autarchy).
4. Conflicts of self-esteem (narcissistic conflicts, value of self *vs.* object).
5. Conflicts of superego and guilt (egoistic *vs.* prosocial tendencies).
6. Oedipal–sexual (genital) conflicts (rivalry).
7. Identity (*vs.* dissonance and other maturity deficits described by Erikson).

human interaction are interconnected not only by the real interaction, but also by some kind of exchange of their intrapsychic states (affects, conflicts, etc.). The way this exchange works is characterised by some typical psychic "mechanisms", known as projection, introjection, and projective identification. The whole ensemble is called a psychosocial arrangement (Mentzos, 1982), or a collusion (Willi, 1975). The best known of these arrangements are collusions between sadistic and masochistic personalities or between narcissistic persons and their environment, the so-called complementary narcissistics.

Conflict, excessive demand, and stress

The psychophysical organism is constantly dealing with the satisfaction of desires and interests as well as the prohibition of danger. The concepts of pleasure principle / disinclination principle and reality principle posited by Freud are identifying those things. Feelings of pleasure or disinclination and their later differentiations (e.g., joy, enthusiasm, well-being, pride, elevated mood, etc., on the one hand, and fear, grief, shame, feelings of guilt, etc., on the other hand) are functioning as indicators in complex systems of regulation. They are indicators that show experiences derived from pleasure (or disinclination) as well as through danger (or safety) and lead to certain reactions. It is important to obtain an optimal (not always constant) level of tension. Extraordinary fluctuations of these tensions are regulated by mechanisms of balance. If the regulation of those tensions is impossible (in one or another direction), emergency mechanisms are activated and other functions are set aside. Both forms of reaction can become what we know as psychic or psychosomatic symptoms or disorders.

Conflicts have great importance in the process of emergence of psychic disorders because they strongly test regulating mechanisms of the psychophysical organism. This organism is able to compensate for even very difficult outer and inner stimulations and their concomitant burdens, but it is extremely prone to burdens caused by inner conflicts.

It is no coincidence that inner tensions and irritability (as well as other symptoms) are common characteristics of many neurotic disorders. They represent the ensemble of motifs that is locked within the conflict, the opposing tendencies keeping each other in check and provoking this increased tension. In the long run, it is an unbearable situation that is comparable with heavy physical stress. As is the case with bodily stress, emergency reactions occur, with mechanisms being mobilised and compromises aimed at which represent a huge part of the clinical picture of neurotic disorders (Mentzos, 1982, pp. 75–77).

Trauma

Recent clinical, theoretical, and research developments in the past two decades show a broad interest in reactions to trauma (such as post traumatic stress disorder—PTSD) and in the field of so-called "psychotraumatology".

However, despite the fact that traumatic reactions have been observed throughout the history of mankind (take, for example, the reaction of Achilles to the death of his friend Patroclus, which is described by the Ancient Greek poet, Homer, in *The Iliad*, which tells the story of the war between the Greeks and the Trojans (Fischer & Riedesser, 1998, p. 31)), it was not until 1980 that PTSD became an official category of such international diagnostic systems as are described in the *DSM* and the *ICD*. Since then, typical psychic reactions to more and more overwhelming experiences are classified as PTSD. This pertains both to individual experiences (death of relatives, assault, rape, severe physical illness, etc.) and to collective experiences, such as wars, ethnic cleansing, including raping and killing people, torture, "man-made" disasters, and natural disasters, such as earthquakes, typhoons, tsunamis, etc.

There are so many clinical, theoretical, and therapeutic developments in different areas of psychology, psychiatry, and neurobiology, but we should say that the psychoanalytical concept of trauma functions as a helpful tool for a more adequate understanding of what is happening in the case of traumatic experiences. Looking back at the concept of trauma which was developed by Freud and Breuer in their studies on hysteria in 1893, before psychoanalysis turned to the drive theory and the conflicts in the inner world of the psyche (inner/intrapsychic conflict between the ego, id, and superego), we can see the relevance of this concept today.

To quote Freud,

> We must presume rather that the psychical trauma – or more precisely the memory of the trauma – acts like a foreign body which long after its entry must continue to be regarded as an agent that is still at work. . . . For we found, to our great surprise at first, that each individual hysterical symptom immediately and permanently disappeared when we had succeeded in bringing clearly to light the memory of the event by which it was provoked and in arousing its accompanying affect, and when the patient had described that event in the greatest possible detail and had put the affect into words. (1895d, p. 6)

Trauma and conflict

Freud's original model consists of the theory of trauma as the cause of neurosis. According to this theory, the neurosis is a result of the inability to cope with the overwhelming affect that has emerged in a (potentially) traumatic situation. The normal mode of working through of an acute affect emerging in a particularly structured situation is seen as a motor discharge or as other, more differentiated, forms of realisation or abreaction: for example, the discourse about it, reactions such as crying, feelings of revenge, etc. If the individual succeeds in this working through, no further complications or disturbances would develop. If not, there is no other choice than to repress this affect and with it many thoughts and images of situations that were connected to this affect through association. Thus, later associations evoking repressed contents (memories) would simultaneously reactivate the repressed or insufficiently abreacted affect, necessitating another and even stronger repression.

> Our observations have shown, on the other hand, that the memories which have become the determinants of hysterical phenomena persist for a long time with astonishing freshness and with the whole of their affective colouring. We must, however, mention another remarkable fact, which we shall later be able to turn to account, namely, that these memories, unlike other memories of their past lives, are not at the patients' disposal. On the contrary, these experiences are completely absent from the patients' memory when they are in a normal psychical state, or are only present in a highly summary form. Not until they have been questioned under hypnosis do these memories emerge with the undiminished vividness of a recent event. (Freud, 1895d, p. 9)

Despite the model of conflict not yet being conceptualised in psychoanalytical theory, a closer investigation reveals the fact that, at that time, Freud identified an intrapsychic conflict as the most important pathogenetic factor. It is not the collision with the environment itself or the affect thus caused, but the absence of abreaction and working through of the affect that becomes pathogenetic. This blockage and this repression are induced by the ego (then called the dominant ego-consciousness).

In further developments of psychoanalysis, this trauma theory of the neurosis was not abandoned, but complemented, modified, and, finally, even integrated in the structural model (ego, id, and superego). The trauma is now not necessarily understood as an acute experience any more, but, more frequently, it is chronic traumatisation, repetitions of traumata. The traumatisation consists either of fear and other unwelcome experiences exceeding the extent that is bearable, or of overwhelming frustration. Therefore, it is not about arbitrary blockages of affects. On the contrary, it is about central, existential destabilisation and/or deep frustration of vital basic needs. At first, Freud thought that this was mainly frustration of sexual instinctual needs. Later on, it was accepted that the sexual needs are just one particular case and that traumatisation also could be provoked by repetitive frustration of contact needs, tendencies to autonomy, or by the lack of a shelter- and safety-providing constant attachment figure, or by narcissistic insult. Essentially, however, the connection between trauma and conflict obtains: the fearful or painful experience generates a greater readiness for reactions of fear, followed by a speedy mobilisation of defence mechanisms. These repress fear and disinclination and—more importantly—block the conscious experience of these frustrated wishes in order to hinder a renewed traumatisation in the future. Hence, safety, shelter, and freedom from pain are achieved through the erection of a counteracting system, but this could be an exchange that might prove expensive: the conflict becomes reinforced and a new source of suffering emerges (Mentzos, 1982, pp. 77–79).

The trauma can be overcome only by new experiences of human interactions, and psychodynamic psychotherapy could offer a helpful and successful way to gain these.

The mechanisms of defence

Alf Gerlach

The psychoanalytical concept of neurosis

The existence of inner conflicts between impulses and the interconnected remainder of the personality, the so-called ego, is the basis for our understanding of neurotic and psychosomatic disorders. Inner conflicts are not themselves neurotic, but are elements of the normal psychic life of everyone. We think there is a fluent passage from the normal way of solving inner conflicts and problems to inadequate forms of trying to master them. In the case of neurosis or psychosomatic illness, the conflicts have not been solved in favour of the impulse or of the ego; when the conflicts are too strong, or the ego has no capacity to handle them, the conflicts become unconscious through a process called repression. Although this repression expels the intolerable impulses from consciousness, it cannot render them innocuous; the repressed impulses find a way back into consciousness in the disguised form of manifestations of neurotic and psychosomatic symptoms.

All manifestations of neurosis, such as irritability, inner tension, anxieties, thoughts, impulses, and enactions, are possible ways to avoid intolerable feelings. Indeed, the patients suffer from their symptoms, which are felt to be alien to the ego, but the neurotic disorder protects them from even stronger feelings of unpleasure in the form of unbearable anxiety, depression, or the sense of guilt and shame. All symptoms of neurosis can be understood as a result of a dialectic process between impulses that would lead to anguish and defence mechanisms against these impulses.

Why can impulses cause anguish? The first intuition that impulses might be dangerous arises in early childhood, because infants are unable to attain satisfaction through their own efforts. They need the help of adults to master tensions like hunger and thirst and to fulfil their wishes for closeness, warmth, and love. That is the reason why they often experience traumatic situations of ungoverned tension; whenever the organism is flooded with excitement, the infant experiences this primary, or automatic, anxiety. Later on, the individual can use the previously automatic anxiety in cases of impending danger. Now, however, it uses anxieties of lower intensity as signals to start defensive actions against uncontrollable tensions.

There are four major anxieties of infants:

1. The fear of losing the object of their primary needs, normally the mother; the child is afraid of being left alone with his impulses (e.g., hunger) and being helpless to satisfy them.
2. The fear of losing the object's love; when children are sure of the existence of their mothers and of other important persons who take care of their needs, they can feel insecurity about the love of these persons.
3. Later on, there is castration fear in boys and its equivalent in girls: for boys, it means fear of losing their penis, or of damage to it, or of being overpowered by stronger males; for girls, it means fear of being deprived of the possessions of femininity, that is, the integrity of the female organs or their attractiveness as women.

4. After the establishment of the so-called superego, or conscience (age 3–5), the anxiety can be replaced by guilt feelings. The guilt feelings represent a special form of anxiety of the ego towards the conscience. In this case, the warning function of conscience expresses the tendency to avoid the pain of intensive guilt feelings. This pain constitutes a special inner displeasure: the fear of losing self-esteem or the inner feeling of well-being, protection, and security is felt. In conscience, this fear is internalised and the danger comes from within the personality. As long as a real, external punishment is feared, we do not speak of true guilt feelings; this fear does not differ from tendencies developed by other anxiety signals.

Defence mechanisms and their functions

These anxieties are common in childhood and in later life. They all appear in the psychoneuroses. The difference between these neurotic anxieties and realistic fear lies in the source of the danger. Real danger threatens from some external object, neurotic danger from an instinctual demand. The intimate relation between anxiety and neurosis derives from the fact that the ego protects itself against an instinctual danger in the same manner as against an external reality danger: it tries to flee from them through defence mechanisms, and, thereby, the neurotic process starts.

Although there are many different mechanisms of defence, each individual uses only a very few. They are the techniques that a person automatically applies in situations of inner danger. Whenever we see a defence mechanism applied in a particular situation, in dealing with a particular challenge, we can accept that this mechanism is applied by this person in many other situations, too. This fact has important consequences for the therapeutic dialogue with patients. Whenever there is a resistance against the free flow of associations and themes in the dialogue, we receive information about the mechanisms of defence in the particular individual. Once our attention has been called to a person's special mechanisms of defence, we are able to spot them in other activities as well; we can then point them out to him, as a proceeding unconsciously and automatically applied by him and characteristic to him. These mechanisms, once established, may then be traced back to their beginnings in childhood. The mechanisms of defence and their early beginnings, once brought to the level of consciousness, will meet with the person's judgement of reality and with his reasoning powers and will become subject to revision.

Specific mental disorders are usually linked with specific mechanisms of defence, as shown in Table 3.5.

Classification of defence mechanisms

Today, we can put the different well-known mechanisms of defence in four divisions, designated "narcissistic", "immature", "neurotic", and "mature" (Table 3.6).

Narcissistic defence mechanisms

These mechanisms are common in all children before the age of five, and also in adult dreams and fantasy. For the user, these mechanisms alter reality; for the beholder, they appear crazy.

Table 3.5. Typical defence mechanisms and mental disorders.

Defence mechanism	Example of mental disorder
Projection	Paranoia, schizophrenia
Splitting	Borderline syndrome
Turning against the self	Depression
Identification with aggressor	Depression
Somatisation	Psychosomatic disorder
Rendering undone	Obsessive–compulsive disorder
Rationalisation	Obsessive–compulsive disorder
Isolation of affect	Obsessive–compulsive disorder
Intellectualisation	Obsessive–compulsive disorder
Reaction formation	Obsessive–compulsive disorder
Displacement	Phobia
Identification	Hysteria
Repression	Hysteria
Dissociation	Hysteria
Emotionalisation	Hysteria

Table 3.6. Defence mechanisms on the early and mature level of ego development (Vaillant, 1971).

Level of maturity	Defence mechanism
1st level (immature, primitive, narcissistic)	Psychotic denial
	Psychotic projection
	Splitting
	Introjection
2nd level (less immature and primitive)	Non-psychotic projection
	Identification as defence (i.e., with aggressor)
3rd level (genuinely psychoneurotic)	Intellectualisation
	Isolation of affect
	Affection
	Rationalisation
	Rendering undone
	Forming reactions
	Displacement
	Turning against the self
	Regression
	Repression
4th level (made up of processes of sublimation)	Sublimation

Normally, they are immune to change by psychotherapeutic interpretation, but they are altered by a change in reality, for example, through the use of drugs such as chlorpromazine, or through the removal of stressful situations. In therapeutic contact, the patient can give up these defence mechanisms temporarily, if the therapist can offer him strong interpersonal support in conjunction with direct confrontation of the ignored reality.

Delusional projection, psychotic denial, distortion, and splitting belong to the narcissistic mechanisms of defence. Delusional projection means obvious delusions about external reality, often in a persecutory sense. Hence, we can find in the patient the perception of his own feelings in another person, resulting in acting in response to the perception (e.g., "The other will damage me, so I have to protect myself"); we can also find the perception of other people or their feelings as being inside one's self (e.g., "The enemy has devoured my soul"). Delusional projection can be distinguished from distortion by the absence of wish fulfilment. Distortion includes unrealistic megalomaniac beliefs, hallucinations, wish-fulfilling delusions, and feelings of delusional superiority and entitlement. It can lead to persistent denial of personal responsibility for one's own behaviour. All external reality is perceived in a way that serves inner needs. Unpleasant feelings are replaced by their opposites, whereas, in delusional projection, unpleasant feelings are alleviated by assigning responsibility for such feelings elsewhere.

Psychotic denial means the denial of facts pertaining to external reality (e.g., "I never had parents"). It includes the use of fantasy as a major substitute for other people, especially absent other people (e.g., "I will make new parents in my own mind").

Splitting as a defence mechanism helps the user to avoid the coincidence of two or more antagonistic contents in his mind. In principle, these contents are conscious, but, from time to time, the one or the other part is denied (e.g., someone says, "You are my best friend". Two minutes later, he is angry and says, "I hate you").

Immature defence mechanisms

These mechanisms are normal in children between the ages of three and sixteen, and they are common in character and affective disorders. For the user, they most often alter distress engendered either by the threat of interpersonal intimacy or the threat of experiencing its loss. To the beholder, they appear as socially undesirable misbehaviour. Normally, they are resistant to change through talk, but they may be altered by repeated and forceful interpretation during prolonged psychotherapy or by improved interpersonal relationships (e.g., by a more mature spouse, by a more intuitive physician).

Immature mechanisms of defence are non-psychotic projection, identification as defence, schizoid fantasy, hypochondriasis, passive–aggressive behaviour, and acting out. Non-psychotic projection means attributing one's own unacknowledged feelings to others. It includes severe prejudice, rejection of intimacy through unwarranted suspicion, and marked hypervigilance to external danger (e.g., "Not I or we are bad, but the others are"). Identification is used as a defence in cases of identification with the aggressor (e.g., "I protect myself against my anxiety by imitating the aggressor"), or in cases of hysterical symptoms: some patients suffer from symptoms (e.g., a cough, or paralysis) that are like the symptoms of their recently deceased parents. Through identification, they defend themselves against the separation and psychic pain of their loss.

Schizoid fantasy as a defence mechanism is the tendency to use fantasy and to remain in autistic retreat for the purposes of conflict resolution and self-satisfaction. Often, it is associated with global avoidance of interpersonal intimacy and the use of eccentricity to repel others. In contrast to psychotic denial, the user does not fully believe in, or insist upon, acting out his fantasies. On the other hand, unlike mere wishes, schizoid fantasies obliterate the overt expression of aggressive or sexual impulses towards others.

Hypochondriasis arises from the transformation of reproach of others for non-acceptance, loneliness, or unacceptable aggressive impulses into (i) self-reproach, (ii) complaints of pain, of somatic illness, and neurasthenia. As distinguished from identification, hypochondriasis produces dysphoria and a sense of affliction, and, unlike hysterical conversion symptoms, it is accompanied by the very opposite of indifference. The mechanism might permit the user to belabour others with his own pain or discomfort in lieu of making direct demands upon them, or in lieu of complaining that others have ignored his wishes, which often remain unexpressed.

Passive–aggressive behaviour is a mechanism of defence in which aggression towards others is expressed indirectly and ineffectively through passivity, masochism, or turning the impulses against the self. It can include failures, procrastination, or illnesses that affect others more than oneself. It can be expressed by silly or provocative behaviour in order to receive attention. The last of the immature mechanisms of defence, acting out, means direct expression of an unconscious wish in order to avoid being conscious of the accompanied affect. It includes the use of motor behaviour and delinquent or impulsive acts to avoid being aware of one's own inner feelings.

Neurotic defence mechanisms

These mechanisms are common in individuals with neurotic disorder and in mastering acute adult stress. For the user, these mechanisms alter private feelings or instinctual expression. To the beholder, they appear as individual quirks. Often, they can be dramatically changed by psychotherapeutic interpretation.

Neurotic defence mechanisms include repression, displacement, reaction formation, and various kinds of defences such as intellectualisation, isolation, rationalisation, undoing, and magical thinking.

Repression consists of an unconsciously purposeful forgetting, or not becoming aware of, internal impulses, perceptions from a selected sense organ or external events, which—as a rule—represent possible temptations or punishments for instinctual demands. The purposeful exclusion of these perceptions from consciousness is obviously intended to hinder their real effects as well as avoiding the pain of becoming aware of them. Although the repressed is not felt consciously, it remains effective in the unconscious. Repression is the main mechanism of hysteria. An example of repression is the simple forgetting of a name or an intention. Analysis reveals that a name or an intention is forgotten if a suppressed motive is in opposition to it, usually because it was associated with some objectionable instinctual demand. In the case of tendentious forgetting, the fact that the repressed still persists in the unconscious is sensed directly in the subjective feeling that one ought to know what has been forgotten, or even that one does know it somehow. Forgetting is often accompanied by highly symbolic behaviour, which suggests that the repressed is not really forgotten. Sometimes certain facts are remembered as such, but their connections, their significance, or their emotional value are repressed.

The mechanism of repression differs from suppression by effecting unconscious inhibition of impulse to the point of losing, not postponing, the desired goals. In contrast to denial, repression prevents the expression and perception of instincts and feelings rather than affecting recognition of, and response to, external events (e.g., if a man were weeping but forgot for whom he wept or denied that he felt sad, this would be repression; if he denied the existence of his tears or insisted that the mourned one was still alive, this would be denial).

The redirection of feelings from a person or situation arousing these feelings towards an object that is relatively less cared about is called displacement. Incidental situations or strangers are substituted for emotionally important people or situations: for example, jokes with hidden hostile intent and caricature involve displacement. A classical clinical example is the phobia that displaces the neurotic anxiety through an unimportant external reason. Small animals or situations such as closed rooms or lifts become a source of anxiety.

Many cramped and rigid neurotic attitudes are obvious attempts to deny or to repress some impulses, or to defend the person against instinctual dangers. They diametrically oppose an unacceptable instinctual impulse and hinder the expression of contrary impulses, which, nevertheless, sometimes break through in various ways. Then we can prove that the original opposite attitude still exists in the unconscious. The secondary opposite attitudes are called reaction formations. Persons with reaction formations do not develop other defence mechanisms when an instinctual danger threatens; they have changed their personality structure to see this danger as continually present, so that they may be ready whenever the danger occurs. The defence mechanism of reaction formation includes overtly caring for someone else when one wishes to be cared for oneself, "hating" someone or something which one really likes, and "loving" a hated rival or unpleasant duty. Clinical examples are the cleanliness or the sense of order of the compulsive neurotic who struggles, by means of those character traits, against his instinctual demand for dirt and disorder. The rigidity of such cleanliness or sense of order, as well as the occasional breaking through of dirtiness and disorder, betray the reactive quality of these character traits. The neurotic defence mechanisms of intellectualisation, isolation, rationalisation, undoing, and magical thinking usually occur as a cluster, although these mechanisms differ from each other. Intellectualisation is thinking about instinctual wishes in formal, affectively bland terms and not acting on them. It includes paying undue attention to the inanimate in order to avoid expression of inner feelings, and paying attention to irrelevant detail to avoid perceiving the whole. Isolation consists of keeping events apart that actually belong together. Sometimes, the user interpolates real spatial or temporal intervals between the two facts or thoughts that are supposed to be kept separate. The most important special case of this defence mechanism is the isolation of an idea from the feelings that originally were connected with it. In discussing the most exciting events, the user remains calm, but, at quite another point, might then develop an incomprehensible emotion, without being aware of the fact that the emotion has been displaced. The normal prototype of this neurotic isolation is the process of logical thinking, which actually consists of the continued elimination of affective associations in the interest of objectivity. The defence mechanisms of undoing and magical thinking can be observed when something positive is done or thought which, actually or magically, is the opposite of something that, again actually or in imagination, was done before. These mechanisms can lead to certain compulsive symptoms that are made up of two actions: the second action is a direct reversion of the first (e.g., to put a stone in someone's way as an aggressive act against that person and then to return and remove the obstacle). A failing of the mechanism of undoing, owing to the invasion of the defence by the warded-off impulses, explains several phenomena frequent in compulsion neurosis: for example, the increase in the number of necessary repetitions of compulsive acts, or the ever broadening scope of the ceremonial assurances, or obsessive doubts as to whether the undoing has succeeded.

Mature defence

These mechanisms can be observed in normal individuals after the age of ten. They emerge during adolescence as a by-product of successful identifications and in the replacement of a primitive conscience with a developed, ideal self-image. They may reflect the increasing complexity of mental integration that Piaget has documented for adolescent cognition. For the user, these mechanisms (e.g., sublimation, suppression, anticipation, altruism, and humour) integrate conscience, reality, interpersonal relationships, and private feelings. To the beholder, they appear as convenient virtues; to a certain extent, they may differ from society to society or from social class to social class. Under increased stress, they may change to less mature mechanisms.

Often, all successful defences are placed under the heading of sublimation. Strictly speaking, sublimation is the indirect or attenuated expression of instincts without either adverse consequences or marked loss of pleasure. It includes both expressing aggression through pleasurable games, sports, and hobbies and tender attenuation of sexual wishes, unlike the case of neurotic defence mechanisms, where sublimation instincts are channelled rather than dammed or diverted. Feelings are acknowledged, modified, and directed towards a relatively significant person or goal so that modest instinctual satisfaction results.

Suppression means the conscious or semi-conscious decision to postpone paying attention to a conscious impulse or conflict. With suppression, one says, "I will think about it tomorrow", and the next day one does remember to think about it. Thus, it includes deliberately postponing, but not avoiding and minimising, acknowledged discomfort. Similar to this mechanism is the realistic anticipation of, or planning for, future inner discomfort. Anticipation includes goal-directed but careful planning or worrying, premature but realistic anticipation of death, surgery, or separations, and the conscious utilisation of insight gained from psychotherapy.

The overt expression of feelings without personal discomfort or immobilisation and without unpleasant effects on others is possible by means of humour. Some games and playful regression come under this heading, too. Whereas wit always involves distraction or displacement away from the affective issue, humour allows overt and direct expression of feelings. In opposition to schizoid fantasy, humour never excludes other people.

Psychosocial mechanisms of defence

All mechanisms of defence described above are inner psychical actions. When the process is not limited to inner psychical changes, and when relations to other people are constituted unconsciously to reaffirm and strengthen the inner psychical changes, these actions are called psychosocial mechanisms of defence. This might happen either by choosing the right partner with a complementary neurotic requirement or by manipulation, seduction, or influence on the partner in the desired direction. For example, parents can assign specific roles to their children in the expectation that they will fulfil the secret dissatisfied desires of the parents. Psychosocial mechanisms of defence are common in many interpersonal relations; above all, their observation is important in psychotherapy with groups and families.

Symptoms and suffering

Wolfgang Merkle

Symptoms, their origin, and their meaning

Neurotic symptoms have their origin in the patient's life history and the investigation of his life will give us insights into the psychogenetic and psychodynamic connection, as shown by the repetitions and conflicting reinforcements in his life.

The reason for these symptoms is generally not known to the patients consciously, and there are different levels of insight of the patients with regard to the connections between the unconscious conflicts and the symptoms.

Sometimes, especially in psychosomatic patients, it is the most difficult step in therapy to convince patients that the somatic symptoms have connections to their life, to conflicts or losses, and are not only due to somatic causation.

Furthermore, in cases exhibiting a stable structuring of symptoms, we find a course in which the primary conditions are so mixed with the secondary motives that they can hardly be distinguished.

In neurotic patients, the traces of the meaning of the symptoms are not as hidden as in psychosomatic patients.

In *Inhibitions, Symptoms and Anxiety* (1926d, p. 98) Freud wrote, "But usually the outcome is different. The initial act of repression is followed by a tedious or interminable sequel in which the struggle against the instinctual impulse is prolonged into a struggle against the symptom".

Somatic symptoms are frequently a concomitant manifestation of psychic suffering with no meaning of their own (for instance, fear is often accompanied by sweating, palpitations, and so on). Nevertheless, these somatic symptoms can become crucial for the development of the patients suffering:

> On the other hand, the same symptoms of anxiety hysteria continue to exist in the "functional syndromes," the increasingly subtle diagnosis of which continues to mount pressure on modern medicine. The disturbed patient—who cannot know that his symptoms are expressions of unconscious emotions—insists that the physician repeat the diagnostic examinations to exclude a hidden and possibly malignant illness.
>
> Frequently the result of these examinations is some harmless deviation from normal that, because of its ambiguity, can become the source of new disturbances and lead to measures that are entirely inappropriate for alleviating the patient's neurotic anxieties. The precise reason for this follows from the structure of these anxieties and the development of a vicious circle in which helplessness, hopelessness, and anxiety reinforce each other. (Thomä & Kächele, 1992, p. 386)

In borderline patients, or in patients with personality disorders, the symptoms are generally represented in behaviour disorders and the meaning must be deduced in a very difficult and exhausting work through the interpretation of countertransference and acting in or out. Sometimes, we need inpatient settings in order to detect and bring together the splitting of the object in different transferences.

Symptoms should always be seen as a creation of the patient of a possibility for him to avoid worse conditions of mind: for instance, helplessness and overwhelming situations. So, symptoms, in the beginning, are helpful not only in surviving difficult situations caused by trauma or conflict, but also to show and to hide the neediness and wish for dependence of the patient.

Symptoms can serve as an attempt to avoid separation from an ambivalent object (because separation would be harder to bear than being unhappy in a relationship). For example, pain can have an important function in adjusting a relationship on the level of intimacy or closeness and distance or in regulating dominance.

Symptoms can be an attempt to avoid psychosis, or autism, or depression. If one can touch a symptom concretely, as in touching a painful leg, there is a concrete danger rather than a vague one, such as helplessness or psychic feeling.

In psychosomatic patients, the symptoms cannot be seen in the same way as in neurotic patients because the symptoms can be unspecific concomitants of stress resulting from the dependence of the specific organ on being the place of minor resistance (disposition factors).

From the very beginning of psychoanalytic theory, it was incorrect to restrict the genesis of symptoms to the model of the genesis of hysterical symptoms.

The individual symptoms, thus, follow biologically given patterns that are rooted in the patient's physical constitution, as described in Freud's notion of complemental series.

Alexander (1935, p. 505) wrote, "It is a methodological error to attempt to interpret psychologically an organic symptom which is the end-result of an intermediary chain of organic processes". This view agrees with Freud's clear methodological guidelines about physical disturbances that cannot be interpreted symbolically (Freud, 1910i, p. 217).

Symptoms and the way to transmit these to the patient in a psychotherapeutic treatment

Patients who have only somatic symptoms, that is, patients with somatoform complaints or psychosomatic patients, often have a long way to go before arriving in a psychoanalytically orientated treatment. On average, it is five years until they are accepted for a psychotherapeutic treatment.

So, we must find ways to convince these patients to come into an adequate (psychotherapeutic) therapy; therefore, we need good techniques to bring us closer to the deficits in the life history of these patients. We must provide our capacity of empathy for these patients to help them to come closer to their original suffering in the pathological situation at the beginning of their repressing process. Because of the defence process of identification with the aggressor, they have lost the capacity to have pity for their own suffering (often there is parental violence in the case history).

Symptoms and the change in them during the past century

During the past century, there was a great shift in the understanding of symptoms from hysterical or conversion symptoms to other themes. These shifts can be seen as an attempt to hide the meaning behind the symptom, and are also due, to some extent, to the fact that the background of neurotic symptoms is understood as common knowledge. Furthermore, in the common symptoms of neurotic patients, we can see conflict themes that exist in reality in society. Therefore, we have more illnesses such as burnout syndromes, fibromyalgia, chronic fatigue syndrome, ADHD, and multiple chemical sensitivity.

What all these diseases have in common is that they have a tendency to mislead the doctor in finding the true reason for the patients suffering, causing her to look for somatic reasons in the patient's body.

Symptoms as an attempt to solve unconscious conflicts

The symptom is an attempt by the ego to limit the damage of a psychically unbearable conflict in a traumatic situation, or a temptation situation, or a heavy disappointment.

The aim of the symptom is to express the drive and the superego equally, and at the same time. Hence, both tendencies are satisfied and there seems to be some logic supporting both sides, even though this logic is not very reasonable. The symptom is the result of a special procedure of a psychic process.

Is the mechanism of repression equal to the mechanism of symptom formation? The formation of symptoms is not only the return of the repressed in the shape of replacement or compromise formations, but also the reaction formation (Laplanche & Pontalis, 1973, p. 389).

Neurotic symptoms can be regarded as being last-resort formations aimed at protecting the individual from conscious awareness of distressing and painful mental content.

Freud's (1926d) theory of symptom formation states, "Since we have traced back the generating of anxiety to a situation of danger, we shall prefer to say that symptoms are created in order to remove the ego from a situation of danger" (p. 144).

Symptoms can serve as a kind of repetition compulsion in order to overcome indigestible traumas:

> The ego, which experienced the trauma passively, now repeats it actively in a weakened version, in the hope of being able itself to direct its course. It is certain that children behave in this fashion towards every distressing impression they receive, by reproducing it in their play. In thus changing from passivity to activity they attempt to master their experiences psychically. (Freud 1926d, p. 167)

> By carrying what is unconscious on into what is conscious, we lift the repressions, we remove the preconditions for the formation of symptoms, we transform the pathogenic conflict into a normal one for which it must be possible somehow to find a solution. All that we bring about in a patient is this single psychical change: the length to which it is carried is the measure of the help we provide. Where no repressions (or analogous psychical processes) can be undone, our therapy has nothing to expect. (Freud 1916–1917, p. 435)

The analytic therapist should pay special attention to the situational factors in and outside the analytic situation that maintain the symptoms. This is very likely to facilitate the discovery of the meaning of the symptom and why it is necessary (primary and secondary illness gain).

Coping with unconscious conflict and trauma

The psychoanalytic theory of symptoms is put together by Thomä and Kächele (1992, p. 461):

Assumption 1: Symptoms are displaced and distorted gratifications of disapproved and repressed desires.
Assumption 2: People attempt with the aid of symptoms to cope with a traumatic situation.
Assumption 3: People unconsciously attempt to falsify their unconscious and pathogenic attitudes by means of their symptoms.

In the first phase of Freud's work, he was convinced of a real traumatic situation (mostly sexual) in the early childhood of each patient. Later, he was more and more convinced that only the fantasy of the patient and his wishes were responsible for the trauma. In the past decades, the real traumas that occur in psychoneurotic and psychosomatic patients were increasingly uncovered. Seduction does not exist only in the fantasy of the child, but there is a high percentage of real violence (sexual or physical). Freud's conviction that it made no difference whether the trauma actually took place or whether it existed only in the fantasy of the child was incorrect, as more recent investigations of the consequences of real trauma on the structure of personality and self have demonstrated.

Of course, this trauma is mostly not a single trauma occurring in childhood, but a repetitive or continuous trauma that is perhaps revitalised at a later stage by an event that is possibly not consciously known by the patient as an important fact. Often, the traumatic situation is unconsciously re-established by the patient himself in order to manage the traumatic situation better now (repetitive compulsion).

Freud (1895d, p. 287) wrote, "We must not expect to meet with a single traumatic memory and a single pathogenic idea as its nucleus; we must be prepared for successions of partial traumas and concatenations of pathogenic trains of thought".

When we have a certain overview of the patient's suffering, it is worthwhile to make the connection between the symptom and the traumata: the therapist

> is supposed to describe the causal factors that led to the development of the neurotic or psychosomatic symptoms or that serve as precipitating factors maintaining the symptoms. At the core of this is a description of the psychic conflicts, especially with regard to their unconscious component and the subsequent development of neurotic compromises and symptoms. Furthermore, the analyst must describe both the point at which the symptoms became manifest and the precipitating factors in the context of the original psycho-genesis. (Thomä & Kächele, 1992, p. 239)

CHAPTER FOUR

DREAMS

Joachim Rothhaupt and Stephan Hau

The history of the theory of dreaming and dream research

Joachim Rothhaupt

Psychoanalytical dream research is concerned with three main aspects of dreaming:

1. How a dream is generated (generation).
2. Whether the dream contents are meaningful (meaning).
3. Whether a dream works for psychological or biological needs (function).

Freud's dream theory

> The theory introduced by Sigmund Freud at the beginning of the twentieth century can be seen as a turning point in the scientific investigation of dreams. The psychoanalytic dream theory has deeply influenced most of the current clinical theories on dreaming and, to some extent, modern experimental investigation of dream states as well. In the 1950s, the discovery of REM sleep and of the profile of typical different sleeping states during the night provided the starting point for modern sleep and dream research. This laboratory research has revealed overwhelming new knowledge about the dreaming mind and about the features of the dream state. I will come back to this type of research and to some of the most important findings later. Freud's "main idea was that dreams serve a function of wish fulfilment. He distinguished between a manifest level of dream content (the dream as it is remembered and reported) and a latent level of dream content that can be inferred by following the associations of the dreamer to the single parts of the dream and by tracing back the different steps of dream work in which the material (infantile material, day residues, etc.) is condensed, displaced, or secondarily revised. The underlying assumption is that the associative chains of the dreamer to every part of the dream will lead to the mental processes that gave rise to the dream and thereby reveal the unconscious (latent) meaning of the dream". (Hau, 2004, p. 1)

So, Freud looks primarily for the function of a dream in order to derive its meaning and generation.

Dream creating motives

According to Freud, unconscious drive wishes (libidinal) are the most important creator for a dream. They are the psycho-energetic source of a dream.

The day's residues are a second source of dreams, which can derive from unimportant, indifferent impressions of daily life as well as from conflicting thoughts loaded with cathectic energy. The latter have passed a conscious examination by the "censor" (or the ego), contrary to the libidinal drive wishes, which derive from the unconscious. The day's residues can be emotions, or matters which are not yet settled, not yet solved, or which were repressed during the day, deriving from real life, which are located in the preconscious (in his conceptualisation of dream theory in 1900, Freud refers to the concept of a topographical model).

An unconscious drive wish is not able to create a dream by itself. It must be attached to a day's residue by means of transference as a precondition for entering the preconscious. Having reached the preconscious, it might become a preconscious dream wish. Thus transformed, it allows the unconscious drive wish to be expressed in a preconscious day's residue.

In reverse, dream wishes empower the day's residues, which are connected to preconscious wishes with energy, so that their latent dream thoughts can be dreamed.

The dream censor is a third source of dream creation. Freud speaks of a psychic agency representing ethics, aesthetics, and social demands which prevent immediate undisguised satisfaction of unconscious drive wishes.

Sleep and dream work

While sleeping, the psychic apparatus tends to conclude its secondary processing, including its reality testing. Censorship is diminished, and the motor discharge is blocked. Only the preconscious remains active by holding the libidinal cathexis of the dream wish and the day's residues and their transformation in the dream work, which is described below.

Topical regression

During the dream, the unconscious system is still active. During a regressive process while sleeping, all conscious and preconscious dream-creating activities retreat into the system unconscious, where preconscious thoughts are fragmented and lose their coherence. Word and thing representations become separated and the themes developing in this state of dissociation can now be visually transformed like thing presentations.

Condensation

Condensation describes the processing of elements of word and thing presentations. To create the manifest dream, condensation leads to the extraction of latent thought fragments necessary for the dream content and the exclusion of others. So, the manifest dream is always a condensed version of latent content.

Condensation is also responsible for the sensory quality of dreams, especially for their visual character. The melding of contents of different elements leads to a summation of their original cathectic energies, and as the sleep interrupts the cathexis of perceptions in the outer world, the energy of the condensed dream elements force the "system perception" (system W) to full intrapsychic perception and cathexis until it reaches the full sensory quality (Illustration 4.1).

Freud used this picture from the Hungarian satirical magazine *Fidibusz* to illustrate the symbolic nature of the urge to urinate as a "wake-up-dream". The sleeping nurse (*bonne*) hears

Illustration 4.1. "The dream of the French *bonne*".

during her sleep the baby's crying but does not want to wake up. The urge to urinate becomes stronger and stronger, so that the nurse has to wake up (Freud 1900a, p. 373).

Displacement

Freud regards displacement as the most important activity for the disfigurement of dreams. It leads to the replacement of dream thoughts. Latent elements are displaced along a chain of conceptual, tonal, or emotional associations to elements further away, which then appear in the manifest dream. For example, allusions appear by transforming a subject into its opposite.

Displacement is also responsible for the fate of the dream affects. Owing to the fragmentation of the dream thoughts, the affects are separated from the thought contents and can be displaced on other contents, or the affect can itself be transformed, for example, into the opposite, or it can be totally repressed, so that it does not appear in the manifest dream.

Secondary revision

The secondary revision serves the coherent composition of the manifest dream. It composes incoherent proto-elements. It separates the manifest from the latent content. Therefore, the dream becomes a unit. The motive of the secondary revision is good composition and consideration of comprehension with regard to the censorship. According to Freud, the secondary revision becomes active after the dream appears in the foreground of the consciousness. Therefore, this is a secondary process activity of the ego during sleep (observing and censoring).

The secondary revision can also be seen during some states of wakefulness: for example, when daydreaming or fantasising.

Special elements of dream presentation

The logical relation of dream thoughts (causality, simultaneity, consecutiveness, contradiction and opposition, neither . . . nor, and so on) are presented by formal aspects of the dream narration, especially by syntactic rows of sequences of dream pictures.

To Freud, dream symbols are constant factors, translations of displaced and condensed dream thoughts and wishes in scenes with typical contents.

He regards dream symbols as universally valid and socially mediated. He thinks dream symbols are always linked to the body, sexuality, birth, death, and members of the family. They are more than associations because they do not only refer to the latent content, but also can be understood as translations of the latent content.

How do anxiety dreams or dreams of punishment fit into Freud's early concept? Concerning anxiety dreams, the censorship did not manage to neutralise the dream wish, and dreams of punishment represent the fulfilment of censorship wishes.

Post trauma nightmares are the exception. They tend to repeat the trauma and resemble a repetition compulsion in the transference relationship. They function like a short-circuit which jumps across the dream work.

After Freud developed the structural model (ego, id, and superego), he corrected his original idea that dreams derive only from the id and added that they also derive from the ego. He pointed out that a dream might give hints for a conflict solution or for the intention to solve a conflict.

In the 1920s, the importance of dream interpretation as the "royal road" to the unconscious, the definition of psychoanalysis as a theory, and the practice of dream interpretation had been established. This process was theoretically supported by Freud's development of the structural model. He developed this concept to better understand and conceptualise the neurotic conflict processes and the transference relationship. This reduces the significance of the pre-conscious (topographic model) as the most important processor for the development of dream and symptom creation.

The development of dream theory after Freud is closely linked to psychoanalytical schools and traditions that refer to Freud, but hold different theoretical assumptions.

The manifest dream becomes more and more important, while the early Freud focuses his interest on the latent dream, caused by sources of drives.

The growing importance of the object relations theory in the 1960s leads to a wider psychoanalytical understanding of dreams. Freud's dictum, that libido is looking for satisfaction, was extended and transformed into "libido is looking for an object". Sharing this assumption must have had consequences for dream theory and the understanding of dreams. The search for an object, its closeness or distance, the treatment of the object, including the satisfaction of drives, becomes the focus of dream analysis. It allows an understanding of transference aspects concerning the therapeutic relationship, its development, and its dramas.

Other aspects, which were very difficult to analyse in earlier times, can now be better understood with the aid of the object relation theory. Authors such as Meltzer and Ogden refer to Bion, who regards dreaming and dreams as a continuous process on the primary level of "unconscious thought".

The concept of "unconscious thought" and unconscious fantasy is based on Klein's theory of inner object relations from birth. To Freud, "fantasies" similar to daydreaming tend towards wish fulfilment. To him, unsatisfied wishes are the drive motive of fantasies, and each fantasy is a wish fulfilment, a correction of the unsatisfying reality. They are mostly conscious or preconscious fantasies, which become repressed if they contain forbidden wishes. Thus, fantasising, for Freud, is a highly developed activity of thinking and, therefore, not within the capabilities of a baby.

In contrast, Kleinians regard fantasies as the mental equivalent or psychic representation of drives. There is no emotion, no drive impulse, which is not experienced as an unconscious fantasy. In this view, unconscious fantasies not only have the function of an imagined gratification, but they are also an expression of destructive drive impulses as well as aspects of a reality of frustrating objects.

Unconscious fantasies are the psychic representation of all bodily and psychic experiences of an individual from the beginning of life. Each experience in the outer reality, as well as in inner drive impulses or another inner mood, is thought to be carried out in an object relation.

Bion (1962) postulates for a baby a concrete, not yet transformed experience in a relationship that he called beta elements. To him, the alpha function of a mother is necessary to transform the beta elements into alpha elements. This means that a concrete, not yet related beta-element experience is transformed into psychic relationship experience elements called alpha elements. Thus, the concrete physical experience acquires a conceivable meaning. To Bion, alpha elements are the building blocks of what he calls "dream thoughts" or "myth". Dream thoughts and myths correspond to the concept of unconscious fantasies.

Meltzer (1984) concludes that there is a formal continuity of different dreams of the same person. He proposes in *Dream Life* (1984) that, to Freud, the dream remained a proof rather than a psychic phenomenon in its own right. Meltzer counters this with his postulation of the dream's own independent symbolic value, appealing to a two-stage model of the development of symbolism and language: symbolisation develops from a close physical interaction between mother and baby, in which rhythmic dancing movements and the mother's humming and singing are answered by the baby, thus initiating the gradual beginning of speech. A first stage of symbolisation and speech formation serves to communicate emotional states, while the communication of information about the external world and its description follows later, in the second stage. These two stages, or levels, in his opinion, correspond to two "grammars". In this, Meltzer seems to get fairly close to Freud's distinction of primary and secondary processes, and also to Fonagy and Target's mentalization concept (Fonagy, Gergely, Jurist, & Target, 2002) and the latest results of infant observation.

Meltzer's opposition to Freud on this point results from his view that Freud placed his main stress on the level of the secondary process, thus considering the verbally formulated thought as the dream's major bearer of meaning; the dream only has an encoding function for him, a code from which the retranslation must be extracted. By attributing the dream to the "primary" level of symbolisation (the symbolisation of emotional states, fantasies, and "unconscious thinking"), Meltzer does not regard dream interpretation as a retranslation, but as the transformation from one symbolic form to another, from a predominantly visual language to a verbal one.

Furthermore, referring to the authority of Bion, Meltzer proposes that dreams are only the particular expression of a continuous process that proceeds on the above-mentioned primary level of "unconscious thought" and primary image-based symbolism like an incessant stream of our inner life—he terms this "dream life".

With Ogden (2005), we can now take another perspective regarding dreams and dreaming. Like Meltzer, Ogden also refers to Bion, but lays more emphasis on his belief that the ability to dream is not an *a priori* primary fact, but a symbolic achievement that is either successfully developed in the course of psychic life or fails to manifest itself. He presents a three-level structure of the ability to dream, as follows.

- The child's night terrors and the adult equivalent. Ogden assumes that the child later has no memory of its night terrors, contrary to the experience of the nightmare, or of a nocturnal event, or of the mother comforting it afterwards; it is also not afraid of going to sleep the next evening. The whole fear and terror experience remains unrepresented, according to Ogden, and cannot be dreamt, thought about, or remembered. Ogden's hypothesis is as follows: in the case of psychotic disorders and severe personality disorders bordering on psychosis, equivalent phenomena occur in adults: these disorders are accompanied by comparable undreamt experiences which cannot be dreamt and which cannot be represented psychically.

- Nightmares from which the dreamer must awake in order to interrupt the dream. For Ogden, nightmares are the expression of neurotic or other non-psychotic disorders.
- "Normal" dreaming in which the dream can be dreamt through to its end.

Ogden justifies his viewpoint with recourse to Bion's concept of the alpha function. The alpha function is the individual's ability to transform beta elements into alpha elements, that is, to symbolically process the crude sense impressions of immediate experience and create a meaningful symbolic inner world. Ogden regards the ability to dream as the expression of an intact alpha function: the ability to dream is coupled with the ability to sleep and being awake. If the alpha function is severely impaired, a person cannot dream, and neither can he really sleep or be awake successfully, for then these expressions of life and ego-states are too much marked by beta elements, the unprocessed, crude data of sense impressions. For Ogden, even more explicitly than for Meltzer, dreaming is a continuous process that goes on in both sleep and at the unconscious level of waking life. Dreaming, for him, is the expression and essence of the unconscious psychological work by means of which we lend our experiences a psychic meaning (Pollak, 2008).

Psychoanalytical and empirical dream research

Stephan Hau

In the 1950s, the discovery of REM sleep (Aserinsky & Kleitman, 1953) and of the typical profile of different sleep stages during the night was the starting point of modern sleep and dream research, which has revealed overwhelming new knowledge about the dreaming mind and about the features of the dream state. In particular, the manifest dream and unconscious cognitions were under investigation. Table 4.1 summarises the main findings of these groundbreaking research activities over a forty-year period.

Dreaming occurs throughout the whole night. Everybody dreams every night. However, only one third of the population report regular dream memories. Lively and vivid dreaming (with complex stories and rich content) occurs for at least 2–3 hours every night. Thus, a seventy-five-year-old human has spent about 6–7 years of his entire life dreaming! In most

Table 4.1. Important findings of experimental dream research.

1. Frequency of dream events.
2. The dream exists in many variations.
3. Qualitative features of dreams.
4. Waking state–dream state continuity.
5. Dreams are not completed formations.
6. Forgetting a dream is not only the result of defence censorship.
7. Multiple functions of dreams.
8. Up to thirteen years development of the capacity to dream.

cases, the length of a dream is approximately 5–20 minutes. Studies of the neurobiology of dreaming have revealed a complete suppression of the release of the neurotransmitters serotonin, histamine, and norepinephrine (Hobson, 2009; Siegel, 2005). As a consequence the motor neurons are not activated. Thus, the muscle tonus is extremely low during REM-sleep which prevents the dreamer for acting out his/her dreams. Even though there is a strong correlation between REM sleep and dreaming, there is no causal connection. Dreams seem to be generated in the forebrain (Solms, 2000) and not in the pons region, as Hobson and McCarley (1977) had suggested.

Another important finding of experimental dream research has been that there is no such thing as a dream. Dreaming occurs in very many different forms and each dream has different qualities and various features. It is possible to distinguish a large number of different types of dreams (e.g., dreams from REM phases, NREM dreams, sleep onset dreams, white dreams, night terrors, nightmares, lucid dreams, "wet" dreams, daydreams, etc.).

In most of the dreams, visual perception dominates (60%), but acoustic phenomena occur also, as do body sensations (smell or taste hardly ever features in dreams). With an even higher frequency than feelings and emotions, thought processes can also be detected in dreams. If emotions occur, they have the same qualities as in waking life (e.g., rage, annoyance, anxiety, disgust, joy, interest, mourning, etc.). The most prominent emotion in dreams is joy, which is more frequent than annoyance or anxiety (Strauch & Meier, 1996).

Day residues can be seen as the most important part of the manifest dream content. More than 70% of the subjects, objects, or scenarios that emerge in dreams refer to incidents from the time period of the last week before the dream. One of the most important findings of experimental dream research is that of a waking-state dream continuity. The prominent affects a person experiences in the waking state reoccur as well in his/her dreams. However, most dream contents seem to be rather banal, by no means bizarre or full of sexual or aggressive connotations, as one might expect.

What is dreamed at night must be considered and described as a process that does not end upon awakening in the morning. Dreams are permanently reprocessed and altered. Dreams that are recounted in the clinical situation must be understood as highly selective products. When a dream is reported several times, it becomes evident that parts of the dream are omitted, changed, or even added (new fantasies, experiences, excerpts from other dreams, and transference fantasies play an important role in these processes of substitution).

The capacity to dream is not present from birth, but develops parallel to cognitive and emotional development. Foulkes (1999) demonstrated that it takes up to thirteen years of human development for the capacity of dreaming to be fully developed. Three- to five-year-old children have short, emotionally neutral dreams without complicated actions. The dream ego does not appear in children's dreams until the age of seven. Thereafter, it takes another 2–3 years until the activity of the dream ego corresponds to those of adult persons. These findings indicate strongly that the dream cannot be seen as a perceptive process, but must be seen as a thought process that is completely dependent on a person's capability to understand and represent symbolically what goes on in the outside world and how the interactions with important others are experienced and encoded.

What has become more and more apparent in recent decades is the relationship between thought activities in the waking state and dream thoughts. High emotional pre-sleep experiences have a strong impact on dream contents (Kramer, 2007). The same author has also demonstrated a mood regulatory function of dreaming (1993), which means that the mood improves during the night: for example, subjects woke up less depressed than the evening before. This effect was also demonstrated in the context of trauma research, for example by the American psychoanalyst Ernest Hartmann, who has conducted extensive research on dreams and nightmares (1995, 1998). The examples given by Hartmann demonstrate that the dream has a "therapeutic function". In finding new contexts for everyday life experiences, an initially overwhelming experience that was expressed in a nightmare can gradually be contextualised. During this process, the dreamer experiences the original nightmare more and more differently, enriched with components of everyday life experiences. Thus, the nightmare gradually develops into a more common anxiety dream. As the process continues, even these anxiety dreams are increasingly altered to become normal dream experiences.

The dream helps to contextualise emotions. Hartmann is convinced that the dream makes connections in a safe place and helps to calm down high emotional states into more manageable ones. What can clearly be demonstrated in dreams after trauma is claimed to be true for all other dream activities. Whenever there are disturbing experiences, conflicts, more general problems, and dangerous situations for the self, and as long as the ego capacities are still intact, the dreaming mind tries to make connections to other experiences of everyday life and to interweave the problematic experience with other experiences of lower affective qualities.

The functions of dreaming

This general model of dreaming is also supported by other findings of experimental dream research. Nowadays, the dream is seen as a multi-functional process (Hau, 2004, 2009). This does not mean that Freud's (1900a) idea of wish fulfilment as an important dream function is wrong—on the contrary. However, seeing wish fulfilment as the main function of dreaming takes a rather narrow perspective, because various other functions of dreaming have been described, as shown in Table 4.2.

Nowadays, dreams are seen as a key process in maintaining the psychological as well as physiological health of a human being.

Table 4.2. Functions of dreaming.

- Wish fulfilment
- Memory
- Consolidation
- Problem solving
- Conflict solving
- Stress reduction
- Creativity
- Mood regulation

Other dream-like mentations

Even in the waking state, dream like experiences are common. Daydreaming can serve as one example. In most instances, narcissistically compensatory fantasies shape the daydream contents. One can compare daydreaming with a relaxing walk through the gardens of fantasies, but, in contrast to the dream state while sleeping, the ego is always aware of a daydream as a fantasy product. However, the fantasy activity activates contents that are also connected to psychological conflicts and unsolved problems, in an often compensating way. The fantasies are not arbitrary. This is also true for the so-called "free associations". Spontaneous ideas, fantasies, and thoughts that seem to be "off track", embarrassing, odd, or negligible turn out to be connected to psychodynamically relevant material. We tend to think logically, in straight lines, in the waking state. However, the mind as a network of content and meanings can also make use of contents that lie more tangentially to straightforward thinking. Metaphors can be understood as such a way of thinking. If someone tries to describe a conflictive relationship, he/she can describe different disputes and conflictive situations. However, it is also possible to use a metaphor, for example, the picture of a "bumpy road" with a lot of potholes. This picture could rise in different mental states, as a part of a daydream, as a free association of a patient in psychotherapy, or as dream content. Artists tend have very good access to these levels of insight.

The dream as therapy material

Joachim Rothhaupt

Dream interpretation, in Freud's sense, serves to decode the latent dream thoughts and dream wishes to reverse the dream work.

In the first interpretation rule, Freud proposes reducing the dream text to its component parts: substantives, verbs, particular events and affects. This means working to oppose the secondary revision. The fragments we obtain by following this first interpretation rule can be (a) part of the undisguised whole, (b) an allusion, (c) a symbolic presentation, (d) a vivid word presentation, (e) an opposite, (f) a pseudo-historical presentation of the latent dream contents, and (g) an inserted day fantasy.

The second interpretation rule, the association rule, helps in choosing the correct translation from the above-mentioned possibilities. As the therapist, you ask the patient to speak about everything he or she thinks about the dream. The underlying assumption is that the associative chains of the dreamer to every part of the dream will lead to the mental processes that gave rise to the dream and, thereby, reveal the unconscious (latent) meaning of the dream.

In his clinical work, Freud focused to a great extent on exploring latent meanings of dreams. However, Erikson, in his 1954 paper titled "The dream specimen of psychoanalysis", set a counterpart to this development. He demonstrates how far one can progress by using only the manifest dream content as a basis for insight into the conflicts and current problems of the dreamer. Dreams are analysed by starting with the manifest configurations of the dream and then looking for connective links between manifest and latent dream material. Then the latent dream material is analysed and, in a fourth and final step, reconstructions of connections to the life cycle and to individual development of the dreamer are hypothetically drawn. In Table 4.3, the different dimensions one has to take into consideration when analysing manifest dream contents are summarised.

Mostly, the dream interpretation leads to a resistance of the dreamer, which might manifest in very bright, detailed, or very hesitant associations.

Most therapists and analysts still work with the association rule, though not as strictly as Freud does. In any case, it is worthwhile to wait for the ideas of the patient as to what he thinks about the dream and to encourage him to go on thinking about it.

The dream interpretation facilitates better and quicker understanding of the actual treatment situation and the transference and countertransference constellations.

The dream allows an exchange between patient and therapist on deep and intimate levels that are difficult to reach otherwise. It often leads the patient and the therapist to the hidden heart of the unconscious matter. Therefore, Freud's dictum of the dream as the "royal road" to the unconscious remains valid.

Compared to the treatment of symptoms, in some cases it is helpful to support and develop a positive attitude towards the dream contents by acknowledging the staging of the dream. This means an acknowledgement of the ego performance in creating the dream. This can be realised, for example, when the patient and the therapist refer back in later sequences of the therapy to the insight and consciousness they gained together through the dream interpretation.

I conclude with an important statement by Hau (2004) concerning the individuality of a dream:

> The process of inference has to be made again and again for every individual dreamer. Each dream is a highly specific individual product and has to be taken as such. Thus each subjective meaning of a dream has to be elucidated by taking the dreamer's actual context into consideration and the situation the dream is embedded in. Even if normative or repetitive dreams exist, no generally valid symbols exist. Trying to create general dream symbols is rather producing fairy-tales than scientific insight.

Table 4.3. Erikson's outline of dream analysis (Hau, 2009).

1. Manifest configurations:
   - Verbal, sensory, spatial, temporal, somatic, interpersonal, affective
2. Links between manifest and latent dream material:
   - Associations, symbols
3. Analysis of latent dream material:
   - Acute sleep-disturbing stimulus, day residues, acute life conflicts, dominant transference conflict, repetitive conflicts, basic childhood conflict, common denominators (wishes, drives, needs, methods of defence, denial, distortion)
4. Reconstruction:
   - Life cycle, social process, ego identity, and life plan

CHAPTER FIVE

THE THERAPEUTIC RELATIONSHIP

Ulrich Ertel, Klaus Kocher, and Hanni Scheid-Gerlach

Expectations and aims of the treatment

Ulrich Ertel

Strictly speaking, the aim of psychoanalysis is to achieve a structural personality change through psychoanalytic treatment. This means a reorganisation of the personality that is profound and lasting and enables the person concerned to best deal with the prospects, challenges, and burdens of his life within the scope of his capabilities and limitations. This far-reaching claim is often made in contrast to therapeutic goals, focusing on the elimination or alleviation of symptoms and on behaviour change. Meanwhile, there is a tendency to acknowledge a floating crossover between goals and aims in psychoanalysis and psychotherapy depending on the length (short- *vs.* long-term) and intensity (frequency) of treatment.

Freud tried to define the aims of psychoanalysis both topographically and structurally. It stretches from his famous principle of making the unconscious conscious, or "Where id was, there ego should be" (1933a, p. 81) to his advice that the analysis should provide the most beneficial conditions for the ego functions. In his *Studies on Hysteria* (1895d), he wrote, "a lot is gained if we succeed in turning the hysterical misery into common calamity; against the latter one will defend himself better with a recovered psychic life" (p. 307). In several places, he mentions the ability to work, love, and enjoy. Many analysts agree that to reach a balance between parts of the id, the ego, and the superego is one aim of psychoanalysis.

The indefiniteness of an aim such as "to make conscious the unconscious" does not hide the fact that the process of establishing consciousness is always carried out with regard to certain goals appearing in valuing nuances.

Admittedly, these goals, which, by the way, are strongly dependent on the theoretical position of the analysts (self psychology, object relational theory, drive theory, etc.), and, in particular, the ways to achieve these goals do not necessarily correspond with the ideas of the patient.

The goals of therapy for patients seeking treatment have to be taken seriously, not least because many studies have identified these goals as important prognostic criteria for success providing an evaluation of the patient's aptitude and willingness to co-operate. Sometimes, behind the often vague complaints and impairments, very ambitious expectations for a happy life free of conflicts are hidden, expectations which the patient believes should be fulfilled with little effort in a short period of time by trusting in the magic omnipotence of the psychotherapist.

Many patients still stick to the medical model of disease that is strongly fostered by the pharmaceutical industry: that is to say, the disease is caused by outside factors or by inner processes not manageable by the patient; through external intervention, with the help of medical apparatus, drugs, or doctor's advice, healing can be achieved without the active participation of the patient. Hence, this model often evokes the hope that it is possible to get rid of psychic problems in a similar way.

The fact that the psychotherapeutic treatment is sometimes a slow and difficult process, highly dependant on the co-operation of the patient, and that real modification and transformation work is necessary, that is, psychotherapy over an extended time, implies an abandonment and a mourning of one's own way of thinking, forms of perception, and experience, old attachments to parents, values, and ideals, which principally can often be discovered only in the course of treatment. So, a patient's quasi-private aetiological theories about the cause of his psychological problems might provide the first clue to the motivation for a causal and revealing form of analytic therapy.

Is the patient inclined to blame his relatives or parents for his fate; does he believe that only external circumstances are responsible for his complaints? And does he at least have an intuition or a sense of psychodynamic constellations and human modes of experience, or does he see himself only as a victim, with his needs being neglected again and again in his life?

In the discussion about goals and aims of treatment, the following compilation, with illustrative examples as summarised by McGlashan and Miller (1982) and in Germany by Mertens (1992, pp. 131–136), has proved useful, and is detailed in the following sections.

Removing developmental restraints

Basic trust and security: the world is no longer perceived as essentially evil and bad; paranoid fears are reduced to a minimum; there is internalisation of a primary good introject; the ability to accept the wealth and satisfaction of other people without becoming too jealous.

Separation and individuation: self-object differentiation with the ability to distinguish one's own feelings and thoughts from those of others; to be able to separate without fear of loss of love; to be able to be alone; autonomy; to say *no* without too intense feelings of fear and guilt; generational autonomy: to work through the influence of one's own parents and to be able to release one's own children.

Conscience: overcoming archaic, primitive superego introjects and reducing this experience and behaviour, which is marked by an irrational sense of duty and moral perfectionism; clear and realistic conscience; ability to appropriate feelings of guilt; the superego should be more tolerant, loving, and understanding and be integrated with the rest of the personality.

Constructive aggression: assertiveness, initiative, and constructive ambition as a result of having overcome the Oedipus complex; decrease of fear of failure—one should and can overtake one's own parents, becoming better than them; motivation to instruct others and to function as a guide and model.

Sexuality: clear gender identity and acceptance of one's own adult sexual body; capacity for orgasmic potency, reducing the obsessive preoccupation with sexual fantasies.

Aspects of the self

Self-responsibility: one can experience oneself as the actor of one's operations and activities without feeling delivered; no more inappropriate external powers; assume responsibility for one's own impulses, emotions, and actions; stick to one's own decisions; the ability to see oneself as a doer rather than a victim leads to tendencies of reparation, compassion, and empathy.

Self-identity: experience of a cohesive self-esteem, sense of one's person as a continuum in time, belonging to a historical and cultural heritage; maintaining a feeling of identity across various moods and activity levels.

Self-esteem: self-esteem, self-love, and self-respect as components of a healthy feeling of self-worth, relative independence of external mirroring and acceptance as well as the relative absence of the urge to idealise others; healthy ego ideal and ability to appreciate other people without having to devalue them at the same time; confidence in the future, integrity, wisdom, and serenity.

Self-experience and continuity with the former disorder: the former disorder should be integrated into the self-experience and not split off or repressed; there should be an understanding of the nature of the disorder and of its development and it should be accepted as part of one's self.

Relatedness to others

Internal vs. external orientation: autistic preoccupation with oneself and schizoid withdrawal reduces considerably; getting satisfaction from the interaction with other people; communicative readiness, responsiveness to the problems of others, and being able to make time for them.

Relationship with parents: the assessment of one's own parents becomes more realistic, balanced, less condemning and less idealising; one discovers new, previously unknown characteristics; the wish that the parents should still change may be abandoned; the inappropriate and irritating preoccupation with them decreases; old family myths may be abandoned, the generation barrier accepted, and the bond between the parents acknowledged.

Relationships with others: to be able to grade relationships with peers, groups, and intimate friendships; to relate to groups and to experience oneself as part of a group without having the feeling of losing one's individuality and independence.

Empathy: the capacity to imagine the emotional experiences of significant fellow men; ability to achieve temporary and partial identification without having to merge totally with the other.

Intimacy: a stable and lasting relationship with a partner experienced as not too incestuous; being able to enjoy the proximity, but also to be alone; to appreciate and accept the love of others; mutual give and take.

Generative aspect: ability to accept triadic relatedness; the desire to leave something for the next generation in the form of one's own children or productive works; the wish to hand on one's experiences to children; charity and concern for one's fellow human beings.

Acceptance of reality

Reduced omnipotence: to accept one's own weaknesses and limitations; recognise that one is not an exception deserving a special status or a narcissistic entitlement; dismissing the wish for unconditional love and compensation for past suffering; giving up oedipal grandiosity and acknowledging the attachment of other people; renouncement of controlling other people; development of gratitude.

Ability to mourn: ability to accept loss and one's own mortality; accepting the inevitability of change and conflict; the impossibility of completely controlling and planning the future; sorrow and grief without longing for vengeance and retribution; ability to yearn.

Drive control and frustration tolerance: to relinquish appropriately; to be able to say *no* to one's own and others' temptations and enticements; to understand the inevitability of the frustration of infantile wishes; to develop a tolerance for frustration, anxiety, misery, and suffering.

Ability to relinquish: to abandon the secondary disease profit aspect and negative therapeutic reactions; to give up destructive envy, claims, jealousy, sadistic desire for control, self-pity, self-righteousness, and masochistic attitudes such as feeling like a victim.

Reality testing: the capacity to distinguish internal from external perceptions and sensations, fantasy from reality, with transference being linked to its reference to the past; truthfulness and honesty.

Richness of experience and liveliness

Feelings: own feelings can be identified and named; competency for a wide range of manifold and appropriate feelings and moods, being differentiated, genuine, modulated, deep thinking, and relatively stable.

Energy: inner liveliness, strength, power, spontaneity, enthusiasm, often metaphorically described as vitality.

Relaxation: the ability for adequate regression, to be childlike; acceptance of one's own wishes for dependency and passivity; the ability for receptivity; to admit helplessness and to ask for help and support if it is necessary, also for therapeutic support.

Ability for happiness: being pleased and satisfied, able to enjoy and relax.

Coping mechanisms

Defence mechanisms: less stereotypical; more adaptive use of defence mechanisms; fewer early, archaic defence mechanisms, such as splitting, projective identification, schizoid withdrawal, or passive aggression; instead, more mature defence mechanisms, such as reaction formation, isolation, displacement, rationalisation, or repression; descendants of conflictual driving impulses and emotions can be allowed without greater fear, shame, or guilt.

Sociocultural adaptation and change: appropriate and creative changes in the environment—for example, a job change—can be accomplished and can be separated; consequences of a pathological identification with one's professional role may be reflected upon and changed.

Integrative capacity

Tolerance of ambivalence: synthesising of good and evil in oneself and in others; the defence mechanism of splitting and the associated processes of idealisation and devaluation are abandoned; the all-or-nothing quality of experience and thinking gives way to a realistic view; there is growing tolerance for ambivalence and ambiguity of contradictions and doubts.

Cognitive economy: the ability for well-functioning, secondary process-like thinking; bothersome desires and emotions do not disturb the course of thinking, can be kept in balance, and lend clarity and vitality to thinking rather than abstract and affect-isolated unimaginativeness; memory takes the place of acting out; planning and proactive action is possible; good memory and concentration without being excessively affected by conflicts is developed.

Transitional capacity: the ability to maintain a tension between the rational and the irrational, to liven up inanimate nature, to create adequate illusions and to live with, enjoy, and experience primary process-like thinking; ability for a sense of humour and an appreciation of the absurd, for imagination and fantasy, regression and loss of control in the service of creativity, flexibility of character structure and readiness for new experiences within a well-established identity.

Self-analytic capabilities

Transference: approximate dissolution of transference neurosis; feelings of negative transference may be tolerated; feelings of inequality compared to the therapist disappear; comprehension of the fact that the analyst has his strengths and weaknesses; the psychic energy invested in the transference neurosis is released for other relationships.

Self-monitoring and self-analysis: the ability for self-reflection, curiosity about psychic and mental processes, repeatedly renewed questioning of perceptions and conclusions; personal experience-based knowledge about the causes and meanings of one's own conflicts, self-destructive actions, neurotic choices of partners, elections, triggering features, and characteristic defence-mechanisms; ability to follow up one's insight with actions. A particular target is the ability for self-analysis acquired through an internalisation of the analytic process or by identifying with the analytic function of the therapist. The acquisition of this ability is important, since catamnestic studies have shown that the classical idea of a complete dissolution of the transference neurosis and its maintaining infantile conflicts is unrealistic. What can be achieved in the case of new conflictual requirements is the possibility of finding new solutions by use of self-analytic capabilities, where previously a repetition of neurotic solutions seemed inevitable.

Discussion

Most of these features can be seen as abilities that are principally accessible to an operationalisation with the help of clinical, observation-based concepts. However, behind each of these abilities there are complex theoretical constructs that describe the psychic and structural conditions for these achievements. If we take as an example the ability to acknowledge reality, which, depending on the theoretical perspective, can be facilitated through the attainment of the depressive position, through internalising triadic relationship constellations on an oedipal level, or through coping with the conflict of separation and individuation by the acquisition of object constancy.

However, the goals and aims may be distorted by the common tendency to view them as perfectionist absolutes. Ticho (1972) pointed out that patients as well as therapists might experience the result of treatment as a severe disappointment if therapists share their perfectionist fantasies with their patients without carefully examining these fantasies as a result of specific transference–countertransference events. The therapist should pay attention to the embedding of treatment goals in life goals. Many therapists are disappointed with their treatment results because treatment goals are not sufficiently distinguished from the fulfilment of general life goals. Since life goals always have elements of a utopia, treatments may result in disappointment, whereas treatment goals should reflect more specific standards congruent with the results of treatment. Ticho warned the analytic community not to share perfectionist fantasies with their patients without examining them as a result of a specific transference–countertransference situation.

Confusing treatment and life goals might be linked to a secret idealisation of psychoanalytic therapy, the idea being that, at the end of treatment, a human being will emerge who is forever able to cope with his problems in life in a mature way. However, psychoanalysis and psychotherapy are not salvation doctrines; at best, they may help to solve problems of an outer or inner nature in a certain life situation or life period.

On the other hand, it is clear that treatment goals and life goals are related to each other, that treatment goals have to fit the life goals, because it is obviously unfavourable if they do not contribute to the attainment of life goals or are incompatible with what the patient is longing for in his life.

We often realise that patients are not able to make clear decisions because of their unclear life goals. Therefore, it might be an important first step in the initial talks to formulate something like a life goal. Life goals play an important role with patients with a chaotic lifestyle, which is often the case with borderline disorders or in the adolescent phase, where focusing on hasty separations and on excessive ideals of independence is common.

Not only are the covert personal norms of the analyst most relevant, but also those of his cultural reference group and society as a whole, so that self-reflection has to be expanded against this background and has to include the implicit valuations in the psychoanalytic theories themselves (see Mertens, 1990, pp. 146–148). The analyst has to mirror the interdependence of his developmental objectives, his therapeutic goals, and the sociocultural background. Much of ethno-psychoanalytic research has shown that our objectives internalised during our socialisation—not least during our psychoanalytic training—are highly shaped by the norms of our western societies and may not be considered as anthropological standards or psychic health *per se*.

The essential asymmetry of the therapeutic relationship

The concept of asymmetry goes back to Parson's (1968) papers on the different roles of patients and doctors in the medical business. From a sociological point of view, the doctor–patient interaction is a structural asymmetric relation for the reasons set out below.

Different distribution and level of knowledge normally result in defining the doctor as an expert and the patient as a lay-person. Hence, the options of information and action that arise bestow an expert's power on the doctor. The different social roles involve the doctor in having the social power of definition (diagnosing, sick certification, right to treatment) through use of a high level of knowledge; the sick role of the patient exempts him from responsibility for sickness, implies the view that he is unable to get better without professional help, and allows him legitimately to withdraw from normal activities and social responsibilities, such as paid work, family duties, and housework, but obliges him to seek competent treatment from a professional health expert and puts him under a social obligation to get better as quickly as possible, having the responsibility and duty to make use of the doctor and to follow his advice.

While the patient's role is defined by elements such as need for help, technical incompetence and emotional dependency, the features of the doctor's role are in contrast: the need of the patient for help matches the "universalism" of the doctor, meaning his readiness to provide help to any person in need of it, irrespective of his social status or any other characteristics; the patient's "technical incompetence" is facing the doctor's "functional specificity', for example, his capability to identify the patient's sickness and treat it. The patient's emotional dependency relates to the doctor's emotional neutrality, his personal impartiality, and his orientation to collectivity. It is his duty not to exploit the patient's helplessness for private purposes, being guided by a professional code of ethics.

The functional specific competence and the imperative of instrumental acting (technics) provide the power of regulation to the doctor in the concrete interaction—such as the definition of the beginning, course, and end of contact, the right to take the initiative, to interrupt, and so forth.

Expert definition and control, or steering power, constitute a principally unequal, asymmetric relationship even in a predominantly verbal interactive activity (such as psychotherapy), where the degree of asymmetry seems structurally less than in an instrumental–technical activity.

This structural asymmetry sets the conditions for a whole set of conscious but precisely unconscious expectations, fantasies, and fears, not only on the part of the patient, but also on that of the therapist.

Professionally practised psychotherapy faces the problem of keeping available the offer of treatment at any time, to apply it to patients largely independent of sympathy or antipathy, and to maintain it unaffected by any possible problems during the performance. It is difficult because one does not associate any kind of service or functioning according to the model of repair through correct application of technique with the idea of therapy. Rather, the realisation of a specific personal relationship is constitutive, thus precisely evoking those parts of behaviour that are prone to fail (such as, for example, "pathologic" behaviour) instead of excluding them as factual, yet it might not fail because of those parts of behaviour.

The power of professionalism is that of being able to integrate these contradictory moments and to provide an institutional model that assures this integration.

The essence of psychotherapeutic action is to show the structure of a personal, not role-shaped, interaction in a frame characterised by the opposite feature of a non-personal, specific role relation (Oevermann, 1996).

Primarily, this action is professional because it implies a rule for establishing and handling this relationship, which is to be addressed by the patient and to address the patient in the mode of a personal relationship, but to reflect and to respect the as-if character of such behaviour by not directly interacting as in everyday communication, but instead with a strategic principle of approach.

Second, it is a technical standard of professionalism. The therapeutic relationship must always contain and actualise the two moments of personal and functional-specific mode with the possibility of realising one mode in favour of the other, but without suspending the dual structure. A purely personal relationship, that obviously might be helpful, is not therapy, and neither does an expert consultation fulfil the conditions.

In the first case, the therapeutic relationship fails because of the dissolution of the professional moment, in the latter because of its absolutism. The therapeutic process can be described as a procedure oscillating between this personal-empathetic pole and the functional-specific, scientific-technical pole, with dynamically (that is, driven by transference or countertransference) induced deviations and distortions in both directions.

However, we have to face the difference between everyday communication and the specificity of communication in the psychotherapeutic situation. This difference can also be described as an asymmetry, being applied and established in a systematic and methodical way by implementing the rule of free association for the patient, that is to say, to talk as freely as possible about his life, his emotions, about whatever comes to his mind, and committing the analyst to the complementary task of *not* telling about his life or his emotions and listening with his free-floating attention.

This kind of social interaction between patient and therapist is characterised by a systematic suspension and refusal of the rules of reciprocity that are followed in everyday communication: for instance, a question asked by the patient is not necessarily answered by the therapist, the therapist does not necessarily take over the speaker's role after the patient has had his say, the therapist remains silent (instead of continuing to talk). As Pollak (2006), referring to Flader and Grodzicki (1978), summarises, "The pre-existing expectation with regard to interaction and language is not fulfilled, the reciprocity of dialogue is suspended. This deconventionalisation must be learnt, not only by the analyst in his/her training, but also by the analysand in analysis, and the continued efforts of both are needed to maintain it against the force of gravity of convention and defences. Renouncing the rule-based behaviour expected by his particular culture induces irritation, anxiety, and regression in the analysand. In order to be able to trust in such conditions, he needs to find a trustworthy guarantee of protection in the analyst's professional standards and ethics" (Pollak, 2006, p. 3, translated for this edition).

It has to be emphasised that—compared to everyday communication—both patient and analyst create an artificial frame allowing the patient to develop his disturbance.

The patient's regression

Körner (2000, pp. 603–609) gave an excellent overview of this concept. This chapter follows his thoughts.

Definition

"Regression"—in its original sense meaning "return" or "withdrawal"—is a descriptive term that signifies a process where an individual leaves or gives up an already achieved psychic structure or function to return to a biographically earlier or less evolved psychic state of thinking, feeling, or acting. We call the process of psychological and psychosomatic disease "regressive" if the patient, in a stressful situation, can cope with his inner conflicts only by going back to earlier, infantile, and, therefore, more crude and primitive modes of processing and experience. Under the conditions of the psychotherapeutic/psychoanalytic treatment, the patient regresses when he shapes the transference situation according to his unconscious fantasies of relationships. From a historical perspective, the central relevance of the concept of regression might, however, be due to the fact that with it and its interaction with the concept of fixation, the possibly most important axiom of psychoanalysis is conceived: the unconscious active attendance of the past in the present, thus introducing an idea of temporality. Some analysts assign to this notion a metaphoric value retaining the connotations of a journey through time and the changes that will be necessary in psychoanalytic treatment.

There is no very precise psychoanalytic definition of the concept of regression. Freud and the analysts of the first generation assigned a central role to the concept of regression in the clinical theory of psychoanalysis and its treatment methods. They described the process of psychological and psychosomatic illness as a regression, and they knew about the regression-enhancing influence of the psychoanalytic contribution on the principle of commitment to free association.

In everyday life, regressions are used for problem solving and conflict resolution, when the individual temporarily retreats from a highly structured, goal-orientated way of thinking to a more holistic, impression-like perception and thinking, or opens himself introspectively to his pre- and unconscious fantasies, such as in creative thinking and artistic productivity.

If regression is understood as a return, or recourse, to earlier and less structured forms of handling things and the psychoanalytic therapeutic work is conceived as moving backwards, then the concept of "progression" forms a counterbalance indicating the more highly structured and adult mode of operation.

In the "classical" psychoanalytic conception, a regressive movement leads back to a point of fixation. A conflictual experience triggers a regressive movement, and the fixation "attracts" the regressive process. The more severe the pathogenic experience in early life, the stronger the effect of attraction; that is, even minor events in the here and now can trigger a regression. Similar to the complemental series of constitution and experience, regression is, thus, based on a dynamic mutual relatedness of early trauma and subsequent conflictual experience.

History of the concept

Myqel (2005) gave a good outline of the development of the concept of regression in Freud's works:

> Sigmund Freud introduced the notion of regression in The Interpretation of Dreams (1900a). The concept was necessary for his description of the psychic apparatus in terms of a topographical model, represented by an instrument whose component parts are agencies or systems with a

> spatial orientation. Excitation traverses the system in a determined temporal order, going from the sensory end to the motor end. In hallucinatory dreams, excitation follows a retrograde pathway. Dreams have a regressive character due to the shutdown of the motor system; the trajectory goes in the reverse direction, toward perception and hallucinatory visual representation. This regression is a psychological particularity of the dream process, but dreams do not have a monopoly on it. In the section of the last chapter of The Interpretation of Dreams titled Regression, Freud wrote that in all probability this regression, wherever it may occur, is an effect of a resistance opposing the progress of a thought into consciousness along the normal path. . . . It is to be further remarked that regression plays a no less important part in the theory of the formation of neurotic symptoms than it does in that of dreams. (Myqel, 2005, p. 547)

In this last chapter of *The Interpretation of Dreams*, Freud had already distinguished between three types of regression: topographical regression, in the sense of the psychic system; temporal regression, in the case of a return to earlier psychic formations; formal regression, where primitive modes of expression and representation replace the usual ones. He also noted, "All these three kinds of regression are, however, one at bottom and occur together as a rule; for what is older in time is more primitive in form and in psychical topography lies nearer to the perceptual end" (Myqel, 2005, p. 548). This basic unity is central to his metapsychological use of the concept.

In *Three Essays on the Theory of Sexuality* (1905d), Freud implicitly invoked the idea of fixation, which is inseparable from regression. In "A metapsychological supplement to the theory of dreams" (1917d), he underscored the distinction between "temporal or developmental regression" (of the ego and the libido) and topographical regression, and the fact that "the two do not necessarily always coincide" (p. 227). Then, in the twenty-second of the *Introductory Lectures on Psycho-analysis* (1916–1917), he distinguished two types of regression affecting the libido: a return to the earliest objects marked by the libido, which is of an incestuous nature, and a return of the entire sexual organisation to earlier stages. Libidinal regression is only an effect of temporal regression, with a reactivation of old libidinal structures preserved by fixation. At that point, he asserted that regression was a "purely descriptive" concept, adding, "we cannot tell where we should localize it in the mental apparatus" (p. 342). In making this assertion, he retreated from his earlier position and denied regression its metaphysical status, which it would regain only after 1920 with the second theory of the instincts. It then becomes constitutive of the death instinct and can threaten to destroy psychic structures, but also becomes a mechanism that can be used by the ego.

Further development of the concept after Freud

The early concept of regression gained some important distinctions after Freud. His suggestion of a distinction between a drive regression and a regression of ego functions became increasingly important for clinical theory and treatment methods. In particular, the differentiation suggested by the ego psychology and its notion of the relative autonomy of the ego implied that even the regressive processes affect the ego functions only in exceptional cases; so, in this conception, the ego became an entity that set the regressive processes in operation and steered them. This relative autonomy of the ego is also rooted in the fact that it is not attracted by fixation points, while the drive regression must follow the pull of a fixation point.

These differentiations were found to be helpful for the further development of psychoanalytic treatment methods. An ego remaining relatively free of regressive influences could now be gained as a partner for a working alliance, even if the drive regression led back to very early stages of psychosexual organisation. Meanwhile, the distinction between a reality competent domain and one being altered by regressive processes turned out to be problematic, but the notion of an ego being not only the object, but also the subject, of regression originated the modern conception of the regressive process being less the result, but more the instrument, of a problem-solving ego.

The observation that not all mental illness starts with the Oedipus complex and must be led back to the regressive fixation points of the psychosexual organisation of early childhood meant that more distinctive features were necessary. Infantile object-relationship fantasies being reflected in the transference might also be an expression of a lack, as a "basic fault" (Balint, 1968). Patients with basic fault, or "structural ego-fault" (Fürstenau, 1977), are not, strictly speaking, regressed patients, and such a regression should not be expected of the patient in the therapeutic process.

In his book *Thrills and Regressions*, Balint (1959) introduced the notion of benign *vs.* malignant regression, distinguishing two types of regression that can appear during analysis, benign regression bringing with it beneficial, therapeutic effects and malignant regression being pathogenic and having the possibility of causing insurmountable problems for the patient and the analysis. Ricaud (2005) stated, "regression, discovered very early on by Freud in its topographical, temporal, and formal aspects as a defense mechanism and therapeutic support, suddenly appeared as a threat to the patient and to treatment" (p. 160).

Balint (1968) showed that a carefully guided process of regression might help severely ill patients to find a new beginning. He also developed the concept of the "therapeutic aspects of regression", referring to Ferenczi, with emphasis on the interaction between two persons in the therapeutic process. With the increased understanding of the interactional aspect of regression, the analyst's role changed from that of an observer of a regressive process to that of the receiver of regressive fantasies of relation. So, along with a concept of regression, which became increasingly understood in terms of interpersonal communication, the patient or the individual in everyday life is seen less as subjected to regressive processes, and more as applying regression instrumentally to cope with inner conflicts.

Kris (1934) described regression "in service of the ego" as a creative movement preceding, and principally facilitating, progression. Thus, regression has a double character—similar to transference, which itself can be understood as a regressive process—as a phenomenon which, on the one hand, facilitates the therapeutic progress and, on the other hand, gets in the way of the process as an obstacle and resistance.

On the one hand, the patient may regress to express his unconscious transference fantasies in a perhaps imperative way, thereby, on the other hand, complicating the process of understanding and working through. Regression can be in the service of defence, especially when the patient avoids the necessary insight into possibly destructive fantasies through a regressive mode. But the patient might also resist the therapeutic process by avoiding the "regression in the service of the ego", thus showing an "anti-regressive tendency" (Sandler & Sandler, 1993), controlling his thoughts, behaving very rationally, and, particularly, preventing the perception of unconscious relation fantasies in himself. Both aspects are demonstrated in the following case.

> For a long time, a young man avoided any comment to his analyst about his relationships by talking in a very rational and objective manner about his everyday experiences with his job, wife, family, and so forth, or by simply remaining silent. To the surprise of the analyst, who, in his countertransference, felt increasingly bored and tired, the patient fell asleep one day during the psychoanalytic session. The analyst first thought the patient might have used this regression (of falling asleep) to avoid talking about what was on his mind. On second thoughts, he considered that showing his regressive needs by being able to fall asleep was an unexpected achievement. The patient commented, somewhat ashamed, that sleeping on the couch was "like lying in Abraham's bosom" and that he never imagined being able to fall asleep. Then, reluctantly, he reported that while sleeping he dreamt that a fire broke out in the treatment room, making it necessary for him to jump out of the window into a net-like elastic pipe provided by the fire brigade which helped him to escape. He then kept himself busy by discussing this strange new rescue system of the fire brigade and how great a threat an outbreak of fire while sleeping could be. The analyst first said, thinking about the patient's reluctance to talk about his "hot" dream, that it had become too hot for him in the room and—referring to the patient's escape from the fire—commented, "And what about me?" The patient then slowly realised that by leaving his analyst behind, he had demonstrated that the relationship had become "too hot" for him, thus sparking a fire with the effect of burning his analyst, whom he suspected of destabilising him by creating a too soft and warm atmosphere. Now he was able to talk about his fears concerning his warm feelings towards the analyst. So, one could say at last that he used his regression (to fall asleep and dream) "in the service of his ego" to recognise the fears, wishes, and feelings described above.

With regard to the above example and to Balint's work, we have to take note that the regression depends on the object; more precisely, on the way the regression is respected by the object, the way it is accepted by the object, and how the object reacts to the regression. To avoid the appearance of a malignant form of regression, Balint recommended the development of adapted therapeutic techniques: the "discrete" (not omnipotent or needlessly intrusive) analyst must create the secure, permissive atmosphere that the patient needs, as well as the time needed for regression and what he called a "new beginning". If regressions do not stand in the service of the ego, the danger of their malignant deterioration becomes manifest. From a relational position, one can argue that as an important aspect of the analytic process, patient and analyst mutually regulate regressive states in each other. Bushra (1998) emphasised that one of the analyst's roles is not simply to foster regression, but "to facilitate the patient's shift into the state best suited for the task of the moment and, often, to improve the patient's ability to internally and interpersonally regulate and move between various states of consciousness" (Sandler & Sandler, 1993, p. 389).

The further development of the concept of regression, resulting in an interactional and instrumental view of it, finally suggested that it had the capacity to capture more precisely the influence of the psychoanalytic situation and, particularly, the influence of the analyst and his countertransference on the regression. The asymmetry of the therapist–patient relationship, the obligation to free association, the minimal structuring, and the abstinence especially enabled and promoted regression. The psychoanalyst contributes in an influential way to the extent that he is able to recognise and accept an offer of relationship (sometimes, it might be a projective identification). In the patient's regression, he enables the patient to use regression not only for the purpose of defence and in therapy for the purposes of resistance, but also in the service of therapeutic progression. And it is of vital importance that the analyst can regress in the service of his ego. If he fears the regression, however, the patient will make use of it merely for purposes of defence.

Authors with a background in object-relation theory have deepened the understanding of regression as an interpersonal process, clarifying that regression takes place between an analyst and a patient. The patient is not regressing "by himself", but, together with his analyst, he is staging a therapeutic situation characterised by infantile fantasies of relationships. In their developmental theory, these authors describe the severe internal conflicts the baby has to endure, with the help of empathetic objects, long before the oedipal triangulation, which may significantly affect its individuation or even arrest it. Thus, the treatment method, being opposed to the "classical" theory of drives and structure, does not aim mainly at searching for, and dealing with, the defence of oedipal conflicts in regressive states. They recommend instead reanimating and working through the very early conflicts regressively.

From this perspective, a psychoanalytic treatment passing through such deep regressive phases may only succeed if the analyst is ready to accept the often troubling and confusing transference of the patient and work it through. Particularly, projective identifications push the analyst to accept very destructive fantasies, to assimilate them, and to offer them to the patient for reintegration.

The concept of regression in the view of other psychoanalytic concepts

The concept of regression and its application in the psychoanalytic therapeutic situation served for many years as a venue for basic controversies between drive and structure theoretical psychoanalysts on the one hand, and self- and object-relation theoretical psychoanalysts on the other. The classical view sees regression essentially as a defence against oedipal conflicts. Accordingly, the patient tries to avoid the oedipal triangulation by reanimating and recathecting pre-oedipal stages of psychosexual development. In the psychotherapeutic process, the patient resists by repeating this regressive movement, but, in working through this resistance, insight and change becomes possible.

Self-psychological psychoanalysts refer to the large number of pre-oedipally damaged patients who appear regressive because they have failed in their self-development owing to their early traumatic experiences. These patients require modifications in the setting and the treatment method. A psychoanalyst who is too abstinent, addressing a healthy ego with his interpretations and aiming for insight, risks overcharging these patients; furthermore, he might repeat those traumatic experiences which such patients had to undergo in their childhood.

By including the results of the research in developmental psychology in the discussion, this controversy has lost its acrimony in the recent past. On the one hand, drive and structure theorists acknowledge that a patient with a personality disorder requires modifications in the treatment technique because only borderline personalities are vulnerable to suddenly beginning deep regressive processes, questioning the analytic work. Self psychologists, on the other hand, insist on the experience of a subtle empathetic object as a prerequisite for the "new beginning" (Balint), but they have come to the conclusion that a deep regression to the level of basic fault is not in itself facilitating therapeutic progress and change.

Although the usefulness of the concept of therapeutic regression is challenged (Spurling, 2008), most of the psychotherapeutic approaches widely agree that a regression that functions by simply evoking a primitive level of experience, or reanimating an infantile stage of relationship or development, must be ineffective. Only the conflictive eagerness created by two persons in the frame of a psychoanalytic situation facilitates a therapeutic progression amid a regressive therapeutic relationship.

The transference of the patient

Klaus Kocher

The concept of transference and the clinical application of transference within the psychoanalytic relationship can be considered one of the most important tools in the psychoanalytic treatment of patients.

One of the challenging aspects of transference is that the phenomenon itself is happening everywhere and at any time in everyday life, but in psychoanalysis we are able to use it as an extremely effective tool in order to understand better the unfolding unconscious dynamic aspects of the patient as they manifest within the clinical setting.

As transference is happening in everyday life as a normal psychic phenomenon, it is necessary to point out that in neurotic patients transference occurs in a much stronger and inadequate way. Transference may occur not only verbally, but also in a non-verbal way.

When the psychoanalyst tries to listen to the unconscious of his patient, he might use the unfurling frame of the emerging interpersonal relationship: everything that is mentioned by the patient will be drawn to his attention, and everything the patient talks about—and even what he does not talk about—will be constantly investigated as to the implication of what it could mean for the understanding of the relationship between psychoanalyst and patient.

So, by listening in that particularly special way, the psychoanalyst may try to catch unconscious aspects of the patient and his feelings towards him in order to understand them better and to make use of this for his work of understanding the unconscious dynamics of his neurotic problems.

As the nature of transference becomes more comprehensible when a conflict in the relationship between the analyst and his patient occurs, it might be helpful to provide a practical example.

Clinical example (from Mueller-Pozzi, 1991)

> A woman in her thirties started her analysis with me soon after the birth of her second child. Her husband worked in the banking business and she had a practice as a doctor. She was able to integrate her professional and familiar tasks quite well, and the couple used to have a satisfying private and social life.
>
> However, soon after the birth of her second baby she suddenly felt more and more restricted and became rather depressed. She had the feeling of not having really lived her life until now. Her social

contacts now seemed simple and superficial to her, and also her marriage did not appear as satisfying as she had perceived it before. In her treatment, she complained of just having left home to be swallowed up in a marriage and not having been able to experience real independent life. As she realised that the life she had been leading up to now was in danger and that the crisis seemed to emerge from herself, she decided to consult a psychoanalyst.

I would like to describe just a little part of our work in order to make evident how transference is actually influencing the psychoanalytic encounter.

After the patient had been working with me in a quite co-operative way at the start, from a certain moment she became more and more silent. The session I want to describe started in a quite peculiar way: I was a little late because of a traffic jam that had made it impossible for me to get to my office on time. She started the session with an unusually long period of silence, and after that she talked about this and that without any particular participation. She seemed irritated. I confronted her, asking if her irritation might be due to the fact that I had arrived a little late. "Of course," she replied, "but it's not your fault that there was a traffic jam." I said, "Yes, that's true. But when you were waiting outside for me you could not know the reason for my being late. I would like to know what you were thinking then." "That would surely be too silly to talk about!" she replied. As I encouraged her to speak, she found it very difficult to talk about her fantasies. But then she told me that while she waited for me she had the strong idea that I preferred another patient who usually comes to his sessions before her and whom she had met by chance sometimes on the stairs. She thought that I would rather work with men, and had taken her into treatment only because there was no male candidate at that time. As she realised those fantasies for the first time during our work, she felt some degree of anger and even hatred towards me. As I encouraged her to talk more about her fantasies, she admitted that she was dealing with the idea that I had gone with the other patient to drink a cup of coffee and had simply forgotten her.

I said, "Isn't this fantasy just silly, because you know, of course, that I would not sit and drink coffee with another patient? And the more you know that this is not the case, the more you have the idea it might have been that way? There must be some reason why you had this particular idea while you waited for me."

She became increasingly overwhelmed with anger, jealousy, and shame as she immersed herself in the mixture of her feelings that had been provoked by this fantasy. Topics emerged that we had already been talking about for some time before, but now they appeared in a different way because they were coloured and brought to life by the vivid emotions caused by her transference feelings.

She started to speak about her brother, who is two years younger than herself. When she was young, she loved and adored him passionately. But now she recalled different memories full of anger and jealousy. She remembered that her father had taught her to ski, but neglected her when her brother was old enough to learn to ski himself. She had felt like a fifth wheel. To an increasing degree, she hated the intimacy between her father and brother and almost felt destroyed by envy. When her father was absent from home she felt relief, because then she was not so dominated by the feelings she always had to hide because she felt so ashamed.

I have quoted this practical example because here we are able to observe the enormous impact of transference in an everyday clinical situation, as occurs so often in our work as psychoanalysts. The example shows how the patient has an unconscious tendency to repeat her infantile conflict of jealousy in the relationship with me. She actualises an unconsciously internalised conflict with her father that she was not able to deal with in her childhood because her feelings had to be repressed at that time.

Transference is always the actualisation of an unconscious fantasy.

In summary, the person we come to know during the analytic process is not the mature woman who is able to control her life, but the little child who is feeling deeply neglected by her father, who frustrated her ardent wish to be loved and admired. Instead, she reacted with hatred because of the frustration of her loving feelings and with jealousy towards her brother, who received what was refused to her.

Even though she had managed quite well in her everyday life, her early conflicts persisted unconsciously until they came back to life during the crisis that brought her to treatment. When they emerged in our therapeutic relationship, there was an opportunity to work them through by realising how they unfolded within the transference.

We used to call transference the enactment of internalised infantile experiences in the presence of a psychoanalytic relationship. If an infantile conflict—as in the above example—is actualised, the analyst inevitably becomes the partner in this conflict, just as if the conflict were absolutely real.

If the transference feelings are characterised by emotions such as hatred, envy, jealousy, or rejection, we speak of "negative transference", and if loving feelings are dominant, we call it "positive transference". In any case, if the patient's behaviour is strongly influenced by transference feelings, it might be difficult to cope with. Thanks to his psychoanalytic training, the analyst should be able to deal with those kinds of emotions, and if he succeeds in perceiving the transference of the patient as an enactment of conflicting unconscious feelings from the patient's past, they lose their strangeness, and all these seemingly inappropriate emotions help in understanding the unfolding unconscious psychic conflict of the patient. If we are able to understand the transference as a kind of meaningful expression of past relations in the here and now of the psychoanalytic situation, it may help us to understand what the patient tries unconsciously to communicate. He tries to enact something he is not yet able to verbalise, and he even does not yet know what to put into words. He does not communicate, therefore he reacts. He does not remember, he just repeats.

Our task as psychoanalysts working with the transference of the patient is to help him to understand what he does and why he does it, and, therefore, we have to take in his feelings, digest them in order to understand them, and look for appropriate words to help him to understand himself in a better way.

The phenomenon of transference—and this is very important to point out—is not at all specific to the analytic situation. What is specific is the use that psychoanalysis makes of it. All human relations are built on experiences of primary relations that have an unconscious tendency to be actualised again in our present relationships. Only in this way are we able to create new experiences. Based on this general human tendency to transfer feelings of the there and then into the here and now, psychoanalysis has created one of its main tools of treatment: the awareness of the importance of these feelings and the capacity of the psychoanalyst to work them through together with the patient.

Freud called this general tendency repetition compulsion. He described the peculiar character of the psyche, compelled to repeat and re-enact unconsciously memorised patterns of psychic conflicts in actual relationships. These patterns remain unconscious because they are repressed, yet they are dynamically active. At the same time, they cannot be processed into consciousness but tend to be repeated continuously in new relations—everything happens again all the time.

The transference and countertransference of the therapist

Like the patient, the therapist has his own conscious and unconscious transference to others. Using his self-experience, the therapist has to recognise his unconscious and neurotic part in the transference, so that he is able to separate his transference from his countertransference (see the section headed "Analyst's resistance" later in this chapter).

The countertransference of the therapist is, in a way, the other side of the coin, which corresponds to the transference of the patient.

In the clinical situation it is very helpful to distinguish transference and countertransference. As a fundamental way of finding out the difference, we might ask ourselves, "How does the patient treat me in a given moment and which kind of person do I represent for him?", in order to get an initial idea of the transference of the patient, and the question, "Which emotional reactions does the patient provoke?" might then lead to further considerations of what the actual countertransference might be (Table 5.1).

In any case, as transference and countertransference are happening everywhere and all the time, it is helpful and necessary for the therapist to distinguish the transference of his own possible neurotic aspects from his countertransference as a reaction to the transference of the patient's feelings. This, incidentally, is one of the very important reasons for a thorough self-experience of the therapist himself.

When we address the countertransference feelings, we consider all possible emotional reactions of the therapist towards his patient. Together with the transference feelings, they form the emotional texture of the bi-personal field which develops between the patient and his analyst to form the ground where the transference neurosis of the patient will be worked through.

After Sigmund Freud discovered the clinical use of transference feelings in psychoanalytic treatment, he later logically found the corresponding situation in himself, and he named it countertransference. He was rather reluctant to make larger use of his discovery and mainly pointed out the necessity to "control the emotions of the psychoanalyst".

It was some years later that Heimann (1950) recognised that the feelings of the analyst are as important a working tool as the transference of the patient. According to her, we may not consider the transference of the patient when we do not adequately bring into consideration

Table 5.1. Helpful reflecting questions about transference and countertransference.

Therapist's reflecting question	
Transference	Countertransference
"How does the patient treat me in a given moment?"	"What about my feelings and ideas?"
"Which kind of person do I present for him?"	"Which emotional reactions does the patient provoke in me?"

the corresponding feelings of the analyst towards the transference. The affective response of the analyst is not exclusively his interpretation of the emotions of his patient. Instead, we should consider that the transference feelings trigger many different and sometimes contradictory emotional reactions in the analyst and allow to come to mind conscious and unconscious fantasies which might be difficult for him to understand, but referring them to his patient in a fruitful way might promote further understanding.

The question may arise as to whether or not countertransference feelings are pure reactions to the patient's transference. In my opinion, this is one of the main reasons for an analyst undergoing his own very thorough psychoanalysis in order to be well prepared to make a distinction. There is no doubt that some patients address the "blind spot" of the analyst, where he may encounter difficulties owing to his own personal conflicts that are not well enough worked through to make a clear distinction. All in all, countertransference feelings may be considered as a kind of compromise between one's own emotional reactions and role responsiveness to what the patient imposes on one.

Transference and countertransference together form the emotional context of the encounter between the analytic couple. Again, it is important to remember that unconscious communication is happening in any meaningful relation between people who are getting in contact with their inner world. In our everyday life, unconscious emotional exchange is only rarely verbalised, and these phenomena happen below the surface of consciousness. It is again the specific use that psychoanalytic technique makes of it within the boundaries of the frame of treatment.

When the analytic couple is working, the analyst tries to listen to his patient with free-flowing attention, which means that he tries to open up emotionally to the messages he grasps from his patient. The analytic relationship is authentic and natural when he is able to respond to the transference of his patient with his own emotional reactions and corresponding fantasies.

The conflicts that may occur in the analytic situation can then be worked through with all their emotional implications. Only if the analyst is conscious of what is happening inside himself will he be able to use his own countertransference feelings as a key to promote a deeper understanding of the patient's unconscious messages, which reach him through his transference. In a specific way, this emotional togetherness also creates the artificiality of the analytic situation, and, at the same time, expresses the art of the psychoanalyst.

When working with his countertransference feelings, the analyst has to be able to contain his stirred-up emotions instead of acting them out (as the patient is encouraged to do). Instead, he has to submit them to the task of digesting these emotions in order to use them for a better understanding of what the patient tries to communicate. In this way, the unconscious of the analyst becomes increasingly able to understand the unconscious of the patient. Therefore, the understanding of countertransference feelings becomes an extremely effective tool to get in touch with the transference of the patient and to understand the analytic situation.

Difficulties in dealing with the countertransference may arise when the analyst is not quite able to get in touch with his emotions, or loses the capacity to perceive and process the patient's emotions internally. Then, the transference resistance of the patient may induce reciprocally a countertransference resistance that might lead to the danger of the reactions of the analyst being acted out instead of being contained for further understanding. Then the analyst is risking becoming caught in the trap of the patient's transference. He might start to act out the roles the patient imposes to him, or else he rejects them and an entangling cycle of mutual transference might begin. The analytic situation is then in danger of becoming a pure repetition of the patient's initial traumatic conflict.

The best way to demonstrate the dynamic and intensity of countertransference feelings is to give again a clinical example.

Clinical example (from Mueller-Pozzi, 1991)

> A quite attractive young woman who was recently divorced used to complain about how she felt deeply neglected by her friends and acquaintances. In her mind, nobody seemed to want to spend time with her, and friendships with either men or women broke up after some time. Everything followed the same pattern: after a short time of mutual enthusiasm, the partners left her.
>
> In the analytic situation, I tried to link these events to her personal behaviour, but she could not understand that her own clinging attitude, mixed as it was with sudden unfriendliness, might be a reason for the reaction of her partners. Either she did not comprehend my intention or she reproached me for being insufficiently empathetic. In fact, she was not completely wrong, because my interpretations were in a way too superficial, not carefully examining what happened between her transference and my countertransference feelings.
>
> Even though my interpretations did not reach her in a fruitful way, they had, none the less, an effect: they increased her transference resistance and induced feelings of impatience in me.
>
> How did these growing conflicts in her transference and my countertransference mould our analytic interaction?
>
> The smallest irregularities concerning the setting irritated her immensely. She became complaining and aggressive, and it seemed that whatever I said was taken as a proof of my incapacity to understand her. She started reproaching me for complaining with her, and became even more furious when I tried to interpret her projections. In that way, she succeeded in causing aggressive emotions in me, which I clearly recognised as a negative countertransference. It became evident that I had difficulty in containing and controlling my emotions.
>
> Things became much more tense when once I had to postpone a session. She became extremely furious, and, as I tried to justify myself, I realised that I became more and more entangled with her. An aggressive power play was about to start that, of course, I had to lose. I felt small and humiliated by her, and, at the same time, I was full of fury. I felt a strong urge to get rid of my patient. To my surprise, I realised that I was tempted to shout at her the question of who it was who was conducting the analysis here—her or me.
>
> It was in this very moment that I realised that my feelings of rage vanished suddenly, giving way to a strong feeling of desperation. And I felt close to tears when she shouted, "You only try to get rid of me!"
>
> It seemed senseless (and untrue, too) to assure her of the opposite because in part she was right, and so I replied, "Yes, you're right. For a moment I did indeed have the wish to get rid of you. Obviously, you can imagine that I would have these feelings when you keep on moaning at me all the time. But if I did really send you away, you would have the same experience you had in all your past relations. Your rage and desperation show me how terrible and destructive this would have been for you, and I can feel what you feel."

> Looking at her personal history, these specific difficulties that reappeared in the analytic encounter can be interpreted as an expression of a very disturbed relationship with her foster parents during her childhood. They were not sufficiently empathetic with her and did not succeed in establishing a good enough emotional contact with their young foster child, even though she was both lively and spontaneous at the beginning of their relationship. Because of their own ambivalence, they never could decide to adopt her. The young girl remained emotionally estranged from them, but, at the same time, she always had the feeling that she had to do everything possible to win their hearts.
>
> This is what she told me later in our analytic work. She had felt emotionally threatened all the time, as if the foster parents were constantly communicating: if you don't like it here you can leave anytime . . . to go into the children's home!
>
> All of her struggle for love and affection seemed to be without success.
>
> Then she became increasingly defiant, isolated herself, and started to show her independence in a demonstrative way, as if she wanted to say: I'm not at all dependent on you!

For a certain time during her childhood, this behaviour might have been appropriate, because it helped to secure her psychic survival and enabled her to get along without love and affection. However, it became a part of her personality and, until now, it had restricted her capacity to love others and to allow others to love her. Intimacy provokes anxieties of becoming dependent and then being rejected.

It became evident that our analytic work was threatening to fail through following these old tracks that were activated by her transference feelings towards me. In my countertransference feelings, I felt humiliated and rejected, and I found it difficult to cope with my emotions. My feelings corresponded with the emotional state of mind she was trapped in, unable to communicate it, but acting out. She had no other language for it.

The scheme below aims to illustrate the above theoretical conclusions: the unconscious communication and interaction between patient and therapist can turn into a conscious communication through the therapist's inner work (Figure 5.1).

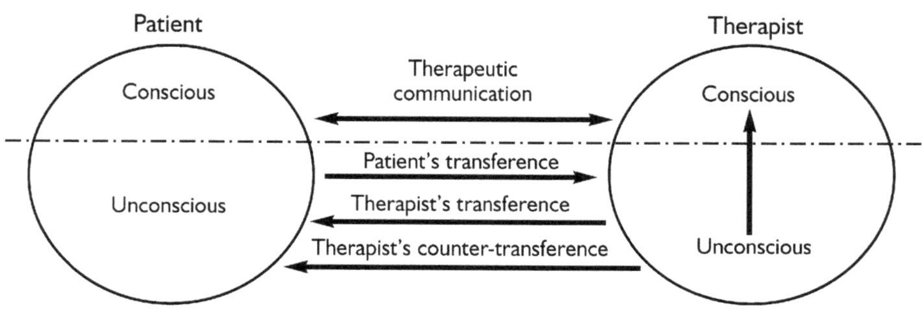

Figure 5.1. The therapeutic communication through transference and countertransference. (Elzer, 2012).

Resistance

Hanni Scheid-Gerlach

Resistance is a central concept of psychoanalysis. Together with transference, resistance is one of the main working subjects during treatment. Resistance is the dynamic aspect of defence in the therapeutic relationship.

The term "resistance" appeared for the first time in Freud's writings in *Studies on Hysteria* (1895d). He discovered that working through resistance is the main task if one is to come into contact with the patient's unconscious material.

Resistance means that unconscious forces hinder the positive process of psychoanalysis. These movements are unconscious defence operations, which always arise in treatment. For example, a patient laughs while talking about sad things; the patient does not use an appropriate affect for mourning—he laughs instead; a defence against sad feelings has occurred.

Resistance is an unconscious force used to maintain the pathological system. This pathological system was built up in childhood, so the former object relations, together with the emotional relationships, will be transferred to the analyst (Gill, 1982). Some of these feelings regarding the old object relations might be very frightening, so they have to be defended against, even in the relationship with the analyst. We can say that at the beginning of the treatment the patient comes with certain defence mechanisms, or with a certain resistance, which he will present in the transference to the analyst (Illustration 5.1). Resistance movements have a very wide spectrum, and can be summarised as set out below.

Picture 5.1. Resistance is like a wall against something (Photo by Elzer).

Conscious or unconscious acting against the analyst

Patients often do not talk about their true feelings about the analyst: mostly they idealise him by paying him compliments about his clothes or his wealth. They would not dare to say something bad or negative about the analyst. Other forbidden thoughts, mostly obnoxious things, sexual ideas, and aggressive impulses, are often not verbalised. Patients do not talk about the furnishings or paintings in the treatment room because they fear the analyst's reaction, just as they fear confrontations with important others in their life.

Against the treatment itself

Some patients tell the psychoanalyst that the treatment is not working and that they do not deserve such a fine person as the therapist. In this case, the patient transfers good feelings to the therapist, yet does not like the treatment. Our task then has to be to work through his fear of, or resistance against, the treatment. This means that we ask the patient for associations about what the treatment is doing to him and how he feels about this form of therapy.

Not profiting from the treatment

The patient explains that every time he leaves the therapy room he forgets what was talked about. He is not able to remember what was spoken about during therapy. In such a case, the patient either forgets at once (defence) or he lacks the structural ability to adopt another point of view, or he has a mentalization problem.

Remaining silent

The patient who is always silent often has a resistance against providing the analyst with material. Thus, the analyst is not able to work. This might be an indirect aggressive impulse against the analyst or other feelings of envy, mistrust, or negative expectations that are in the inner world of the patient. In this case, most patients hide their feelings towards others and are not able to solve conflicts with others.

No associations or too many associations

Dreams are very important for treatment. If a patient has no other ideas about his dream than the content, he is hiding something or he is unable to associate.

The opposite could also be a method of resistance. In this case, a patient talks about a dream and cannot stop having more and more associations regarding the dream. With such an overload of associations, it is very difficult to find the real meaning of the dream. The patient is not really searching for a meaning—he is just proud of producing a great deal of material. In this case, the analytical couple cannot co-operate to find the meaning of the patient's dream.

Leaving out certain subjects of life

If you have known the patient for some time and you notice that the patient never speaks about his mother, his father, his sexual life, his spouse, his income, or his living costs, you become aware that he is omitting certain subjects. This means that the analyst has no chance of working these topics through with the patient. This is also a form of resistance.

Fast relief of symptoms

After three to five hours of therapy, the patient tells the therapist that all his symptoms have vanished, whereas analytical work has not really started at that point. In this case, the patient could have a resistance against the treatment and he is not really interested in continuing.

Acting out

"Acting out" means revealing feelings and thoughts in actions, instead of speaking about them. For example, a patient brings flowers to the first session, before he even knows what kind of relationship he will have with the analyst. The patient acts as if he is a guest. He is not aware of the fact that he is trying to please the analyst. So, instead of talking about his wish for the analyst to be kind and thoughtful, the patient acts it out.

Function of resistance

From an economic perspective, the function of resistance is to maintain an inner stability. Inner conflicts are destabilising when defence breaks down.

In this case, too many fears cause an imbalance of the inner stability.

With the defence operations, certain conflicts undergo a change, which means that unpleasant feelings are no longer conscious—they are "gone" or transformed into physical symptoms which cause suffering to the patient.

The resistance must be worked through to find the unconscious roots.

To clarify the resistance, we need certain words to help the patient find another viewpoint from which to look at his problem. We can ask the patient what frightens him about the content of his fears. In another approach, the patient may tell the analyst that he is the best therapist. We can confront the patient in this case, asking him if he could imagine that an analyst could also be disappointing.

Resistance and defence

The concepts of resistance in treatment and defence as a general operation of the psyche belong together. Freud put it this way: resistance is mainly that someone does not want to know something, because this knowledge triggers feelings of shame and fear of narcissistic hurt. In Freud's thinking, the concept of resistance is also close to the concept of dream censorship. Both concepts have the function of changing something unbearable into something bearable. The dreamer is unable to understand his own dream.

Working on resistance

To find out the meaning of the resistance phenomenon, we use the technique of free association. We ask the patient what comes to mind when he thinks about his fears. Since Freud, the work on resistance was reserved for the so-called transference neuroses. A change occurred in the theory with the advent of ego and self psychology. More importance was later given to narcissistic needs, self-confidence, and how to keep up "good" relationships.

In further developments of the theory, especially in the treatment of personality disorders (Balint and Winnicott), it was found that resistance in these cases was something else, for the regression of these patients is more profound. It goes back to an early stage of development. This means that these patients reach a stage of inner development where verbalisation is not yet developed. So, in these cases, we have no resistance against verbalisation but we have a "level of not yet being able to verbalise".

Analyst's resistance

The analyst, even having been analysed, can build up some resistance, which is called countertransference resistance. This concept was not mentioned by Freud, but, for example, by Little, Reik, Glover, and Racker in the further development of the theory.

This concept means that the analyst can defend associations and feelings in his self when his inner feelings are touched by the patient's material. This is possible because not everything can be analysed in the self-experience of the therapist. Hence, we should always be aware of what kind of topics and feelings the patient transfers to us and what these projections trigger in us.

The process of analysing oneself should be installed during the own process of analysis. Using this instrument we can feel when a patient touches us with feelings of shame or hurts us. The analyst also should take care that he does not always agree with the patient. This means we have a different point of view and no working through is possible. Another side of this problem is that we behave in just the way the patient expects. So, we have to be consciously aware of what kind of relationship the patient transfers to us. For this reason, self-experience is very important for doing good work with patients.

The treatment alliance

Treatment alliance is a therapeutic concept of psychoanalysis, which was formed after Freud. Greenson, Zetzel, Sandler, Dare, and Holder, and Langs and Luborsky worked in this field.

The therapeutic alliance should be orientated towards the needs of the patient. The patient should feel engaged in the therapeutic work and he should have the feeling that the working alliance is confidential and safe.

The therapeutic alliance should aim at realistic treatment goals. These aims should be found jointly as a common goal. The patient should also feel that the analyst listens empathically and tries to understand the patient, his history, and his special dynamics. It is also important that the analyst can hold back his interpretations. The analyst should not be ahead of, or lagging behind, the patient's thoughts. The timing, when to say something to the patient, is very important, because interpretations that come too soon might have an impact on the defence more than the progressive tendencies in the patient.

The therapist should encourage the patient to talk about his inner thoughts or fantasies. In other words, to talk freely about everything he wishes. The therapist should follow the associations of the patient and he should put these associations together like a puzzle, because these elements are the inner reality of the patient.

Both the analyst and the patient have special work to do. The analyst should be aware of how the patient presents his material, bringing in certain emotions and relationships with others. These object relationships that are presented will let the analyst know how the patient deals with, and thinks about, the people he interacts with.

The treatment alliance in the interaction with the patient starts with the first contact. Depending on the patient's structure and his defence mechanisms, we might experience problems in building up the treatment alliance.

If the patient feels good about the analyst from the start, the treatment alliance is mostly good. Further "good" interactions of the analytical couple will support the process of treatment. If a patient has defences such as splitting or projective identification, we mostly have negative reactions and a difficult treatment alliance. To explain to the patient how the treatment works, we should offer him some help, such as telling him that he will learn a new way of dealing with his feelings and relationships. We might also say that we will put together the personal story of his growing up in order to better understand how he deals with daily life. Hence, we will find some "patterns" in the inner life which are responsible for his suffering.

In the beginning and during further work we should try to explain and show the patient his transference to us. This means that the patient transfers his feelings for the object relations of his childhood to the analyst. The patient is not conscious of this fact, so we have to work on this field. We may ask the patient if he recognises these feelings from other times, so that we can find other situations in the past where the patient's feelings were the same. A further step towards increasing the working alliance is when the patient is able to understand that certain feelings towards people can trigger or re-awaken feelings which he has had for a long time—since his childhood, for example. If the patient understands these movements, he will experience that the old unconscious processes still hurt. At the same time, he can feel that mourning these hurts is a relieving act and is an important step towards changing childhood behaviour.

To strengthen the treatment alliance, the analyst should become somewhat less active verbally; he should omit his own personality and try not to mix his own personal story (countertransference) with the story of the patient. This more abstinent behaviour increases the patient's fantasies about the analyst and might increase transference. A further method to improve the work is to encourage the patient's associations so that he can spread out his own story, which makes the analyst's work easier. As mentioned in the chapter about resistance, in the free flow of speaking we may find blocks (resistance), for example, when a patient stops talking at a particular point because the topic he is talking about triggers negative feelings.

Further factors, such as the treatment room, environment, and regulation of payment are also part of the treatment alliance. All these details flow together into a whole and form the treatment alliance. How the patient uses the different parts of the treatment depends on his inner structure, his level of fixation, and his particular defence mechanisms.

Ethical aspects

Ethical rules for the therapeutic relationship are necessary as the relationship between the therapist and the patient is an artificial one and has to be protected against sexual and narcissistic abuse. This is important because this relationship is unequal, as the patient comes with an inner suffering. He is in regression and wants to be helped by the therapist. The transference of the patient is either idealised or hopeless. This means we do not have a realistic relationship.

Common ethical rules

The patient should become able to develop himself during treatment. The therapeutic process aims to loosen the fixations of the patient. In this process, we should help the patient to become conscious of his neurotic inner world.

The process works through transference and countertransference. In this work, the analyst has to take care of the patient's regressions and he also has to keep an eye on his own regression, which may be triggered by the patient.

Special ethical rules

The psychotherapist should be aware of the patient's dignity and integrity.

The analytic process is protected by the rule of abstinence. This means that the analyst does not abuse his authority. He should not profit from the patient or his family. The analyst has no economic or private relationship with his patients, and neither should the therapist abuse the patient for his own narcissistic needs, such as being admired or idealised.

Regarding sexual needs, the therapist should never have a sexual relationship with the patient during or after treatment. Even when the treatment is over and some time has elapsed, the identification with the therapist is still internalised, so a sexual relationship could, in fact, destroy the therapeutic work afterwards.

A patient's relationship with the psychoanalyst is purely voluntary and the patient may discontinue treatment or seek other treatment or advice at any time.

Regarding confidentiality, the psychoanalyst should take care of all documents he collects from the patient. He should not speak about his patients with others by revealing names or other personal details. He should not give any information to other institutions without the permission of the patient. The material the patient talks about is confidential, even after the patient's death. Scientific publications about the patient can only be written if the patient has given his consent.

Financial arrangements should be clarified with the patient before treatment starts. Termination of treatment should also be talked about clearly. If the psychotherapist decides to discontinue a patient's treatment, he should respond to the patient's treatment needs and reasonable request for information about possible alternative sources of treatment.

Finally, a psychotherapist should be informed about relevant professional and scientific developments and their application to the practice of psychotherapy. He should also be informed about legal conditions of his profession and he should not damage the reputation of any person or organisation recklessly or maliciously.

CHAPTER SIX

THE SETTING IN PSYCHOANALYTIC PSYCHOTHERAPY

Christine Gerstenfeld and Hanni Scheid-Gerlach

Frame and setting of the psychotherapy

Christine Gerstenfeld

What distinguishes the psychotherapeutic dialogue from the patient's talk about the same problems with a friend, a relative, a religious mentor, or a doctor of another speciality? What makes clear to the patient that in the psychotherapist's office he or she receives psychotherapy, and additionally, a psychoanalytically orientated type? It is the *frame* of the treatment that carries the fundamental function to initiate, to maintain, and to protect the essence of the psychotherapeutic process and which, at the same time, becomes a most valuable tool for the understanding of the unconscious psychic conflicts of the patient.

Components of the frame or setting of psychoanalytic therapy

In order to understand what is encompassed by the concept of "frame" or "setting", consider the list set out in Table 6.1, which contains factors that have been considered in the literature to belong to the frame or setting of psychoanalysis or psychoanalytic psychotherapy.

Definition of the concept: as we can see, the concept of the frame is a concept consisting on the one hand of general norms like ethical rules, of abstract concepts such as the "therapeutic attitude" (one could call these the "general principles of psychotherapy"), and, on the other hand, very practical, personal factors like the office of the therapist—the "local factors". In many articles, the terms "frame" and "setting" are used interchangeably, but recently there is a trend to reserve the term "setting" for the local factors, and for the sake of clarity this is how I will use it in this context.

As one attempt to define the frame, one could say that it encompasses the implicit and explicit rules that create the distinctive set of conditions that characterise psychoanalytic psychotherapy as opposed to any other human social activity. This basic set of conditions

Table 6.1. Components of the frame (setting) of psychoanalytic therapy.

1. *General codes of conduct*
Classical ethical rules of the medical or psychological professions (for example, confidentiality) adapted for psychotherapy
2. *Therapeutic stance or attitude*
Abstinence, neutrality, anonymity
Techniques for discovering the unconscious
Letting the unconscious speak: free association
Listening to the unconscious: free-floating attention
Noticing the enacted unconscious: role-responsiveness
3. *Setting components*
Time arrangements
Spatial arrangement
Payment arrangements

applies to all forms of psychoanalytic therapy, whether a once-per-week short therapy or a five-times-per-week analysis. The frame is the same, but the technique differs.

The establishment and maintenance of the frame is the responsibility of the therapist. It is important to note that the frame is established during our training as therapists as an internalised structure of our own minds (see example A), long before the first patient comes to our office, that it continues after the death of our patients (for example, we cannot divulge the communications of the patient to anybody, even after the patient has died), and also after our own death, as it is our duty to protect the confidentiality of our written files even in the case of sickness or death.

Example A: A therapist has a patient who is a successful painter, but who never speaks about her paintings. The therapist becomes increasingly curious, and one day, at home, she accesses the Internet and "Googles" the patient. Just as the websites come up, she realises that she is about to "break the frame" by collecting "external" information about her patient. She understands that she was not able to tolerate the feeling of being excluded and that this feeling reflects an important feeling of the patient herself. She does not call up any of the websites and uses the insight for interpretations.

Ethical dimension and rules of conduct

Although these principles are well known to you, I would like to say a few words about their implication for psychotherapy. We notice that the frame reflects the historical development of psychotherapy itself, in the sense that it is based on classical medical rules of conduct (e.g., the Hippocratic Oath). When Freud developed psychoanalysis, he was already a doctor, and many of the medical rules of conduct were automatically applied to his way of working. During his clinical practice, he developed additional specific principles designed to establish the best conditions for the unfolding of the analytical process; however, he did not define these as a frame. Historically, the pioneering years of psychoanalysis, prior to the understanding of the *specific needs* of an analytic frame, were marked, from our modern point of view, by frequent and often massive deviations from the analytic frame—including by Freud himself.

Today, most medical and psychological societies formalise their ethical codes according to the four bio-ethical principles specified by Beauchamp and Childress (2001) (for one example of how a psychoanalytical society codifies these basic rules, see APsaA, 2007).

- Respect for the autonomy of the patient: in psychotherapy this would mean, for example, informing the patient about the way the therapy works, the freedom of the patient to choose his therapist or the method, not collecting information from any source other than the patient. (Respect for autonomy can also extend to other persons in psychotherapy, e.g., we do not attempt to analyse dreams of relatives that the patient may bring to us.)
- Obligation to give assistance (adopting an attitude of care and concern for the patients; this principle may override other frame aspects, see example under "emergency").
- Duty to prevent harm to the patient (not abusing the patient for one's own needs, for example, no sexual, social, or financial transactions with patients or their families; not letting patients wait too long for therapy; seeking supervision in cases we cannot handle properly and not ending the psychotherapy unilaterally just because it is difficult; not "labelling" patients with diagnoses after only brief encounters; giving tactful reasons to patients whom we decide not to take into treatment).
- Fairness (not selecting patients according to their wealth, status, insurance, religious or ethnic background, or severity of disturbance).

Some of these rules of conduct have the character of immutable ethical laws: that is, any violation of them irreparably damages the therapy and leads to professional and legal penalties (e.g., embarking on a sexual relationship with a patient). Thus, the frame provides a protective dimension for both patient and therapist (as the patient, too, has to accept limits in the way he can make use of the therapist—if a patient threatens or endangers the therapist or his privacy, the therapist may terminate the treatment). Studies on the subject of sexual abuse in psychotherapy show that it ranges from 7% to 12% for male therapists and 2–3% for female therapists. Here is an example of where a sexual relationship was about to begin:

Example B: A therapist is single and has an attractive female patient. By chance, one day, the patient sees the therapist entering his private home, which is located near to her home, and quite far away from the psychotherapy office. In the next session, the patient asks the therapist to give her a lift in his car to her early morning sessions, and he agrees. After some drives in which there were somewhat flirtatious conversations, it becomes clear that this is a massive obstacle to therapy and he understands that he has avoided confronting his erotic countertransference. He stops driving her and seeks supervision, but the treatment has been heavily compromised and the supervisor decides that he must refer the patient to another colleague.

An emergency overrules the frame. There are, of course, psychotherapeutic emergency situations in which concern and worry for the patient's life and well-being may lead at times to changes to the frame, as illustrated by the next example.

Example C: A heavily traumatised patient in her third year of analysis calls the therapist on a Sunday. She has never done this before. The therapist feels the desperation of the patient and offers her an appointment in the office. It is clear that the patient is unable to guarantee that she would not harm herself, and the therapist is genuinely worried that she might kill herself. The therapist proposes to the patient that a short treatment in a psychiatric hospital would be advisable, and personally drives her there. The patient is discharged after a week and expresses both gratitude and anger at having been "abandoned" by the therapist for a week. She is able to make creative use of the multitude of transferential aspects of the joint ride in the car for the analytic process: for example, seeing the full ashtray in the therapist's car provides a link to her chain-smoking, alcoholic mother, who had often actually abandoned her and disappeared from home (compare this with the very different outcome of almost the same behavioural action in example B).

The long-established and well-known medical principle of confidentiality (included under "obligation not to harm the patient") is of paramount importance in psychotherapy. It extends from the simple fact that the patient is in treatment with us, to the spoken communications of the patient during the sessions, to our written notes and documents about the patient, and to special rules that apply when we decide to present case material (or to publish it; since I will not explore this last subject here, I have included a reference below, see Gabbard (2000)).

As a rule, we are allowed to speak about our patients only to colleagues who are themselves working within a psychotherapeutic consultative, educational, or scientific frame: that is, our own training analysts/therapists, our supervisors, seminar teachers, or intervision groups. Even in these situations, the identity of the patient must be sufficiently disguised so as to prevent identification of the individual.

Preserving confidentiality applies to sending case material by post or e-mail, to carefully selecting supervisors for patients that are themselves part of the medical or psychological community, and to many other situations that need special reflection.

Functions of the frame

The British analyst Donald Winnicott wrote about the distinction between the technique used by the therapist and the milieu in which he carries out his work. His analysand Marion Milner first used the metaphor "frame" instead of "milieu" in 1952. She noted that the frame of the treatment separates the sessions from the everyday life of the patient, in very much the same way that a frame separates a picture from the wall on which it hangs, thus using this concept in a similar way to the sociologist Erwin Goffman, who showed that it is a basic human capacity to register and adhere to frames that characterise all social situations. (Consider, for example, our confusion if an actor on stage suddenly shouts "Fire!" Is he saying this word within the frame of the play or in the frame of everyday life? Depending on how we interpret his exclamation, we either remain seated or run out to the street.) This is the sociologic dimension of the frame, which enables the patient to recognise that the session is a "time out" of his usual life in which he enters a unique human dialogue very different from the outside world. This aspect of clear delineation of a space reserved for psychotherapy explains why breaking the frame is called a boundary violation.

Although some aspects of the frame are so variable that each therapist develops his or her own personal style, there is good reason why we should try to develop a personal frame that we can keep fairly stable and constant: by keeping some variables constant, we establish a background that enables us to notice even slight differences in the way a patient relates to us and to the frame, and in the way we change it with a specific patient. This could be called the diagnostic function of the frame. A standardised personal frame is, thus, especially beneficial for enhancing our awareness of the psychic conflicts, object relationships, and structural deficits of the patient (or, indeed, the therapist), that will manifest themselves in specific attempts to change the frame. This is the "container" function of the frame, in which it serves as a projection space for unconscious conflicts that cannot be symbolised sufficiently into words. Traumatised patients, those with structural deficits, or deeply regressed patients actually transfer their symbolisation deficits into the frame. Thus, it becomes obvious that the work focusing on frame distortions or enactments of the patient is, at the same time, a work on core conflicts.

The frame needs constant attention because it gives the patient a feeling of security—this is its "holding" dimension. This aspect enables the patient to develop trust in the therapy, allowing him to open up sufficiently. In a way, this aspect of the frame provides patients with a "good enough" environment that is comparable to "good enough mothering". Attachment theory has emphasised the need for dependable, trustworthy relationships in order to achieve psychic growth. Patients observe very keenly how the therapist protects the frame, and if frame infringements are tolerated conclude (sometimes rightly) that the therapist lacks the competence to handle the process adequately. Frame changes might cause considerable anxiety to the patient, who must fear that his psychic conflicts are too difficult to be contained by the therapist. However, when unconsciously motivated, spontaneous minor enactments of frame changes are understood and "repaired", the insight in therapy often deepens considerably, as shown in the following example.

Example D: A therapist has a patient in once-per-week psychotherapy who routinely rejects interpretations as having no significance. One day, the therapist forgets the session and goes shopping. The patient waits a while in front of the door and then goes home. The therapist realises her mistake, calls the patient, apologises and gives him another appointment in the same week. It is clear to the therapist that she has forgotten the session because of her feelings of frustration, but the frame has been adequately "repaired" and the patient can reflect on the distress he has felt while outside the door. His emotional relationship with the therapist deepens and he is able to acknowledge her importance for his inner world.

Another function of the frame is providing a triangulating factor that lies outside both patient and therapist, a third entity in an otherwise exclusive dyadic relationship. The third creates an oedipal situation: patient, therapist, and the frame. Thus, by protecting and repairing the frame, the therapist conveys that he is not caught up with the patient in an exclusive symbiotic relationship or *folie à deux*, and ultimately conveys that the therapist is a separate object with his own concerns and needs. In this triangulating function, the frame also represents the larger social context, thus serving as an aid to symbolisation (much in the way language helps the child to learn about the world and to articulate his separate identity from his parents). Some authors regard this aspect as a "function of the father". It is this function especially that leads patients to make "oedipal attacks" on the frame. We can now understand why a sexual relationship in therapy carries for both participants the unconscious meaning of an incestuous relationship and an oedipal triumph.

We can summarise the functions of the frame for the therapeutic process (Table 6.2). Naturally, in all forms of therapy (such as cognitive–behavioural, among others), these dimensions

Table 6.2. Functions of frame (setting) for the therapeutic process.

1. Protective function for both participants.
2. Sociologic function of demarcating boundaries.
3. Diagnostic function for the unconscious of both participants.
4. Container function for the patient.
5. Holding function for the patient.
6. Triangulating function for both participants.

of the frame are present in the background, but they are not routinely used as an instrument for understanding the unconscious of the patient.

The rule of abstinence

I would now like to highlight some of the frame components of the therapeutic attitude specific to psychoanalytically orientated therapeutic processes.

The concept of abstinence developed by Freud means initially that the therapist should not gratify the patient's instinctual desires. Freud formulates the rule of abstinence in the context of patients desiring the love of the therapist:

> I have already let it be seen that the analytic technique requires the physician to deny the patient who is longing for love the satisfaction she craves. The treatment must be carried through in a state of abstinence; I do not mean merely corporal abstinence, nor yet deprivation of everything desired, for this could perhaps not be tolerated by any sick person. But I would state as a fundamental principle that the patient's desire and longing are to be allowed to remain, to serve as driving forces for the work and for the changes to be wrought, and one must beware of granting this source of strength some discharge by surrogates. (Freud, 1915a)

Here Freud makes clear that—generally—a direct gratification of a desire destroys the possibility of symbolising it, understanding its unconscious motives, and, thus, using it for the actual scope of therapy, the removal of symptoms, and the psychic growth of the patient.

Abstinence does not refer only to sexual wishes, but also to other instinctual wishes, and, naturally, excludes gratification for both patient and therapist. This is why, in general, neither patient nor therapist eat or smoke during the sessions; in the case history of the Rat Man, one can immediately follow in Freud's handwritten notes the disruptive effects of the meal that Freud served to his patient. It also refers to narcissistic gratifications: we should not praise the patient too much, thus creating a suggestive process, and should not allow "special rules and exceptions" for famous or powerful patients who might be providing us with narcissistic gratification.

Neutrality and anonymity

The term "technical neutrality" is centred exclusively on the therapist, meaning that he or she should not impose on the patient any *extra-therapeutic* (religious, moral, political, social) goals or ideals. Additionally, the therapist should also abstain from expressing his opinions or letting himself be dragged into discussions on these matters. The therapist should not make moral judgements, not take sides in conflicts that the patient relates to him, and not be over-intrusive into the life of the patient. This tenet is especially important in cases of patients whose lifestyles and life goals run counter to the accepted conventions of a given culture (e.g., gender roles, sexual orientation). Thus, neutrality is closely linked to the first principle of Beauchamp and Childress (2001) in the field of psychotherapy and reflects the respect of the therapist for the unique individuality of the patient.

Neutrality and abstinence are also closely related to the technical rule of relative anonymity that intends to promote the undisturbed unfolding of the patient's transference by restricting the amount of personal information given to the patient. Freud's famous metaphor of the analyst as mirror conveys this: "the doctor should be opaque to his patients, and like a mirror should show them nothing but what is shown to him" (Freud, 1912e, p. 117).

Although today this metaphor is thought to place the therapist in too rigid a position, it still holds sway with regard to revelations of the therapist about his private life, his personal history, his personality, or his own problems. Self-disclosure of this kind in most cases distorts the transference and burdens the patient. As psychotherapists, we must be aware from the start of the profession that our work carries with it considerable frustration of our normal narcissistic needs: we conduct hours of therapy without being ourselves *as a person* at the centre of attention.

Thus, one can try to formulate more explicitly some practical consequences of these three concepts for the psychotherapeutic profession and we can see how some of these differ from other medical or psychological branches:

- bodily contact other than the conventional greeting and parting rituals specific to the given culture are to be avoided (in Germany, patients do occasionally spontaneously embrace the therapist, especially at the end of the therapy). It also follows for hospital settings that patients who are taken into psychoanalytically orientated psychotherapy should not normally be medically examined by the doctor who conducts the therapy;
- *planned* meetings outside the consulting room/hospital are not allowed (except in emergency situations);
- the patient must not be asked to provide "expert" information or help that benefits the private life or professional career of the analyst;
- no financial transactions other than the paying of the fee are allowed;
- providing the patient with information on aspects of our private life in excess of what the patient can infer from the setting, or about our beliefs and political, religious, and social affiliations should be avoided;
- one should strive for as much mutual anonymity prior to the treatment and during the treatment as possible—one cannot take into treatment relatives of the patient, or one's own relatives, friends, colleagues, employees, or superiors, or the neighbour living next door to us.

The rule of free association

In discussing the technical aspects of the techniques that are considered to belong to the framework of analytically orientated psychotherapy, I would like to start with a quote by Freud explaining the rule of free association. Freud addresses an imaginary patient directly:

> One more thing before you start. What you tell me must differ in one respect from an ordinary conversation. Ordinarily you rightly try to keep a connecting thread running through your remarks and you exclude any intrusive ideas that may occur to you and any side-issues, so as not to wander too far from the point. But in this case you must proceed differently. You will notice that as you relate things various thoughts will occur to you which you would like to put aside on the ground of certain criticisms and objections. You will be tempted to say to yourself that this or that is irrelevant here, or is quite unimportant, or nonsensical, so that there is no need to say it. You must never give in to these criticisms, but must say it in spite of them – indeed, you must say it precisely because you feel an aversion to doing so. Later on you will find out and learn to understand the reason for this injunction, which is really the only one you have to follow. So say whatever goes through your mind. Act as though, for instance, you were a traveller sitting next to the window of a railway carriage and describing to someone inside the carriage the changing views which you see outside. Finally, never forget that you have promised to be absolutely honest, and never leave anything out because, for some reason or other, it is unpleasant to tell it. (Freud, 1913c, pp. 133–134)

Compare this to his explanation of the free-floating attention of the therapist, which states that it

> rejects the use of any special expedient (even that of taking notes). It consists simply in not directing one's notice to anything in particular and in maintaining the same "evenly-suspended attention" (as I have called it) in the face of all that one hears. In this way we spare ourselves a strain on our attention which could not in any case be kept up for several hours daily, and we avoid a danger which is inseparable from the exercise of deliberate attention. For as soon as anyone deliberately concentrates his attention to a certain degree, he begins to select from the material before him; one point will be fixed in his mind with particular clearness and some other will be correspondingly disregarded, and in making this selection he will be following his expectations or inclinations. This, however, is precisely what must not be done. In making the selection, if he follows his expectations he is in danger of never finding anything but what he already knows; and if he follows his inclinations he will certainly falsify what he may perceive. (Freud, 1912e, pp. 110–111)

We realise that these two techniques are analogous to one another: one is directed to the therapist, the other to the patient. Freud asks that we both try to learn a certain kind of attention: the patient needs attention to when he feels a resistance to say something, and the therapist needs attention that freely roams among everything that is said and that also covers the therapist's feelings, the countertransference.

We can see that the rule of free association is the only one that is actually the responsibility of the patient, but today we know that it is only a very limited responsibility, because, in the modern understanding of transference as a process, it is clear that the unconscious conflicts of the patient will manifest themselves as resistances in the free association in an unconscious way. Thus, we realise that the patient cannot possibly be in a position always to obey the rule, even if he consciously very much wishes to do so. So, then, why tell him the rule at all? One reason for telling the patient about the technique of free association is to enhance his own awareness of unconscious manifestations, to allow him to discover it himself. Another reason is that to start interpreting without telling the patient how we arrive at our hypotheses about his unconscious conflicts may carry with it an omnipotent attitude. Some therapists explain this to the patient in very similar words to those of Freud's at the beginning of the treatment, but make it seem more like an invitation than a rule.

Regarding the therapist, Sandler (1976) has developed an additional and very useful concept to free-floating attention, which he called "free floating role responsiveness". It is based on the theory that the early relationships of a child result in the internalisation of these relationship patterns (internalised object relations) and that patients in the course of therapy will try to induce us to become similar to their inner internalised relationship patterns, thus unconsciously asking us to take up a role. In order to recognise these roles into which we are unconsciously cast, we must be free to recognise our feelings in regard to a patient and to initially allow ourselves, to some degree, to respond spontaneously in the role. An example follows.

Example E: The patient starts crying and asks for a paper tissue, and the therapist gives her one, although the patient could easily take it herself from the table. In the course of the following sessions, this happens again a few times, in the end with the crying patient just holding up her hand in the direction of the therapist. The therapist, somewhat annoyed, thinks to herself "That is enough now!" She realises that she is playing some role, but which? She asks the patient to say something about her feelings about the paper tissues. The patient answers spontaneously, "I think I am trying to see when your goodness will end!" Then a memory from her childhood emerges: her mother often told her that as an infant she had been like a vampire because she had sucked the breast very forcefully. Now she was "forcefully sucking paper tissues", and unconsciously enacting the probability of being again rejected.

Setting components: time and room

Aspect of time

The time arrangement is very significant for the setting, because it is here that "attachment and separation" are most often felt and enacted. Special attention to the feelings of the patient with regard to changed times, frequency of sessions, or to vacations of the therapist provides important information about his unconscious relationship patterns. The higher the frequency of the treatment, and the more regressed a patient is, the more intensely the effects of separation are felt by the patient.

Generally, one should aspire to schedule appointments at regular times each week (e.g., Tuesday 11.00), and to ensure both stable frequency (e.g., once a week) and stable duration of a session (e.g., fifty minutes). Of course, changes in the times or frequency might arise, but their emotional meaning for the patient should be always explored. I recommend pauses of ten minutes between patients to facilitate the relaxation of the therapist, and also because then the patients do not meet each other. Except in emergencies, one should not schedule appointments on bank holidays, at weekends, or at very unusual social times (such as very late at night). Patients should be notified of vacations well in advance.

Aspect of room (office)

Generally, patients get used to the appearance of our office and expect it to be the same every time they come, which reflects a need for a safe and stable environment. As with all aspects of the frame, the office itself and all pieces of furniture in it may assume important symbolic meaning to patients at different stages of the therapy. Because of this, we must be aware that—in a sense—everything that is in the consulting room does not belong exclusively to us, but also to the patient. This is why we should avoid making too frequent changes in the furniture, and should alert patients if we intend to renovate or change its appearance.

Example F: A therapist informed the patients of an imminent renovation and most of them developed spontaneous fantasies about it. One patient asked, "Will my plant remain there?" The therapist had not known that this specific plant was important to the patient, who had emigrated from her homeland and had lost almost all personal belongings from her past. Another patient exclaimed after the renovation, "Oh no, you have put the pictures back wrongly! The one with the boat was on the other wall!" To this patient, this was an important aspect of transference—she assumed that the therapist did it deliberately in order to annoy her.

Our offices should aspire to convey a tranquil, quiet, and safe environment: the sessions should not be disturbed by telephone calls. The office should be protected from the intrusion of other people, from views inside it, and the spoken words should not be heard outside, for example, through a thin door (these are especially important aspects in hospital settings). The therapist should furnish her office in such a manner that she feels comfortable in it, but I recommend reflecting on the amount and the kind of personal information that is visible (e.g., photographs, etc.). Therapists who have their consulting rooms inside their own homes should carefully reflect on the transference to their visible personal life. Regarding the geographic position, one should avoid sitting behind a desk, and choose a distance between the armchairs that is neither too distant nor too close. Generally, one should try to have armchairs that are similar in comfort and "status" for both patient and therapist.

I would like to comment on the transition time between the greeting or parting at the door and the armchairs where we conduct the therapeutic dialogues. Often, the things that are said spontaneously by the patient in this "transition space" are of great psychic importance. Generally, I think it is best not to make specific therapeutic interventions during these transitions, but to keep in mind what is said or enacted and come back to it later when appropriate. Often, the feelings we have during these times convey better than words the unconscious conflicts of the patient, though it might take some time for us to understand what we are feeling and why.

Additional remarks

The frame carries a dual character that, ideally, combines both stability and flexibility. On the one hand, the constancy and the protection of its components give the patient a feeling of security, trust, and coherence. On the other hand, the frame should not be so rigid as to prevent us from noticing the patient's and our unconscious little deviations from the usual frame. These provide us with excellent opportunities for understanding the conflicts of the patient and for therapeutic work around frame aspects. This does not mean that we should dogmatically interpret all frame aspects that we become aware of, which might actually promote conformity rather than understanding. As with all things, we need good balance. With more clinical experience, the frame becomes something like an internalised "auto-pilot" that naturally belongs to our personal professional identity and that we learn to use as easily for the understanding of the patient as his spoken words or his dreams.

Other aspects of the setting

Hanni Scheid-Gerlach

In the following sections, further clinical and technical aspects of the setting are discussed.

The fee

The question of the fee belongs to the topic of framework and setting. Before treatment starts, the patient and the analyst should determine the cost of the treatment. With regard to the fee, the analyst should follow some ethical rules. The analyst should not exploit his patients by enriching himself and impoverishing the patients. We should find a socially acceptable way appropriate for the patient's means. The fee and other conditions of the framework should be fixed in a written or verbal form to establish a good and secure working relationship. Paying for missed appointments must be clarified. The rules or framework we lay down stabilise the working alliance. How the patient uses these financial rules depends on his particular inner structure. Money is part of the basic constraints and, therefore, part of the analytical process which should also be worked through. Most patients have problems with money and they associate it with fantasies of dependency, emotional supply, or feelings of guilt or deprivation. In particular, the question of the patient's reaction to paying for missed appointments is a delicate one. We should not morally judge why patients do not come to sessions and refuse payment. We should try to understand their disappointment better, and the feelings of anger which are certainly connected to their inner life and the experience with the objects of their childhood.

In clarifying the financial problem, it is helpful to use the term "renting hours", as renting other things in daily life is very common to all of us; nobody would get the idea that a rented car or house would be free when we go on holiday.

Changing the setting and the therapeutic method

Resistance is the central concept of psychoanalysis. It is, therefore, the main problem when patients do not want to go on with their psychoanalysis, want to change to another setting, or reduce the number of sessions. This problem is partly predictable when you have a differentiated interview at the beginning and you are aware of the negative objects inside the patient (negative transference).

It could be that a patient is directing his unconscious forces against you and tries to put you in a negative role, without realising that he is transferring a negative object relationship to you. In this case, the patient might want to change to another therapist. Patients might think that behaviour therapy, or any other form of therapy, would be preferable. In these cases, the analyst should try to confront the patient with his resistance, pointing out that he might fear his own negative side and probably has some negative feelings of disappointment towards his therapist (working through the idealisation).

If work on the resistance is not fruitful, we have to inform the patient about other methods. The therapist should not try to retain a patient at all costs. We have an obligation to tell the patient that he might be choosing something that will not be helpful for him (such as witchcraft, religion, or "re-birthing"). It might even be detrimental rather than helpful.

In some cases, the wish to reduce the frequency of sessions is connected with a fear of being emotionally too close to the other. This means that the inner object relationships of the patient do not allow this process of coming closer. In this case, the analyst is a danger for the objects in the inner world, from whom the patient does not want to separate, because the feelings of mourning involved with separation hurt.

Parallel treatments and medication

Often, we see patients who are in a desolate psychic situation. They are unable to bear their emotional state of confusion. In these cases, the patients are treated by a psychiatrist with psychotropic medication (antidepressant or antipsychotic drugs or tranquillisers). We know that medication and the relationship to the doctor also have an influence on the symptoms and the emotional tension of the patient. Medication is often an easy way for patients to experience relaxation quickly; the effects of psychotherapy are slower and take more time, but the results last longer.

It is very helpful if the two functions, giving medication and being the analyst, are not combined in the same person. At first sight, it seems that the two treatments are complementary, but if we take into account that medication is given by an "object" that interacts with the patient, we have a different point of view.

We always have a process of interaction in different ways:

1. The doctor and the patient.
2. The patient and the medication (function).
3. The patient and the analyst.

Thus, between the doctor and the patient we also have a process of transference and countertransference, with conscious and unconscious attitudes. In the worst case scenario, a patient's inner dynamics might lead to defiance of the doctor if the patient does not follow the doctor's advice.

It is important in this case to work on the function of medication. We know that a confused patient has a lack of inner structure. In this case, medication might take over an inner structural function: for example, the "function of a calming object". If the doctor is unaware of this function, it could happen that the patient becomes dependent on the medication and does not really improve. On the other hand, medication might disturb other ego functions: for example, the patient might have problems thinking or visualising. Most medications change a patient's narcissistic self-awareness and confidence and reduce the feeling of being strong enough to deal independently with a crisis. Therefore, it is very important to observe a patient during his medication process with the other object, the psychiatrist. Perhaps the psychiatrist and the analyst have conflicting ideas about which treatment is the most appropriate. This could lead to a splitting process in all the people involved, which is not very efficacious for the further process of treatment.

In the worst case scenario, a doctor acts out through his method of treatment; for example, because he does not believe in psychoanalysis, he could have a negative influence on this method of treatment. Then the medication therapy could be less helpful, because the patient will be confronted with a new conflict that he is unable to solve, or the patient believes in medication and leaves his other conflicts unsolved.

Patients, especially those with personality disorders, always act out their defence by splitting in this setting. This process works through projective identification, whereby transference of the negative and the idealised side will be transferred. The therapist and the doctor are both in unrealistic roles, into which they are forced by the compulsive repetition of the patient.

In conclusion, we can say that medication can take over the following functions:

- the good object (symbiotically);
- the transitional object (substitute object with a special value, enabling toleration of separation);
- the splitting of the object;
- the function of fear;
- the negative object (reduced object constancy);
- the steering object (function of control or abuse by the object);
- the object as a persuader or liberator (paranoid function).

The patient and his relatives

The patient who comes to the therapist always brings along his whole family in his inner life. The patient carries all emotional interactions from birth to the present; most of these emotional bonds are unconscious. During analysis, we understand how the patient developed according to his circumstances.

In contrast to the inner family we just mentioned, we have another conflict when the patients bring relatives in person.

In your cultural reality, you often see that the family or other relatives accompany the patient. In such cases, we know that the patient cannot show his feelings or talk about his problems in front of his relatives. He will show us his symptoms or how he thinks and acts, but in a way which is influenced by his defence mechanisms. In this situation, we are confronted with two aspects: one is the patient who suffers as a "victim" and the other relates to the people who "caused" his neurosis.

If you choose an individual therapeutic setting, it may be that family members, spouses, or friends try to interfere with the individualised process. In this case, the patient might show feelings of disappointment in his parents, because he does not live and act the way his parents wanted him to. Here, we have a conflict between two generations who are very different in their inner life. We have to take into account that different circumstances of the parents build up different inner structures, so we have different inner solutions. Further conflicts might arise when incest barriers cannot be accepted and sexual fantasies confuse the family system. Often, we can see that feelings of loss and disappointment are unconscious and the whole family system is not aware of this emotional problem.

Finally, different identities, which contain different moral identifications, cultural and political backgrounds, are causes of further misunderstandings.

Modification and application of the psychoanalytical method

In the history of psychoanalysis, a large amount of knowledge about psychic illnesses and their treatment has been collected. Through further developments of the theory and the application thereof in practice, a broad spectrum of treatments was constructed by means of the psychoanalytical theory.

The different settings for treatment in Germany are shown in Table 6.3.

Frequency of the treatment in psychoanalysis and psychotherapy

The features that Freud recounted in "On beginning the treatment" (1913c) include the analyst's position outside the patient's vision, regular sessions, and prescribed duration and terms for payment of fees. High-frequency analysis works with the standard technique.

This is a method of treating psychic suffering by advancing self-knowledge. It is characterised by the interpretations of the free associations of a patient, who should become aware of his feelings and forgotten memories.

The development of the transference neurosis, whose infantile origins are revealed in analysis, is the central moment of the treatment. This may arouse highly ambivalent feelings in the patient towards his analyst.

The density of the frequency and the length of this form of treatment allow intensive working through in the transference. More time and a closer relationship enable the analyst to understand more of the structure of the inner representations.

As well as the frequency of sessions and the function of the couch, everything that belongs to the analyst's room (pictures, pillows, chairs, etc.) may be infused with meaning in the relationship of the analytical couple. The meaning of these objects that belong to the analyst might interfere with the fantasies of the patient and should be analysed when they are mentioned.

Interpretation of dreams is also a very important part of the analytical work. Free association is the fundamental rule for working on dreams.

The termination of analysis generally is an aim discussed between the patient and the analyst. Curing the symptom has never been the most important function of the analytical work. The patient should obtain relief from his psychic suffering and find a better way to deal with his inner world, including his defences.

In the decades after Freud, psychoanalytic treatment was extended to more severe pathologies, to borderline conditions and psychotic disorders.

Table 6.3. Applications of psychoanalysis in different settings.

Method	Qualification of the therapist by training programme in:	Frequency of sessions	Duration of one session	Duration of the treatment (number of sessions; months, years)
Psychoanalysis	Psychoanalysis	3–5 per week	50 min.	200–500 sessions over several years
Psychoanalytically orientated psychotherapy	Psychoanalysis or psychoanalytically orientated psychotherapy	1–2 per week	50 min.	50–100 sessions for 1–2 years
Psychoanalytical short-term therapy	Psychoanalysis or psychoanalytically orientated psychotherapy	1 or less per week	50 min.	10–25 sessions over several months
Crisis intervention	Psychoanalysis or psychoanalytically orientated psychotherapy	1–2 per week	50 min.	10–25 sessions lasting some months
Focal therapy	Psychoanalysis and special training should be requested	1 per week	50 min.	About 25 sessions over ome months
Psychoanalytical couple therapy	Special training requested for psychoanalyst or psychoanalytically orientated psychotherapist	Varies, 1–2 per month	50–100 min.	Counselling (5 sessions). Long term (25 or more sessions) lasting some months or years
Psychoanalytical family therapy	Special training requested for psychoanalyst or psychoanalytically orientated psychotherapist	Varies, 1 per month	90–120 min.	Counselling (5 sessions). Long term (25 or more sessions) over months or years
Psychoanalytical therapy for children and adolescents	Special training programme is necessary for psychoanalyst or psychoanalytically orientated psychotherapist	2–3 per week + one with parents	50 min.	Short term 25 sessions Long term 80–120 sessions for months or years
Psychoanalytical group therapy	Special group training is necessary for psychoanalyst or psychoanalytically orientated psychotherapist	1 or 2 per week	90–100 min.	Short term 25 sessions Long term 80–120 sessions for several years

The termination of treatment does not mark the end of the analytic process. Analysing oneself should be an ongoing task. The process of self-analysis, which is learnt during the analysis, should be internalised, so that the patient has the possibility of working through his conflicts by himself. No one should be ashamed of going back to treatment, if he is in a new situation, because no one can analyse situations that have not yet happened.

Psychoanalytic psychotherapy

Full psychoanalysis is appropriate and feasible as a treatment for only a minority of patients. For this reason, psychoanalytical psychotherapy is a method that is often used in daily practice. Patients who are motivated and who can quite clearly identify their problem and who are aware of some kind of aim they want to reach can be treated in this setting. In this kind of treatment we use the couch one to three times; sometimes the patients are sitting, depending on their inner state of regression.

Transference interpretations and the work on regressions should be used in a more limited way, in comparison with psychoanalysis proper. The low frequency and the time limitation reduce the opportunities for working through, so we have more limited aims. The analyst works with the metaphoric memories of childhood, which are presented as figures of daily life. In this treatment, we prefer to work less with the transference neurosis in order to keep regression within limits.

Analysts mostly choose this setting for reasons of time, cost, and the special mechanisms of a disease. All neuroses can be treated with this method. Further indications are: personality disorders, perversions, and borderline cases, and, to a certain degree, psychosis.

Psychoanalytic short-term therapy

This kind of treatment often takes 10–25 sessions. To use this form of treatment for a patient, it is necessary for the therapist to quickly have an idea (differential diagnostic) of the patient's internal structure and conflicts. Working with this form of therapy is a challenge, so it is good to be experienced with long-term therapies.

General indications for short-term therapy include a clearly defined actual conflict, good motivation of the patient, and limited goals. Specific indications for this treatment include that it is possible to find a relationship between the patient's present conflict and the inner conflict of his childhood. We may see that the patient suffers severely from a separation, but the patient is unconscious of the fact that he suffered from the same feelings during childhood. Oedipal conflicts might be triggered through certain constellations in daily life.

The analyst practising short-term therapy needs to be more active; he must always keep the actual conflict focused in his mind. The interpretations should be based on the conflict, which is in relation to the present and the past.

The available time—as an essential in all short-term treatments—should always be kept in mind. This is of special importance because we have to find out which projections the patient is applying to this setting. The limitation of time may arouse separation problems or feelings of loss.

The psychoanalytically orientated short-term psychotherapy can help the patient solve an actual problem, such as the loss of a person, a terminated relationship, the process of mourning, fatigue syndrome (burn-out), or help him cope with narcissistic hurt as a crisis intervention. Short-term therapy can also be used as a probe to see whether a long-term therapy might be indicated.

When crisis intervention is indicated, we take patients who suffer from an actual conflict. The patient in this state is in personal distress; he is unable to think about his crisis or to understand what is going on in him emotionally. Within this setting, we try to build up a structure of progression which helps the patient understand what has happened to him. In such a setting we use no transference interpretations, the analyst verbalises more, and he gives more supporting interpretations with regard to the patient's daily life. The theoretical concept behind the model of mental and somatic decompensation is that the ego has a synthesising function. In a crisis the ego cannot form a synthesis and, therefore, is somehow falling apart.

During treatment, the analyst takes two roles. At first, he is a kind of mother substitute who takes over the role of being close and creating safety. Second, the analyst has to frustrate this mother-substitute role, for separation has to take place. In this ambivalent conflict, it might happen that the patient cannot tolerate the separation and acts out his problem while frequently calling the therapist on the phone.

One special application of the psychoanalytical short-term psychotherapy is that of focal therapy. It is a very ambitious method of short-term treatment, which should be used only by psychoanalysts with special experience in this method. At the beginning of the treatment, the analyst has to formulate the focus through his psychodynamic understanding of the patient's core conflict. The focus is a complex hypothesis, which has to be communicated to the patient right from the beginning of this limited treatment. The focus consists of the patient's main symptoms, the defence mechanisms, the defended content, the actual conflict, and the transference situation.

Psychoanalytic couple therapy

The common element of couple therapy is the focus on the couple as a disturbed unit. This means that the way of satisfying each other is disturbed, perhaps through hurting each other in a narcissistic way: for example, by using destructive words. In the treatment, the inner structure, including the defence mechanisms of both, must be analysed. In working through the couple problem, we will find that the two people are interacting with their inner unconscious patterns. They will even use the other partner as a projection to rid themselves of some of their own parts.

During the work, the analyst should be very careful not to side with one person. To avoid this problem, it is useful to work in this setting with a couple of therapists, male and female.

If we have a couple problem, we will choose a setting in which we see both of them. We should interview both together, because the interview of each one alone would bring up fantasies in the absent person.

The co-operation of the partners in working together on the "problem" is of great diagnostic importance. A bad working alliance bodes ill for reaching a solution to the couple's problem.

For example, one of the two insists that the other one is responsible for the problem and he or she is blamed and accused.

Couple therapy can be conducted in various settings: either a couple meets a therapist couple or a couple works with one analyst. It is also possible to have a group setting where three to four couples meet with one or two therapists. Another possibility is to have an individual setting, where each partner works with a different therapist.

Couple therapy cannot be conducted when we have patients who are not functioning as fully separated individuals with the defence of projective identification.

Psychoanalytic family therapy

The analytical family-therapy concept deals with the idea that parents who deal unconsciously with their inner world will transfer some of their problems to their children. As with couple therapy, we see the family as a disturbed unit with an imbalanced use of feelings or fantasies in the relationships (the attuned psyches are connected by primary identifications). Further indications are: psychosomatic, personality, and eating disorders, and even families with a psychotic member. Often, one person in the family is accused, very often the weakest person, such as a child. A very extreme example is where a member of the family is falsely consigned to a mental hospital by his relatives who want to get rid of him. Carrying out this treatment in a clinic allows a suitable setting: sufficient chairs in a circle in a quiet room and enough space for children to move around.

The reasons why family groups become sick are often seen in changes of cultural morals, political changes, and catastrophes in the society. The family group shares daily life under different inner situations, with a different past and present. It has to adapt to these changes, which gives rise to several problems in the inner life of the whole group. For example, inner representations of how men and women should behave might not match the "new way", and there might be confusion as to what a family should be like when old patterns of living together are not suitable any more. The concept of family neurosis is the model that is used nowadays. With regard to the family's problems, a good prognosis is likely when the whole family is interested in changing their interaction.

The method of working in the therapy is determined by talking about the subjects that have been avoided up to now, for example, family secrets, disappointments, unfairness, and damage to confidence. The analyst acts as a mediator to enable a constructive dialogue among the family members. Interpretations of transference and resistance are the main methods used to change the unconscious to the conscious and to let the family develop. The essential goal for therapy is to work with the paradoxical narcissism and anti-narcissism duality that is active from the very beginning in each subject and is a primal component of the familial psychic apparatus. Also, the goal is to achieve autonomy for the individual psyche and access to the oedipal conflict through sufficient development of the couple/group tension.

Psychoanalytic therapy for children and adolescents

The treatment of children was established by Anna Freud, Hermine Hug-Hellmuth, and Melanie Klein. Differentiations and modifications to their methods were developed later. The development of this type of therapy promoted the role of the mother–child relationship in the development of the child.

The medium in which child therapy takes place is play. The analyst plays, observes, and interprets simultaneously. The analyst in this setting will be projected with a multi-dimensional network of transferences. It is usual to have contact with the parents in order to realise the difference between the child's fantasies and the real parents.

The most important concepts that are needed to work in this form are those of infantile sexuality, transference, the unconscious, resistance, repetition, drives, and interpretation. *Analysis of a Phobia in a Five-year-old Boy* (Freud, 1909b) is a very good example of how to observe and swap ideas with a child. With the analytical work, the child or adolescent should make changes to his dependency on his parents. The process of individualisation should grow and the patient should use fewer defence mechanisms and should become almost free of fears. In this sense, child analysis can be seen as the application of psychoanalysis in all its facets.

The treatment is not limited to neurosis, but has also been extended to various forms of psychosis, autism, mental retardation, and psychosomatic disorders. In the case of borderline patients, it is very helpful for the theory and technique to study the child–mother interaction, especially when the mother object is depressive.

Special training in psychoanalytical psychotherapy is necessary and indispensable for treating children and adolescents in a professional way.

Psychoanalytic group therapy

In our daily lives, we all live in social or family groups. The interaction between the individual and the group is known to all of us and we interact everywhere, even in our training course. In contrast to individual psychoanalysis, the group experiences the inner world as composed of, and profoundly affected by, relationships with others—families, societies, and cultural patterns.

Today, with increasing job insecurity and pressure at work, greater social mobility, broken families, etc., changes in society often disrupt supportive networks or impede their development. Group therapy can help to restore or provide a sense of connectedness, and enhance confidence in oneself with others.

Groups are able to provide powerful support and encouragement and a vivid setting in which problems can be explored and treated.

In considering group therapy, it is useful to distinguish between homogeneous groups, where patients share the same problem, and more heterogeneous groups.

There are two settings for groups:

- closed group: the patients start and finish together over, say, two years. If one patient leaves the group, no other new patient can join it. The process of the members of such a closed group is similar and parallel;
- slow open group: this concept of group therapy is different from the closed group in so far as the group continues for many years; if a patient leaves the group, his or her place will be taken by a new patient. The process of each patient is individual and different, as in a family with older and younger siblings. The German–British group analyst, Foulkes (1992), developed the concept of the "matrix of the group".

A special training programme and group self-experience is necessary and indispensable for working as a group analyst or group psychotherapist.

Group therapy is possible in two settings:

- outpatients: in this setting, the group meets once or twice a week, for two to four years for one and a half hours.
- inpatients: two to three sessions a week, one and a half hours lasting 6–12 weeks. The work in this setting deals with regressive processes that trigger special transferences to the analyst. In this way, the material can be worked through.

CHAPTER SEVEN

DIAGNOSIS AND TREATMENT IN PSYCHOANALYTIC PSYCHOTHERAPY

Matthias Elzer, Wolfgang Merkle, Hermann Schultz, and Alf Gerlach

The initial interview

Matthias Elzer

In general, psychotherapy is a conscious and intentional process of interaction that can be described as follows.

1. It aims to influence behavioural disorders and states of suffering in a patient.
2. It should take place with the consensus of the doctor and the patient.
3. It uses psychological means (of communication).
4. It has defined aims (i.e., reduction of symptoms, healing, ending of suffering).
5. It is based on teachable techniques founded on a theory of normal and pathological behaviour.
6. Its fundamental premise is patient-centred, not disease-centred. (Strotzka, in Hoffmann & Hochapfel, 1999, p. 405, translated for this edition).

Before we start any kind of psychotherapeutic treatment, a diagnostic phase to assess the patient's complaints and illness is necessary. The initial interview is a very important and interesting first step towards understanding the patient and clarifying the indication for treatment.

In his paper "On beginning the treatment" (1913c), Freud compared psychoanalytical treatment with the game of chess, where we can learn only the beginning and the end of the game by reading books. This means that we can learn how to begin a therapy by systematically using techniques. Nevertheless, Freud did not describe any technique for an initial interview; he used the first weeks as a test run for therapy.

Influenced by psychiatry, some concepts of a structured interview were developed, for example by Gill, Newman, and Redlich (1954) and Kernberg (1981). Psychoanalysis offered different forms of therapy (psychoanalysis, psychodynamic, or psychoanalytic psychotherapy, short-term therapy, group therapy) not only for patients with neuroses, but also for patients with severe personality disorders, and psychosomatic and psychotic disorders. The questions of indication and contraindication were raised when considering the most suitable form of psychoanalysis for each case.

The demands of field of psychiatry, as well as health insurance systems, necessitated the formulation of a diagnosis and an indication of the psychotherapy; insurance has been termed "the Latent Presence of Third Parties" (Thomä & Kächele, 1987, p. 169). Today, the potential, as well as the limitation, of the psychodynamic diagnostic is well covered in scientific literature, but the discussion still continues.

Generally, the initial interview is the first contact between the patient and the therapist. This meeting is a very special one: it is a unique situation of great intensity, which requires deep understanding and a professional way of dealing with the situation.

Patient and psychotherapist begin to develop a relationship that is equal but asymmetric: the patient is the suffering person (patient: from Latin *patire,* meaning suffering, enduring) because he or she is in a regressive psychic and/or somatic state, and, under the pressure of suffering, the patient opens up his inner world of unconscious conflicts and traumatic experience. The therapist is the expert and tries to help the patient to come closer to his inner world; through regression and the dynamics of transference, the therapist will become a part of this inner world and will offer him/herself as an object for transference.

During the initial interview, the patient unconsciously undergoes a therapeutic splitting of the ego, as in therapy: on the one hand, he knows that the therapist is a stranger and an expert; on the other hand, he is developing an unconscious emotional bond to the therapist in the same way as he did to another significant person in his life (offer of transference).

The therapist undergoes a splitting, too: first, he offers himself as an object for transference, and accepts this role; second, he steps out of this relationship structure and, together with the patient, looks at something; third, the unconscious meaning of symptoms or behaviour and the dynamics of transference and countertransference is brought into play. The therapist switches between a dyadic and triadic relationship structure.

The first contact

Usually, the first contact between patient and therapist happens before the initial interview: for example, the patient might contact the therapist by phone. The patient listens to the therapist's voice on the answerphone or voicemail system. Personal phone contacts occur if a patient calls the therapist at the time suggested on the recorded message. If the therapist offers to return the call in his recorded message, as he does not interrupt sessions with other patients, he must call the patient back if the patient so requests. The therapist should demonstrate that he is a reliable object. During the first contact, each will receive a first impression of the other. The phenomena of transference and countertransference begin to develop. Generally, the patient asks for an appointment, perhaps talks about his affliction, and asks for therapy.

It could be that the patient has been recommended by a colleague, a relative, or a friend. In such cases, the therapist receives first impressions and information through a third person, as he has not yet come into contact with the person concerned. Many psychoanalysts do not want to be given much information about the patient by the referring person, in order to keep the initial interview natural and unbiased.

In principle, the patient should come into contact with the therapist or the staff of the outpatient clinic personally, and not anonymously via a third person. For example: perhaps a wife believes her husband should contact a psychotherapist, but he does not think so.

Appointment for initial interview

It should be clear that, for the patient, the first contact is connected with shame and fear because he has to ask for help, expecting relief or healing. The request for an appointment for therapy is connected with the fear of being rejected by the therapist. The wish for an appointment is disappointed.

My personal way of dealing with appointments for initial interviews is as follows.

I offer an initial interview subject to two conditions:

1. As clarification or counselling: if a patient is asking for therapy and I have no spare capacity for this, I offer two or three sessions for a psycho-diagnostic clarification, or counselling with five to eight sessions. In this way, the patient knows that he cannot expect to get therapy in the near future. If there is an indication for psychotherapy, the patient has to look for a different therapist on my recommendation. If the patient wants clarification or counselling only, he is permitted an interview. If not, he has to look for another therapist. Frequently, the diagnostic interviews and a few more sessions are sufficient to reduce the suffering or to solve a current problem.
2. As implementation of the therapy: if I have the capacity for short-term or long-term psychotherapy or psychoanalysis and a patient is asking for therapy, I offer an initial interview and some more sessions to establish the indication and to become acquainted with the patient. For the patient, it is very important to check whether or not I am the right therapist for him.

The appointment for the initial interview also contains information about time, place, and duration. I suggest, "Please, come precisely at 11.00 a.m. You will not have to wait and we have 50 minutes for our conversation." Furthermore, I ask for a referral by the patient's general practitioner, and give information about the fees. I tell the patient that the time is reserved for him, and if he does not want to make use of the appointment, he has to cancel it at least two days in advance. I ask for the patient's phone number and sometimes for his address.

The first contact should explore the psychoanalytic attitude in connection with the increased dynamics of transference and countertransference on the one hand, and, on the other hand, the scene will be set by dealing clearly with reality.

Referring of the patient

The path to the patient's referral begins in the medical history. Sometimes, many other doctors have been involved with the patient's suffering.

During the first contact, the patient mentions the recommendation he has had from friends, relatives, other patients, or from another doctor. Sometimes, patients come having consulted the Yellow Pages or the Internet. If the patient does not mention how it has come about that he is seeking therapy, the therapist should ask explicitly.

Ethical aspects

By giving an appointment for an initial interview, the therapist takes responsibility for the diagnostic phase and has to apply his professional expertise. Between patient and therapist there is a contract only for the diagnostic phases; it is not a promise of, or an appointment for, therapy itself. The patient is free to discontinue contact during the diagnostic phase, but the therapist is not. After this diagnostic phase, the patient should have the next procedure, should it be deemed necessary, explained to him.

How to deal with the first interview

We can be sure that most patients do not know how a psychotherapist works, or what is going on during the initial interview. The patient wants to communicate his complaints or suffering and wants treatment, advice, and a prescription.

The therapist generously satisfies the first expectation: he listens actively to the patient patiently and at length. In comparison, international studies about general practitioners show that patients, when talking about their complaints, will generally be interrupted by the doctor after eighteen to twenty-six seconds.

The second expectation of the patient will be frustrated by the therapist: he does not provide suggestions, gives no advice, no indication of what is wrong or what is right; most of all, he listens and tries to understand the patient in a psychodynamic way.

The patient enters the consulting room. Patient and therapist shake hands and introduce themselves by name. The first visual and tactile contact is intense; both are receiving a great deal of non-verbal information about each other: Feelings of interest, curiosity, surprise, sympathy, antipathy, disappointment, and fear will be activated. In particular, the contact of hands can express much: perhaps the therapist is offered a cold, limp hand (like a wet fish), or the dynamic patient tries to grasp the therapist's hand in a contra-phobic way (like a bone crusher)—two extreme examples.

After introductions, the patient should be led into the consulting room and possibly shown where he can leave his coat. The therapist points out the armchairs standing in a special arrangement; the patient should choose which one he prefers. The chairs should be comfortable and similar. Patient and therapist are equal partners in an asymmetric conversation. If the therapist is sitting in a comfortable, executive-type chair behind his desk and computer and the patient is sitting in a simple chair in front of the table opposite to him, the setting poses a big problem for the therapist.

The therapist opens the interview with some information: "For our conversation we will have 50 minutes." This information is important for the patient: he has a lot of time to talk, but the time is limited, too. The therapist can announce the end of the interview by reminding him of the time. After this information has been imparted, the therapist asks the initial question: "Why have you come to see me?" (summarised in Table 7.1).

Table 7.1. The initial interview.

The therapist opens the interview by saying:
1. "For our conversation we will have 50 minutes."
2. "Why have you come to see me?"

Above all, this question is the stimulus for the patient to talk about his suffering and problems, about the reason for his coming, and his expectations and hope for help. The therapist should keep the first sentences in his mind (in the patient's own words) and should write them down after the session. At the start of an initial interview, the patient is suffering high emotional pressure, so that he expresses his central problem unconsciously in his own way. This situation is unique and not repeatable.

The initial interview is not an interview conducted in the way a journalist would conduct one. The therapist may have a lot of questions, but "interview" in this case means that the patient is talking and the therapist is listening. Using the "active listening" technique, the therapist offers his attention in a kind way and builds an atmosphere of trust, so that the patient can overcome his fears, open his mind, and show his feelings. The silence and attentiveness of the therapist stimulates the patient to reveal more of himself: generally, silence motivates others to talk. If the patient stops speaking and keeps silent, the therapist should wait, listen to the silence, and tolerate it for a while. The passive patient stimulates the inexperienced young therapist to fill the silence with questions. Balint (1965, p. 1178) said, ". . . he who asks questions will get answers, but not much else".

If the kind of suffering and the duration of it are known to the therapist, it is important to hear the patient's ideas about the symptoms and the beginning of the suffering. For example, the therapist says to his patient, "You told me the panic attacks started with the birth of your son. Maybe the fact that you are a father now has stimulated something in your mind. Do you have any ideas about what it could be?"

Besides the history of the symptoms and other diseases, the story of the patient's life is very important for the psychodynamic understanding of the patient. This part of the interview can be introduced in the following way: "Please tell me something about your childhood and your family. How did you grow up?"

The therapist should obtain an overview of the patient's biography from early childhood to the current situation. Covering both aspects (actual suffering and biography) will generally require about 50 minutes of the initial interview. Through the biographical details that have come to light, the therapist can recognise some connections to the actual complaint, so he can formulate an interpretation. The interpretation tries to bring unconscious meaning to consciousness. During this experience, the patient is sometimes touched, and emotions like fear, pain, shame, grief, and rage, to mention but a few, can be aroused.

There are three main types of interventions: clarification, confrontation, and interpretation of unconscious material. We can separate interpretation into two subtypes: the interpretation of biographical (psychogenetic) material and the interpretation of the actual dynamics of transference and countertransference between patient and therapist. Sometimes, the therapist can connect the interpretation of psychogenetic material and the actual transference, which is very effective.

The end of the interview should be announced some minutes before: "We have to end our talk in a few minutes." The therapist should then offer a second interview. He and the patient should fix the next appointment to take place, for example, in one or two weeks' time.

In my opinion, the initial interview consists of two appointments. Very often, the first meeting reveals some material and opens up old wounds, and this process needs to continue.

After the patient has left the consulting room, the therapist should take notes. There will be more on this topic later.

Second interview

The second interview can be introduced by the therapist like this: "Today we have 50 minutes again. Maybe you have been thinking about the topic of our last meeting?" (Table 7.2).

Generally, the patient accepts this invitation and talks about the topic of the first interview, very often about the test interpretation of the therapist. The therapist can see if the psychoanalytical point of view was useful to the patient and assess his ability for introspection.

Sometimes, the patient brings up more material, perhaps a memory of something, a new experience, sometimes a dream or a parapraxis (slip), for example.

The first and second interviews belong together and form the initial interview, which has a diagnostic and therapeutic function. The patient should recognise some new aspects, insights, and understanding of his inner world, conflicts, and motives.

The patient and the therapist come into contact in a very special, intense relationship. It is a therapeutic relationship. This diagnostic stage is a complete unit and if there is no possibility of continuing the therapy, the patient and the therapist have to separate.

If the diagnostic stages are not clearly structured and run for many sessions, the patient and the therapist slide into a kind of therapeutic process and the separation is difficult.

Scenic information from the patient

The report of the patient can be divided into three levels (Argelander, 1970): the objective, the subjective, and the scenic, or situational, information (Table 7.3).

Objective information is mostly biographical data. For example, the patient is a man and has six brothers and sisters. Thus, the objective level is quite clear.

Table 7.2. How the therapist begins the second interview.

Inital question of the therapist: for example, "Today we have 50 minutes again. Maybe you have been thinking about the topic of our last meeting?"

Table 7.3. Three levels of information (Argelander, 1970).

1. Objective	Unbiased, verifiable
2. Subjective	Meaning of the patient
3. Scenic/situational	Non-verbal, gesture, acting, behaviour

Subjective information is what the patient means about the objective information. For example, "I'm a man, but I feel like a woman." Or, "I was hungry all the time and had the feeling I had to fight my brothers and sisters for my food." Or, "It was wonderful; I was never alone." The subjective level of information represents the exclusive understanding of the patient. The information induces a lot of fantasies and interpretations in the therapist's mind, of course, but the therapist should come into contact with the patient's subjective understanding. He can use his own understanding of this information in his own transference and the countertransference of the patient in a second step.

Scenic information is the non-verbal information imparted by the patient through gesture, facial expressions, and behaviour during the interview situation.

The scenic, or situational, level of information has to be explained: very often, when the patient comes in contact with the therapist, he unconsciously presents his central problem as if he were on stage. He acts out his problem.

For example: a young patient was transferred by the department of surgery to the department of psychosomatics. The patient enters my room on two crutches and throws himself down in my analyst's chair, puts his legs on my stool, pointing his crutches like two machine guns at me. He starts to rail about the doctors, saying he has a problem with his leg, not with his brain. I could, at this stage, write him off as being rather crazy. Yet, as I listen to the patient, I perceive his aggressive and provocative message with some amusement. Because I do not react, he talks about the accident he had on a stolen motorbike, the row with the policemen, the row with his boss, and the row with the doctors. Congenially, I suggest, "Oh, and now you come into my room, plop down in my chair, and rail about the stupid doctors, among others. It seems you are eager to get into a row with me, too. I think you have a need for a row."

At first, the patient looks very angry and ignores my intervention. As he continues his story, I get the information I need: he has always struggled against the authority figures in his life ("They are all fucking fools"). He describes an old conflict with his father ("the boss of the fucking fools") and its origin. What I hear is that the patient is always criticised by his father, and it seems that what he wants is to obtain the acknowledgement and love of his father, but, instead, he manages to get punishment rather than respect and love (in German, "Hiebe statt Liebe"; in English, "beatings instead of love"). Unconsciously, he tries to get the attention of other figures of authority, such as his boss, the police, or the doctors, and to fight with them, instead of with his father. My interpretation: "The result is that you behave like a fool who makes a lot of trouble. You are trying to get the attention of your father, but instead, while dealing with others, like policemen and doctors, you make them responsible for your troubles."

Initial interviews and transference and countertransference

The scenic information is a kind of acting-out with high content, which comes about through the minimal situation structure of the interview. The therapist can become an object of transference, which is connected with the patient's central conflict or trauma. As well as the transference, the therapist should pay attention to his own fantasies, ideas, and feelings. He should try to understand his countertransference by the contact he has with the patient in this concrete situation.

I compare the phenomenon of countertransference with the acoustic phenomenon of resonance in physics: a status of activity of an instrument will be transferred to another, both instruments sound in the same way.

By asking the following question: "How does the patient deal with me?", or "Which person in the patient's life should I be at this moment?", his transference can be better understood.

To uncover the therapist's countertransference, ask this question: "What kind of feelings and fantasies does the patient produce in me?"

For example: A thirty-year-old man tells me that he has not been able to have long-term relationships with women, because they generally leave him, although he tries his best not to make any mistakes. While I listen to him relate his problem haltingly, a feeling of being dead tired overcomes me, and I cannot suppress a yawn. This is very embarrassing for me, so I explain, "I'm awfully sorry for yawning. I think I had enough sleep last night so this tiredness must be the result of the situation between the two of us here." The patient answers, "Don't worry, this often happens to me. One girlfriend once said I have the same effect a sleeping pill would have on her." First we laughed about this aspect, but, while listening, I became aware that the patient was controlling and hypnotising me by the way he talked. I remembered the film *The Jungle Book* and the snake, Kaa. Yawning is a physiological reaction against falling asleep. I interpreted that he unconsciously tries to lull as well as to dominate other human beings. There might be some danger in this. The patient did not react and his speech continued to meander along like a murmuring stream.

In the second interview, the patient expressed his sexual fantasies, which were connected with the fact that he would like to tie up a woman to have sex with her. His perversion made him suffer, but he never carried out his wishes. Because of his shyness, he used a style of communication that, in effect, allowed him to creep up on unware victims and hypnotise them.

Diagnosis, indication, and contraindication

From a technical point of view, the first and second interviews contribute to assessing the patient's suffering as a temporary problem, or an illness, and to formulating a diagnosis and clearly defining the indication or contraindication for a therapeutic treatment.

During the years of our training course in Shanghai, we used an assessment list made up of questions that should be formulated and answered by the therapist. This list is not meant as a questionnaire for the patient. The therapist should obtain the answers by listening and talking to the patient, being flexible in his technique. None the less, it is often not possible to find an answer to every question after only two sessions.

A note about the use of a questionnaire: many colleagues and clinics use questionnaires for different aspects, such as lists of symptoms and sufferings as well as of the biography or family history. These questionnaires are quite informative, but they have to be completed during the sessions; if not, they form an information gap and might lead to misunderstandings.

Sometimes, what one does not know is interesting. For example, after many sessions, a female patient mentioned a younger brother. I was very surprised, as I did not know of his existence, although I had asked the patient about siblings while researching the family history. The unconscious meaning of the suppression of her brother's existence was clear: envy and rivalry.

Assessment for psychoanalytic psychotherapy

The word "assessment" comes from the Latin word *assidere*, and means: to sit beside somebody. Assessment means not to explore and to "squeeze out" the patient through questions; this is the job of a psychiatrist. Assessment means to be aware of the patient with all one's senses, consciously and unconsciously.

Check list for assessment

The psychodynamic assessment is carried out using a standardised pattern: the therapist starts the interview with some central questions and is mostly passive. He listens to the patient and he listens to his own ideas; he should try to answer the following questions by listening and additional questions (Table 7.4).

Documentation of the diagnostic interviews

Figure 7.1 is a reproduction of a documentation sheet which I have been using in my practice for many years. I try to fill in the findings directly after the initial interview or some hours later. On a second and third page, I write down the interview in my own words.

Indication and contraindication for psychoanalytic psychotherapy

The psychoanalytical standard method leads to a "selective indication" (Thomä & Kächele, 1987, p.4); the patient has to accept the condition of psychoanalysis. The modified psychoanalytical techniques (like psychoanalytic psychotherapy) offer an "adaptive indication"; they adapt to the need of the patient: age, kind of disorder, aims, etc.

Table 7.4. Check list for assessment.

1. Who referred or recommended the patient?
2. What are the sufferings and the symptoms of the patient? (Note patient's words.)
3. Does the patient formulate an aim for the interview and for a later psychotherapy?
4. Why has the patient shown up now? (Not earlier or later.)
5. What happened, when the symptoms started? Are there any precipitating events?
6. Does the patient have any ideas about the causes of his/her suffering?
7. Does the patient have the ability for insight?
8. Is he/she motivated to learn something about his/her inner world and conflicts?
9. What is the therapist's first spontaneous impression (countertransference)?
10. What is the spontaneous offer of transference?
11. What are the psychological findings? (cognition, affects)
12. Does the therapist have any ideas about the defence mechanism?
13. Can the therapist define an intrapsychic conflict or trauma?
14. Can the therapist formulate a diagnosis (symptomatically and structurally)?
15. What about the prognosis? Is therapy indicated to help the patient?

Documentation Sheet of Initial Interviews:
Prof.Dr. med. Matthias Elzer (Germany, 2010)

Date of intial interview ____ Patient's code (sex-birthday) ____ Name of psychotherapist ____

Patient's age:

Patient's complaints/ symptoms (in patients own words):

First manifestation of the complaints/ symptoms. (when, which biographical situation?)

Referral mode: by the patient himself ☐ from phone book ☐ from Internet ☐ recommended ☐ by ____

Referred by professionals ☐ Dr. ____ Diagnosis ____

Patient's wish: screening of indication ☐ counselling ☐ crisis intervention ☐ short-term psychotherapy ☐ psychodynamic psychotherapy ☐ psychoanalysis ☐ counselling (couple/family) ☐ group psychotherapy ☐ psychiatric threatment ☐ no explicit wish mentioned ☐

Initial offer of transference: "scenic behaviour":

Spontaneous countertransference:

Results of mental status: (cognition, emotions, communication, suicidal ideas)

Main defence mechanism:

Symptomatical diagnosis ICD 10: ____

Structural diagnosis:

Level of neurotic main conflict: pre-Oedipal ☐ Oedipal ☐ :

Traumatic disorder? ☐:

Differential diagnosis: Diagnosis unsure: ☐

Former diseases of the body ☐ Which?
Operation ☐ accidents ☐ trauma of the body ☐ Which?
Actual somatic diseases ☐ Which?

Social situation: single ☐ married ☐ in partnership ☐ separated ☐ divorced ☐ widowed ☐
Living situation: together with parents ☐ alone ☐ with partner ☐ others: ____ Children: son ____ (Age) daughter ____ (Age)

Level of education: school, professional, academical:
Profession, actually working as:

Former treatment (psychotherapy = pt):
Outpatient: psychiatrist ☐ short-term pt ☐ psychodynamic pt ☐ psychoanalysis ☐ behavior therapy ☐ other pt ☐ TCM ☐ When?

Inpatient: psychiatric hospital ☐ psychosomatic hospital ☐ TCM hospital ☐ When?

Has the patient used psychopharmacological medication in the past? ☐ Which?
Does the patient use psychopharmacological medication now? ☐ Which?

Parents: Age, diseases, death, when?

Brothers: ____ Sisters: ____
Distance of years to the patient

Next page >

Number of diagnostic, probationary sessions: ____ Ended on: ____ Offer/Agreement for psychotherapy yes ☐ no ☐

If recommendation: Letter/feedback to referring Dr. ☐ ____

Process of interviews and other probationary *sessions on page 2 ff*

Figure 7.1. Example of documentation form used by M. Elzer for the initial interview.

The decision about indication or contra-indication for therapy depends on two aspects: the diagnosis (symptomatically and structurally) and the patient. In others words, the indication has an objective and a subjective aspect.

An example. A patient is suffering from neurotic depression (*ICD-10* dysthymia); this is an objective indication for psychoanalysis or psychoanalytic psychotherapy. But this patient only wants to get help. He does not want a deeper understanding of his conflicts and the unconscious meaning of the symptoms. He shows no motivation and no desire for insight. "I don't want to know" is an expression of anxiety and resistance.

The patient can see how the therapist is dealing with the significance of the material during the initial interview. The therapist might win the patient over to this method of understanding, but the therapist should not try to persuade the patient or sell the therapy to him. For this patient, there is no indication for a psychodynamic therapy. Possibly, a supportive therapy or a behaviour therapy might be indicated. The objective indication is present, but not the subjective indication.

Another patient wants to know something about himself, therefore the subjective indication exists. However, the therapist cannot see any relevant conflict or suffering and cannot formulate a diagnosis. There is no objective indication here. The motivation of intellectual curiosity is not sufficient for a long-term psychotherapy, but is an indication for counselling.

The scientific discussion about indication is a lot more widespread in psychoanalysis than in psychodynamic psychotherapy. The indication for psychoanalysis is rather strict, because this method is more intensive than psychotherapy. The aim of psychoanalysis is to change the psychical structure of the patient by using the regression of the patient and the dynamics of transference and countertransference. Thomä and Kächele describe the indication for psychoanalysis in this way: "The patient has to be sick enough to need it and healthy enough to stand it" (1987).

This is not the aim of psychoanalytic psychotherapy. The aim is to understand the actual conflicts against the background of the biography using the dynamics of transference and countertransference. The psychic structure of the patient cannot generally be changed by psychoanalytic psychotherapy . The face-to-face-setting makes it more difficult to use the fundamental rule of association of the couch–chair setting. The regression of the patient is not that intense.

The indication for psychoanalytic psychotherapy is broader than that of psychoanalysis.

The therapist should reflect on his own motivation if he offers a therapy after the diagnostic phase. Motivation is related to the dynamics of transference and countertransference, but also to the personality and structure of the therapist. Here are some possible motives: he offers therapy because he is in need of money; he has the fantasy of helping and rescuing the patient from his unfortunate life; he needs the patient for his own narcissistic satisfaction; he wants to show his colleagues that he is a successful therapist, etc. These kinds of motives for offering psychotherapy have to be worked through in self-experience.

Operationalised psychodynamic diagnosis (OPD)

Operationalised Psychodynamic Diagnosis (*OPD*) is a diagnostic manual, which was developed by psychoanalysts from Germany and other European countries during the past twenty years.

Those involved included M. Cierpka, University of Heidelberg, S. O. Hoffmann, University of Mainz, J. Kuechenhoff, University of Basel, G. Schuessler, University of Innsbruck and others. The first edition was published in 1996, the second in 2006 (*OPD-2*).

OPD functions as a supplement to the *ICD-10* and *DSM-IV* and tries to offer a diagnostic instrument by looking at scientific criteria (objectivity, reliability, validity) from a psychoanalytical point of view. It is also an instrument for describing and evaluating the therapeutic process and outcome. The *OPD* consists of five axes, as shown in Table 7.5.

The *OPD* manual offers questionnaires for every axis, with which the therapist can assess the mental state of the patient during the process of therapy (*OPD*, 2008).

Table 7.5. The five axes of *OPD*.

Axis	What the axis examines
Axis I	Experience of illness and prerequisities for treatment, i.e., severity of somatic and mental illness, patient's subjective suffering, motivation for therapy
Axis II	Interpersonal relations, i.e., patient's relations to others and others to patient; therapeutic relation as transference and countertransference
Axis III	Conflicts 1. Dependence *vs.* autonomy 2. Submission *vs.* control 3. Desire for care *vs.* autarchy 4. Conflicts of self-value 5. Guilt conflicts 6. Oedipal sexual conflicts 7. Identity conflicts 8. Limited perception of conflicts and feelings
Axis IV	Structure 1. Self-perception 2. Self-regulation 3. Defence 4. Object perception 5. Communication 6. Bonding
Axis V	Syndromal (according to Chapter V(F) of *ICD-10*), i.e., psychic and psychosomatic disorders

The therapeutic contract of psychotherapy

Wolfgang Merkle

The initial interview is of both diagnostic and therapeutic importance. At the end of the interview, we need to draw the therapeutic conclusions.

If we decide on therapy, very important rules must be established for the further course of the therapeutic situation. It is important to lay down these rules at the beginning.

In the transition from initial interview to therapy, it is important to leave as much room as possible for flexibility and to create an atmosphere of freedom that provides space for hope. At the same time, sound conditions for the work must be established, one of which is the framework. The patient should have an approximate idea of the duration of the therapeutic process suggested, whether it is a short-term psychotherapy (some weeks), a psychoanalytically based therapy (several months to years), or a psychoanalytic therapy (years).

At the beginning, the analyst must always take into consideration that the patient is at liberty to interrupt or terminate the treatment at any time.

If the therapy needs more than one hour per week, it is better to spread them over the week: for example, one hour at the beginning of the week, the other at the end.

You must discuss the financial situation with the patient: he should be informed of the regulations covering psychoanalysis, including those pertaining to public and private health insurance.

You should define and possibly negotiate an adequate fee per hour that you will charge him. It is also important to make clear in advance what will happen if the patient does not keep the arranged appointment, in order to limit acting out. Should he have to pay a fee for this, or would it depend on how much prior notice he gives of his absence?

If you have intense psychoanalytic work to do, it is advisable to explain to the patient that it would not be beneficial to have long breaks during the therapeutic process. Therefore, he should, if possible, arrange his holidays to coincide with yours.

The patient should know how to contact you in an emergency outside working hours. For example, he should know at what times he can call you or leave messages.

The working alliance

This has been discussed in previous chapters. In the following section, I will concretise the meaning of working alliance during treatment by means of questions. How do patient and therapist work during the therapeutic relationship?

There are many differences between working in psychoanalysis (couch–chair setting, more than one session per week) and in psychodynamic psychotherapy (chair–chair setting, one session per week), but they also have many theoretical and technical aspects in common.

How does the patient work?

Generally, the patient does not know how he or she should "work" during therapy. At the start of therapy, the therapist should provide information about the setting and the way of working together in psychoanalytical psychotherapy.

Fundamental rule

In the psychoanalytic setting, we invite the patient to tell us everything that comes to mind, whether it is important or unimportant, decent or indecent. He should let his associations come freely into contact with the unconscious meanings of his thoughts or behaviour.

The definition of the association rule that is most frequently communicated to patients seems to be: "Say what is in your mind". The formalities of the treatment, such as the fixed arrangements regarding payment, appointments, and holidays, none of which arouse particularly pleasurable feelings in most people, are often discussed in the same session and almost in the same breath as the fundamental rule. The various aspects of the agreement become so closely associated that the fundamental rule is very often seen, mistakenly, as almost equivalent to a contract, like the arrangements concerning fees and the procedure to be followed in the event of interruptions and missed sessions. The patient's already existing anxieties are strengthened by the unaccustomed prospect of having to disclose his best-kept secrets to a stranger. While being informed about the fundamental rule, many patients think of something that they decide to keep to themselves, which, if we are lucky, we hear about later.

Initially, at any rate, not much remains of the pleasure of telling stories. Freud attempted to clarify why the patient cannot be allowed to make an exception and keep a secret by means of an anecdote: if an extraterritorial refuge in St. Stephan's Church had been created for the tramps of Vienna, that is exactly where they would have stayed (Freud, 1916–1917, p. 288).

Of course, you must first win the patient's confidence before you can expect him to reveal all his shameful secrets.

There are many methods of self-assertion. Analytic experience teaches us that many patients keep some secrets for a long time, or even forever.

What sense is there in obliging a patient to be honest and open if, at the same time, one knows that complete honesty is prevented by inner resistances? The demand for absolute honesty augments the patient's bad conscience and his unconscious feelings of guilt, leading to reactions that have a negative effect on the therapy. Freud seems to have had similar experiences: "How small is the effect of such agreements as one makes with the patient in laying down the fundamental rule is regularly demonstrated" (1913c, p. 135).

This can lead from the strict obligation of "you *must* say everything" to the inner freedom of "you *may* say everything".

Transference

Transferences arise in all human relationships, and this fact gives Freud's discovery wide significance. Initially, however, he based his definition of transference on observations made in the course of therapy:

> They are new editions or facsimiles of the impulses and fantasies which are aroused and made conscious during the progress of the analysis; but they have this peculiarity, which is characteristic for their species, that they replace some earlier person by the person of the therapist. To put it another way: a whole series of psychological experiences are revived, not as belonging to the past, but as applying to the person of the therapist at the present moment. Some of these transferences have a content which doesn't differ from that of their model. These then to keep to the same metaphor are merely new impressions or reprints. Others are more ingeniously constructed: by cleverly taking advantage of some real peculiarity in the therapist's person or circumstances and attaching themselves to that. (Freud, 1905e, p. 116)

Later, however, he generalised:

> Transference arises spontaneously in all human relationships just as it does between the patient and the physician. It is everywhere the true vehicle of therapeutic influence, and the less its presence is suspected, the more powerfully it operates. So psychoanalysis does not create it, but merely reveals it to consciousness and gains control of it in order to guide psychical processes towards the desired goal. (Freud, 1910a, p. 51)

Transference is, thus, a generic term in both senses of the word: first, since a person's past experiences have a fundamental and persistent influence on his present life, transference is universal in Homo sapiens. Second, the concept embraces numerous typical phenomena that are expressed uniquely in each one of us. Special forms of transference are found in psychoanalysis. Transference phenomena, including resistance, are dependent on the analytic situation and its shaping by the analyst, starting with the appearance of his office and continuing with his behaviour, his sex, his countertransference, his personal equation, his theory, his image of man, etc.

Experience has taught us that it is not easy to grasp how the view of transference shifted from its being the major obstacle to treatment to the most powerful aid. Of course, the bewildering multiplicity of transference and resistance phenomena had not yet been recognised at the time of the original discovery.

Thus, the transference activates conflicts in the relationship, any obstacle to this being termed transference resistance, though, more accurately, one should speak of resistance against transference. The psychoanalyst has the greatest difficulty in mastering these transference phenomena, but we must not forget "that it is precisely they that do us the inestimable service of making the patient's hidden and forgotten erotic impulses immediate and manifest. For when all is said and done, it is impossible to destroy anyone in absentia or in effigy". With these famous words, Freud (1912b, p. 108) characterised the here-and-now actuality of transference, which is convincing because of its immediacy and authenticity: nothing can be dealt with successfully "in absentia", that is, by talking about the past, or "in effigy", by symbolic indirect representation.

Transference and transference neurosis

The development of transference, whether positive or negative, is not only opposed step by step by the most varied forms of resistance, but the transference can itself become resistance if there is an imbalance between the repetition in present experience and the patient's ability or willingness to replace the transferences with memories or, at least, to relativise them.

Theoretical postulates have contributed to the conceptualisation of the transference neurosis in the ideal psychoanalytic process as something apparently independent of the participating observer: it develops in the reflection of images by the analyst, who is, ideally, free of all countertransference blind spots.

Resistance

The patient seeking help comes to realise, just like his therapist, that the process of change itself is unsettling because the balance that the patient has attained, even at the cost of serious restrictions of his internal and external freedom of movement, guarantees a certain degree of security and stability. On the basis of this balance, events are unconsciously expected and imagined, even though they might be unpleasant in nature. Although the patient consciously desires a change, a self-perpetuating circle is created, maintained, and reinforced because the balance, however pathological its consequences may be, contributes decisively towards reducing anxiety and insecurity. The many forms that resistance takes have the function of maintaining the balance that has been achieved. This reveals different aspects of resistance, as listed below.

1. Resistance is related to the change that is consciously desired but unconsciously feared.
2. The observation of resistance is tied to the therapeutic relationship, whereas parapraxes and other unconsciously motivated phenomena can also be observed outside therapy. Resistance is part of the therapeutic process.
3. Since the continuation of the analytic work can be disturbed in a multitude of ways, there are no forms of behaviour that cannot be employed as resistance once they have attained a certain strength. The co-operation between therapist and patient suffers if the resistance surpasses a certain level of intensity, which can be detected in a wide range of phenomena. An increase in transference to the level of blind infatuation can become resistance in the same way as excessive reporting of dreams or overly rational reflection on them does.
4. Thus, qualitative and quantitative criteria are used in the evaluation of resistance. For example, positive and negative transference become resistance if they reach an intensity that inhibits or prohibits reflective co-operation.

There are some crude forms of resistance, such as arriving late, missing sessions, talking too much or not at all, automatically rejecting or misunderstanding all the analyst's utterances, playing ignorant, constantly being absent-minded, falling asleep, and, finally, terminating the treatment prematurely.

Since resistance to the psychoanalytic process is observed as transference resistance, this form of resistance has always been the centre of attention.

The relationship between transference and resistance (in the concept of transference resistance) can be described schematically as follows. After overcoming the resistance to transference becoming conscious, therapy, in Freud's theory, is based on mild, unobjectionable transference, which thus becomes desirable and the analyst's most powerful tool. Positive transference in the sense of a relationship *sui generis* forms the foundation of therapy.

This working relationship, as we would call it today, is endangered if positive transference is intensified and if polarisations—transference love or negative (aggressive) transference—are created. Transference, thus, again becomes resistance if the patient's attitude to the analyst is erotised (transference love) or turns into hate (negative transference). According to Freud, these two forms of transference become resistance if they prevent remembering.

Finally, in the resistance to the resolution of transference, we find a third aspect. United in the concept of transference resistance are resistance to transference becoming conscious, resistance in the form of transference love or negative transference, and resistance to the resolution of transference.

Acting out

The general issue of action in psychoanalysis and the generally negative appraisal of acting out are good indications that it is easier for us to deal with the word than with the action. Despite the efforts of some psychoanalysts to provide an adequate treatment for acting out from, for example, the points of view of developmental psychology and psychodynamics, the term is still used to refer to forms of behaviour which are undesirable and may even endanger the analysis. Specific phenomena in the psychoanalytic situation have made this concept necessary and given it its negative image.

Freud says,

> If we confine ourselves to this second type in order to bring out the difference, we may say that the patient does not remember anything of what he has forgotten and repressed, but acts it out. He reproduces it not as a memory but as action: he repeats it, without, of course, knowing that he is repeating it. (1914g, p. 150)

He also said, "The patient . . . acts it out before us, as it were, instead of reporting it to us" (1940a, p. 176).

Acting out is not only related to remembering and repeating, but also has meanings and functions that make a purely technical classification and differentiation appear insufficient. Laplanche and Pontalis (1973, p. 6) have, therefore, recommended that the psychoanalytic theories of action and communication be subjected to a reconsideration that would have to include the following topics: affective and impulsive abreactions and controls; blind acting out and goal-directed action; motor discharge and highly organised acts such as play and scenic representation; structuring of relationships; creative achievement, and other ways of resolving tensions and conflicts by means of differentiated and complex courses of movement and action; acting out as the result and resolution of defence; and adaptation potentials in the repertoire of an individual in relationship to his environment.

There is a large number of unconscious conditions which might increase the tendency to acting out. They include early traumas with a deficient capacity for the formation of symbols, since memory and remembering are connected with the acquisition of word symbols, which themselves lead to a state in which the memory apparatus has a useful structure. Disturbances of the sense of reality, visual sensibilities, and fixations at the level of the "magic of action" are different kinds of conditions that might emphasise action language in contrast to verbal language. At the same time, fantasies and action are possible preverbal means of problem solving and communication.

Blos (1963) described acting out as a common and appropriate solution for the problems of separation in adolescence. The ego impoverishment resulting from the withdrawal of libido from the important (parental) objects is compensated by overcathexis of the external world or of the possibilities for interacting with it (which is, naturally, a source of important new experiences). In our opinion, this experience also throws light on the role that acting out plays during separation from loved ones as well as in the stages of development and the consequent separation from the past.

It is essential for analysts to evaluate their competence realistically and to retain a feeling of security in the treatment situation. One aspect of this is that the analyst needs to maintain an overview of what is happening in the analysis by limiting the number of variables and possibilities for expression. This is a precondition for the treatment to which a patient is entitled.

Whether the analyst allows acting out, how he works with it in the analytic situation, and how he makes new solutions possible probably depend to a large degree on the capacity and flexibility that the analyst demonstrates in confronting and reviewing the present analytic situation, and not only the psychogenesis. In other words, they depend on his ability to be receptive for phenomena in the current encounter (forms of behaviour, ideas, and sensations) which are usually more difficult to thematise in the here-and-now than as repetitions from the past. By following this principle of paying attention to current dynamic and intensive affects and ideas, it may be possible to recognise the past better and, thus, to make the present "more present", that is freer of the past. Most patients with traumatisation and sexual abuse tend to act out, because they can only show it in this way. Also, many patients who were disturbed early in their development act out because they do not have enough capacity to symbolise.

How does the therapist work?

Rule of abstinence

There are two aspects to abstinence in psychoanalysis: as a rule, it aims to impose specific limitations on the patient; as a recommendation of analytic neutrality, it aims to place restrictions on the therapist. Laplanche and Pontalis (1973) define the principle of abstinence as the "rule according to which the analytic treatment should be organized so as to ensure that the patient finds as few substitutive satisfactions for his symptoms as possible" (p. 2). Neutrality is "one of the defining characteristics of the attitude of the analyst during the treatment" (p. 271). Substantively, the two aspects belong together; they are based, on the one hand, on the characteristics of all professional relationships and, on the other, on the peculiarities of the analytic situation. Cremerius (1984) has described the destiny of the concept and rule of abstinence in striking terms. He points out that Freud's first resort to this rule was necessitated specifically by the problems Freud encountered in treating women suffering from hysteria. Their desire for concrete love relationships threatened the professional relationship. First of all, then, the commandment of abstinence has the function of a "game rule" to ensure the continuation of the analysis: "The love-relationship in fact destroys the patient's susceptibility to influence from analytic treatment" (Freud, 1915a, p. 166).

However, the rule of abstinence derives its greatest significance from Freud's attempt to replace normative argumentation with one based on his method. While medical ethics would urge strict rejection of the patients' feelings of love, Freud recommends that their development should not be disturbed, but, rather, that they should be used in order to reach and better analyse the impulses that arise from the suppressed wish. So, it was not only for reasons of medical ethics, but also for methodological reasons that he stated that erotic wishes should not be satisfied.

We have already explained that derivation of rules from theory is utopian and often harmful, because the question of the suitability of the rules is relegated to the background. The rule of abstinence is a particularly good example, having had clearly unfavourable effects on the development of psychoanalytic technique. Cremerius (1984) points out that the specific features of the treatment of hysteria were, without justification, incorporated into the treatment of other forms of neurosis. Wishes that are quite characteristic of resistance in women suffering from hysteria can have completely different meanings in obsessives, phobics, and anxiety neurotics. The analyst's concern that a patient might find secret substitutive gratification in the transference leads to a defensive approach. The function of the rule of abstinence is no longer to produce the potential for favourable tension and, thus, actuate development, but, rather, to prevent developments which are viewed with apprehension. The conception that frustration is necessary for the constitution of the motive force for change has become more than questionable and has, above all, distracted attention from the unfavourable consequences that exaggerated neutrality on the part of the analyst has on the therapeutic process.

Arguments derived from instinct theory are not necessary to justify the demand for neutrality on the part of the analyst, as it can also be substantiated methodologically. The call for neutrality refers to various areas: with regard to work on the material offered by the patient, the analyst should not pursue his own advantage; with regard to therapeutic ambition, the analyst should renounce suggestive techniques; with regard to the problem of goals, the analyst should not pursue his own values; and, finally, with regard to the problem of countertransference, the analyst should reject any secret satisfaction of his own instinctual wishes.

The experience that sometimes more and sometimes less gratification had to be allowed moved Freud to take a flexible attitude toward the rule of abstinence. We also have nothing against pragmatic compromises, as long as they are compatible with medical ethics and can be vindicated methodologically. We would like to go a step further, and believe that nowadays psychoanalysts can, for fundamental reasons, face the rule of abstinence with greater assurance.

As long as approval and gratification are not misunderstood as sexual stimuli, the analyst's anxiety that the slightest concession could lead to the wrong path is unfounded. The liberation from the chains of the rule of abstinence can be seen most clearly in Kohut's technique of narcissistic gratification. In view of our strong doubt about the existence of an independent narcissism, we would assume that narcissistic gratification might have an oedipal connotation, so that it will definitely have a bearing on libidinal transference.

Psychodynamic listening: "the third ear"

Psychoanalysis is, in this sense, not so much a heart-to-heart talk as a drive-to-drive talk, an inaudible but highly expressive dialogue. The psychoanalyst has to learn how one mind speaks to another beyond words and in silence. He must learn to listen "with the third ear". It is not true that you have to shout to make yourself understood. When you wish to be heard, you whisper (Reik, 1949, p. 144).

One of the peculiarities of this third ear is that it works two ways. It can catch what other people do not say, but only feel and think, and it can also be turned inward. It can hear voices from within the self that are otherwise not audible because they are drowned out by the noise of our conscious thought process (Reik, 1949, pp. 146–147).

Freud defines the particular kind of attention as *gleichschwebend*. This word is difficult to translate: together with its connotation of equal distribution, it also has the meaning of revolving or circling. The closest I can come to the German is "free floating". Another possibility, which emphasises the psychological balance rather than the motion, would be "poised attention".

Two factors induced Freud to recommend such free-floating attention: it saves tension, which, after all, cannot be maintained for hours, and avoids the dangers that threaten in the case of deliberate attention directed toward a particular aim. If we strain our attention to a certain point, if we begin to select from among the data offered and seize upon one particular fragment, then, Freud warns us, we follow our own expectations or inclinations. The danger naturally arises that we may never find anything but that which we are prepared to find. If we follow our inclinations, we are sure to falsify the possible perception. The rule that we must note everything equally is the necessary counterpart to the demand we make upon the patient to tell everything that occurs to him without criticism or selection (Reik, 1949, pp. 157–158).

Free-floating attention—evenly suspended attention

Freud (1912e, p. 115) described the close links between the analyst's evenly suspended attention and the patient's free association. The complementary nature of the two processes is underlined by some writers' preference for the term "free-floating attention", although this is an incorrect rendering of the original German *gleichschwebende Aufmerksamkeit*.

The analyst who follows this rule remains open to all the patient's associations and allows him complete freedom to unfold his ideas and fantasies. Most important of all, he does not permit himself to be influenced by his abstract theoretical knowledge, but sees every patient as unique and incomparable and is eager to hear and experience something new. He deliberately avoids drawing comparisons in order not to hinder his access to the unknown. If he follows Freud's recommendation (1912e, p. 114), he swings over "according to need from the one mental attitude to the other" and postpones the "synthetic process of thought" to the end of the treatment. As long as the treatment continues, new material can constantly emerge that can correct the previous image (that is, the provisional reconstruction). The technique of evenly suspended attention should remind the analyst that every case could turn out differently than one might be led to expect by the general (and always provisional) theory and by one's limited personal experience.

While listening passively, the analyst tries to let everything impress him to the same degree with his attention evenly suspended; he tries not to select. In the process, he discovers his own limitations, which exist on two levels. His evenly suspended attention is disturbed by his countertransference (in the traditional sense), which results from his personal presuppositions regarding particular human problems. In the newer understanding of countertransference, disturbances of evenly suspended attention can be rendered therapeutically productive. In addition, the analyst notices that his evenly suspended attention is steered involuntarily in certain directions: not everything can be kept evenly suspended. When an interpretation comes to mind, he has chosen one of many possibilities, for both the patient's free associations and the analyst's interpretations are motivated.

On the basis of these considerations, we see the rule of evenly suspended attention as containing the demands—far from easy to fulfil—for self-critical examination of one's own attitude to this patient at this moment and for constant grappling with the general and specific problems of psychoanalytic theory and treatment technique. We also share Freud's opinion (1915c, p. 117) that we always listen actively, in as much as our understanding of what we observe is affected by pre-existing ideas. Therefore, it is, in principle, impossible to devote the same attention to everything, and we do not do so in practice. However, it is both possible and necessary to account for our ideas, and for what lies behind them, to ourselves and to the scientific community, and to correct presuppositions in the light of observations.

Countertransference

"The analyst's counter-transference is not only part and parcel of the analytic relationship, but it is the patient's creation, it is part of the patient's personality" (Heimann, 1950, p. 83).

If countertransference had until then been regarded as a (more or less) strong neurotic reaction by the analyst to the patient's transference neurosis that was to be avoided as far as possible, now it became part and parcel of the analytic relationship and, later, "comprehensive" countertransference (Kernberg, 1965). For Heimann, countertransference includes all the feelings the analyst experiences toward the patient.

Her thesis is that the analyst's emotional response to his patient within the analytic situation represents one of the most important tools for his work. The analyst's countertransference is an instrument of research into the patient's unconscious.

> . . . It has not been sufficiently stressed that it is a relationship between two persons. What distinguishes this relationship from others is not the presence of feelings in one partner, the patient, and their absence in the other, the analyst, but above all the degree of the feelings experienced and the use made of them, these factors being interdependent. (Heimann, 1950, p. 81)

It is essential that the analyst, in contrast to the patient, does not abreact the feelings released in him. They are subordinated to the task of analysis, in which the analyst functions as a mirror for the patient.

> The analyst, along with this freely working attention, needs a freely roused emotional sensibility so as to follow the patient's emotional movements and unconscious fantasies. Our basic assumption is that the analyst's unconscious understands that of his patient. This rapport at a deep level comes to the surface in the form of feelings which the analyst notices in response to his patient, in his "countertransference". This is the most dynamic way in which his patient's voice reaches him. In the comparison of feelings roused in himself with his patient's associations and behaviour, the analyst possesses a most valuable means of checking whether he has understood or failed to understand his patient. (Heimann, 1950, p. 82)

Methods of talking to the patient: general and special intervention techniques

The psychoanalytic dialogue and the counter-question rule: the patient comes to the analyst seeking answers to questions he cannot solve by himself. In none of his many discussions—with friends and colleagues, with clergymen, doctors, and quacks—has he been given satisfactory answers, that is, answers that cure his symptoms. We have already spoken of the profound, agonising questions that the patient cannot formulate but with which his unconscious conflicts confront him. It no longer needs to be emphasised that, ultimately, the revealing of these unanswered questions constitutes the beneficial effect of the analysis. However, what about the questions the patient can and does ask? How should they be dealt with? Let us first give some examples. Will the treatment cure or at least improve my symptoms? How does it work? How long will it last? Have you treated similar illnesses before? Do I have the same illness as my father? Soon, the patient takes an interest in the analyst's private life and family, wants to know his holiday address or, "for emergencies", his home telephone number.

You will sense something of the tension these questions create. They force the analyst's hand: the patient has urged him to give an answer, and will understand everything he now does as a response. Even silence is, in this sense, an answer.

Through the patient's questioning, the initiative passes to the analyst, whether he likes it or not. The compulsion arises from the fact that analyst and patient have entered into a dialogue and are, therefore, subject to rules of discourse, on which they must be in at least partial (tacit) agreement if they want in be in any position to conduct the dialogue in a meaningful way. It is in the nature of a question that the person asking it wants an answer and views every reaction as such.

The patient, who is not yet familiar with the analytic situation, will expect the conversation with the analyst to follow the rules of everyday communication. If questions are left unanswered, he might take it as a sign that the analyst cannot answer, is not willing to answer, or both.

Is this a means by which one person can induce another to enter into a verbal exchange, a dialogue? Since psychoanalysis lives on conversation, from the "interchange of words" (Freud, 1916–1917, p. 17), it is extremely important what and how the analyst replies—and not just to questions. Questions serve here as an excellent example of a broad spectrum of direct and open attempts by the patient to involve the analyst *ad hoc* in an exchange; requests and criticisms are further examples. Questions can also contain hidden attempts of this nature; also, something that initially seems to be purely a question to obtain information can later turn out to be, for example, an accusation. Questions are difficult to deal with because they invite interaction in such a multiplicity of ways. Which mother has not occasionally been exasperated by her child's insistent inquisitiveness? The analyst's situation is very similar when questions are put to him under pressure.

One rule of treatment, which has ossified into a frequently encountered stereotype, seems to cut through all difficulties just as Alexander's sword did through the Gordian knot. This stereotype is to respond to a question from the patient with a counter-question: "What leads you to ask that question?" For example, if a treatment report mentions that a given question came up and was "analysed", one can be fairly sure that the patient asked a question which was then thrown back at him with a request for the thoughts behind it. Such information is also often invited indirectly by silence. This answering of questions with questions is, for the general public, one of the characteristic features of analysis.

It is assumed that the withholding of an answer will result in the patient more quickly expressing thoughts that will lead to the latent meaning of the question. Thus, the rule is justified by the hoped-for gain in therapeutic insight. An unintended result, however, is that the patient often interprets the failure to answer his question as a rejection. What influence does this rejection have on the transference relationship and on the desired process of restructuring the patient's self- and object-representation? We believe that we have to assume that only a few patients have an ego so intact that they experience the rejection represented by the stereotyped non-answering of questions without feeling offended and without all the implications this has for unconscious defence mechanisms.

In a therapeutic relationship, the therapist must decide if the patient is at a level of ego stability that is sufficient to deal with confrontation and interpretation, or if he first has to

Table 7.6. Overview of ten most important talking and listening techniques (Elzer, 2009b, translated for this edition).

Technique	Application and effects	Hint, beware of
1 *Questions*		
Closed questions	Yes/No	Beware: don't use too often
Semi-closed questions	More scope	Who, how, where, what, when, etc. Why-questions are difficult to answer
Open questions	Very stimulating, enlarging the potentiality of answers	Beware: answers can be abundant
2 *Active listening*	Verbal feedback ("hmm", "yes") or non-verbal mimic feedback (nodding) stimulates the willingness to speak	Requirements: 1. Interest 2. Willingness to listen 3. Capacity to listen 4. To be completely present
3 *Pauses and silence*	Pressure to talk	Beware: being silent produces fear, i.e., trauma and shame
4 *Mirroring and paraphrasing*	Feedback, confrontation with own statements	Beware: not too often, can be parrot-like
5 *Probe*	Step-by-step approach to a subject	Don't leave the leadership to patient
6 *Clarification*	Request clarification	If there are unclear contents
7 *Confrontation*	To confront with contradictions or unconscious contents	Perceptively, not in a know-it-all fashion
8 *To talk about contents*		The talk leads in a certain direction
To talk about cognitive contents		Cognitive contents
To talk about emotional contents		Affective contents
9 To talk about physical contents		Like confrontation, very embarrassing
10 Interpretation	Unconscious meanings	Caution and empathy

support the patient and do some uncovering psychotherapy with ego-strengthening to stabilise the patient. If, later on, the patient is in a trustful relationship with the therapist, this can enable the him to deal with shameful parts of the self or with shameful parts of the drives, where he has the ego strength to deal with guilt feelings, and so on.

In therapy, the first part is that the patient comes to us because of his suffering. Generally, however, therapy only continues if we manage to induce some curiosity in the patient to investigate himself and to be interested in finding deep structures within himself.

Often, we must be content if we succeed in symptom alleviation. However, in a long therapy, we can also achieve structural changes that mean more stable success, the longer the therapy has continued.

The therapeutic process

Hermann Schultz

General definition and typical characteristics of the psychotherapeutic process

In general usage, a "process" is a course of events. We may distinguish certain characteristics of such a process:

- by "psychotherapeutic process", we mean an interpersonal process going on between patient and therapist and, at the same time, an intrapsychic process going on within the patient, continuing between sessions and also beyond the formal ending of the therapy;
- the therapeutic process, on the one hand, is an emotional and relational process, unfolding naturally and spontaneously as soon as patient and therapist feel safe enough to let it happen and not to disturb its development. On the other hand, it is a planned process, controlled by a framework of setting conditions, aims, and goals, rules and regulations, as well as the therapist's interventions (and the patient's conscious intentions), in order to make sure that this process will be therapeutic and help the patient to alleviate suffering, lose his symptoms, gain insight, solve his problems, and learn to live with the realities of his life.

Resistance

There are patients who seem to be unable to enter into this kind of therapeutic process, or are resistant to doing so: in other words, patients for whom it seems difficult to get into contact with their own emotions and to develop a deeper emotional relationship with their therapist. There could be various reasons for such a resistance against the therapeutic process: for example, opening up to emotions makes them feel unsafe and vulnerable, stirs up distrust, or causes them to fear that their emotions—or perhaps the therapist's emotions—might run out of control, with the result that they may be confronted with dangerous aggressive impulses, with uncontrollable sexual excitement, or with the panic of unbearable traumatic memories. The primary reason for these fears lies, of course, in certain negative experiences of the patient's past, which he anticipates may be repeated in therapy. There is a chapter in this volume dealing with resistance, its different forms and functions, illustrated with clinical examples. In the present context, it should only be emphasised that resistance might serve a self-protecting and tension-regulating function; therefore, we should not take the patient's resistance as directed against our therapeutic efforts, but, rather, accept it and try to understand it with the patient's help.

Therapy as a safe place

Because the psychotherapeutic process stirs up old fears and anxieties, it is all the more important that therapy should be a safe place for the patient and, we may add, also for the therapist, where both can be sure that there is (as far as possible) no realistic basis for such fears. Under this precondition, the patients can dare to go deeper into the therapeutic process, face those aspects of their self, which they had avoided becoming aware of, gain more insight and tolerance, and re-emerge with a new feeling of personal strength and competence. What makes therapy a safe place? The answer is clear: the precondition for the development of a deeply emotional psychotherapeutic process is a reliable therapeutic frame. These two concepts—process and frame—are complementary: the frame is a stable set of conditions, which enables a dynamic process to develop.

The concept of frame is very important; it has already been dealt with in earlier chapters and will certainly be taken up again and again in other contexts. Let us sum up some important aspects of the therapeutic frame.

We distinguish between an external frame and an internal frame. The external frame is what we also call the therapeutic setting: the location of therapy (hospital, counselling centre, private practice, etc.), time (dates of sessions), duration and frequency of sessions (e.g., fifty minutes once or twice per week), fees (how much per session, how cancelled sessions will be dealt with, etc.), planned length of therapy (short-term, long-term), method of treatment, etc. We discuss these setting conditions in detail with the patient in the beginning phase of therapy as part of the therapeutic contract with the patient.

This external frame is complemented by an internal frame, which is a kind of mental setting, consisting of two parts: the therapist's part is the so-called therapeutic attitude (openness, empathy, non-judgemental, abstinence, neutrality, psychodynamic understanding, professional responsibility, etc.), whereas the patient's part is what we call therapeutic alliance: an attitude of willingness to co-operate in a psychodynamic type of therapy (including self-observation, control of self-destructive behaviour, verbalising one's associations, honesty, responsibility, etc.).

Reality and fantasy in the psychotherapeutic process

The frame concept is useful because it helps us to understand that what is going on in a psychodynamic psychotherapy is different in character from normal interpersonal relationships and normal everyday conversation: on the one hand, the psychotherapeutic process is psychologically real; it is a deeply meaningful experience which can change patients' attitudes towards themselves and others, help them to gain insight, master their problems, and develop towards maturity. On the other hand, the therapeutic situation has something artificial about it: the emotions of love and hate, guilt and shame, envy and jealousy, etc., feel very real, but, at the same time, these emotions appear more or less inadequate towards a therapist who, outside of the therapy sessions, remains a stranger for the patient. In our understanding of the psychotherapeutic process, typical patterns of emotional object relations and conflicts, which the patient has experienced in the course of his/her life, tend to be re-experienced in memories, fantasies, and in the transference relationship with the therapist.

In other words, the patient's (and therapist's) emotions belong to the world of transference and countertransference fantasy and memory, enacted unconsciously in the therapy situation like a theatre play on the stage, and it is the therapist's task to recognise which play is on the programme today and which are the roles the patient assigns (by transference) to the therapist and to him-/herself (see Chapter Five (pp. 104–111), and Chapter Seven (pp. 152–160), in this volume, with clinical case examples).

We can see now that the psychotherapeutic process is something real, but its reality is different from normal "matter-of-fact" concrete reality; it is, as Freud says, psychic reality, or, as others say, symbolic reality, comparable to the symbolic reality of a dream, a film, or a theatre drama.

Taking an example from the world of the theatre, when, in Shakespeare's *Othello*, the protagonist in his jealous rage is attempting to murder his beloved Desdemona, the spectators will not feel urged to rescue her—they know her death belongs to the play, she will not really die. What happens belongs within the frame of the theatre stage and not to the reality without. Nevertheless, such a stage play can be deeply moving.

So, the frame (or setting) defines the kind of reality we are dealing with. In psychotherapy, it should always be clear that what is going on here is therapy, with clearly defined roles, tasks, and responsibilities, and not a situation, for instance, of real fighting, of erotic intimacy, of regressive nursing, etc. Within the frame of psychotherapy, the patient should feel safe enough to experience the full range of his emotions and fantasies and express these in words, but should strictly refrain from direct actions. The therapist, too, must know the responsibility and the limits of his/her role and act accordingly.

Specific characteristics of the psychotherapeutic process

If the frame is created as a stable, protecting structure, the therapeutic process can develop in a way that is unique and characteristic for each specific patient. It should be emphasised that, on the one hand, the psychotherapeutic process is of a personal and most individual sort, because each individual patient is different from others in character, life history, symptoms, and problems; on the other hand, there are some general characteristics of the psychotherapeutic process which can be taught and learnt in clinical theory and in case supervision.

Three aspects of the psychotherapeutic process are of particular practical importance, as listed below.

1. The balance between the extremes of letting the process develop spontaneously without interventions of the therapist and structuring and focusing the process.
2. The balance between feeling and thinking: in other words, between therapy as a corrective emotional experience and therapy as insight into the reasons and origins of the patient's problems and developing strategies for solutions.
3. Typical features of three phases of the psychotherapeutic process: beginning phase, middle phase, terminating phase. Since the beginning phase and the terminating phase will be dealt with in other chapters, this section will be focused upon the middle phase and what is called "working through".

Let us go into these aspects in more detail: the therapeutic process, on the one hand, is an emotional and relational process, unfolding naturally and spontaneously as soon as patient and therapist feel safe enough to let it happen and not disturb its development. On the other hand, it is a planned process, controlled by a framework of setting conditions, aims and goals, rules and regulations, as well as the therapist's interventions. There are big differences between individual therapists in their general style of working and sometimes also in their dealing with different patients. These differences may be characterised within a continuum: at one extreme, we find those therapists who try to facilitate a regressive emotional process, mostly through their "holding" and "containing" presence, concentrating on empathising with the patient and restricting interpretations of conflicts as far as possible, because they feel that the emotional experience of the patient is the most important healing process. At the other extreme, we find those more active therapists who are convinced that confronting the patient with his habitual character patterns and resistances, reconstruction of traumatic childhood situations, gaining insight into the reasons of conflicts, working through the central conflict patterns, is the most important part of therapy and might help the patient best.

During the history of psychoanalysis, there have been fierce debates about these fundamental questions of therapeutic technique, the opponents accusing each other of "too much thinking" or "too much feeling". The majority of therapists will situate themselves between the extremes and say that there should be a good balance between the spontaneous development of the emotional process on the one hand and the structuring activities of the therapist on the other. Rational insight into conflicts is not enough; in order to gain a deeper conviction regarding the truth of his insights and to change his habitual pattern, the patient needs the full experiencing of the emotions in the transference relationship with the therapist. On the other hand, a patient might experience strong feelings in his therapy without learning from that, without drawing conclusions, taking responsibility, and changing accordingly. Rationalisation and intellectualisation ("too much thinking") as well as "affectualisation" ("too much feeling") might be used as mechanisms of defence and resistance against therapeutic change. However, for an efficient psychotherapeutic process, both feeling and thinking are necessary: the courage to open up towards vital emotions, wishful and fearful fantasies, and unknown areas of one's inner world, and the ego functions of self-observation, discrimination, insight, and responsible action. Both partners in the psychotherapeutic process, patient and therapist, will have to invest the full potential of their feeling and thinking abilities, each of them in his or her specific role, so that the therapy can effect change and help the patient to take the necessary steps towards maturity.

Acting-out, enactments, action dialogue

A special problem in psychotherapy can be what we call acting out, especially in the form of violent, impulse-ridden behaviour, such as openly aggressive attacks against the therapist or self-destructive actions, for example, suicide attempts, self-cutting, excessive drinking, etc. This might happen with severely disturbed patients when, in the course of therapy, they are confronted with internal or external situations that they are unable to deal with. The therapist has to counter such destructive behaviour through a mixture of firm containment, clear rules and regulations, and understanding and interpreting the patient's inner conflict situation. This might help to restore the psychotherapeutic frame and continue the psychotherapeutic process. However, if the patient's acting out presents a real danger to himself or other people, psychiatric hospitalisation should be considered.

In his fundamental paper, "Remembering, repeating and working through", Freud (1914g, pp. 145–156) used the term "acting-out" (German: *Agieren*) for the first time: the patient "does not remember what he has forgotten and repressed, instead he acts it out. He does not reproduce it as a memory, but as an action, in other words: he repeats it, of course without knowing what he repeats."

For instance, instead of remembering how his father treated him, the patient unconsciously treats his therapist (or feels treated by his therapist) in the same way, that is, without being aware of doing so. Of course, this is what we call transference. But there is more about this phenomenon. As can be seen from the quotation above, what Freud discovered and described in his 1914 paper was the fact that there are fundamentally two different kinds of memory: explicit and implicit memory, as they are known today. The contents of explicit memory can be recalled and verbalised in the form of memorised scenes and narratives. But, besides this explicit memory, there exists a second and more fundamental memory system: we call it "implicit memory", or "action memory", the contents of which are remembered by being actualised in certain situations. Clinical experience shows that certain traumatic experiences that are stored in implicit memory can be actualised automatically in certain situations and deeply influence the patient's way of relating and interacting with others. Our implicit memory is a memory of action and interaction patterns, a memory of patterns of object relations, a memory of emotional states in relation to typical situations. In the context of psychotherapy, this is the non-verbal (feeling and action) part of the therapeutic interaction.

So, we must distinguish between two very different kinds of acting in psychotherapy.

1. Violent acting-out behaviour, usually occurring in patients with a deficient impulse control and in situations of high pressure that cannot be managed otherwise.
2. A different kind of phenomena, which we should not call "acting-out", but, rather, "enactments" (Jacobs, 1986) or the "nonverbal part of the therapeutic interaction" (Langs, 1976), or even the "unconscious action dialogue" between patient and therapist (Klüwer, 1983; Sandler 1976). These phenomena usually do not appear as a sudden release of unbearably high tension, but more like free associations in the form of bodily actions.

Regarding these two kinds of action phenomena in psychoanalytic psychotherapy, the therapist needs both: on the one hand, a greater tolerance for acting out in therapy, until the therapist has understood what is going on, and which "scene" of the patient's past is being replayed here and now in the therapy room, so that he can formulate an interpretation and regain distance. On the other hand, in dealing with dangerously acting-out patients, we recognise the necessity of a firm therapeutic frame as a holding structure to "contain" the patient's high tensions. The frame must be flexible enough, not rigid, and stable enough, not weak.

These considerations are especially important in the psychotherapy of patients with severe complex personality disorders who suffer mainly (and make others suffer) from their disturbed interpersonal relationships. In such therapies, the informative content of what patient and therapist say is less important, whereas the performative or "action" dimension of language dominates the scene: they try to put pressure upon the therapist and provoke him, seduce him, control him, threaten him, shame him, make him feel guilty, or angry, or anxious, or flattered, or impotent. Accordingly, interpretations are not understood, because, on the action level, the patients are unable to reflect their behaviour from a third point of view outside the interaction (triangulation, reflective capacity, Sterba's (1934) "therapeutic ego dissociation"). They take the therapist's interpretations as interactional moves, as if he aimed at criticising them, or confusing them, or trying to be more clever than the patient, etc. So, with these patients, we should be careful with interpretations. Instead, what they need is an adequate interactional answer, which helps them to become aware of their own feelings and what they make others feel by treating them in this manner.

Kleinian authors describe these processes in terms of projective identification, but the process is not one-sided from patient to therapist; it is, rather, a kind of unconscious interaction with contributions from both patient and therapist.

Working through

Earlier, I mentioned "working through", as an important characteristic of the psychotherapeutic process during its middle phase, when the process—after some uncertain lingering in the beginning phase—"has found its direction" and concentrates upon the "core conflictual relationship themes" (CCRT), as Luborsky and Crits-Christoph (1998) formulate it. These core conflicts, or focal conflicts, will appear again and again in the patient's life outside of therapy as well as in the transference relationship with the therapist; although the actual circumstances and contexts will vary, the fundamental pattern remains the same. As always, these conflicts will show a "wish or drive aspect" and a "fear or resistance aspect"; both aspects need to be worked through again and again in the context of new experiences in therapy in order to achieve lasting structural change to neurotic personality patterns. In other words, the patient must really feel his emotions towards himself and others, his longing, his fear, his resisting and struggling. Only in this way can he gain the convincing experience of being understood and accepted, in contrast to his unconscious negative beliefs and expectations, which were formed during traumatic experiences of his childhood (Weiss & Sampson, 1984). This new experience enables the patient to dare to change and give up his habitual security strategies—tentatively at first, then with increasing confidence. This process of increasingly getting in touch with one's own deeper conflicts, struggling for solutions, trying out how it feels to be that way, finding a new relationship to these parts of oneself, sorting out what to accept, what to reject, and how to live with this new experience of self and others—this is the very essence of working through. Experience shows that most patients need the therapist's help in order to transform the insights gained in therapy into real life changes. Little wonder that this process needs time in order to effect real structural change in depth, which is necessary if patients present some circumscribed neurotic symptom which was triggered by some actual conflict, or suffer from longstanding personality problems. In these cases, besides clarification and interpretation of unconscious conflict, structure-building interventions are often necessary—for example, building up more efficient capacities for affect tolerance, impulse control, affect differentiation, self-object differentiation, anticipation, and reality testing.

Indicators of progress in therapy

Matthias Elzer

Psychotherapy is a continuous process from beginning to end, and very often the progression continues after the therapy has ended. There has been progress when the patient's development is positive, but what about negative development, backward steps, stagnancy, and crises within the process? Sometimes, the patient will break off the therapy, sometimes the therapist will. What about the termination phase of the treatment? And what about the therapeutic relationship after the end of the therapy? These things are illustrated in Table 7.7.

These problems occur in nearly every therapy and we have to understand and handle them professionally.

We can form an impression of the process through considering the following points.

1. *Using the setting and entering into a working alliance*
   A clear and safe setting is the precondition for every kind of psychotherapy, especially for psychodynamic psychotherapy and psychoanalysis. One indicator of therapeutic progress is that the patient should be able to understand and accept the setting as a helpful framework in which to work on his or her problems. Generally, patients do not know how psychotherapy works; thus, very often, patients expect to be treated and advised by the doctor. This is not the case in psychodynamic psychotherapy. The patient has to treat himself by understanding the unconscious meaning of the symptoms underlying his conflict or trauma. If only the therapist works, the therapy will be unsuccessful. The

Table 7.7. The process of a long-term psychotherapy.

Number of sessions (more or less)										
1–2	3–5	10	20	30	40	45	50	70	80	90–100
Initial interview	Probationary appointment	The main therapeutic process, including phases of progress, and phases of step-back, stagnation, and crises								Termination

therapist should demonstrate the way psychotherapy operates as "team work" through his own behaviour, empathic attitude, and how he, the therapist, thinks and talks about the patient's material.

In my experience, the setting is to be understood as a triangular relationship: the patient does not know the theoretical background of psychodynamics, but he is an expert on his own life and suffering. On the other hand, the therapist does not know the special aspects of the patient's life and suffering, but his expertise lies in the theory of psychopathology. We can formulate it as follows: two people come together; one is blind in his left eye and the other in the right eye. The material (biographic information, ideas, fantasies, dreams) is like a third entity, and the patient and the therapist work with this material from different points of view (Figure 7.2).

The questions to be asked are:

- Can the therapist implement the setting as a helpful framework for the therapeutic relationship?
- Can the patient accept and use the setting to work on his problems?
- Can the patient use this therapeutic communication to offer new material?

2. *The increase of the patient's understanding (insight, introspection)*

The therapist has to win his patient over to understanding psychodynamics through his professional communication of the patient's material. The patient learns to use and to work with the material with the help of the therapist.

During therapy, especially during long-term therapy, we can see some changes and progressive behaviour in the patient's current life and in his private and professional relationships to others.

For example: A patient, Miss T, who is suffering from a neurotic depression (*ICD*: dysthymia), could finally understand—after many repetitions and through her own psychoanalytical work—when she was being rejected by other people. She understood that she unconsciously induced or transferred a self-fulfilling prophecy to others in a masochistic way: "Reject and disappoint me". At the beginning of contact with others, nobody seemed to dislike her, but after some time the prophecy began to work. During the therapy, and through some interventions of the therapist, she became able to revive her childhood experience of being an unloved child. She could feel and recognise the

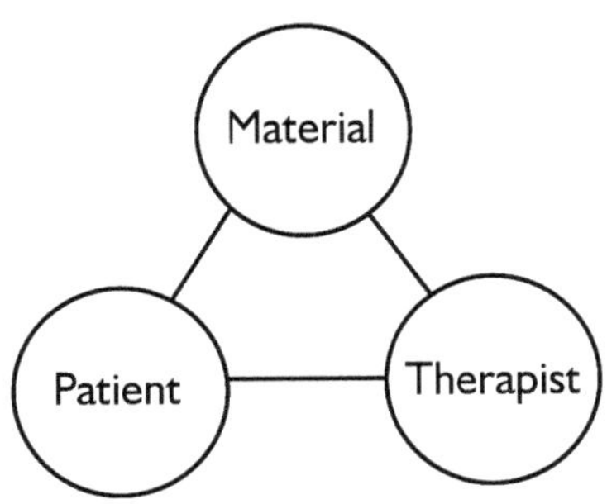

Figure 7.2. The process of a long-term psychotherapy.

neurotic repetition and the interpersonal dynamics. This is called the defence mechanism of projection and projective identification.

We can formulate a second indicator of progress by asking ourselves the following questions:

- Is the patient able to develop more insight into the problems and conflicts of his current life?
- Is the patient able to recognise the biographical roots of these problems and conflicts?
- Is the patient motivated to try some of the steps necessary to relinquish his neurotic behaviour?

3. *The understanding and development of the patient's main symptoms*
The external changes of the symptoms are very important for the patient who comes for therapy because he is suffering. Most patients expect to be treated passively by the therapist similar to being in an operating theatre under anaesthetic, where the symptoms can be "cut out". This is not the way psychoanalytic therapy works. For some patients, it is difficult to realise that they need the symptoms to express an unconscious problem (conflict, trauma). The patient needs time to understand the unconscious meaning of his symptoms. It is an important signal, like a red flag, and the patient will no longer need it if the reason for this signal is identified and repaired by working through it.

Sometimes, the symptoms disappear very quickly at the beginning of the therapy, as if a ticket has been obtained to enter the patient's internal world and neurotic life story.

One indicator of progress is that the patient can understand the sense and meaning of the symptoms: for example, the depressive feeling of loss and narcissistic hurt, or the panic of the revival of a traumatic experience in childhood.

Often, the cognitive understanding of the symptoms happens rather quickly, but the emotional understanding needs much more time and occurs in many repetitions in the patient's life and in the therapeutic relationship within the phenomenon of transference.

We can formulate a third indicator of progress by means of the following questions:

- Can the patient imagine that his symptoms have an unconscious meaning and that they belong to his current life and to the history of his life?
- Is the patient motivated to recognise the meaning of his suffering?
- Is the therapy helpful to the patient's understanding of himself?

4. *The dynamics of the therapeutic relationship*
The phenomena of transference and countertransference exist in every therapeutic relationship at an unconscious level, but do they surface at a conscious level, too? Do they only exist in the mind of the therapist, or are they articulated and communicated between patient and therapist?

For example: The depressive patient, Miss T, seemed to be disappointed by the (male) therapist (Dr S). She misses one session and explains later that Dr S is not really interested in her, because other patients are in greater need of his skills and care. Subsequently, she rationalises that others are more attractive than she is. Dr S, in turn, feels warm and empathic towards Miss T, but he has the fantasy that he is an inadequate therapist and cannot give her enough support. By means of the interpretation ("You are disappointed by me, and I have the feeling that your needs exceed my capabilities, so I am not good enough"), the actual therapeutic relationship is described in terms of transference and countertransference.

For the process and for progress it is important that the transference becomes more vivid and more dynamic; the patient brings more material, for example, by means of ideas, fantasies, memories, dreams, as well as acting out.

In the case of short-term therapy, it is sometimes very difficult to recognise and to work with the dynamics of transference and countertransference on a conscious level. The therapist should ask himself what is going on at that moment, or what went on during the previous sessions. He should also communicate his thoughts through interventions such as clarifications, confrontations, and interpretations in a professional way.

We can formulate another indicator of progress by asking ourselves the following question:

- What is the actual relationship between patient and therapist, and how can we describe the dynamic of transference and countertransference?

5. *The progressive change of the defence mechanism and of resistance*
Psychoanalytic treatment is like a walk along a wall. It is a journey with many barriers, obstacles, and difficulties. Because of that, psychotherapy is not boring; on the contrary, it demands a lot of energy, activity, and patience to overcome these obstacles. Like symptoms, the patient needs his defence mechanisms to use against the recognition of the unconscious conflict or traumatic experience during his daily life and he needs the resistance against working in therapy, too. The patient feels and shows anxiety if his defence mechanisms and resistance are challenged or exposed by the therapist or by therapeutic work. This resistance should be worked on step-by-step from the surface to the core.

Resistance in therapy is connected with the patient's defence-mechanism structures. Typical mental disorders have typical defence mechanisms and typical forms of resistance during therapy. The knowledge of psychopathology helps to deal with the patient's structure of defence and his expected resistance during therapy.

We can formulate a fifth indicator of progress through the following questions:

- Is there any understanding and progressive change in the patient's defence mechanism and the resistance against the therapeutic process?
- Is there only a repetition of these dynamics or is there movement, whether it is regression or progression?

Different aims in psychoanalytic psychotherapy and psychoanalysis

These five indicators of progress—(1) working alliance, (2) introspection, (3) symptoms, (4) transference and countertransference, (5) resistance—are most important for the setting of the psychoanalytic therapy and psychoanalysis. It is easy to understand that the indicators of process and progress are better recognised in long-term psychodynamic psychotherapy and psychoanalysis, where we can have 50, 100, 200, and more sessions.

The aims of psychoanalytic psychotherapy and psychoanalysis are different. The changing of the patient's intrapsychic structure is an important aim of psychoanalysis. It is very difficult to achieve a change of the intrapsychic structure, for instance, of the mental apparatus: the development of the id, the ego, the superego, and the ideal ego, through psychoanalytic psychotherapy. The scientific discussion of the psychotherapeutic process is well developed in psychoanalysis. Here, we find different constructs of process from different points of view. For example, one construct stresses the concept of psychological stages of the development of the patient from the oral and anal stages to the oedipal stage to overcome infantile neurotic fixations. Another construct says that the process is like a chain of one focus point after the other (Thomä & Kächele, 1987, p. 349).

The aim of psychoanalytic psychotherapy is to work through the unconscious psychodynamics of the active neurotic conflicts by using the dynamic of transference and countertransference. Compared to psychoanalysis, psychoanalytic psychotherapy has a narrower aim: a conflict-centred procedure limited by the constraints of the patient's regression. The progress of therapy has to be seen within this framework.

Indicators of stagnation and crisis

Nearly every psychotherapy and psychoanalysis has phases of stagnation and crisis. They are unavoidable, interesting, and fruitful, if the stagnation and crisis can be overcome by the therapist's and the patient's work.

If there is stagnation, or an impasse of the therapeutic process, we should try to understand the reasons for it, although the therapist should wait patiently and look at, and listen to, his own fantasies and ideas (countertransference). He can formulate an intervention such as this: "During the previous sessions, I got the impression that the therapy is not going anywhere. Nothing is happening. It's like sailing without wind. What is your impression?" It is good to give an intervention as a revelation of the therapist's own feelings or ideas and not as criticism or as an accusation that the patient has stopped working.

Stagnation in therapy is quite interesting; it is like standing in front of a high wall and not being able to see a door or a hole. The main question is: against what has the patient built up this wall?

Perhaps stagnation is a precursor of a new stage with new material, but most of all the phenomenon of stagnation is a sign of resistance. The therapist has to understand the kind of resistance, for example:

- resistance against new material (association, fantasies);
- resistance against the transference;
- resistance against the continuation of the therapy in general.

Resistance is an expression of anxiety and fear about facing repressed conflicts.

However, the phenomenon of stagnation, impasse, and crisis can also be a misunderstanding caused by the therapist through

- his own unconscious transference to the patient;
- his resistance against the countertransference;
- his fear of regressing and coming into contact with his infantile anxiety and experience;
- his unconscious wishes or drives (i.e., erotic fantasies or aggression).

If the therapist is involved in his own deeper neurotic problems, the therapy will be influenced negatively. For example, perhaps the therapist cannot tolerate the patient's depressive or aggressive feelings, his mourning, traumatic experience of loss and deprivation. Because of this, the therapist is touched and moved by his own biography. He might want to transfer the patient to another doctor, prescribe medication, etc. In this case, it is an acting out by the therapist and he himself would seem to be the reason for the stagnation and the crisis. He should visit a supervisor, or an experienced colleague, in order to understand his own resistance against the patient and the therapy.

We should understand stagnation, or an impasse, as a "joint problem to which both patient and analyst contribute" (Bateman & Holmes, 1995, p. 188).

Sometimes, I compare the therapeutic process with surgery. The patient should not jump from the operating table, and neither should the therapist leave the theatre before surgery has been completed professionally. The decision to undergo this therapy must be shared by both in the diagnostic phase.

Breaking off the therapy

The topic of stagnation and crisis leads us to the problem of dropping out and breaking off the therapy. I quote Schultz from his paper, "On premature termination (drop out, forced termination)".

> 'Premature' means 'too early' or it means: 'The patient quits therapy earlier than the therapist thought it would have been good or necessary for the patient'. So it is an 'unexpected' or unplanned termination – contrary to natural, planned termination. Premature termination may be initiated either by the patient (this is what we call 'dropout') or by the therapist (this is what we call 'forced termination'). (Schultz, 2008, p. 1)

Schultz refers to the small number of publications about premature termination: in the scientific literature, he found that nearly 40% of the outpatients of psychotherapy in all settings terminate by dropping out. Compared to my own experience, this figure is too high. Nevertheless, we have to understand every drop-out and forced termination and deal with it.

Schultz mentions some studies in which it is pointed out that most patients who break off their therapy said that they felt better at the end than at the beginning of the therapy.

The most common reasons for breaking off the therapy are listed below.

1. *Diagnostic*
   The indication for psychotherapy and the diagnostic assessment are faulty, incomplete, and unprofessional. Some aspects are:

- the pressure of the patient's suffering is too low and superficial;
- the motivation of the patient for the psychodynamic approach is insufficient;
- the ability for insight does not exist;
- the mental structure of the patient cannot tolerate the psychoanalytical method of uncovering unconscious conflicts in a regressive therapeutic relationship through the dynamics of transference. Extremely narcissistic or severely depressive, psychotic, or suicidal patients need more supportive or behavioural psychotherapy and psychiatric treatment in general.

2. *The motivation of the therapist*
The motivation is not only related to the dynamics of transference and countertransference, but also to the personality and neurotic structure of the therapist. Maybe the patient was "pushed into psychotherapy" by the therapist. Here are some examples:

- he offers therapy because of his own financial needs;
- he has the fantasy of rescuing the patient from his unfortunate life;
- he needs the patient for his own narcissistic satisfaction;
- he wants to show his colleagues that he is a successful therapist.

3. *The setting*

- After the diagnostic phase, the appointment of the treatment was not clearly implemented.
- The setting is not clear and safe and allows many opportunities for acting out.

4. *Therapeutic relationship*
A good, empathic, helpful, and resilient relationship and alliance cannot be established by the patient and/or by the therapist. This disturbance has many different aspects, as shown in the section headed "The indicators of stagnation and crisis".
Some aspects of the patient:

- resistance against the therapy;
- resistance against the progress and development ("negative therapeutic reaction");
- deep regression of the patient (psychotic, depressive, suicidal crisis or disorder)'
- strong erotic sexualising transference and acting out.

Some aspects of the therapist:

- late recognition, understanding, and working through of negative transference and countertransference feelings of patient and therapist, for example, in cases of forced termination by the therapist;
- acting out of the therapist, for example, by changing the setting, abandoning abstinence, relinquishing the psychodynamic attitude of listening, understanding, and communication.

If the premature termination through drop-out or forced termination is unavoidable, both the patient and the therapist should take some time to try to understand and communicate the reasons for this untimely and unhappy end. The therapist should avoid apportioning some of blame and moral guilt to the patient. He should accept the patient's decision, even if he would have preferred another decision.

Most break-offs happen during the beginning phase of therapy. I prefer to reach an agreement with the patient that the therapy is on probation for a number of sessions. Both can test whether or not the patient is able to use the therapeutic method, and if he is, the therapeutic relationship can begin to develop.

The process of termination

During open-ended therapy, the "real" and mature end of the therapy is difficult to recognise. In my experience, it is necessary to talk with the patient about the expected duration and the method of termination at the beginning of therapy, while the therapist and the patient are formulating a contract agreement. The patient should have an idea about the duration and type of therapy.

1. In case of short-term therapy, the end of treatment is fixed and clear-cut from the beginning. In Germany, the maximum duration of short-term psychotherapy is twenty-five sessions.
2. If the therapy is conducted as a long-term psychotherapy, we have two possibilities: a limited long-term psychotherapy, or an open-ended psychotherapy.

It is helpful and necessary that the patient is given information about, and has an idea of the "dosage", for example, one session a week, and the expected duration (say, fifty sessions) of his therapy. In Germany, medical insurance offers long-term psychoanalytic orientated psychotherapy (*tiefenpsychologisch fundierte Psychotherapie*) with a maximum of 100 sessions in three steps: fifty, thirty, and twenty sessions. At every step, the patient has to complete and sign an application form stating his willingness to continue the therapy. So, he is involved in the decision of continuing or terminating the therapy. The therapist has to write a case report to a surveyor of the medical insurance company. The insurance system is "the third entity" in the therapeutic setting. After the medical insurance institution has made its payment, the patient and the therapist could agree to continue the therapy with private fee payment.

In case of time-limited or open-ended psychotherapy, the question is: what is the right time to finish the therapy and how to handle the termination?

Bateman and Holmes say,

> As a general rule the topic of finishing should come from the patient rather than the analyst, although there may be exceptional circumstances when the analyst needs to broach the subject himself because of personal reasons, because he feels the patient will not get further with the treatment, or even because he cannot tolerate the emotional burden he experiences in relation to a particular patient. (Bateman & Holmes, 1995, p. 178)

When the patient talks about his wish to finish the therapy, the most important fact to clarify is whether or not this wish is an expression of resistance against the therapy, an acting out, a negative therapeutic reaction, or an inevitable disappointment, because the goals of the treatment are different from the goals of the patient's life.

Ursano, Sonnenberg, and Lazar formulate some criteria for terminating psychodynamic psychotherapy (1998, p. 156): the patient . . .

- experiences relief of symptoms
- experiences symptoms as alien
- understands his characteristic defences
- is able to understand and recognize his characteristic transference responses
- engages in ongoing self-inquiry as a method of resolving internal conflicts.

Ursano and colleagues describe the work of termination (1998, p. 158): the patient . . .

- reviews the therapy
- experiences and masters the separation and loss
- re-experiences and re-masters the transference
- begins self-inquiry

The patient and the therapist . . .

- identify disappointments, limitations and unsuccessful aspects of the therapy
- discuss the possibility of future psychotherapy
- discuss plans for the future.

In simple words, the patient becomes an expert on his own personality in the past, in the present, and in the future by better understanding the dynamics of his inner world and the strong and weak points of his personality ("empowerment"). He should be able to feel and act in a less neurotic or non-neurotic way. This extends to the patient's drives, object relations, and narcissism (self-esteem).

The ending of therapy is a process of separation: the patient has to leave his therapist and the therapist has to let his patient go. It is a separation from both sides. The process of separation needs some time. It is important to fix the end of the therapy as an intermediate aim, for example, in two months (after eight to ten or more sessions). During this process of ending, the patient sometimes exhibits some symptoms such as those displayed at the beginning of therapy, as an expression of fear of separation. Sometimes, the patient has ambivalent feelings: on the one hand he wants to be separated from the therapist, and on the other he does not, because he doubts that he will be able to deal with his significant problems on his own.

The therapeutic relationship after the end of the therapy

In the setting of the classical psychoanalysis, the patient's transference should be dissolved in the terminal stage. This is ideal, but, in reality, the transference continues on a lower and realistic level. The therapist should be aware that the patient's transference is still working after the therapy, but with decreasing tendency. After the end of the therapy, the therapeutic process still continues in the patient's mind. The therapist is an important object for the patient, so the internal dialogue continues; the patient may ask himself, "What would Dr X say about this problem?"

After the end of the therapy, the fundamental rule of abstinence exists in the future, too.

Sometimes, the patient comes back to the therapist for some sessions to work on an actual problem, such as the death of a father or mother, or any other type of loss or crisis.

If the therapy is a self-experience of a psychotherapeutic training programme for the candidate, it is sometimes difficult to meet his therapist in a non-therapeutic setting. On the one hand, this experience disturbs the prolonged transference relationship; on the other, it does make the candidate understand the reality of the therapist as a human being and leads to a de-idealisation.

How to present or to write a case report

Matthias Elzer and Alf Gerlach

One part of a training in psychoanalytical psychotherapy is the presentation and discussion of a continuing or finished therapy. The case report can be given to a teacher and colleagues during a clinical seminar, in a single supervision, or as a final case report at the end of the training. It can be presented verbally or in written form.

This section of the chapter will provide an outline for case reports and case presentations that was developed by some of the authors of this book during the training course at the Shanghai Mental Health Centre in 2006.

Generally, the report should show the process of the therapy, the therapeutic relationship, the therapist's understanding of the patient. The report should also contain how the patient can use the therapist's understanding to work on his or her psychic conflict or trauma. Sometimes, the therapist can show a successful treatment. Often, the presenter will speak about problems or crises of the treatment, and the ideas of the supervisor and the colleagues can be helpful.

The case presentation or the written report should have the structure shown in Table 7.8.

We shall now list what these elements of the structure comprise.

Table 7.8. Structure for presenting and writing a case report.

1. The initial interview.
2. Biography.
3. Patient–therapist relationship.
4 Diagnostic and psychodynamic considerations.
5 The frame/setting.
6 Treatment plan.
7 Results.

1. *The initial interview*

   - The referral: preconditions for consultation.
   - The suffering and complaints of the patient (in the patient's own words) and the reasons for the patient to consult the therapist (manifest symptoms).
   - Observation of the scenic, non-verbal behaviour of the patient on the first contact.
   - The spontaneous impression of the therapist.
   - Emotional condition, state of mind, the way the patient describes his illness.
   - Preliminary diagnostic and psychodynamic considerations (transference and countertransference).
   - Reasons for the therapist to accept the patient for therapy.

2. *Biography*

   - The patient's personal development, family history, and present psychosocial situation. This includes professional development, school, university, current job, profession of father, mother, age of parents, how long they have been married, and whether there are siblings. If there are, how many, and what are their ages? It also includes diseases, accidents, trauma in childhood or adolescence, death of grandparents, parents, or siblings, moves in childhood, separation, loss, and changes of care-giving person, and asks how often and when. What is the patient's marital status? Does he or she have children? If so, how many, and what are their ages?
   - How does the patient judge his development in childhood and adolescence?
   - Has the patient had previous treatments? If yes, when, which kind, and for how long? Has he or she received medication?

3. *Patient–therapist relationship*

   - The transference and countertransference in the beginning and their development during the therapy.
   - Important moments and shifts within the therapy.
   - Sequences of concrete dialogue between patient and therapist: the topics of the patient, the understanding of the therapist, formulation of interpretations. How does the therapist talk with his patient (give interpretations) and what is the answer and reaction of the patient? (The therapist should write down the material after the session; using a tape recorder is not allowed for ethical reasons, unless the patient agrees to the recording.)

4. *Diagnostic and psychodynamic considerations*

   - What is the patient's central conflict (focus)?
   - Is there a trauma or a traumatic cause?
   - How does the therapist understand the symptom formation?
   - What are the unconscious compromises?
   - Which defence mechanisms can be seen?
   - Is there a development of the therapist's hypothesis during the treatment?

5. *The frame/setting*

- What are the arrangements concerning the time (sessions per week), expected duration of treatment (short-term or long-term treatment), the fee, the handling of vacations, and if the patient did not come to a session, etc?

6. *Treatment plan*

- Aims of the treatment.
- Development and present state of the therapy.
- Prognosis.

7. *Results*

- Which aims of the patient could be reached?
- Which aims of the therapist could be reached?
- Any other comments about the therapy.

To present or to write a case report about a still extant or finished psychoanalytical treatment is often not so easy. It is sometimes hard work, but it is a good exercise and provides reflection about the complexity of psychotherapy.

CHAPTER EIGHT

PSYCHOPATHOLOGY AND PSYCHODYNAMICS OF NEUROSIS

Matthias Elzer, Michael Wolf, Hermann Schultz, Irmgard Dettbarn, and Anne-Marie Schloesser

General theories of neuroses

Matthias Elzer

Historical aspects of the term "neurosis"

The term "neurosis" was first used by the Scottish physician, Cullen, in 1787; he wanted to express his understanding that mental disorders are caused by the nervous system. He collected typical neuroses and psychosomatic and neurological disorders together under this term.

Freud used different terms for, and concepts of, neuroses, which changed during later decades. Table 8.1 provides an overview of the terms used in Freud's literature.

Freud tried to avoid differentiating between neuroses and psychoses and he separated neurosis from perversion.

The actual understanding and use of the term neuroses is described later.

Trauma vs. conflict

In the beginning of psychoanalysis, Freud and others, such as Breuer, assumed from their clinical experiences that the origin of suffering from neuroses is a sexual seduction or abuse in the patient's childhood. The reason for a neurosis is a traumatic experience. We call this the trauma theory. This was the beginning of a "trauma model of mental disorders".

However, with further clinical experience, Freud recognised that very often the sexual seduction and abuse existed only in the infantile fantasy of the child, especially in the context of oedipal stage, where infantile sexual fantasies and explanations are vivid in the child's mind.

Freud amended his understanding of neurosis from the theory of trauma to the theory of conflict, an infantile conflict, which was unsolved and repressed in childhood into the unconscious and reactivated in adolescence and adulthood by similar circumstances.

Table 8.1. Overview of the terms related to "neurosis".

Term	Meaning in Freud	Relevance today
Actual neurosis	Neurasthenia and anxiety neurosis. Caused by problems of being sexually unsatisfied	No different to neurosis, "neurasthenia" (*ICD-10*)
Psychoneurosis, or neurosis	Symbolic expression of an intrapsychic conflict, based in childhood, a compromise-formation of (drive) wishes and defence	Neurosis, in Freud's sense
Narcissistic neurosis	Early use, psychoses Later, affective psychoses only	Today, we use only the term psychosis (schizophrenia, affective psychosis). "Narcissistic neurosis" in sense of "narcissistic personality disorder"
Transference neurosis	Psychoneurosis, such as forms of hysteria, obsessive compulsive neurosis, but no narcissistic neurosis (psychosis)	No relevance
Neuropsychosis	Differentiation from actual neurosis, partly the same as psychoneurosis	No relevance
Neuropsychosis of defence	A very early term; he pointed out the function of defence	No relevance
Perversion	Deviation from "normal" sexual activity, change of sexual object or sexual modus, e.g., exhibitionism	The same meaning; homosexuality is not psychopathological

In the history of psychoanalysis, the trauma theory and the theory of intrapsychic conflict existed in parallel. During the past decades, however, the trauma theory (i.e., trauma experienced through sexual abuse, violence, and emotional neglect) received more attention.

Neuroses were and are one of the main areas of responsibility of psychoanalysis and psychodynamic psychotherapy. During the past thirty years, behaviour therapy discovered neuroses, especially phobia, panic disorders, and obsessive–compulsive neuroses.

The disappearance of the term "neurosis" in ICD-10 *and* DSM-IV

In the past twenty years, the term "neurosis" has disappeared in the classification systems of *ICD-10* and *DSM-IV*; these publications use only the term "neurotic disorder", and have eliminated some historical diagnoses. The same happened with many psychosomatic disorders. These classifications want to give a description of the disorders only through collection of significant symptoms; they have no causal concept in the sense of nosology (theory of psychopathology).

To give an example of the disappearance of the diagnosis, in *ICD-10* the concept of "neurotic depression", or "depressive reaction", or "depressive personality disorder" was omitted. In Chapter F, we find, under "affective disorders", "depressive episode" with differentiation in "low", "middle" and "severe" episodes with and without psychotic symptoms.

In *ICD-9*, we could find the diagnosis "neurotic depression". In *ICD-10*, neurotic depression changed into "dysthymia" (F, 34.1) and means a chronic depressive mood, running for a minimum of two years without severe or repeated episodes.

The same thing happened to the old analytic diagnosis "hysteria". It changed to "dissociate disorder" (F44) or into "histrionic personality disorder".

Many textbooks in psychoanalysis, psychotherapy, and psychiatry followed the classifications of *ICD-10* and *DSM-IV* and gave up the historical psychoanalytical concept of neurosis. None the less, it is practical to use both the historic causal concepts and the descriptions of the classification systems.

The systematics of mental disorders

On the subject of medicine and psychology, the mental disorders are divided in three groups, as shown in Table 8.2.

Mental disorders of human beings have psychic and somatic parts and reasons. The mixture of these parts is different, related to the disease but also variable in individual cases during the process of disease (Table 8.3).

Table 8.2. Overview of mental disorders.

	Neurosis	Psychosomatic disorder	Psychosis
Clinical examples	Hysteria	Conversion phenomenon	Organic psychosis (i.e., dementia)
	Depression Anxiety disorders (phobia, panic attack, anxiety neurosis) Obsessive–compulsive neurosis Traumatic neurosis Personality disorder, etc.	Psychosomatosis (i. e., asthma, stomach or bowel ulcer inflammatory bowel disease disease, hypertension) Somatisation (i.e., heart phobia, vertigo, acute or chronic pain) Hypochondria Eating disorders, etc.	Schizophrenia Affective psychosis (major depression, megalomania) etc.

Table 8.3. Somatic and psychic parts of mental disorders.

Mental disorders								
Neurosis			Psychosomatic disorders			Psychosis		
Somatic	Psychic		Somatic	Psychic		Somatic	Psychic	
0	50	100%	0	50	100%	0	50	100%

Epidemiology of mental disorders

During the past twenty-five years, many epidemiological studies have increased our knowledge about the incidence of mental disorders. The epidemiological studies in both Germany and more widely in Europe show similar findings and are related to the design and research question.

If we collect two studies together, one from a psychiatric point of view (Dilling, Weyerer, & Castell, 1984) and the other from a psychosomatic angle (Franz, Lieberz, & Schepank, 2000), we can present the data about the prevalence of mental diseases in the population in Germany (prevalence = how many people are suffering at the time of research) in Table 8.4.

From this, we can extrapolate the epidemiology of the German population as follows.

1. Approximately 31% of the population were suffering from mental disease which needed treatment.
2. Approximately 24.5% (80% of them) were suffering from neurotic and psychosomatic diseases and needed a psychotherapeutic treatment.
3. Approximately 6.5% (20% of them) were suffering from a neuro-psychiatric disease and needed psychiatric treatment.

This is summarised in Table 8.5.

Table 8.4. Epidemiology of mental diseases of the German population: I.

	Neurotic and psychiatric diseases[1] (percentage of population)	Neurotic and psychosomatic diseases[2] (percentage of population)
Population suffering from mental disorders	40.9	50.0
Needing no treatment, because temporary, transient	22.3	24.0
Needing treatment	18.6	26.0
Diagnoses:		
Neuroses and personality disorders	12.0	12.9
Psychosomatic disorders	*	11.6
Schizophrenic psychoses	0.4	*
Affective psychoses (depression, mania)	1.3	*
Addiction (alcohol, drugs, narcotics)	1.8	1.5
Organic brain disorders (dementia)	1.4	*
Other brain injuries	0.6	*
Mental deficiency (imbecility)	1.0	*

* Was not studied in this research.

[1] The representative field study by Dilling, Weyerer, and Castell (1984) researched the rural population of Bavaria, Germany in respect of psychiatric and neurotic diseases; psychosomatic disorders were not studied.

[2] The research group of Franz, Lieberz, and Schepank (2000), from the famous Zentralinstitut für Seelische Gesundheit Mannheim, conducted a representative long-term study starting in 1979 (*Mannheimer Kohortenstudie*) on how many people were suffering from psychosomatic and neurotic diseases and how the process of the diseases was progressing.

Table 8.5. Epidemiology of mental diseases of the German population: II.

Population needing treatment treatment for mental disease	Population with psychosomatic and neurotic diseases	Population with psychiatric diseases
Approx. 31%	Approx. 24.5%	Approx. 6.5%

Actual tendencies of mental health in Germany

In recent years, the German health insurance companies describe an increase in psychosomatic and neurotic diseases such as acute and chronic vertebral pain syndrome of the back, so-called fibromyalgia, so-called chronic fatigue syndrome, and so-called burnout syndrome. We can interpret the incidence of these diseases as a somatic expression of depression and psychosocial pressure and stress. Further, the insurance companies register an increase of the diagnosis of depression.

The statistical data of the German health authorities show an opposite trend with regard to suicide: compared with 1980, the number of people who committed suicide was halved in 2010, going from 24.6 to 11.8 suicides per 100,000 people (*Statistical Yearbook of the Federal Republic of Germany*, 2011).

One possible interpretation of these counter-tendencies in mental health is that mental disorders increase concomitantly with psychosocial stress and that the people suffering from these disorders demand more help from health professionals such as psychiatrists and psychotherapists.

What is neurosis?

Very often, neuroses and psychosomatic diseases are difficult to differentiate clearly. For example, the heart phobia is a typical neurosis, but it can be classified as a psychosomatic disorder, too, because bodily symptoms (the fear of dying from a heart attack) are at the centre of the patient's suffering. Another example is the conversion symptom of hysteria: the symptoms are primarily somatic (i.e., pain or dysfunction of the motor or sensitive nerve system).

Nearly every neurosis has a somatic part because of the sympathetic reaction of the vegetative nervous system. Anxiety is a common symptom of the neuroses: it is a bodily reaction.

In the early days of psychoanalysis, the psychopathology did not differentiate between neurosis and psychosomatic diseases. Psychosomatic medicine started to develop more by the internal medicine as by the psychiatry and neurology inside and outside the psychoanalysis. The term "psychosomatic medicine" was first used by the internist and psychoanalyst Felix Deutsch, in 1922 (Meyer, 2005, p. 1)

It is useful to separate neurosis from psychosomatic disorders. In the next part of our chapter, we will discuss the general aspects of psychosomatic medicine.

Hoffmann and Hochapfel have provided a definition of neuroses:

> Neuroses are psychogenetic, mostly environmental diseases, which determine a disorder in the psychic and/or somatic and/or personal field.
>
> The psychoanalytical understanding of neurosis is that it is an insufficient attempt at processing unconscious conflicts and traumata which are caused in childhood.

> Behaviour theory points out the genetic role of conditioning as a consequence of missed, too strong, or too weak learning processes. (1999, p. 8, translated for this edition)

The systematics of neuroses

There are some different systematics of neuroses occurring in the psychodynamic literature, which are explained in the following subsections.

The classical systematic of neuroses and personality disorders

There are three groups of disorders, symptom neurosis, traumatic neurosis, and personality disorders.

Symptom neurosis

Symptom neuroses are identified by the main symptom of this disorder, for example, depression, anxiety, or compulsion. Neurosis is the symbolic expression of an intrapsychic conflict, which is based in childhood. The common conflicts of psychosexual development are unresolved and fixed. The content of the conflict is repressed into the unconscious by the defence system. Later, mostly in early adulthood, the conflict is forced out of the unconscious into consciousness through the failure of the defence mechanism. The conflict is revived by a similar event in the patient's present life. The symptom is a compromise formation.

Resolving symptom neuroses is the main task of psychodynamic psychotherapy and psychoanalysis.

Traumatic neurosis

The reason for this type of neurosis is not a conflict, but a real trauma in childhood, adolescence, or adulthood. An overwhelming emotional stimulus takes over psychic capability and the defence system. The traumatic experience (sexual abuse, violent acts, emotional neglect, deprivation) cannot be completely repressed, so the emotional parts are split from the cognitive content. The emotional reaction (i.e., anxiety or panic) is still able to be invoked.

The impact of the traumatic experience is particularly strong if it meets a childhood conflict that has not been resolved or if the person has no social and psychological support after the traumatic event.

Post traumatic stress disorder (PTSD) is a modern term for traumatic neurosis.

Figure 8.1 illustrates in a simple form the process of symptom reaction for symptom neuroses and traumatic neurosis.

The personality disorders

During psychosexual development, every person develops a personality or a character, which is stable throughout life. The personality influences the use and handling of emotions, drives, relationships, styles of communication, and social behaviour. It is like colour or an individual style. Biological aspects (temperament) work together with personality.

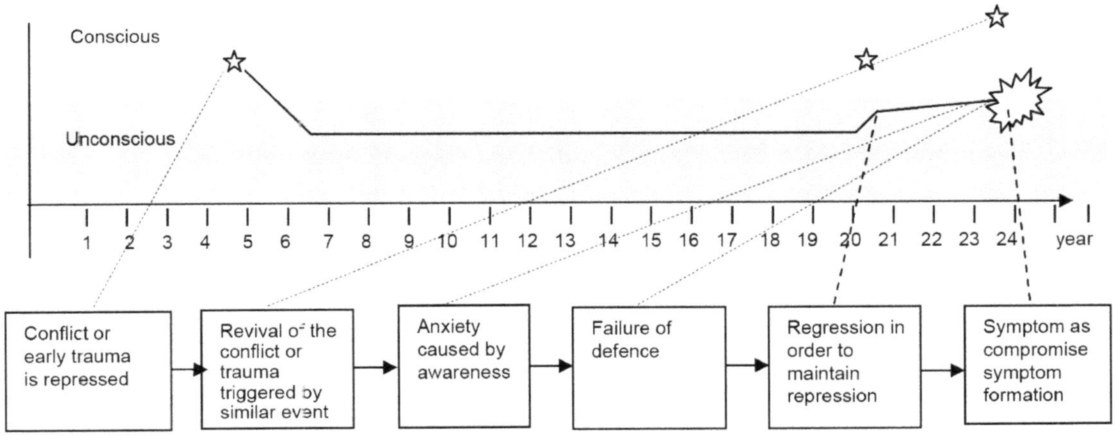

Figure 8.1. The process of symptom reaction (Elzer, 2012, translated for this edition).

In the terminology of psychoanalysis, we talk about the personality structure of a person, and sometimes we add an evaluative adjective, such as hysterical, narcissistic, depressive, inhibited, aggressive, or schizoid personality, but this is not pathological.

There is a fluid transition to personality disorder, where the main symptom influences social interaction. We can describe this as moving from personality to personality disorder and ending with symptom neurosis.

Example: A person with a compulsive personality likes to do every thing perfectly and exactly. There are no significant problems in the environment and relationships of this person. He does his job thoroughly and responsibly. A person with a compulsive personality disorder will experience many problems and conflicts with others, because his behaviour causes them to suffer. Very often, the person with the personality disorder has no insight into these problems, or any understanding of them; his behaviour is consistent within himself ("ego-syntonic") and he is not suffering.

Another level of intensity and disorder occurs if the person is suffering from a symptom neurosis of obsessive compulsive neurosis.

For the general diagnosis of patients with personality disorder, it is helpful if at least three of the six criteria given in Table 8.6 exist.

Table 8.6. Criteria of personality disorders (Hoffmann & Hochapfel, 2004, p. 181, translated for this edition).

1	Emotions, impulses, perception, thinking, and arrangement of relationships are clearly unbalanced.
2	These patterns of behaviour are enduring.
3	Through the patterns of behaviour, many disturbances are manifested in personal and social situations.
4	The beginning of these disorders is in childhood or adolescence and they manifest in adulthood.
5	The long-term suffering of the patient as a result of the disorder is sometimes obvious.
6	The disorder prevents the patient from developing and using his/her social and professional potentiality.

Mode of neurotic conflict processing

The German psychoanalyst Mentzos (1982) criticised the nosology of neuroses, because there is a big difference between the theory and the clinical reality. Very often, we can see that the neurotic symptoms are not specific to the conflict and stage of development.

For instance, the diagnosis of hysteria is not only the result of an oedipal conflict; we often see a conflict of the oral stage, conflicts of separation, narcissism, and self-esteem. In the nosology, we can say that there are oedipal and pre-oedipal types of hysteria. So, Mentzos suggested a three-dimensional model of the neurosis:

1. The central conflict and other secondary conflicts.
2. The structure and maturation of the ego (self).
3. The defence processing as a "mode of neurotic conflict processing".

Mentzos substitutes the term "neurosis" with the term "mode": hysterical mode, narcissistic mode, and psychosomatic mode.

The symptom systematic of neuroses

Hoffmann and Hochapfel (2004, p. 181) classified the neuroses by the main symptoms listed in the *ICD-10* (Table 8.7).

Another diagnostic instrument, which combines descriptive and psychodynamic aspects, is the "operationalised psychodynamic diagnostic" (OPD) desiged by Cierpka and colleagues (2001), which uses five axes to assess the indication of psychodynamic psychotherapy.

Diagnostic instruments are helpful, but it should be borne in mind that a nosological systematic is no substitute for psychodynamic understanding.

Table 8.7. Systematic of neuroses (Hoffman & Hochapfel, 2004, translated for this edition).

Specific neurosis	Symptoms according to *ICD-10*.
Neurosis with expressed development of anxiety	Panic attack, generalised anxiety disorder, phobia, heart phobia, hypochondria, neurasthenia, anxiety related to natural environment
Neurosis with expressed auto-aggression	Depression (dysthymia, depressive episodes, recurring depressive disorders) psychological masochism, artificiality, and self-harm
Obsessive–compulsive disorders	Different forms of OCD
Dissociate (conversion) disorders, including depersonalisation	Dissociate amnesia, fugue, stupor, trance state, convulsion, Ganser syndrome, depersonalisation syndrome, derealisation syndrome, dissociative identity disorder
Reaction to severe stress and adjustment disorders	Acute stress reaction,post traumatic stress disorder, adjustment disorder

Patient-orientated and psychodynamic thinking

The psychotherapist needs professional knowledge of the mental disorders as a theory of psychopathology, but he also draws on his clinical experience, understanding that the patients are not necessarily as described in the textbooks: they are much more different and complex.

Psychodynamic understanding and treatment is patient orientated, or person orientated, rather than disease orientated. This means we treat patients who are suffering from mental or somatic disorders, and not merely disorders and diseases.

The therapist has to understand the disorder of a patient by studying the biography, the psychosexual development, as a dynamic process; it is not a static state. The special dynamic of the patient also influences the therapeutic relationship through the phenomena of transference and countertransference, with particular defence mechanisms and kinds of resistance during therapy.

This is what we describe as being "psychodynamic".

Hysteria: dissociative and somatoform disorders

Michael Wolf

Preliminary remark

The psychoanalytic concepts of hysteria, phobia, and anxiety neurosis belong to a nosological tradition that was based on so-called "disease-units" (named by the German psychiatrist, Kraepelin). This meant units consisting of interrelated causes, processes, and symptoms of diseases. In this manner, the psychoanalytical concepts of diseases, and the psychiatric ones, too, have been conceived during the twentieth century up to new classifications of *DSM* and *ICD* beginning in the 1980s. From this time on, first research, and later clinical practice, abandoned the idea of a disease unit in favour of a differentiation by symptoms, now renamed "disorders", and different levels of phenomena which were related to them but which where not supposed to be clear "causes" and have typical courses. However, psychoanalysis did not embrace this change, holding on to the traditional and, in some sense, more intellectual and, perhaps, also clinically satisfying concept of the disease unit. For the problems resulting from giving up this tradition, one may look, for example, at the OPD (operationalised psychodynamic diagnostics), which provides a very differentiated system for psychodynamic diagnoses related to the disorder diagnoses of *DSM* and *ICD*, which is also splitting off typical forms of neuroses artificially into different symptoms/disorders/diagnoses.

The English version of *ICD* (2010) that I am referring to here has also given up this "disease unit" concept, but psychoanalytical considerations about neuroses are still holding to it.

Neuroses are primarily consequences of conflictual, more or less traumatic and disturbing experiences of the personality. The varieties of personal development, structures, conflicts, defences, coping mechanisms, and other factors lead to neurotic solutions of conflicts appearing as symptoms that are not so easy to diagnose with reference to such seemingly clear cut types of neuroses. Nevertheless, for both the theoretical and the practical (therapeutically) concept of understanding, it is useful and helpful to classify typical constellations with apparently similar psychodynamic causes, courses, and symptoms

It was Freud who first explored and developed an understanding of the aetiology (i.e., the psycho-genesis, the psychodynamic of the usually known clinical "pictures") of phobia, compulsion, hysterical neurosis, anxiety neurosis, and depression. He devised a theoretical model for the development of neurosis and tried to classify the neurotic "pictures" according to specific causes, conflicts, structures, and defence mechanisms of the personality. So, diagnosis nowadays refers to different levels: the manifest symptoms, the neurotic mood of the conflict and its typical defence mechanisms, and the psychogenesis in life development or/and traumatic experiences.

In the *ICD*, in contrast, the psychoanalytical concept of hysteria is split into its two main symptoms: dissociation and somatisation.

In F44, the *ICD-10* speaks of dissociative (conversion) disorders, defined by

> a partial or complete loss of the normal integration between memories of the past, awareness of identity and immediate sensations, and control of bodily movements. All types of dissociative disorders tend to remit after a few weeks or months, particularly if their onset is associated with a traumatic life event. More chronic disorders, particularly paralyses and anaesthesias, may develop if the onset is associated with insoluble problems or interpersonal difficulties. These disorders have previously been classified as various types of "conversion hysteria". They are presumed to be psychogenic in origin, being associated closely in time with traumatic events, insoluble and intolerable problems, or disturbed relationships. The symptoms often represent the patient's concept of how a physical illness would be manifest. Medical examination and investigation do not reveal the presence of any known physical or neurological disorder. In addition, there is evidence that the loss of function is an expression of emotional conflicts or needs. The symptoms may develop in close relationship to psychological stress, and often appear suddenly. Only disorders of physical functions normally under voluntary control and loss of sensations are included here. Disorders involving pain and other complex physical sensations mediated by the autonomic nervous system are classified under somatization disorder (F45.0). The possibility of the later appearance of serious physical or psychiatric disorders should always be kept in mind.

In F45, somatoform disorders are presented, with the main feature of

> repeated presentation of physical symptoms together with persistent requests for medical investigations, in spite of repeated negative findings and reassurances by doctors that the symptoms have no physical basis. If any physical disorders are present, they do not explain the nature and extent of the symptoms or the distress and preoccupation of the patient.

This includes, particularly, "Somatisation disorder", with the main symptoms of various, often changing, physical symptoms.

The psychodynamic concept

Symptoms of hysteria and hysterical character formation

The word hysteria has its origin in the Greek word *hystera*, which means womb (uterus) and was used in the pre-scientific area of medicine to describe the somatic symptoms of women, which, as we know today, are often linked to sexual conflicts of both women and men and have nothing to do with the womb as an organ.

The symptoms comprise functional disorders of the body, paralysis, anaesthesias, complications with seeing or hearing, being voiceless (aphonia), disturbance of one's sense of balance, etc., that imitate organic illnesses but for which no organic reason can be found (all reflexes are present, pupil reaction is normal, muscles are in good condition, etc.).

They also include phenomena of mental dissociation: amnesia, mental gloom, and hysterical pseudo hallucinations.

Hysterical character formations include dramatisation, partial inability to differentiate between fantasy and reality, extraordinary susceptibility to suggestions of others, delicacy (an expressive coquetry, coquettishness, theatrical ability, impressionistic cognition.

What these groups of different phenomena have in common is the style of the neurotic conflict solution.

Freud conceptualised hysterical symptoms as an unconscious compromise between an impulse which is defended and the ego, which is defending this impulse. Hence, conversion has become the typical concept of hysteria while the original concept of this is a physical one: the accumulated libidinal energy is transformed or converted into somatic nervous tension. The accumulation of the libidinal energy is caused by a conflict. Freud had the idea that the libidinal energy needed to be separated from the original but intolerable image, so that it had to be split off and became repressed and converted into nervous energy, which, in turn, leads to a somatic symptom with a symbolic function ("reappearance of the repressed").

Case examples

The female patient with the disabled arm. The symptom started after a conflict with her friend which took place while she was ironing. She wanted to hit him with the iron, but forbade herself at the same moment. Hence, the symptom appeared as a compromise between aggression and punishment of the aggression.

The frigid patient who developed vertigo during the sessions, which she described as being as if she might fall down and lose herself. The working through of the symptom led to her sexual thoughts, which were aroused after an intervention by the analyst turned into sexual wishes (appearing in dreams) that she could not consciously recognise. She could then speak about having fantasies of soon having intercourse, and other sexual fantasies that she immediately repressed. Here, the symptom of vertigo represents the compromise between the wish to lie down or to fall down and lose herself in sexual satisfaction on the one hand, and the anxiety connected with sexual experiences and the threat of punishment for her desires.

So, here, the model of conversion as a compromise between repressed wishes and impulses on the one hand and punishing tendencies on the other hand is obvious.

Processes of identification can lead to hysterical symptoms. Freud referred to the case of a girl who collapsed in joyful excitement after she had received a love-letter from her friend (a boy) in the classroom. The next day, other girls collapsed, too, in the process of resolving the conflict between envy of their schoolfellow and the desire also to receive a love letter through identification with her.

Other defence mechanisms are repression (one of the most important preconditions for unconscious processing), dissociation, which leads to separate conscious states of mind that are contradictory, but exist in parallel ("the right hand does not know what the left hand is doing"), and emotionalisation as an opposite to intellectualisation.

The most specific in the hysterical style of conflict resolution, according to the psychoanalyst Mentzos (1980), is an unconscious enactment of the self for both an inner observer (ego and superego) and an observer (or an audience) in external reality. The enactment provides partially hidden satisfaction, a binding of affects, and, at the same time, allows, as its main function, the temporary alteration of self-representation in order to appear in a particular manner in front of the inner observer (ego/superego) or an external observer.

A patient with hysterical paralysis enacts and presents himself to others and to himself as a person that cannot "stand" any more, that cannot "go" any more; a patient with aphonia cannot speak; one with vertigo cannot be in clear conscience; someone with amnesia cannot remember, and there are other symptom formations with evident symbolic content.

When these patients appear to be more ill and "weak" than they really are, then we call them pseudo-regressive or, similarly, when they appear stronger than they are, we speak of a pseudo-progressive dynamic.

Psychogenesis of hysteria

Originally (with Freud), hysterical symptoms and character formations were linked to conflicts of the oedipal phase (Oedipus complex). At this stage of psychosexual development, the psyche is occupied with repressed incestuous desires towards the parent of the opposite sex, and with hostile affects towards the parent of the same sex. These emotions are—according to Freud´s early model—unconsciously reactivated in the adult's life by some analogous life experiences (e.g., jealousy, loss of a beloved partner, etc.). In the subsequent course of clinical and theoretical development, psychoanalysis has learnt from its patients that oral conflicts, as well as narcissistic conflicts, can be responsible for hysterical symptoms and hysterical character formations.

Rupprecht-Schampera (1995) presents and discusses those early "oedipal" aspects of hysteria that could be considered as very important for the understanding and treatment of it, especially the so-called early triangulation: that is, the triangulation function of the father in the early stages of development and the role of father in general (Lacan). Here, the hypothesis is that the non-accessibility of the father in the early stages might lead to disturbances with the "oedipal" father relationship, such as splitting of the idealised–absent and the "seducing" real father, the devaluation of the mother, and the search for other idealised father representations, and, finally, the idealised phallus (in the patient´s phantasy).

Primary and secondary gain resulting from the hysterical symptoms is particularly relevant in hysteria, in the hysterical enactments. Each neurotic symptom leads to partial reduction of anxieties through repression and partial satisfaction through the neurotic compromise. That is what is meant by primary gain. Because of their neurotic solutions, the patients are regarded as ill and, as such, they receive more care and rest and increased attention. Some patients are unable to go to work any more, and might retire. That is what is meant by secondary gain.

Anxiety disorders

Preliminary remark

As explained in the subsection headed "Hysteria: dissociative and somatoform disorders", above, there is a nosological difference between the psychoanalytical way of thinking about neuroses as illness units and the psychiatric viewpoint, which is based on a disorder orientation. These two positions are only sometimes bridged by concepts such as those in the OCD.

Phobic disorders

In the *ICD-10*, phobic anxiety disorders are defined as a

> group of disorders in which anxiety is evoked only, or predominantly, in certain well-defined situations that are not currently dangerous. As a result these situations are characteristically avoided or endured with dread. The patient's concern may be focused on individual symptoms like palpitations or feeling faint and is often associated with secondary fears of dying, losing control, or going mad. Contemplating entry to the phobic situation usually generates anticipatory anxiety.

The *ICD-10* defines agoraphobia as a

> cluster of phobias embracing fears of leaving home, entering shops, crowds and public places, or travelling alone in trains, buses or planes, social phobias with the main symptom of avoidance of social situations, and specific isolated phobias, which are restricted to highly specific situations. This can be a nearness to special animals, the experience of heights, of darkness etc.

Psychodynamic concept of phobic neurosis

Phobic individuals are suffering from anxieties related to objects and/or situations that are not reasonable in an objective sense. The symptoms are agoraphobia and claustrophobia (respectively, wide open or closed rooms containing other human beings), animal phobia, bridge phobia, fear of heights, more general social phobia, and others.

Case example: Bridge phobia: The patient with the bridge phobia developed the symptom when she drove for the first time over a bridge with her mother-in-law, with whom she had had many conflicts in past weeks. During the analysis, the patient discovered that while she was driving over the bridge, she had the impulse to turn the car to the right and drive into the abyss with the mother-in-law. The aggressive and auto-aggressive impulse was immediately repressed. The anxiety about a reappearance of the impulse was replaced by the bridge phobia, which also occurred when she drove alone. Later on in analysis, it became clear that the actual conflict with her mother-in-law repeated earlier conflicts with her own mother. Therefore, her fears about driving over a bridge could be analysed as displaced anxieties deriving from murderous feelings of aggression towards her own mother. The primary gain of the phobic symptom in this case derives from the (unconscious) displacement of the original aggression, leading to the reduction of anxiety, and from the expression of that aggression in the disguised symptomatic form.

Psychogenesis and psychodynamics

Phobias are the result of the defence against fantasies and emotions that provoke anxieties. These original anxieties are displaced (displacement is the most important defence mechanism in phobia) on to situations or objects which are considered to be less dangerous. The main defence mechanism is repression, so that the conflict becomes unconscious. By means of the subsequent displacement, the original intrapsychic danger and anxiety become (virtually) danger and anxiety related to the outside world. As it now seems to be a conflict outside the anxiety-provoking situation, it is possible for it to be avoided. Avoidance is another important defence mechanism in phobia.

Originally (in instinct theory), phobia was linked to oedipal genital conflicts. A classic example is Freud´s case history of "little Hans", where the ambivalence (love–hate) towards the father was displaced on to a horse, which he feared would both fall down and bite him.

Today (in object-relations theory), attention concerning phobic symptoms is much more focused on the fear of the loss of an important object, which is an anxiety deriving from a conflictive mother–child relationship. In human development, conflicts in the mother–child dyad are precursors of triadic conflicts (oedipal), as Freud posited, and both are important as causes of anxieties and phobias. Phobic persons often live in a partnership in which they are very dependent on the partner, so that being away from this partner, for whatever reason, can provoke anxieties. On the other hand, the presence of the partner calms the anxieties of the phobic person. Transferred to the oedipal level of conflict, it can be seen as comparable: distance can provoke anxieties (seduction by others, fraud, etc.) and presence can provide feelings of security (e.g., no anxiety). Conscious and unconscious wishes about being cared for and being satisfied with dependence on others are also often found with phobic patients, as well as the need to control such persons and partners, displaced from the phobic object or situation.

Concerning phobic choice, the symbolic aspect can be important. The fear of walking on a street, for example, can derive from exhibitionistic tendencies (anxiety about presenting oneself naked in public, or walking the street in the sense of being a prostitute). Knives or other similar objects that carry displaced genital or aggressive (phallic) connotations might become objects to be feared and avoided.

Lichtenberg (1991a) discusses the differences between fear, anxiety, and phobia. In early infant development, fear as a basic affect is part of aversive affects, one of the "motivational systems" leading to and protecting the interaction with others. Fear as an indicator and motivator for the anticipation of danger is essential for infants because they "are remarkably ill prepared innately to perceive danger" (Lichtenberg, 1991a, p. 396). So, "stranger anxiety" (or eight-month-anxiety, as it was once termed by Spitz) is essential for existence and development. This is particularly affirmed by Volkan (1988), understanding the need to have allies and enemies(!) as an overall condition of human existence, based on the earliest stages of child development as well as the earliest relations with other significant persons (e.g., parents). Given stable and trustful early experiences, normal babies (and adults) explore their environment lustily and with interest, developing efficiency, competence, and a sense of security (through control). Disturbed babies (and adults), however, experience failed efforts when confronting novel aspects, with feelings of humiliation, etc., mobilising the activation of aggression as a means of getting help. Lichtenberg continues by saying that phobias, or phobic symptoms, appear as a compromise between different tendencies (avoidance, interest, and attachment, thrill, anxiety, pleasure, or lust). A phobia creates a safety-providing pseudo-solution, organised as a story containing a "cause" of the fear (horse, tiger, etc.), which disguises more severe and painful or conflictive feelings such as shame, guilt, greed, or sexual rivalry.

Other anxiety disorders as defined by the ICD-10

The *ICD-10* defines other anxiety disorders as disorders "in which manifestation of anxiety is the major symptom and is not restricted to any particular environmental situation". The most prominent is the panic disorder (episodic paroxysmal anxiety) with

> recurrent attacks of severe anxiety (panic), which are not restricted to any particular situation or set of circumstances and are therefore unpredictable. As with other anxiety disorders, the dominant symptoms include sudden onset of palpitations, chest pain, choking sensations, dizziness, and feelings of unreality (depersonalization or derealization).

Another type is the generalised anxiety disorder with often "free-floating anxiety".

The psychodynamic concept

Anxiety is at the core of the psychoanalytic theory of *affects* (feelings), and, from the beginning of psychoanalytic thought, anxiety has been recognised as central to an understanding of mental conflict (for it is through bad feelings that conflicts are felt and known). In his early work, Freud, in keeping with his early discharge model of mental function, considered anxiety to be a "toxic transformation" of undischarged libido. This failure of discharge could either be physiological ("realistic"), as in *coitus interruptus* or other incomplete or unsatisfactory sexual practices, resulting in "actual neuroses" or "anxiety neuroses", or it could arise from repression (or its failure), as a symptom of the continued pressure of unacceptable desires, which led to the "psychoneuroses"—hysteria and obsessions.

In 1926, Freud radically revised his ideas about anxiety, abandoning the distinction between neurotic and realistic anxiety, together with the claim that repression caused anxiety. In this new theory, Freud distinguished two types of anxiety, a traumatic, reality-orientated "automatic" anxiety in which the system was overwhelmed, and a secondary, "neurotic" anxiety in which reprisals for these situations were anticipated, thus setting defensive processes in motion. "Automatic anxiety" was an affective reaction to the helplessness experienced during a traumatic experience. The prototype for this experience lies in the helplessness of the infant during and after birth, in which the danger came from outside and flooded a psychic system essentially unmediated by the (as yet unformed) ego.

The second form of anxiety originated within the psychical system and was mediated by the ego. This "signal anxiety" presaged the emergence of a new "danger situation" that would be a repetition of one of several earlier "traumatic states". These states, the prototype of which lay in birth, corresponded to the central preoccupations of different developmental levels, as the infant's needs become progressively abstracted from the original situation of immediate sensory overload to more sophisticated forms of need regulation capable of synthesising the many elements facing it (from the reality and pleasure principles and the object world). These moments, *loss of the object, loss of the object's love, the threat of castration,* and *the fear of punishment by the internalised objects of the superego,* which were experienced serially during the developmental process, could re-emerge at any time in a person's subsequent adult life, typically brought on by some conflation of reality and intrapsychic conflict, as a new occasion for anxiety.

This new way of conceptualising anxiety was an outgrowth of Freud's late revisions of his theory (1923b) with the structural theory and his formulation of the mediating agency of the ego, and it had the effect of shifting clinical work on anxiety into the realm of the ego. The correlation of the dangerous situations with developmental stages also suggested a diagnostic aspect to anxiety, with the earlier types of anxiety indicating earlier fixations. In the work of later theorists, the presence of the earliest anxieties in clinical work have been thought to be indicative of pre-oedipal disturbances in development, and of corresponding structural deficits in the ego.

The psychoanalyst and psychiatrist Mentzos has differentiated anxieties in two dimensions: body related *vs.* only or mainly psychic anxieties, and diffuse *vs.* specific anxieties, the latter better known as fears (Table 8.8).

Table 8.8. Dimensions of anxiety (Mentzos, 1984, p. 19, translated for this edition).

	Level of anxiety (A–F)								
Body related diffuse	11							12	Psychic, desomatised, specific
				F			1		
				E		2			
				D	3				
	10	6	5	C					
		9	7	B		4			
		8		A					
									(continued)

Table 8.8. (continued)

Level and content of anxiety		Type of anxiety disorder/neurosis
F Castration	12	Normal, non-neurotic fear
E Loss of love and/or autonomy	11	Panic anxiety with natural catastrophes
D Loss of self-esteem	1	"Ripe" phobia
and mirroring	2	
C Loss of object and self-object	3	Oedipal phobia (Little Hans)
B Destruction of "good objects"	4	Phobia with narcissistic disorder
A Disintegration (psychosis)	5	Phobia with borderline disorder
	6	Agoraphobia/social phobia
	7	Panic attack
	8	Diffuse anxiety with borderline disorder
	9	Diffuse anxiety with psychosis
	10	Panic attack with borderline decompensated anxiety, early stage (eight months)

Depression (dysthymia)

Hermann Schultz

First, an introductory remark concerning depression (and obsessive–compulsive disorders as well, see Chapter Nine): today we know much more than in Freud's time about the role of organic and genetic factors, brain functions, neurotransmitters, etc.; therefore, besides psychodynamic psychotherapy, other treatment approaches (antidepressant medication, CBT) have been developed, and there is often the question of indication: finding out which form of therapy will be the most effective one for the patient. No doubt there are patients who profit best from psychodynamic psychotherapy; others need medication, combined with psychodynamic psychotherapy or CBT. We will try to formulate criteria for the decision.

Depression has many faces

The term "depression" covers a broad spectrum of apparently very different clinical syndromes. I, as a psychiatrist and a psychoanalytic psychotherapist, during my training as a psychiatric resident, worked for several years in a psychiatric university hospital on closed and open wards where I saw many patients with severe depression.

Later, when working in a psychosomatic clinic, I often observed that the psychosomatic symptoms of this patient group—especially chronic pain syndromes, such as, for instance, chronic headache or fibromyalgia (chronic pain in muscles, without clear organic causes)—are often an expression of an underlying depressive condition. In our diagnostic manuals, this type of disorder is listed not as a form of depression, but as "somatisation disorder", whereas, from a psychodynamic point of view, we often find that while the symptoms are those of a somatisation disorder, the underlying dynamic condition is rather depressive—psychic pain (depression) transformed into somatic pain. Other diagnostic groups of patients whose symptoms often had a depressive background were alcoholics, patients with eating disorders, and overweight individuals.

Finally, during many years of private practice as a psychoanalyst and psychotherapist, I often treated depressive patients in long-term psychodynamic psychotherapy. Here, I had to deal not only with depressive states, but mostly with depressive traits, that is, depressive personality traits and depressive lifestyle, chronic unhappiness, anhedonia (not being able to enjoy life), low self-esteem, inferiority feelings, ambivalent dependence on others, and self-denigrating or self-destructive tendencies.

So, while working in different fields of our profession (in the psychiatric hospital, in a psychosomatic clinic, and in private practice), I met with rather different kinds of depressive patients. On first sight, you might think these different groups of patients do not have much in common. Indeed, their descriptive symptoms and *ICD* diagnoses are very different. However, in spite of their different appearance, from a psychodynamic point of view, essentially all these patients may suffer from a basic depressive disorder with typical symptoms and typical psychodynamic characteristics. Some of them feel and present like typical depressives; with others, the depressive state may be repressed or defended against by flight into work and other activities, such as drinking alcohol, focusing on bodily complaints, or other "masks" for an underlying depression.

Typical symptoms of depression: a depressive core syndrome

In spite of individual differences, we can discern a depressive core syndrome, which is more or less common to them all, although, in less severe cases, part of the symptoms may be lacking or defended against. The typical symptoms of depression appear in the following areas of the patient's mental state.

- Mood and affect: low-key ("depressed") mood, reduced pleasure in life (anhedonia), low self-esteem, loss of self-confidence, ideas of guilt and worthlessness, possibly suicidal ideation, and on a deeper level, often feelings of despair and helpless rage, guilt, and shame, or emptiness, meaninglessness, loss of aliveness.
- Energy and vital functions: reduction of energy and activity, psychomotor retardation (or agitation), inhibition of personality functions (movements, speech, thinking etc.), loss of interest and concentration, decrease in vital functions: sleeping disorder, loss of appetite, weight loss, loss of libido.
- Self and object relations: withdrawal from others or clinging to others,preoccupation with self, often somatic symptoms such as pains, etc.
- Precipitating factors: experiences of loss or defeat, guilt and shame conflicts.

Psychodynamics of depression

These depressive symptoms are the result of long-term developmental processes, with contributions of manifold factors. We may distinguish between two groups of factors: (a) developmental deficits contributing to a life-long vulnerability or disposition for depression; (b) a typical basic depressive conflict, together with typical defence mechanisms to deal with this conflict. We shall first examine vulnerability to depression.

Vulnerability (disposition) to depression

By this, we mean a typical tendency of some patients to react to certain stressful life situations with a depressive mode, that is, easily giving up or feeling given-up, feeling helpless and hopeless, whereas other people would deal differently with the same stresses, for example, through active coping, fighting, and self-assertion. The "depressive mode of dealing with stress" might be easy to recognise in people with a "dependent personality" structure; with others, it might be hidden for a long time behind a façade of overactivity and exaggerated optimism. The origin of the "depressive mode" can be found in the past history of the patient.

- In the family history, we look for possible genetic factors: depression, psychiatric hospital treatment or suicide among family relatives, indications of bipolar affective disorder, etc.
- In the personal developmental history of our depressive patients, we look for the developmental conditions under which the patient grew up as a child and adolescent, and what they may have meant to him in terms of phase-specific developmental needs. In severe cases, we regularly find early developmental deficits and/or severe traumatic experiences.

First of all, we often find a lack of adequate mothering (attachment): perhaps the patient was an unwanted child or lost his/her care-giver very early, or mother was physically present but emotionally not available to help the young child to feel and regulate his emotions, express his feelings, become familiar with himself, and develop an adequate basic feeling of "being-in-this-world" and having the right to exist. In terms of attachment theory, we call this an insecure attachment: either characterised by rejection and loneliness or by symbiotic clinging and separation anxiety.

In our depressive patients, we typically also find a deficit in mastering the next developmental step: separation–individuation, recognising oneself as an individual person, freeing oneself from symbiotic ties, growing more independent in thinking and self-esteem, having one's own will. For this process of separation–individuation, the child (and later the adolescent) needs encouragement, support, and guidance; here, the father, as a person different from mother, can be very helpful. In the case of our depressive patients, father was often absent, or, if present, he was usually very strict, severely punishing, demanding obedience, and disregarding the developmental needs of his child for affirmation as a growing person.

Object loss and separation trauma (also loss of a parent by divorce) happened much more frequently in the life of individuals who later became depressives than with other kinds of patients. About one third of them lost one parent through death before they were sixteen years old (Will, 2000). As a result, they often feel helpless, hopeless, and unable to influence the course of their life.

This is why depressive personality types so often, in a dependent way, keep clinging to the persons they have, on whom they feel dependent, always fearing losing them or losing their love and approval. Because their inner feeling of self-worth is not strong and stable enough, they need these "idealised objects" from which they expect approval and affirmation in order to feel they are valuable persons, spouses, mothers, or members of the group. Therefore, they are willing to go very far in sacrificing themselves, renouncing personal needs to fulfil others' expectations.

Besides what they had been lacking in terms of developmental needs, there is another factor: what has been done to them. By this, I mean psychic trauma, especially early loss of important self-objects, neglect and loveless treatment, and, still worse, physical, emotional, or sexual abuse, which can really crush personality development.

All these repetitive early experiences are internalised into the psychic structure: they become fundamental patterns of self-concept and interpersonal relations. Instead of good experiences of being held, supported, and appreciated by understanding parent figures, we find, in the inner world of depressive people, images like that of a "dead mother" (Green), a threatening or absent father, a lonely or devalued self. Some of our patients feel unable to express their depressive mood in words or find an image for it; these are areas of non-mentalised (often traumatic) experience, which they fear approaching in therapy.

The typical basic conflict of depressive patients

Along with these fundamental developmental deficits, in our depressive patients we find a *typical basic conflict*: on the one hand, they feel a deep wish for a very close relationship with one person (an idealised mother, such as the patient never had), whose love and appreciation is longed for. The quality of this relationship shows clearly symbiotic and oral features. On the other hand, they constantly fear and expect that this longing will again be rejected and frustrated, they will be left hungry (for affection and appreciation). Therefore, they try to control their aggressive impulses (anger about their dependence, narcissistic shame and rage emanating from hurt feelings, reproach as a result of disappointment about the object not being totally at their disposal) for fear of destroying or losing the urgently needed relationship with the idealised object. Such aggressive impulses typically will be turned against oneself (self-reproaches, guilt feelings for fear of having destroyed the object's love), whereas desire for autonomy and independence, for separation and individuation will be defended against. The result is an ambivalent dependence on others (needy and aggressive). Living with this basic conflict means permanent stress connected with efforts to gain others' approval, a constant fear of losing their sympathy, the necessity of adapting to other people's expectations, and suppressing one's own wishes for independence and one's inner rage over being disappointed.

People with a depressive personality structure like this develop various coping or defence strategies to deal with this conflict and obtain a certain amount of satisfaction and security in their life. In our clinical experience and daily life we can observe that:

- the anxious, clinging type is often submissive and self-defeating, living with a constant fear of losing the urgently needed object;
- the altruistic type ("helper syndrome") is self-sacrificing, postponing his own needs and doing his duty;
- the narcissistic type pretends he does not need others, and makes others dependent on him;
- the schizoid type does not fear loneliness, he makes loneliness his preferred state of being, he avoids feelings and close contact with others and tolerates only contact with non-human objects, such as nature, animals, or absorbing subjects such as mathematics and science;
- the regressive type flees from the real world into dream worlds of addiction, etc.

Precipitating factors

Actual depressive states often result when these coping strategies break down for some reason, for example, if anxious clinging and self-defeating submission cannot prevent object loss, or if an altruistic helper feels exhausted and exploited by others, or if they leave him, if the narcissistic type suddenly loses power and attractiveness, if a schizoid person gets more and more isolated and alienated, or if an addictive person is no longer able to anaesthesise his growing despair.

Let us keep these psychodynamic patterns in mind when we now turn to questions of therapy.

The depressive patient in the diagnostic interview

In the initial diagnostic interview, these are our most important aims:

- To establish contact with the patient, offering him a space for presenting—in words or otherwise—his personal condition, building a basic relationship of safety and trust in the therapist's competence and good will. In every case, the therapist should try to find out the precipitating cause that triggered the depressive episode, so that the patient's depression appears as an understandable human reaction to conditions that he was not able to cope with.
- To observe the typical depressive symptomatology and assess if the patient is suffering from (a) "organic" depression (*ICD-10*, F06) caused by organic disease—these patients need organic diagnostics and treatment; (b) "endogenous" depression (*ICD-10*, F31, F32, F33), which means severe "major" depression, with a family history of depression, typically recurrent phases, sometimes manic and depressive (bipolar), lowered vitality, sometimes psychotic symptoms—these patients need antidepressants, supportive psychotherapy, probably hospitalisation; (c) chronic "neurotic" depression (*ICD-10*: F34.1 Dysthymia, F60.7 Dependent Personality Disorder, F.62.0 Post traumatic Personality Disorder), with typical patterns of object relations; in this case, we should determine the structural level: low-level (borderline), middle-level (most chronically depressed patients),

or higher-level neurotic depression. This is important for our style of intervention. These patients need long-term psychodynamic psychotherapy to work through their dysfunctional patterns of self and object relations, deeply ingrained in their life history and personality structure. (d) Finally, some patients do not show the typical depressive personality patterns, but their acute depression is rather a reaction to overwhelming life events, such as a severe loss—for example, of a child, spouse, parent, job, health, etc. In *ICD-10*, the reactive depressions are classified as "Adjustment Disorder, Depressive Type", F43.2. These patients need psychotherapeutic support and help in their mourning process, often also for their conflict reactions: short-term or middle-term psychodynamic psychotherapy is a good choice. In most of our patients, we have to deal with a combination of (b) or (c), that is a structural vulnerability for depression, and (d) an acute triggering stress situation (loss, defeat, conflict).

- To look for additional risks and complications: risk of suicide or other kinds of self-destructive behaviour, addiction, somatic or psychosomatic disease (e.g., anorexia nervosa, etc.). Such risks need clarification and open discussion to prevent acting out; in case of suicidal risk, also clear statements about what the patient will have to do if he feels unable to control his suicide impulses.
- To decide on therapeutic measures: therapy will start from the first moment, with establishing contact, finding out and explaining to the patient what the therapist thinks is the patient's problem, what psychotherapy is about, how it can be helpful, and what will be the patient's own contribution. The initial interview with a depressive patient should always end in some helpful result. If the therapist cannot help the patient himself, he should recommend a colleague, refer the patient for psychiatric treatment, or include a family relative or friend of the patient to care for him, etc.

The depressive patient in psychodynamic psychotherapy

I shall describe this only briefly. My remarks mainly focus on the chronically depressed patient with a depressive personality disorder or depressive lifestyle, which is the most frequent type of patient in long-term psychodynamic psychotherapy. Although some depressive patients need psychopharmacological medication (antidepressants such as SSRI, etc.), medication alone is not enough. The central therapeutic approach must always be a psychotherapeutic one, because these patients need help to deal with their basic conflicts and to overcome their developmental deficits. In therapy, we may distinguish a beginning phase, a middle phase, and a final phase.

In the *beginning phase* of psychodynamic psychotherapy with depressive patients, usually an idealising transference is in the foreground. We often recognise that the patient is trying to be a "good" patient, ready to adapt to our expectations, so she tries to make it easy for us to like her, appreciate her, and "do something for her". At the same time, as we observe the transference, we can often feel an undercurrent of ambivalence: the patient doubts that the therapist is really interested, whether this kind of therapy can really be helpful, or whether the therapist will be able and willing to give the patient what she really needs. There is no open critique or reproach against the therapist, however; instead, the patient protects him and turns her aggression against herself in the form of self-doubt and self-reproach. This indirect aggression may stir counter-aggressive impulses in the therapist, but it is too early to interpret this, because the patient still cannot feel her own aggression. Therefore, the therapist should tolerate the patient's neediness, her mistrust, and her constant fear of being hurt or let down; he must understand these tendencies from the context of the patient's early life experiences and help the patient—through affirmative interventions—to understand and accept such tendencies in herself without feeling bad or worthless.

Most short-term psychotherapies of depressive patients will remain on this level, concentrating on the actual stress situation, trying to help the patient with the work of mourning losses, working-through actual conflicts and learning to live with the new situation. In a long-term psychodynamic psychotherapy, we can go deeper (if the patient is willing): we try to work through the basic depressive conflict, as it is re-experienced in the transference situation between patient and therapist, in order to enable a deeper personality change. We will help the patient to overcome his symbiotic needs, work his way through the process of separation and individuation struggle in order to achieve more freedom and independence, and gain more self-esteem, first within the secure frame of the therapy relationship, then in his life outside. This is a long process, deepening in the middle phase.

The *middle phase* of treatment is often the hardest part for both therapist and patient. Now the patient feels safe enough to dare to bring his negative feelings into the relationship with the therapist. If the therapist listens carefully to the emotional dialogue between them, he will detect that typical mixture of dependency and anger over frustrated wishes for closeness that is very typical for the transference of depressive patients. The aggression is often expressed indirectly, or by devaluing the therapist's efforts, letting her feel that her therapy is useless, she does not help the patient, does not understand him, is not caring, not interested in him, etc. It is important that the therapist survives these attacks against her identity, competence, and good will, without sinking into depression herself. She should realise that a big part of the patient's aggressiveness comes from despair, from psychic pain that the patient tries to get rid of by turning it against the therapist, making her feel the same. The therapist must remain emotionally available, in contact with her patient, holding and containing the patient's and her own violent feelings and trying to understand. Thus, the patient regains hope that he might also be able to believe in life and in the strength of love against hate, hope against despair. All our depressive patients who could profit from their psychoanalytic therapy told us afterwards that this was the most decisive factor for their healing process.

I want to mention briefly two additional aspects of the middle phase: first, the importance of working through resistance against remembering (and this means re-experiencing) traumatic experiences of the past in order to overcome this traumatic past through a process of mourning and accept the chance of living in the present, instead of repeating the past again and again. Second, working through and revising unconscious negative beliefs, such as, "My parents did not love me—because I do not deserve to be loved; I can get some appreciation only by dedicating myself to others; as soon as I express my own wishes, I will be let down and disappointed." Such negative beliefs are not easy to correct; patients cling to them because they often have a protective function: better to think of the "worst case" so you need not fear being disappointed. However, the price for this "protection" is a very restricted life, and often these negative beliefs act as "self-fulfilling prophecies".

In the *final phase*, it is time to prepare for separation. Meanwhile, the basic conflict over the desire for dependency *vs.* that for autonomy will have been alleviated, and the focus of therapy will be more on oedipal conflicts. However, in view of the forthcoming separation, traumatic experiences of object loss will reappear in the transference and need to be worked through. As a result of a successful termination process, the patients will be able to take their leave, without feeling "let down" and without having to devalue the therapist and his treatment; they feel they have taken a step forward in terms of personal maturity and psychic stability. In view of the severe pathology of many of our depressive patients, the outcome is not always so successful; often we have to be content with a "good enough" result.

Obsessive–compulsive neurosis (OCD) and obsessive–compulsive personality disorder (OCPD)

Epidemiology

Obsessive–compulsive disorders are by no means rare; about 25% of all patients with mental disorders are given this diagnosis and lifetime prevalence is nearly 2%, but only a quarter of them seek professional help, often not until years after onset. Most OCD patients feel ashamed of their symptoms and try to keep them secret, for fear of other people thinking they are crazy. The average age at the onset of OCD symptoms is in the early twenties. No major gender difference between men and women has been found.

Course of illness

Transitory obsessive–compulsive symptoms as a reaction to stressful life events (e.g., death of a relative) are quite common, and the prognosis is good. More frequently, we see episodic forms of OCD; the most frequent form is the chronic type of OCD, which can be rather incapacitating. The most severe form (very rare, only about 1%) is the progressive malignant form, in which the obsessive disorder completely dominates the patient's life.

Co-morbidity

Obsessive–compulsive symptoms frequently appear together with depression, phobia (avoidant behaviour), anxiety disorders, eating disorders (anorexia, bulimia), and focal dystonia (stuttering, tic disorder, torticollis spasticus, writing cramps), and also with certain psychosomatic disorders such as tension headache, functional bowel problems, etc.

Clinical picture

We distinguish between *obsessional symptoms* (OCD = obsessive–compulsive disorder, *ICD-10*, F42) and obsessional *personality traits* (OCPD = anankastic or obsessive–compulsive personality disorder, *ICD-10*: F60.5).

Among obsessive–compulsive symptoms (OCD), we can list the following.

- Obsessions proper: spells of doubting and brooding: "swinging back and forth between the same set of pros and the same set of cons without being able to reach a decision" (Rado, 1959). Examples: recurrent doubt about themes such as
  - "Am I a homosexual or not?'";
  - constant fear of possibly harming or having harmed some other person;
  - blasphemous or sacrilegious thoughts, for example, do saints have sexual intercourse?
  - health: constant fear of contamination, for example, of having contracted a disease by having eaten poisonous food, having touched a door knob which might have been touched by some ill person, etc.
- Compulsions (compulsive acts, rituals): certain repetitive acts that are performed by the patient, sometimes for hours, as a protective measure against feared dangers. If the patient is prevented from executing these ritualistic acts, mounting tension, even panic, will occur. Examples of such compulsive behaviours are:
  - controlling and checking compulsions: checking again and again if the front door has been locked before leaving, if electric equipment has been turned off, etc.,
  - washing compulsion: washing one's hands again and again and still feeling they are "not clean";
  - obsessively counting specific things (such as footsteps) or in specific ways (for instance, at intervals of two) and performing other repetitive actions, often with atypical sensitivity to numbers or patterns;
  - having to turn lights on and off, or touch objects, a certain number of times before exiting a room, or walk in a certain routine way, etc.
- Obsessional impulses: fits of horrific temptation: for example, a mother fearing she might, as a result of a sudden uncontrollable impulse, harm or even kill her baby; a person who fears that in a church he might shout out an obscene and sacrilegious curse. Consequently, the patient often shows phobic avoidance of situations in which such impulses may occur (avoidance of knives and scissors, of churches, etc.).

Obsessive–compulsive personality disorder (OCPD) should be distinguished from OCD, since these patients typically do not suffer from ego-dystonic obsessions and compulsions, as described. They are characterised by a pervasive pattern of

- orderliness (preoccupation with details, rules, lists, order, organisation, or schedules to the extent that the major point of the activity is lost);
- miserliness towards both self and others; money is viewed as something to be hoarded for future catastrophes;
- rigidity and stubbornness;
- over-conscientiousness, scrupulousness, and inflexibility;
- perfectionism that interferes with task completion; procrastination;
- "workaholism", to the exclusion of leisure activities and friendships;
- reluctance to delegate tasks or to work with others unless they submit to exactly the patient's way of doing things.

Psychodynamic understanding of OCD and OCPD

The patients themselves often emphasise the "unreasonable" and "meaningless" nature of their obsessive and compulsive symptom behaviour (their endless doubting, their horrifying impulses, their ritualistic counting, checking, cleaning, etc.) which is ego-dystonic, that is, contrary to their conscious reasonable attitude; nevertheless they feel forced to do it again and again. In OCD symptoms, we see the expression of a neurotic conflict between "unreasonable" impulses and a "reasonable" attitude, in other words, a conflict between—on the one hand—aggressive, rebellious impulses (for instance, to harm, to hurt, or even to kill someone, to soil what should be kept clean, to desecrate the sacred atmosphere of a church, to rebel against imposed order, against rules of decent behaviour) and, on the other hand, the effort to restore order, cleanliness, rational and conventional behaviour according to expected rules and roles. Lang (1997) calls these patients "inhibited rebels".

Dating from Freud's early papers on this topic (1909d, 1913i), and that of Abraham (1924), it has been one of the fundamental insights of psychoanalysis—valid still today—that this conflict has its roots in the so-called "anal-sadistic phase" of psychic development. This phase of development occurs in the second and third year. The central achievements of this phase are:

- growing psychomotor and cognitive capacities (walking, speech, the wish to know);
- gradual "hatching" from symbiosis, beginning separation–individuation phase, "rapprochement" conflicts, conflict of need for autonomy *vs.* that of dependency;
- the child's growing awareness of his power to act and to affect others, whose reactions may signal he is a "good child" or a "bad child";
- autonomy and pride *vs.* shame and doubt (Erikson);
- first "No", refusing *vs.* giving, egoism *vs.* altruism, ruthlessness *vs.* caring for others, conflicts with adult care-givers over having one's own way *vs.* having to submit to their demands, defiance/rebelliousness *vs.* obedience, dominance *vs.* submission, sadistic *vs.* masochistic attitude, power struggles, sibling rivalry, competitive attitude;
- connection with "anal" interests: faeces as a product of one's own, as a possession, as a gift (achievements according to expectations of others), as a weapon (for soiling, degrading, making a mess, rebelling against parental demands);
- first ideas of life and death, giving rise to questions such as where do I come from?, where are dead persons now? Individuals who later became obsessives often experienced early loss of important persons through death or early separation, about which they felt guilty and responsible and, therefore, expect to be punished;
- the anal phase is of central importance, its course will strongly depend on the family situation in which the child grows up, the parents' relationship with their child and their support or lack of it for the child in mastering these developmental tasks.

For our psychodynamic understanding of obsessional patients, the adverse family situation, in which the child grew up, is very important. As Barnett (1969, citing Sullivan, 1956) describes it, the obsessional's early life experience is often marked by hostility, rejection, and power struggles. "But", he continues,

> such experiences are common in the history of many other neurotic patients. What seems specifically true in the case of the obsessional, as Sullivan pointed out, is the hypocrisy typical of his family experience. In such a family, the parents camouflage hostile behavior toward the child with a facade of love and concern. They rationalize their own needs as being objectively right, and self-assertion by the child as wrong. This private, arbitrary system of morality is mediated through interpersonal operations creating anxiety, shame, and guilt. I have observed that the discrepancy between the hostility implicit in the parents' destructive behavior and their explicit avowals of concern creates a dichotomy in the experience of the child. This dichotomy forms the nucleus around which a characteristic cognitive disorder develops which, I feel, is the central fault of obsessional living. (Barnett, 1969, pp. 48–49)

In other words, in order not to be aware of the parent's hidden rejecting and hostile attitude, as well as his own anxiety, shame, and rage, the child develops a cognitive style which focuses on what the parents explicitly say (instead of what the child feels they implicitly mean), taking this as "objective facts" and ignoring his own implicit perceptions as "only subjective emotions" which cannot be trusted. The result is a cognitive deficit in the perception and inference of what is going on in interpersonal relationships. As Barnett describes it,

> The obsessional patient desperately refuses to make interpersonal inferences that most of us would find blatantly obvious. [It seems . . .] that the obsessional is absorbed in maintaining a sort of innocence about himself and the nature of his relations with others. . . . The obsessional's outward reason and competence screens an underlying *unwillingness to know about himself, the impact he makes on others or they on him.* By this abdication from selected areas of cognition, he can maintain his innocence even in the face of behavior baldly indicating power motives, hostility, competitiveness, etc.
>
> Clinically, this phenomenon is reflected in the almost unbelievable lack of awareness that obsessional patients frequently show about their parents and their own relationship to them. Such patients often start their analysis with recitations about their happy childhoods, the closeness of their family group, or their loving parents, only to convey considerable loneliness, isolation, rejection, and often even brutality on the part of one or both parents. (Barnett, 1966, pp. 124–125)

Typical defence mechanisms/coping strategies of obsessional (OCPD) patients are listed below.

- Isolation (of affect from thought), rationalisation, intellectualisation: adopting a "reasonable", "objective" attitude, keeping emotional implications outside of awareness.
- Mainly aggressive impulses (hate, hostility, sadism, death wishes) must be repressed and counteracted because, for these patients, an aggressive impulse or thought is equivalent to an aggressive act (magical thinking, narcissistic phantasies of destructive power).
- Hypervigilant control of self boundaries in both directions, fearing that harmful influences from outside might damage the self (fear of contamination, avoidance of contact with potentially harmful objects) or hostile impulses of the self might inadvertently hurt or even kill other persons whom the patient loves and needs. Ritualistic checking of situations for which the patient feels responsible, in order to prevent damage to others.

- Magical undoing in order to counteract possibly harmful acts and restore the balance between impulse and defence, between defiance and obedience, hostility and reparation, guilt and repentance, attacking and protecting the object, messiness and orderliness, etc.

Diagnosis

OCD is often kept secret by the patient for a very long time, because of shame or fear of being thought crazy. So if there is some indication, we should actively ask for typical symptoms.

Distinguish between:

- OCD (obsessive ruminations about topics such as fear of contamination, illness, protection against damage, etc., obsessive impulses, obsessive rituals such as checking and control, washing and disinfection, etc.);
- OCPD (dysfunctional obsessive personality traits: extreme orderliness, perfectionism that interferes with task completion, miserliness toward both self and others, rigidity and stubbornness, etc.),
- an obsessive–compulsive façade as a protective defence structure in a latent schizophrenic patient: in this case, therapy should not focus on the OCD or OCPD symptoms (which the patient needs as a bulwark against psychotic decompensation); what is more helpful for those patients is antipsychotic therapy.

Look for special forms of OCD spectrum disorders, such as, for instance,

- hoarding ("messy house syndrome"): being unable to discard worn-out or worthless objects;
- stuttering, tics (Tourette's syndrome), focal dystonias (writing cramps, etc.);
- functional somatic disorders often associated with OCPD traits: difficulties falling asleep (because of obsessional brooding and doubting), tension headaches, functional bowel problems, etc.

Look for other psychic disorders frequently associated with OCD, such as, for instance,

- phobia and other anxiety disorders;
- depression;
- schizophrenic disorder (rare but important).

Therapy

Today, for this group of patients, we have different treatment approaches at our disposal. Therefore, it is the responsibility of the therapist, as an expert, to find out which form of therapy will be the best one for the patient: medication, cognitive behaviour therapy, or psychodynamic psychotherapy.

- Medication: neurobiological research findings indicate certain regular abnormalities in OCD patients (Baxter, 1992): it seems there is an over-activation of certain brain circuits between the orbito-frontal cortex, the striatum, the pallidum internum, and the anterior thalamus, repeatedly stimulating OCD ritualistic behaviour in thinking and acting without being able to complete the action with a satisfactory result; at the same time, other regulating brain circuits are under-activated, and there is an imbalance in neurotransmitters. Therefore, medication with specific antidepressant drugs (selective serotonin reuptake inhibitors (SSRIs) such as imipramine, fluvoxamine, escitalopram, paroxetine, etc.) can be helpful in ameliorating OCD symptoms, but only in high doses, administered regularly over months or years. When the OCD symptoms are ameliorated by therapy, the neurobiological situation will also be normalised. However, as soon as medication is discontinued, symptoms will come back.
- SSRI medication in combination with cognitive behaviour therapy is much more effective (see Reinecker's chapter on OCD in Senf & Broda, 2007) in ameliorating severe OCD symptoms. CBT is similar to the approach with phobic disorders: a combination of exhibition and symptom prevention. More than two thirds of the patients respond positively, but the symptoms are only reduced, at most by 50%.
- Indication for psychodynamic psychotherapy (PDPT): notwithstanding the role of medication and CBT, psychodynamic psychotherapy (alone or in combination with CBT and medication within a multi-dimensional treatment plan) is still very important, because its aim is not only the alleviation of symptoms, but the modification of emotional conflicts and personality patterns through work in the relationship with the therapist (Gabbard, 2001).
    - Psychodynamic psychotherapy is indicated mainly for patients with an obsessive–compulsive (anankastic) personality disorder (OCPD). The therapeutic approach must be geared to the specific conflicts and deficits of these patients. Since the fundamental patterns of object relating, self-protection, and affect regulation are implemented in implicit—not explicit—memory, verbal interpretations on the declarative level alone will not reach these patients. Much more important is the therapeutic interaction here and now—*how* patient and therapist *deal with* each other and the *function* and *meaning* of their interaction in terms of the emotional process between them. The therapist should be aware of the function of obsessional interaction patterns to regulate interpersonal distance and to keep others excluded from the patient's inner world and secret personal life, which is dominated by magical thinking, anal–sadistic phantasies, power struggles, and guilt and shame feelings. Therapy must help the patient to bridge the gulf between his inner world and the interpersonal world, to assimilate new experience and modify his rigid patterns.
    - Sometimes, a psychodynamic psychotherapy can also be successful in cases of OCD symptoms as an expression of an acute neurotic conflict, triggered by some external event, for example, death of a close relative.
    - Psychodynamic understanding can also be helpful within a multi-dimensional therapy plan, for example, for inpatient treatment of OCD patients. Here, the contribution of a psychodynamic approach is an understanding of the interpersonal meanings of the symptoms as well as conflicts with aggression and with autonomy *vs.* dependency

> needs. Moreover, while OCD symptoms may call for medication and CBT, personality aspects of individuals with OCD or OCPD may respond dramatically to dynamic psychotherapy so that these patients can lead much more gratifying lives (Gabbard, 2001).

Generally, whereas medication and CBT aim at symptom alleviation, a psychodynamic approach (in individual or group therapy) will help patients to change their personality structure and attitude by opening up to a more satisfying interpersonal emotional experience. In Barnett's words, "Much of the grimness of obsessional living revolves about the dynamics of aggression. It is therefore essential that these patients understand and resolve these problems in psychoanalytic treatment if they are to escape the isolation and loneliness they themselves perpetuate" (1969, p. 56).

Traumatic neurosis: post traumatic stress disorder (PTSD)

Irmgard Dettbarn

History and definition of trauma and PTSD

The Greek word *trauma* means injury or wound. It was first used in the field of medicine to describe physical bruises or wounds to the body. At the end of the nineteenth century, *trauma* was introduced into the language of psychiatry, when the neuropathologist Oppenheim used the term "traumatic neurosis" to refer to a condition caused by train accidents, which had previously been known as "railway-brain" (Oppenheim, 1889).

The man-made disasters of the First World War, with its shell-shocked soldiers and their other war-related neuroses, along with the consequences of the Holocaust in the Second World War have consistently led to psychoanalysis and psychotherapy research examining the issues surrounding both the trauma of the individual and of entire peoples and populations. As a result of the Vietnam War, the term trauma, F43, was added to the World Health Organization's (WHO) International Classification of Mental Disorders.

In terms of the development of psychoanalysis, Freud regarded trauma, especially the sexual seduction of a child by an adult, as the fundamental cause of all mental disorders. He later went on to qualify or relativise this view, after he had learnt from his work with patients that internal factors, such as fantasies associated with intense and unbearable sexual desires also have a traumatic effect. This development meant that Freud had not only recognised an external event as the cause of neurosis but also the related inner experience process. In the development of a traumatic neurosis, the ego helplessly experiences an overwhelming situation involving stress and anxiety, which can be triggered by external or internal events. Thus, the human ego, with its protective function, essentially collapses or falls apart. The ability to symbolise is destroyed.

Ferenczi dealt especially with trauma and its destructive effect, which, in turn, gives rise to a "dead ego-piece and agony". In his clinical work with patients, Ferenczi "found the splitting off of the ego in an observational instance and in a revealed body; the paralysis of the emotions (numbing) and in particular the effect of silence and the perpetrator's speechlessness or silence on the traumatised child" (Bohleber, 2000, p. 803, translated for this edition). He described how the child, in his extreme state of fear, helplessness, and vulnerability, feels compelled to identify with the perpetrator or aggressor in order to survive emotionally.

Whether in a clinic or in private practice, when a patient is diagnosed with PTSD, the practitioner uses a term taken from the WHO's diagnostic guidelines. Post traumatic stress disorder may be summarised as a severe anxiety disorder which develops following exposure to any event resulting from psychological trauma. During this event, death may be a real threat either to oneself or another, or this event might include the threat of harm or damage to an individual's physical, sexual, or psychological integrity, thus making them unable to cope. In terms of psychological trauma, PTSD is less common and more long-term or long-lasting than post trauma stress (also referred to as acute stress response), which is more frequent. Repeatedly experiencing the original trauma in the form of flashbacks or nightmares, evading stimuli associated with the trauma, combined with raised levels of arousal (including problems such as the inability to sleep properly, dealing with anger and hyper-vigilance), comprise the diagnostic symptoms of PTSD. Both *DSM-IV-TR* and *ICD-10* specify that the symptoms have to endure for period of over one month and they must significantly impede how the individual functions in social and work settings or other important areas of daily life.

Psychodynamic consideration

Traumatic experiences often cause people to become dumb or speechless, as they affect their ability to express themselves; they are unable to put into language or words what they have experienced (Laub, 2000, p. 863). It becomes the unspeakable. The trauma robs one of the ability to speak about what has happened because, as previously mentioned, the trauma damages or destroys man's ability to symbolise (Bohleber, 2000), which is a prerequisite for a linguistic or spoken form of communication.

Over the course of time, an inflated sense of the term "trauma" evolved to a certain extent. "This category has led to a questionable broadening of the concept, for it tends to water down the specificity assigned to trauma in Freud's early works" (Brette, 2005, p. 1802). However, not every sense or feeling of helplessness automatically leads to a collapse of the ego, and not every external disaster (such as earthquakes, war, etc.) or internal event (imagined situations of terror, fantasies, overwhelming changes in sexual drive) is equally or similarly traumatic for every human being. Each person has his or her own individual, psychological disposition. The relationship or interaction between the real situation and the individual's mental disposition determines if a traumatic effect is created. "Whether a psychic dream occurs depends solely on whether a given internal or external threat is subjectively considered or assessed as inescapable or subjectively deemed to be inescapable" (Bohleber, 2000, p. 812, translated for this edition).

A large percentage of people (50–90%) experience trauma during their lifetime, with approximately 20–30% of them developing PTSD; however, more than half of these people recover without treatment. The interaction of biological diathesis may well affect the pre-deposition or tendency towards PTSD; that is, developmental experiences in early childhood and the degree of severity of the trauma. If an individual who never established secure relationships and ways of coping as a young child is then faced with a traumatic experience, then there is an increased likelihood that they will develop PTSD, when compared to the person who developed good coping skills and a support network.

Childhood trauma, chronic adversity, and familial stressors have been consistently found (by predictor models) to increase the risk of PTSD, along with the risk of biological markers in relation to the risk of PTSD subsequent to a traumatic event in adulthood. Peri-traumatic dissociation in children can act as a predictive indicator of the development of PTSD in mature adulthood. Although it still has to be comprehensively understood, the effect of childhood trauma can possibly provide a marker for both traumatic experiences and attachment problems. Contributing factors are immediacy of, or closeness to, the trauma, and the length and severity of it; furthermore, more problems are caused by interpersonal traumas than impersonal ones.

The traumatic effect of an event not only leads to the occurrence of psychological defence mechanisms, but these defence mechanisms are also determined by physiological responses. Horowitz (1976) describes the normal response to trauma as the alternation between denial and sensory overload, which is an emergency measure to integrate the traumatic experience. Accordingly, the traumatic reaction is a normal response to an extraordinary situation.

Because the traumatic events are unpredictable, any examination of the emotional, cognitive, and neurobiological states of those affected before and after the traumatisation is virtually impossible. Nevertheless, it has been possible to observe several mental health issues and neural changes in numerous studies on traumatised people: in cases of traumatisation, the resulting immense release of neurohormones causes a malfunction within the hippocampus formation. This leads to a major disruption in the spatial and temporal acquisition or recording of sensations, which means that they are no longer realised or recorded in categories, but rather the various sensations (acoustic, visual, olfactory, and kinaesthetic) are then perceived as unrelated information. Moreover, the incoming traumatic sensations are not fed into the conscious, explicit memory (hippocampal) and consequently stored there, but are fragmented in the unconscious, implicit memory (amygdaloidal) instead. This process often leads to an "endlessness of the historicization process" (Baranger, Baranger, & Mom, 1988, p. 125): the traumatic event cannot become a part of the past, but belongs to the present of the patient and cannot become assimilated into the personality (Barwinski, 2005).

Occasionally, such dissociated or "split-off" memories may unexpectedly erupt into the human consciousness. The affected person is unable to alter or control them. They act as a trigger, which is a disturbing reminder of a traumatic event, although the trigger itself need not be traumatic or alarming. A trigger can have many different forms, ranging from a particular person, animal, or place to sounds, smells, pictures, emotions, films, seasons, tones of voice, body gestures, etc., or, indeed, it can consist of a combination of many of these factors. These triggers, which may often intensify and worsen the PTSD, can be very subtle and diverse in nature.

Fragmented memories, referred to as flashbacks, also play a role. Studies carried out on the persistence of traumatic memories in Second World War prisoners concluded that the persistence of severely traumatic autobiographical memories can continue for up to a period of sixty-five years. In comparison to healthy individuals, trauma patients show an increase in the noradrenergic stress system's activity. This change in the hormonal stress system causes accompanying symptoms such as insomnia, lack of concentration, over-excitability, or nervousness. Some studies indicate that the release of cortisol can be lowered and the sensitivity of glucocorticoid may be increased.

A variety of "trauma terminology" is used to refer to different traumatic events. A shock trauma (Fenichel, 1945) is triggered by massive external events such as rape, or experiences of war or natural disasters. In contrast to a shock trauma, a cumulative trauma is not a unique (one-off) event.

> Cumulative trauma has its beginnings in the period of development when the infant needs and uses the mother as his protective shield. The inevitable temporary failures of the mother as protective shield are corrected and recovered from the evolving complexity and rhythm of the maturational processes. Where these failures of the mother in her role as protective shield are significantly frequent and lead to impingement on the infant's psyche-soma, impingements which he has no means of eliminating, they set up a nucleus of pathogenic reaction. (Khan, 1963, p. 297)

The term "sequential traumatisation", coined by Keilson (1979) describes the long-term effect of manifest damage as the effect of a sequence of several similar negative psychological experiences. Bergmann compiled a number of facts which, following the Holocaust, forced psychoanalysis to look at trauma in a new way:

> In relation to the survivors of the Holocaust, the issue of pre-trauma personality was often irrelevant. The length of detention or imprisonment and the horrors they had witnessed played a much more significant role. The massive trauma did not result in regression but the destruction of the psychic structure.
>
> 1. The need to mourn changed their inability to do so into melancholy.
> 2. The ability to speak and act metaphorically was lost. The survivors lived in a dual reality. In everyday life, they behave "realistically". From time to time, however, the psychological reality of the Holocaust breaks through and disrupts their lives. In some emotional areas, the trauma has destroyed their mental capacity to distinguish between reality and fantasy.
> 3. Many years, even decades, often passed between their liberation from the concentration camps and the onset of neurosis. This latency was found to be an essential characteristic of traumatic stress. (Bergmann, 1996, quoted in Bohleber, 2000, pp. 814–815, translated for this edition)

Psychoanalytical research on children of survivors of the concentration camps in the Second World War made evident that the extreme catastrophe of the Holocaust (*Shoa*) had a severe impact on the following generation. The trauma that their parents had suffered became an "organizing factor" in the lives of their children (Bergmann, quoted in Kocher, 2011). The "complex of the survivor" is unconsciously handed down to the next generation. There is frequently a deep empathetic failure within the traumatised parents, which then results in a disturbance/breakdown in the attachment relationship. The parents are unable to function adequately in critical periods during the child's life, when the parents' containing function is needed. On the other hand, the child makes an active attempt to repair the parents' trauma by identifying with them, turning passive into active. There is an active unconscious "pushing" by the parents, who place (project) aspects of their own internal unbearable world on the child. This is mostly achieved by means of projective identification (Kocher, 2011).

Since a trauma can be found and expressed in a variety of symptoms and disorders, essentially, when all patients first come to psychoanalysis, the possibility of a trauma experience cannot be ruled out. Therefore, it is always necessary to take a cautious and careful approach in the first interview/analytic session and in the subsequent probationary meetings/sessions in order to (help to) avoid retraumatisation.

Targeting the promotion of regression in a trauma therapy may be contraindicated, seeing as a therapist's neutral attitude unconsciously reinforces the self-blame tendencies of trauma patients (identification with the aggressor), or the return of stressful memories regarding the trauma can be promoted, which in turn can cause re-traumatisation.

The relationship work requires the analyst to flexibly commute between identification and distancing. As with any new treatment or human relationship, at the beginning there is a conscious or unconscious test of the partners' trust. On the one hand, the traumatised patient's trust test can be very subtle, but, on the other hand, it can also be violent, for example, it can be presented as enactment (Holderegger, 2012). In the traumatic situation, the patient, possibly even as a child, lost his sense of basic or fundamental trust. If he has now taken it upon himself to come to therapy, it seems that he will use every means available (to him) to convince himself that he can trust the therapist. In such situations errors often "happen" to the therapist, which he only notices in hindsight. Ferenczi points out that in such situations, the analyst has to be absolutely honest; for example, he should admit his mistake: he has recognised "the effect of lies and deception as a traumatizing moment and the danger of their repetition in the therapeutic situation. The trust which can now develop due to the presence of honesty and sincerity makes up the difference to the traumatogenic past and allows their therapeutic treatment" (Bohleber, 2000, p. 802). Dealing competently with transference and countertransference, closeness and distance, is also necessary, in order to protect the therapists themselves from becoming traumatised.

The fact that, despite traumatising living conditions, not every individual automatically develops a trauma disorder, has led researchers to pose the question of whether "invulnerable" people exist. Bergman's findings on extremely traumatised Holocaust survivors resulted in the answer to this question being "no". However, all the sources of resistance, as investigated by the research done into resilience and on salutogenesis, describe how they also provide important background knowledge to support the psychotherapy–psychoanalytic treatments.

Is it not already possible to consider the wish for treatment of a traumatised patient as an indication of an existing inner resolve and hope that, with the help of another person, the language lost in a trauma can be found again; that at least a part of the "dead ego-piece" can be brought back to life again and the ability to symbolise can at least be partially recovered?

Personality disorders

Anne-Marie Schloesser

In our wards and private practices, we treat patients with different diagnoses: neurotics, psychotics, and patients who do not fit into either of these categories. This last group of patients, those who suffer from the so-called personality disorders, are the topic of this section, dealing with pathological narcissism and borderline personality disorder.

The section begins with an overview of general features of the topic. Then there is a large subsection on patients with a narcissistic disturbance, who are then compared to patients with a borderline disorder. I shall try to make a clear-cut distinction between them by pointing out the differences in terms of symptomatology, developmental background, and structures. Questions of treatment will conclude the section.

Personality disorders: general features and critical aspects

There have been several attempts to classify personality disorders, two of which are of main relevance. According to the American Psychiatric Association (APA), personality disorders are defined as "a class of personality types and enduring behaviours associated with significant distress or disability which appear to deviate from social expectations particularly in relating to others" (*Diagnostic and Statistical Manual of Mental Disorders* (*DSM-IV*)). Similar to the WHO's *ICD-10* (*International Classification of Diseases*) classification, it follows a categorical approach in contrast to a trait approach.

Looking at the prevalence of personality disorders, we see that, starting from the 1990s, there have been numerous surveys on national and international levels. The results show that the rates cover a wide range going from 2% to around 10%, depending on differences in demographic and socioeconomic factors (Huang et al., 2009; Lenzenweger, 2008). In a UK national epidemiological study where the criteria were classified into levels of severity (low/high), the majority of people showed some personality difficulties, and the prevalence of the most complex and severe cases was estimated at 1.3%.

There have been attempts by researchers (predominantly in the USA) to identify the traits and structure of human personality that identified five broad factors (Digman, 1990). By taking well-known personality traits and factor-analysing hundreds of measures of these traits (subjective measures from questionnaires and objective measures from experimental settings), they found five underlying factors of personality (five factor model: FFM): openness to experience, conscientiousness, extroversion, agreeableness, neuroticism (Costa & McCrae, 1992). This was followed by many years of research aiming at finding the basic factors of the normal and the disturbed personality. The results were, in spite of different techniques, highly intercorrelated.

Critical comments

Regarding these attempts to describe traits and features of normal personality against those of personality disorders, and also taking a look at the figures given in the prevalence surveys mentioned above, we see that the term personality disorder is not a very clearly defined one. The *DSM-IV* defines disorders by their symptoms, and, if we imagine that the majority of a population were to show personality difficulties such as those mentioned above, this would indicate that by talking of "disorders" we might have transformed normal disturbances and/or personal sorrows into a disorder of the whole personality. There is an ongoing critical discussion of this issue. Jerome C. Wakefield, professor at the New York State University and specialist in the history of psychiatric diagnoses, points out that our diagnostic standards are too broad (see Buchholz, 2008). The criteria used in the *DSM* specify the symptoms that must be present in order to justify a given diagnosis. But any reference to the context in which they have developed is ignored. To talk about personality disorders means that the specification "without a cause" in the criteria cannot be a very clear one, since the cause might be one the patient has become used to and, therefore, does not think worth mentioning.

"The distinction between personality and personality disorder is becoming a minefield. It cannot be a border" (R. Spitzer, in Buchholz, 2008, p. 14). It is possible that we try to operationalise conventions of everyday language or social stereotypes in order to create categories of illnesses.

Pathological narcissism

Narcissistic problems occur in many psychic disorders: in psychosomatoses, hysteria, compulsive neurosis, anxiety neurosis—in fact, there is no psychic illness without some disturbance in the sense of a narcissistic problem. The illness in which narcissistic problems in the sense of disturbance of self esteem play a central role is the narcissistic personality disorder.

The symptoms

We can see that, in social relations, the patient is incapable of understanding other people's needs and feelings. He has no feeling for the right proportions or measures. He seeks limitless adoration and tends to exploit others. His egocentrism and his phantasies of greatness are a problem for his relations to the people with whom he is in contact. Others may be idealised, but only as long as they promise narcissistic gratification, and they are devaluated as soon as they become disappointing. This disappointment incites uncontrolled fits of rage. Behind the charming façade, we sense something cold and rigid.

The capacity for maintaining relations is disturbed in a fundamental aspect: a true dependency on others must not develop; there can be no reliance on, or trust in, another person. Narcissistic personalities are full of distrust and devaluation. At the same time they are tortured by intense feelings of envy towards others. They may be funny but are not really humorous.

In the realm of sexuality, the distorted relations show up in perverse fantasies or in a lack of sexual interest. Narcissistic personalities often suffer from psychosomatic complaints or a fear of becoming ill; sometimes the patient is focused on their somatic or psychic health in a hypochondriac fashion.

Sometimes these patients are vague when we ask them to talk about their problems. Such a patient might say, "I don't know what's wrong with me, but something is basically wrong in my life."

From the symptoms alone, we cannot conclude what the underlying disturbance might be. What is more important is the specific spontaneous transference–countertransference constellation. Here, the context counts. The therapist may, for example, feel a boost in the perception of their value or, conversely, feel devaluated and timid. Both reactions may be interpreted as hints that there is a narcissistic distortion lying behind the complaints. This can also be true if the therapist notices that he is choosing his interventions extremely carefully. This might be a countertransference reaction to the patient's tendency to be easily hurt or insulted. In contrast, a borderline patient will evoke feelings of being puzzled or wanting to act in some way.

Early theoretical considerations

Before Freud, narcissism was understood as a sexual perversion where one's own body is treated like the body of the sexual object. Freud accepted this clinical point of view, but developed it further. He added an (onto-)genetic aspect: narcissism is a normal period of development, called the autoerotic stage. The child then moves on to direct its libido at objects.

Today, we no longer accept this way of understanding. The results of modern research in infant observation clearly show that the relatedness to objects starts much earlier than psychoanalytic theory had predicted. In addition, the economic implications of this theory would be that everybody has a limited amount of libido to turn towards either the self or the object. If the self is already too highly libidinised, there is no psychic energy left for the objects. This idea cannot be supported any longer. Experience tells us that persons with high self-esteem tend to show deeper commitment to, and engagement with, others than those with lower self-esteem. Narcissistic cathexis and object cathexis obviously are not conjoined. Besides this, the fact that someone has no, or few, manifest relations to other people does not mean that others play no role in his fantasy. Clinical experience shows the contrary: narcissistically disturbed persons seem to be even more dependent on others.

Freud also added an aspect of object relations: narcissism indicates a type of object choice. We love a person who is what we want to be or a person that has been part of our self. Narcissism also means a kind of not relating to the outer world, a lack of relatedness. Furthermore, Freud pointed out that narcissism has to do with the feeling of self-esteem.

What is this self? It is something between the superego and the id, but it is not the ego. It encompasses all of them. It is the wholeness of the person in contrast to the object. It is that part of the psychic instance which becomes relevant when the subject takes itself as an object. So, when someone says, "I am a young man who would like to go out dancing but sometimes I am afraid of young women", this is a statement about the self.

For today's psychoanalytic theorists, the question of cathexis of the self is no longer interesting. The question now is not that of a quantitative aspect but, rather, of a more qualitative aspect, not of the amount of libidinous energy, but of affective states in the sense of "is the feeling of self-esteem good or bad?" Whether it is viewed as good or bad depends on the agreement or discrepancy, respectively, between the real self and the ideal self, called the ego ideal; in short, between the notion of who I am and the idea of who I would like to be. Am I able to come to terms with the distance between those two, and what are the mechanisms regulating the feelings of self-esteem? What can I do when feeling miserable and small? I could try to devaluate others, try to force others to admire me, or flee into daydreams, etc. These are common mechanisms of people with a narcissistic disturbance.

Further developments

There are two prominent protagonists in the discussion of narcissism: Kohut and Kernberg. Both come from a German-speaking background from which they had to flee to the USA when central Europe was taken over by the Nazis.

Looking at Kohut's theory, we find that the idea of narcissism as libidinous cathexis of the self is the core of his definition of the narcissistic personality. He states in his book *Analysis of the Self* (1971) that the main source of suffering lies in the incapability of the psyche to regulate the self esteem and keep it at a normal level. He takes up Freud's criticised concept of primary narcissism and postulates a line of narcissism developing side by side with the drives. When the child is very young, it is in the balanced stage of primary narcissism. But this ideal state is distorted by the natural limitations of his mother's caring practice. This leads to the child having to compensate for the lost perfect state by developing images of a grandiose and exhibitionistic self. However, this is not enough. The child also projects the lost perfectness of the mother-object to an admired omnipotent self-object: the idealised parent imago.

These two mechanisms exist side by side from the beginning, but we may look at them as being nearly independent from each other. Under optimal developmental conditions, grandiosity of the archaic and grandiose self is tamed step by step, meaning it is adapted to reality. The emerging structure is then integrated into the adult personality, providing it with drive energy for our ego-adapted actions and for important aspects of our self-esteem.

At the same time, the idealised parent imago is integrated into the adult personality and also becomes part of it. It happens like this: the child feels frustration when being looked after; this is only natural because no mother is perfect. If these frustrations are not too significant, just occurring in small doses, the child will withdraw its cathexis step by step. It is most important that the frustration is not too huge. In that case, the child would be forced to take the entire cathexis from the disappointing parent. If the frustration occurs infrequently and/or only in small portions, the child can internalise functions of the mother: first of all, her capacity to reduce physical or psychic tensions in the child from the object to the self. Kohut called this operation transmuting internalisation, normal development. Transitional objects play an important part in this process.

However, if the child is severely hurt in its narcissistic harmony with the mother, the grandiose self will not be tamed by a confrontation with reality. It is then conserved in its archaic shape and demands fulfilment of its grandiose needs. Furthermore, if the child experiences traumatic disappointment in the admired parent, the idealised parent image will also survive in its unmodified shape. In this case, it is then not transformed into a structure that reduces tension and might, therefore, continue to exist as an archaic transitional object needed for the maintenance of the narcissistic balance.

These disorders also occur in the transference situation. One possibility is that the grandiose self might be reactivated and we may observe a situation called mirror transference. The idea behind it is "I am perfect and you realise how perfect I am". Or, the other possibility is that the reactivation of the ego-ideal object might lead to an idealised transference: "You are perfect, but I am part of you".

So, we see that Kohut interprets pathological narcissism as an interrupted maturation process.

Kernberg's understanding of pathological narcissism is different. He sees it as a defence formation. Its features are:

- great frustration in the first years of life;
- or, a huge aggressive drive due to personal constitution;

- or, also due to personal constitution, an anxiety tolerance which is too weak to manage aggressive impulses.

All of this might lead to the formation of a massive oral aggression. This must be defended against. The frustrations usually reside in the needs of the child being misused for the needs of the parents, so that, in consequence, the child is afraid of engaging in deeper relations. In other words, a fear of becoming dependent emerges.

The defence formation against these two threats—aggression and dependency—is the merging of diverse self- and object representations: the ego ideal, the ideal object, and the real self. The real self is what I perceive as being myself, what I am (as an example, "I am afraid of being rejected by young women and therefore I don't go out dancing"). The ego ideal is what I want to be ("I want to be self-confident and strong and be able to make someone love me"). The ideal object is someone else whom I admire.

These three images or representations merge. The new structure is called the grandiose self. At the same time, those aspects of the self that are not acceptable are projected to objects of the environment that are then devaluated. This is a way to get rid of feelings of guilt and paranoid fears.

We might now formulate the way the narcissistic patient would describe himself according to Kernberg's view: "I am great. I don't need to be afraid of being rejected by others because I don't fulfil their expectations. I am great and capable of fulfilling all expectations. Others can never reach the level of perfectness I display. This is why I feel completely indifferent towards them. The only thing is that I have to defend myself against their envy."

Through this defence operation, the fear of becoming dependent can be controlled. A discrepancy between the real self and the ego ideal—meaning a distance between what I am and what I want to be—is not felt. Mourning and feelings of guilt do not reach consciousness. The consequence is necessarily an impoverishment of the inner world. Narcissistic personalities have difficulty in saying "sorry", or "thank you", because this would mean that they are not perfect. As these persons are not able to live in more profound relationships, other people are experienced as being pale and somehow not alive. The consequence is a feeling of inner emptiness.

In the treatment of narcissistic patients, Kernberg notices an alternation between narcissistic grandiosity and inaccessibility on the one hand, and paranoid anxieties on the other. The patient does not perceive the therapist as an independent person. Narcissistic patients are not able to accept something good from the therapist. The deep envy and the guilt feelings emerging from their destructive aggression would then become unbearable. The patient withdraws into a world of "splendid isolation" so that he does not have to realise that someone else could arouse something within him. This is why the therapy and all possible improvements need to be devaluated.

This resistance is prominent in the therapy for long periods of time. The patient tells the therapist how incompetent the therapist is and says that the treatment makes no sense. Nevertheless, strangely enough, the patient attends the sessions regularly and punctually.

Let us now differentiate between the concepts of Kohut and Kernberg. In the eyes of Kohut, pathological narcissism is—as has been mentioned earlier—a fixation to a stage of childhood development in which the development is in some way frozen or stuck.

For Kernberg, narcissism is a kind of defence process that is completely created anew by the ego. The evidence for that idea is the observation that the narcissism of the small child is absolutely different from the narcissism of adult patients. He mentions the following points.

1. The fantasies of grandiosity of normal infants are more realistic.
2. Children do not only show strong reactions to critique, failure in attempted achievements, or guilt. They are also capable of showing deep love, being thankful, and interested in others. Most importantly, they are able to develop dependency relations with relevant objects.
3. The demands of children refer to real needs. The infant demands food, love, consolation, and comfort. Pathological narcissism expresses itself in unachievable expectations.
4. Children usually do not devaluate others, but instead relate to them in a warm and pleasure-orientated fashion.
5. Infantile demands for possession and power are not exclusive, but are intended by the child to make him or her become lovable and acceptable to those people whom he or she loves and by whom he or she wants to be loved in turn.

In spite of this strong critique of Kohut's concept of narcissism, it adds much to the understanding of narcissistic personality disorders. On the other hand, Kernberg's concept is not sufficient to explain all facets of pathological narcissism. His statements refer to those forms of pathological narcissism in which the formation of a grandiose self plays an important role. Other variations—for instance, the predominance of strong feelings of inferiority—would need different models of explanation.

Borderline personality disorder

In 1994, the APA published a list of personality disorders that belong to the category defined as borderline:

- borderline personality disorder;
- schizoid personality disorder;
- schizotypical personality disorder;
- paranoid personality disorder;
- histrionic personality disorder;
- narcissistic personality disorder;
- antisocial personality disorder;
- dependent personality disorder.

We see that, here, borderline personality disorder appears together with other personality disorders, which indicates a high co-morbidity. Following Kernberg and Caligor (1996) there are other personality disorders belonging to this group, for example, the syndrome of malign narcissism, hypochondria, hypomanic and sadomasochistic personality disorders.

These patients suffer from a dysfunction in the areas of affects, thinking, acting, and a distorted relation to others and themselves. Symptoms such as dissociative disorders and multiple forms of self-injuring behaviour are often associated.

According to the *DSM-IV* classification system of the APA, at least five of the criteria in Table 8.9 have to be fulfilled in order to secure the diagnosis of a borderline disorder.

As some of these symptoms can also appear with other disorders, for example, depression, schizophrenia, schizoaffective psychoses, schizoid personality disorders, and narcissistic personality disorders, careful differential diagnosis is required.

We will concentrate here on the borderline personality in a stricter sense and try to understand psychodynamically the processes of the inner world of these patients. In doing this, we see a syndrome characterised by identity diffusion and the use of mainly immature defence mechanisms, with splitting as the main defence operation.

Identity diffusion

The borderline patient has no integrated concept of himself. Contradicting views and judgements about himself are uttered (and felt, of course) without any signs of recognising the need to integrate them. We also observe a severe lack of the ability to bring together aspects that would enable coping with complex structures. However, as the intelligence of these patients is not disturbed, complexity can be dealt with if it occurs in non-relationship contexts. Disturbed intelligence processes have to be understood as due to internal conflicts and not as enduring deficits.

Patterns of thinking and feeling: defence mechanisms

Borderline patients show characteristic patterns of thinking in the sense of experiencing others in a "black-or-white" manner. In fact, it would be more appropriate to speak of "patterns of feeling", as it is more a process that takes place beneath the secondary process than is part of it. These patterns of primitive defence mechanisms manifest themselves in behaviour patterns that harm the patient in his relation to himself and others. Idealisation and devaluation oscillate swiftly, and experiencing a constant feeling towards emotionally relevant persons is rare. The self-image also changes from feelings of inferiority to phantasies of omnipotence, which

Table 8.9. Clinical criteria of borderline personality disorders (*DSM-IV*).

1. A strong wish to avoid being abandoned, either real or phantasised
2. A set of unstable but intense interpersonal relations, characterised by a constant oscillation between idealisation and devaluation
3. Strong and enduring distortion of identity in the sense of lacking stability of the self-image or self-perception
4. Impulsivity (in at least two areas), potentially self-damaging (not including suicidal or self-injuring behaviour)
5. Recurrent suicidal behaviour, gestures, threats, or self-injuring behaviour like cutting, excoriation, or picking at oneself.
6. Affective instability due to a marked reactivity of mood.
7. Chronic feelings of emptiness.
8. Inappropriate anger or difficulty in controlling anger.
9. Transient, stress-related paranoid ideation, delusions, or severe dissociative symptoms.

reminds us of the narcissistic personality. These patterns have the function of splitting operations and of immature or primitive defence mechanisms. They are predominantly used in situations of interpersonal conflicts when the patient is in emotional distress and cannot deal in a mature way with the affects, which, in that case, are aggressive. The patient then fears being overwhelmed by his destructive affects. Splitting is a means of evacuating the bad object in order not to experience disappointment and suffer from it. The bad object is pushed away, or split off into total indifference, so that the danger no longer exists, but feelings of emptiness are the result. This operation also takes place when the patient is disappointed with himself: self-esteem goes down immediately, and self-hatred and despising take the place of the feeling of omnipotence.

The second effect of this splitting process is the maintenance of an inner image or representation of the "only good" object or self, which has to be protected against one's own destructiveness.

Differential diagnosis

How can we differentiate pathological narcissism from other psychic diseases? We have to look in two directions: upwards, to where we find the neuroses (the most mature psychic illnesses), and downwards to borderline disorders as the other important type of personality disorder. Borderline disorders are a severe distortion, but not as severe as psychosis. Let us take a look at the central problem, the defence mechanisms, the level of achieved self-integration, and the capacity for reality testing.

The central problem

The neurotic patient has to cope with the Oedipus conflict, castration anxiety, and guilt feelings. The main problem of the narcissistic personality is the regulation of his self-esteem.

The borderline personality has to hold out against psychic disintegration and dissolution, and against loss of control of impulses.

The psychotic patient is lost in disintegration and dissolution already having taken place.

The defence mechanisms

Another important criterion is the level of functionality of the ego and the defence mechanisms. This level of functionality can also be viewed as being on an incline, increasing from borderline to neurosis. Narcissistic and borderline patients use primitive defence mechanisms: idealisation, projective identification, projection, and splitting. Neurotics bring into action repression, avoidance, disavowal, and sublimation.

Level of achieved self-integration

Narcissistic personalities and the neurotics have an integrated self, even if that of the narcissists is highly pathological. Borderline patients have disintegrated (split) self-representations and diffused identities, especially in the realm of aggression.

The perception or testing of reality is not disturbed in neurotic, narcissistic, and borderline patients, whereas with psychotic patients, it is severely disturbed. Psychotic patients completely project their problems into the outer world, to people or other objects. For them, it is not themselves who feel aggressive towards others, but they feel threatened and persecuted by others.

It will be noticed that the severity of the disorder decreases from psychotic to borderline to neurotic patients, from a state of permanent and complete disintegration (psychosis) to partial disintegration (borderline) and via regulation of balance (narcissism) to conflict (neurosis).

Some aspects of treatment

After all we have established so far, I think it is obvious that the therapeutic treatment of these patients should facilitate the maturation of the true self (a term created by Winnicott, 1965), which would mean coming into contact with one's own feelings and strivings and accepting them. The false self ("I am strong, independent and invulnerable") has been built up against feelings of impotence, of not being loved, of insecurity and reactive anger. Consequently, the therapist should accept any and every transference offered by the patient, idealised transference as well as mirror transference. When the therapist comes to be like an understanding mother who sees and mirrors what the child / the patient offers, then he is, of course, well aware that the transference offered may be a defence formation against unbearable feelings. This function of defence should be explained to the patient.

When mirroring the feelings of the patient through being empathetic, this empathy is always limited, and, as a consequence, the patient will be frustrated. These frustrations should not be so significant that they might cause a new trauma. In this way, it should be possible for the patient to gradually develop a more mature structure.

Since, for Kernberg, pathological narcissism is a defence formation, his treatment is different. He stresses the necessity to keep an eye on the aggressive conflicts. The therapist should systematically interpret both idealisation and aggression in the transference. Aggression may be expressed, for example, by being silent or through coming late to the session, or by rejecting any interpretation . . . it is through countertransference that one can find out whether this behaviour is aggressive or not.

The aim here is to bring to the patient's conscious mind that he has impulses both to idealise the therapist and devaluate him. The devaluation serves to avoid the defended feelings of rage and envy—the therapist could react vengefully. This is what the patient is afraid of: revenge and feelings of guilt, and this has to be made conscious. Similarly, what has to be made conscious is the fear of becoming dependent, which is expressed by trying to induce the therapist to submit to the patient's total control. This would seem to control the aggression. It is as if the patient were to say, "Either you are the way I need you to be or you will not exist".

All of this, the unrealistic idealisations of the therapist, the disappointment, and the manifold motives for the narcissistic withdrawal, as well as the devaluation, has to be analysed carefully.

A specific problem occurring in the treatment of borderline patients is the impulse to act out. It is a defence mechanism aimed at getting rid of unbearable inner tensions by acting, usually in a destructive way. This is a challenge for the therapist, who has to maintain the frame of the treatment, a space where everything can be put into words and communicated to the therapist, but in no way be brought into action. The aim of the therapeutic work, then, is to translate the actions into understanding of the intolerable aggressive forces and impulses as symptoms of disappointment and the affects of anger and hate being concomitant with it.

But—of course—there is not only a negative transference. There are also impulses of identifying with the therapist, listening to him, and exploring one's own self together with him. But these functions often are split off, since they are neither spectacular nor grandiose.

Through the realisation of these aspects of the self and through holding and enlarging them, the patient can change his own negative self-image. This is true for the narcissistic patient as well as for the borderline patient, whose problem is to maintain the difference between the self and the object. With borderline patients, this happens when the patient feels frustrated and aggressive impulses are on the rise. The patients might then start to injure themselves by cutting their skin—a form of aggression that is originally meant to strike at the disappointing therapist. Self and object merge into one undifferentiated structure, this being the result of getting rid of destroying impulses. The primary process takes over, and the patient slips into a state of psychotic functioning.

What happens when the aggressive impulses are not worked through? In such cases, the patient might show progress concerning his social functions, his relations become more intense, since he can understand better what is going on in other persons. His ambitions will become less grandiose, as well as his feelings of restlessness and boredom. What will remain, however, is the lack of the ability both to deeply and empathetically understand others and to have and maintain fully developed love relations.

CHAPTER NINE

PSYCHOPATHOLOGY AND PSYCHODYNAMICS OF PSYCHOSOMATIC DISORDERS

Matthias Elzer, Wolfgang Merkle, and Michael Wolf

General aspects of psychosomatic medicine

Matthias Elzer

The history of psychosomatic medicine in Western countries

The roots of the psychosomatic approach go back to Ancient Greece, more than 2,300 years ago. On the one hand, there was the famous physician Hippocrates (460–377 BC), whose understanding was based on the "humoral model" of the body and its diseases.

Today, many medical terms reflect this understanding (e.g., melancholia (Greek: black bile)). This model is similar to traditional Chinese medicine. But Hippocrates' understanding was mostly somatically orientated.

On the other hand, there were some philosophers, such as Aristotle and Plato (427–347 BC), who were interested in questions about human beings and about the science of nature, too. Plato wrote that the human body should not be treated without the psyche and the body has to be treated by "nice words". The word "psychotherapy" could have been used first by Plato.

During the Middle Ages, the understanding of the human body and its diseases were influenced by a pre-scientific magic thinking regarding bad influence. The therapy was a kind of cleaning and detoxification (catharsis). Mental disorders were seen as the results of sins and as signs of guilt. Better understanding of the physical and biological processes of nature led to a focus on the aspects of natural sciences. The French philosopher and scientist Descartes (1595–1650) postulated a splitting into matter (*res externa*) and cognition (*res cogitans*). Since that time, medicine was divided in two parts, which we term the dualism of body and psyche. Developing medical science was much more interested in somatic and natural scientific understanding of the human being and its diseases and neglected the social and psychic dimension of illness, which was finally brought into focus at the end of the nineteenth century. However, some physicians pointed out the influence of psyche somewhat earlier, such as Heinroth in 1818, in Germany, who used the word "psychosomatic" first.

Around 1900, the role of the psyche was rediscovered by Freud (1856–1939) and later by some German physicians of internal medicine. Psychosomatic medicine is a so-called "German invention". In the Nazi dictatorship in Germany (1933–1945), the new psychosomatic thinking was suppressed; many psychoanalysts, psychosomatic physicians, and researchers emigrated from Europe to the USA and other countries, although some of them returned in the 1960s.

In the German-language countries (Switzerland, Austria, and Germany), the study programmes of medical universities have taught the subject of psychosomatic medicine since the 1970s. Every student has to learn the basics of psychosomatic medicine. However, in reality and the everyday practice of the medical system, psychosomatic medicine plays only a small role. The historical influence of somatic and natural scientific medicine is dominant.

In Germany today, there are two concepts of psychosomatic medicine.

1. The basic psychosomatic approach: the fundamentals of psychosomatic understanding and competences are practised in every area of medicine (general medicine, intern medicine, surgery, neurology, psychiatry, etc.). Every physician should have a basic psychosomatic approach, acquired through study at university and through clinical experience, to diagnosing and treating his patient. However, this psychosomatic approach is mostly obscured by the daily practice of the disease-orientated understanding of medicine.

   Nevertheless, physicians, mostly general practitioners, can obtain, by means of special training, an additional qualification in "psychosomatic basic support" (*psychosomatische Grundversorgung*). This training consists of theoretical seminars on psychosomatic medicine and case discussion as clinical reflection: that is, a Balint group. The aim is to treat the patient with more psychosomatic understanding; for doing that, physicians are paid a higher fee by the insurance system. This additional basic training is not a qualification to do psychotherapy.
2. Specialisation in psychosomatic medicine. Physicians can acquire a further training as specialists in psychosomatic or psychotherapeutic medicine. In the health system of Germany, two psychotherapeutic schools are accepted: psychoanalysis and psychoanalytically orientated (dynamic) psychotherapy, and behaviour therapy. These training programmes run over many years and comprise self-experience, attendance at theoretical and clinical seminars, and psychotherapeutic experience controlled by supervision. In psychotherapy, trained physicians and also psychologists can work as psychotherapists and can treat patients suffering from psychosomatic disorders.

General psychosomatic medicine

There are two preconditions for general psychosomatic medicine.

1. Psychosomatic medicine uses a unitary model of the patient and his illness: it is a bio-psychosocial model (Engel, 1975) (Figure 9.1).
2. Psychosomatic medicine uses a patient-orientated rather than a disease-orientated approach. We do not treat diseases; we treat patients who suffer from diseases. That is an important difference. The disorder of a patient has to be understood by studying the biography and the psychosexual development as a dynamic process; it is not a static state.

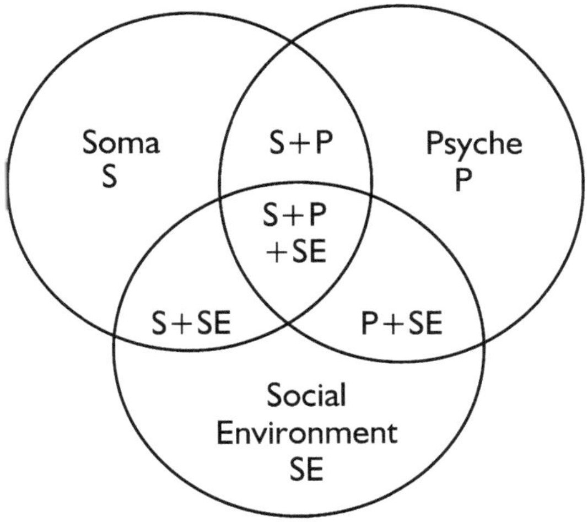

Figure 9.1. The bio-psychosocial unitary model.

Von Uexküll (1908–2004), an important German professor of psychosomatic medicine, criticised somatic medicine, saying that it understands the human body as if it were a machine, and the doctor is like an engineer who checks and repairs a defective organ as if it were part of a machine: his approach is bio-mechanical (Figure 9.2).

Psychosomatic disorders and ICD-10

In the past twenty years, the terms "neurosis" and "psychosomatic disorder" disappeared from classification systems such as *ICD-10* and *DSM-IV*; they use the term "neurotic disorder" or "somatization" and have eliminated the historical diagnoses. These classifications seek to give a description of disorders only through a collection of significant symptoms; they have no context in the sense of nosology (theory of psychopathology).

Example: The old diagnosis "hysteria", as a neurotic and psychosomatic disorder, disappeared from *ICD-10*. It changed to "dissociate disorder" (F44) or "histrionic personality disorder".

Epidemiology

The mental disorders are divided into three groups:

- psychoses;
- neuroses and personality disorders;
- psychosomatic disorders.

Somatic medicine		Psychosomatic medicine
Model of machine disease-oriented	⟷	Model bio-psycho-social entity patient-oriented

Figure 9.2. Different models of medicine.

In Table 8.4 (Chapter Eight), the epidemiological data of mental disorders were listed. Psychosomatic disorders occur to a similar percentage of the population as neurotic disorders: approximately 12% (Table 9.1).

Definitions

What is "psychosomatic medicine"? "Psychosomatic medicine is the science of the somatic–psychic–social interactions in the origin, the course, and the treatment of human diseases. Psychosomatic medicine has to be a person-centred medicine" (Hoffmann & Hochapfel, 2004, p. 195, translated for this edition).

What is the meaning of "psychosomatic"? It is derived from Greek: Σομα (Soma), meaning body, and φυχη (Psyche), meaning breath.

The term is used in many ways and it describes different kinds of interaction between the body (soma = S) and the psyche (P). We should differentiate between the following terms:

- psychogenetic, meaning that the organ has no somatic deficiency, but expresses a psychic conflict in a symbolic way, like a body language. Example: the function of the arm is affected by pain with no organic source; the pain prevents the patient from hitting someone as a result of rage and hate.
- somatopsychic or somatogenetic, describing the opposite interaction to "psychogenetic". Example: A primarily bodily disease, such as a complicated fracture of the leg or the loss of an organ through cancer leads to an anxiety disorder or kind of depression as a pathological way of coping;
- psychosomatic, meaning that an organic (genetic or acquired) disposition will be triggered by a psychic conflict or trauma or emotional stress. Example 1: Genetic atrophy of immune system + the unconscious conflict generated by fear of loss: attack of obstructive asthma. Example 2: Deformation of the spine/disc + hypertension of the paravertebral muscular system as a result of somatisation of aggressive inhibition through persistent emotional

Table 9.1. Epidemiology of psychosomatic disorders (German population).

Diagnoses (selected)	Neurotic and psychosomatic diseases[2]	Neurotic and psychiatric diseases[1]
Neuroses and personality disorders	12.0%	12.9%
Psychosomatic disorders	*	11.6%

* Was not the topic of the study, not inspected.

[1] The representative field study by Dilling, Weyerer, and Castell (1984) researched the rural population of Bavaria, Germany in respect of psychiatric and neurotic diseases; psychosomatic disorders were not studied.

[2] The research group of Franz, Lieberz, and Schepank (2000), from the famous Zentralinstitut für Seelische Gesundheit Mannheim conducted a representative long-term study starting in 1979 (*Mannheimer Kohortenstudie*) on how many people were suffering from psychosomatic and neurotic diseases and how the process of the diseases was progressing.

stress: slipped disc and compression of the nervous ischiaticus lead to attacks of pain and paralysis.

These terms and the effects they define are summarised in Table 9.2.

Psychosomatic diseases are complex disorders, which contain a somatic and a psychic part. These component parts differ:

1. The somatic part can consist of a disturbed function without any morphological defect; a psychic conflict or trauma causes an organic symptom which functions like a body language (psychogenetic).
2. The somatic part causes a secondary psychic or bodily reaction (somatogenetic or somatopsychic).
3. The somatic part is involved with a morphological deficiency caused by genetic or acquired predisposition and will be triggered by a psychic conflict or traumatic experience (psychosomatic).

The psychic and emotional part contains a neurotic quality (Elzer, 2012, translated for this edition).

The classification of psychosomatic disorders

Classical systematisation of psychosomatic disorders

From a historical point of view, we have four groups of psychosomatic disorders, which are based on a psychodynamic understanding.

1. Conversion phenomenon: in 1895, Freud, together with Breuer, described the psychic causes of many neurological disorders that influenced the motor and the sensory nervous systems and named them "hysteria".

Table 9.2. Interaction between body/soma and psyche (Elzer, 2012, translated for this edition).

Interaction		Term	Example
Psyche influences soma	P ⟶ S	Psychogenetic	Dissociative (conversion) disorders, dissociative motor disorders, dissociative anaesthesia and sensory loss, persistent somatoform pain disorder, types of migraine, psychic vertigo
Soma influences psyche	S ⟶ P	Somatogenetic or somatopsychic	Reactive depression or anxiety disorder after trauma or loss of organ as a narcissistic hurt
Soma and psyche influence each other	S ⟷ P	Psychosomatic	Obstructive asthma, ulcerative colitis, gastric and duodenal ulcers, types of migraine, slipped disc

The diseases are pseudo-neurological, such as paralysis or spasticity of the extremities (arms, legs), fainting, dysfunction of sensory perception (visual, acoustic, olfactory, tactile).

"Conversion" means the turn over or transformation of an intrapsychic conflict into a symptom of the body. It is like a "language of the body". Von Uexküll (2003) named it "Disease of expression" (*Ausdruckskrankheiten*): the patient expresses his problem/conflict in body language. Example: in a conflict of aggression, the desire to hit somebody with murderous rage is converted into motoric adynamia and pain in the dominant arm.

The *ICD-10* names this "monosymptomatic phenomenon of conversion" as "dissociative (conversion) disorder" (F44).

2. Psychosomatosis, or "organ-diseases with psychosocial components". Alexander (1950) postulated the "holy seven" of psychosomatic disorders: peptic ulcer, ulcerative colitis, obstructive asthma, ideopathic hypertension, atopic dermatitis, hyperthyreosis, rheumatoid arthritis. These diseases contain dysfunctions of organs of the vegetative nervous system. Alexander described them as "organ-diseases with psychosocial components", Engel (1967) named them "psychosomatoses". Genetic or acquired somatic disposition will be triggered by an intrapsychic conflict or by the overwhelming effect of a traumatic experience. In the scientific discussion, the concept of "epigenetic" explains how the genetic disposition (a sequence on the DNA) can be switched on and off by psychosocial experience.

   Von Uexküll named these psychosomatoses as "diseases of provision" (*Bereitstellungskrankheiten*), because the body offers a continuous vegetative provision for reaction to flight or to fight. Example: continuous stress and chronic excessive demands lead to high blood pressure and developing hypertension or peptic ulcer.
3. Psycho-vegetative syndrome, functional syndrome, or somatoform disorder (*ICD-10*): here we can find different dysfunctions of the organs and organ systems without any morphological defect of the organ. Only the function is pathological. The patient is suffering, but the physician cannot find any somatic pathology. Sometimes these functional syndromes are similar to the phenomenon of conversion, but the symptoms extend to the motor and the sensory nervous system. The symptom can be understood as an equivalent of fear. Example: cardiac arrhythmia, vertigo, tinnitus, chronic pain.
4. Somato-psychic or somatogenetic disorder: this disorder is a secondary psychosomatic or neurotic reaction to a primary somatic disease. It is a somatisation that occurs in place of mourning another somatic disease or depression. Example: panic attacks after suffering coronary–vascular heart disease.

Figure 9.3 shows the prioritisation of the somatic and psychic factors.

The descriptive classification

This classification abstains from concepts of causes of the disorder; instead, it simply describes the symptoms as given in the *ICD-10* and their effect on the body and behaviour. The systems of the body affected by psychosomatic disorders are listed below:

- digestive system (upper, lower);
- respiratory system;

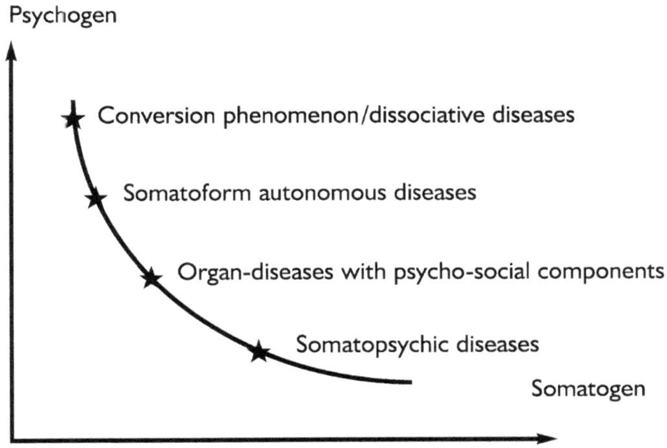

Figure 9.3. Prioritisation of the somatic and psychic factors (Hoffmann & Hochapfel, 2004, p. 216, translated for this edition).

- cardiovascular system;
- skin system;
- motor apparatus;
- urogenital system;
- central nervous system;
- endocrinal system, etc.

Very often it is useful to combine these two concepts (descriptive and classical classifications), even if by doing so the diagnoses might seem a little clumsy. Example: instead of the somatic diagnosis, "back pain syndrome", we can formulate a psychosomatic diagnosis: "back pain syndrome as expression of a conversion phenomenon caused by a chronic relationship conflict".

Psychoanalytical models of psychosomatic diseases

Preliminary remarks

A model is just a model—nothing more. A model tries to describe and illustrate a theory and to explain the clinical reality of the suffering patients.

There is no psychosomatic model that can explain every kind of psychosomatic disorder. However, such models are helpful in understanding the individual patient and talking with him about this understanding.

During the history of psychosomatic medicine, there have been many concepts and models to explain and understand patients who were suffering from psychosomatic diseases. Some of these models are old, but still important today. Other models have been disproved by research. One of them is the theory of "typology", in the sense of a patient as an "ulcer-type", a "heart-attack-type", and so on. As another example, Alexander postulated specific conflicts for specific disorders. Both the diseases and the patients suffering from them are much more complicated than the theory.

In psychosomatic medicine today, there is no single theory or concept to explain all diseases. The question of the symptom reaction and the choice of organ keeps psychosomatic medicine busy with continuing research.

Now we shall discuss the most important models of psychosomatic medicine in detail. They help us to understand the patient and they are also suitable for helping the patient to understand what is going with him or her.

Conversion model (Freud, 1895d)

This is the oldest model. In 1895 Freud and Breuer formulated the phenomenon of conversion (Latin, *conversio*: transformation) in their clinical case reports of some patients who were suffering from hysteria. It posits that the intolerable unconscious imagination will be rendered harmless by transforming the psychic energy into an expression of the body. Freud calls this conversion a "mysterious jump" from the psyche into the body.

The phenomenon of conversion was the first model to attempt to explain and to treat hysterical disorders. Hysteria and conversion were synonymous at that time. Conversion is a psychosomatic concept, but we know that there are patients with hysterical neurosis or hysterical personality disorder where the body symptoms are not in focus as are the symptoms and conflict arising from interpersonal relationships.

The concept of conversion is still valid today. *ICD-10* uses the term "dissociation". Dissociation is the most important defence mechanism for the phenomena of conversion. *ICD-10* abolished the term "hysteria" and talks instead about dissociation or conversion. In F60.4 of *ICD-10*, the "hysteric personality" is renamed as "histrionic personality" (Latin, *histrion* = actor).

The diseases are "pseudo-neurological", meaning that they influence the motor and the sensory nervous systems: paralysis or spasticity of the extremities (arms, legs), fainting, dysfunction of sensory perception (visual, acoustic, olfactory, tactile).

"Pseudo-neurological" means that there are no somatic pathological findings. Freud was a highly experienced neurologist and neuro-physiologist, and, through the neurological examination of the patient's body, he could identify the "pseudo-neurological" symptom.

Today, it is much easier to arrive at the right diagnosis through the various neuro-physiological tests, such as EEG, EMG, AEP, VEP, SSEP, CT, NMR, PET.

At the beginning of psychoanalysis, Freud's theory of drives (libido and destrudo) was the most important element of theory. The model of conversion means:

1. A strong drive conflict (sexual or aggressive impulses, intensive affects, and wishes are denied by the superego and the ego develops feelings of shame and guilt.
2. The wishes or emotions are defended from becoming conscious, but only partially.
3. Psychic energy is dissociated and transformed into the activation of the motor and the sensory nervous systems and produces a bodily symptom as compensation for the conflict. The patient is relieved and derives a benefit from the symptom.
4. The symptom acts as a symbol and expresses the conflict in a kind of body language.

The model of conversion is shown in Figure 9.4.

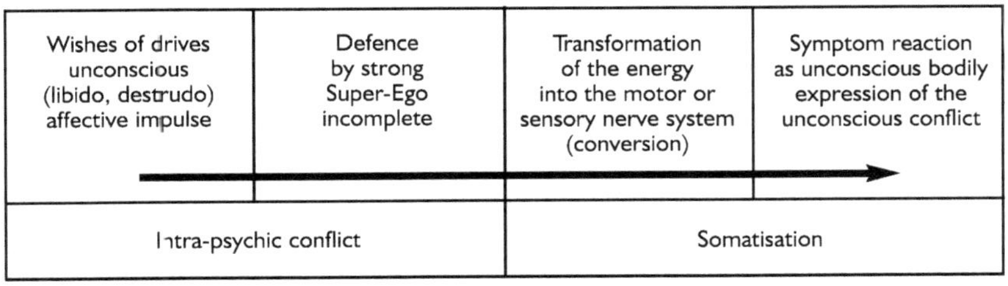

Figure 9.4. The model of conversion.

Drive conflicts are the main conflicts of the conversion phenomenon from the perspective of the drive theory, but conflicts of relationships could also cause the conversion phenomenon.

Drive aspects cannot be separated from the aspects of object relations; they belong together. Drives need objects for satisfaction and object relations are related to drives.

Model of "organ neurosis" (Alexander, 1950)

Freud's model of conversion highlighted the transformation into the motor and sensory nervous systems and the production of pseudo-neurological symptoms.

Alexander's (1935, 1950) theory of "organ neurosis" pointed out the reaction of the vegetative (visceral or autonomous) nervous system and its organs to every kind of emotion. He formulated that every emotion has bodily reactions and, conversely, every bodily function has a reaction in the mood.

The homoeostasis, the neuro-endocrine balance of the vegetative organs such as heart, lungs, stomach, bowels, etc. are at the centre of his theory: in the case of psychosomatic disorders, the balance between the sympathetic and parasympathetic parts of the vegetative nervous system is disturbed. Every organ is influenced by sympathetic and parasympathetic activities except the kidneys and the adrenal gland. Generally, organs are innervated by the sympathetic nerves (transmitters: adrenalin, noradrenalin), and their activity is inhibited by the parasympathetic nerves (transmitter: acethylcholin). However, the innervation and inhibition of one system, the stomach and bowel system, is inverted: the parasympathetic nerves stimulate the activity of the bowel (digestion) and the sympathetic ones inhibit the bowel activity.

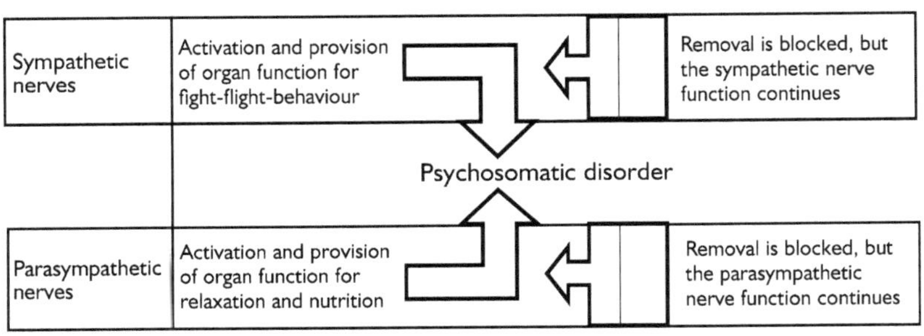

Figure 9.5. Organ neurosis (following Alexander).

This is necessary for basic flight/fight behaviour: in this case, all organs are activated (heart, lungs, vascular system), but the bowel system is inhibited. The organs of the body provide the flight/fight activities through sympathetic nerves, and the retreat into passivity through parasympathetic nerves. The need to react will be steered by the central and vegetative nervous system, both consciously and unconsciously.

Alexander introduced a second model, in which he focused on the dysfunction of the vegetative system. His main hypothesis was that "the organ neurosis" develops from chronic suppressed emotions. The central conflict is that of autonomy and dependency related to the sympathetic (autonomy) and parasympathetic (dependency) nervous systems. Both can become pathologic, if the organ provides a reaction, but the satisfaction or removal (ready for fight/flight or for support) will not come about; thus, the vegetative homoeostasis will not be restored. This status can be very prolonged.

As an example, a chronic feeling of anger and powerless rage can lead to high blood pressure or hyper-secretion of the gastric juices, but the bodily reaction cannot be satisfied. The patient can develop a chronic hypertension, or gastritis, or a gastric ulcer (Figure 9.5).

Critics of Alexander's hypothesis of the specification of conflict pointed out that it could not be verified. Nevertheless, his model is helpful in understanding and explaining the interplay between the somatic disposition or dysfunction of visceral organs and the neurotic conflict in developing a psychosomatic disorder. His model is also useful for understanding the process of stress reaction and stress disorders, which was developed after Alexander by physiologists such as Selye (1974).

Model of de- and re-somatisation (Schur, 1955)

Schur (1955) described a simple and general model of the psychosomatic symptom reaction: the psychosexual development from child to adulthood is a continuous process of de-somatisation; the strong and spontaneous emotions of the child become calmer (decathexis of the emotions from the body) and the adult uses more verbal symbolisation and cognition. The adult develops the ability to abstain from libidinal and aggressive drives and sublimation.

The psychosomatic symptom reaction can be explained as the reverse process, that the conflict of the adult person leads to a psychic and somatic regression to the level of a young child. This is called re-somatisation (Figure 9.6). Example: we can understand the fear of failing an examination through the model of re-somatisation and "organ neurosis". The person will feel anxiety, the vegetative nervous system is dominated by the sympathetic reaction of flight or fight (cardio–vascular system is stimulated), the parasympathetic function of calming and relaxation is inhibited, the function of the bowel (large intestine) cannot regulate the water

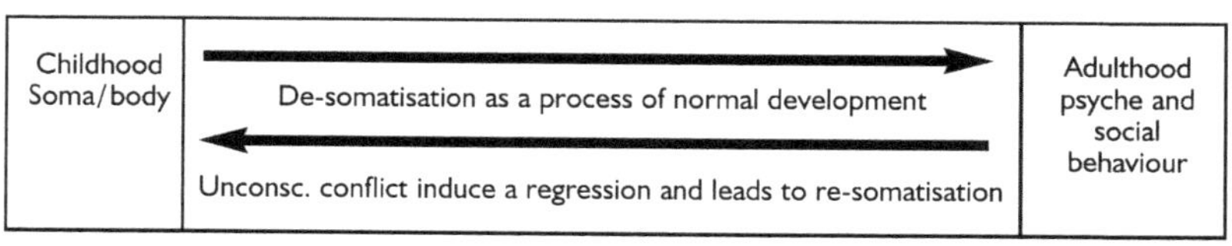

Figure 9.6. Model of de- and re-somatisation (following Schur).

in the stool (faeces), so the person suffers diarrhoea. In German, we have a vulgar word for anxiety: "*Schiss*", which in English means "shit".

Model of alexithymia (Marty & de M'Uzan, 1957)

Patients who are suffering from psychosomatic diseases seem to have difficulty in verbalising emotional topics and conflicts; they seem to suffer from a paucity of feelings and to lack imagination. Often, they cannot express their bodily complaints, feelings, and emotions through words.

The term "alexithymia" comes from the Greek and means the inability to read emotions. The model of alexithymia devised by some French and American psychosomatic physicians postulated a kind of "psychic defect" of the patient's personality. The patient cannot read his feelings and emotions because of his "emotional blindness".

The model of alexithymia is criticised in many psychosomatic studies; one criticism relates to the hypothesis of defect. In our daily practice, it is seldom that we find patients who are unable to verbalise their emotions. But this "defect" could also be understood as a kind of defence mechanism (avoidance, isolation of affect, rationalisation). This emotional blockade can also be caused by a traumatic experience or a massive intrapsychic conflict.

Model of two-phasic repression (Mitscherlich, 1974)

The model devised by Mitscherlich (1974) can be understood as a critical answer to the model of alexithymia. Mitscherlich posited a model that describes the relation between the conscious and unconscious affects and their somatic correlation on two levels. A conflict is repressed into the unconsciousness. There are two phases or levels: in the first phase, the conflict will be defended on a neurotic level. This can be seen as a neurotic symptom: the patient is suffering from anxiety or depression and he feels his suffering. In the second phase, if this defence is insufficient, the repression can enter the second level, where the neurotic symptom formation will be defended against and the symptom reaction appears on a somatic level. The patient feels no suffering from anxiety or depression; now he has an organic problem, i.e., pain (Figure 9.7).

During psychotherapy, the patient has to pass through a contra-rotation from the somatic symptom formation to the conscious level. At level 1, the patient feels more ill, because he is in contact with his suppressed emotions.

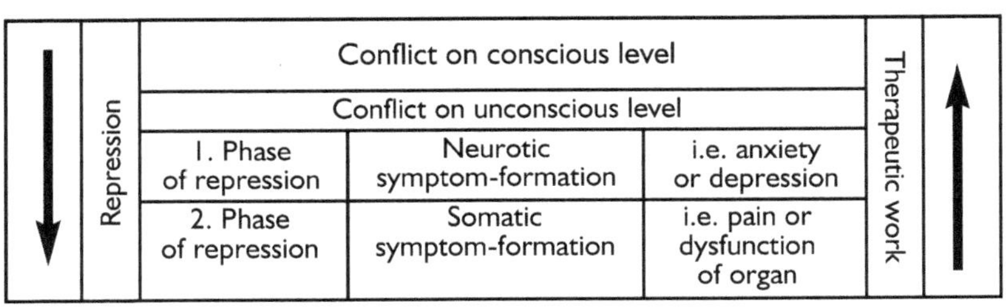

Figure 9.7. Model of two-phase repression (following Mitscherlich).

As an example, the psychic pain of anxiety or a depressive mood changes into a somatic symptom such as asthma or low back pain. The patient suffers from an acceptable and communicable symptom of the body and feels relieved.

If the patient can leave the second level of repression through psychosomatic therapy, he will enter into the first level. On this level, the patient suffers more from his emotions. Sometimes he will say, "Now I'm feeling more sick than before," but this represents progress, because he is in contact with the emotional aspects of his conflict or trauma, thus better enabling him to work through his problem.

Model of stress

Everybody knows the phenomenon of personal stress. We feel that something is "too much" for us, we become aware of aroused emotions and somatic reactions, we feel pressure and anxiety, and perhaps we want to run away or fight against this threat.

Stress is a difficult term and there are many models and concepts. In psychosomatic medicine, stress is an important term encompassing such things as post traumatic stress disorder and so-called burn-out syndrome. Anxiety disorders and panic attacks are evidence of the phenomena of stress, as are severe depression or psychotic states. The phenomenon of stress can often be seen in daily situations as part of many disorders and as psychophysical reactions.

The psychoanalytic concepts of mental disorders do not use the term stress directly, but the phenomenon of stress is ubiquitous on the somatic and the emotional level.

Historical aspects

Biological models of stress

Emergency reaction: The technical term *stress* comes from material testing in engineering. We know that a stress test can determine the durability of a system or a material by pushing it to its limits.

The American physiologist Walter B. Cannon (1871–1945) discovered the important role of the balance (homeostasis) of the autonomous, vegetative nervous system (sympathicus and parasympathicus). He described the "emergency reaction" to a dangerous situation: The body reacts by pouring out catecholamines for the flight-or-fight reaction of the individual. The ideal emergency reaction is shown in Table 9.3.

General adaption syndrome: The physiologist Hans Selye (1907–1982) researched the unspecific reaction of the body to extreme physical and chemical exposition (stressors). The reaction

Table 9.3. Emergency reaction (Cannon, 1939).

4	Relaxation	↑
3	Adaptation	│
2	Activation	│
1	Orientation	│

of the body was like an inflammatory reaction of the vegetative and endocrine system. Selye formulated the "General adaption syndrome", in three steps, as shown in Table 9.4.

If the body has no more capacity to resist stressor exhaustion, breakdown is imminent. The worst case could mean death of the organism.

Selye also mentioned positive and negative aspects of stress and called them "eustress" and "distress". A bit of stress can help to optimise the energy for solving a problem or a conflict.

Psychoimmunology: Psychoneuroendocrinology and psychoimmunology deal with immunological processes on the cellular, humoral, and neurophysiological parts of the body. All models of stress describe the exhaustion and breakdown of somatic functions after resistance. Psychoimmunology can offer answers to the complex question of what exactly is going on in the body.

Roth (2001) describes the normal stress reaction in two phases:

1. Primary reaction: the brain perceives the stressor and responds with subcortical and cortical activation of the hypothalamus, mesolimbic system, and amygdala. The subcortical reaction is followed by the cortical reaction. Noradrenalin will be released by the locus coeruleus. In the truncus cerebri, the origin of the twelve brain nerves, the sympathetic nervous system will be activated and the parasympathetic nervous system like nervus vagus will be inhibited by the hypothalamus. Through the hypothalamic–pituitary–adrenal axis (HTPA axis) adrenalin and noradrenalin will be released from the suprarenal glands and will stimulate the ergotopic functions of the vegetative organs (heart, lung, vascular system, etc.) for the fight-or-flight reaction (top-down).
2. Second or late reaction: some minutes later, the hypothalamus and amygdala produce releasing factors (CRF) and stimulate the suprarenal glands with adrenocorticotrope hormone (ACTH) via the hypophysis (the pituitary gland), which causes an increase of glucocorticoids such as cortisol. Cortisol leads to the mobilisation of glucose and blood lipids or fatty acids, which are necessary for the metabolism of energy. Through negative feedback, cortisol inhibits the excretion of CRF and ACTH in the hypophysis, so that the stress reaction will be limited and the organism will be protected (bottom-up) (Table 9.5). Other anti-stress hormones, such as neuropeptide Y and b-endorphin, help to limit the alarm reaction.

In plain words, between the brain and the peripheral nervous system there is intense communication of activation and inhibition; the aim is to keep energy ready for the activation of fight-or-flight behaviour and to limit this stress reaction to protect the body.

Table 9.4. General adaption syndrome" (Selye, 1950).

3	Exhaustion	↑
2	Resistance	
1	Alarm reaction	

Table 9.5. The normal stress reaction (following Roth, 2001).

1	Primary reaction	Top down
2	Secondary or late reaction	Top down and bottom up

Chronic stress can be caused by two factors: the permanent influence of stressors and the inability of the system to defend itself against the stressors. Permanent stress suppresses the parasympathetic nervous system and the calming function of the body and the emotions, which are operating at a high level of activity. For instance, the symptom of insomnia is the expression of the inability to relax and find a psychoneurological balance; the body is a permanent state of activity of fight-or-flight, because the activity cannot be used to terminate this state (see subsection headed 'Model of "organ neurosis"', above). Permanent stress influences the function of tissue immediately and changes the organic structure thereof later, for example: the vascular system of the heart, the intestines or the neural network of the brain (dentrites). The somatic defence is weakened by the reduction of the *leukocytes* and T-lymphocytes and other elements of the cellular and humoral defence system.

Psychosocial models of stress

The somatic models of stress are based on stressors that originate outside the person. Other stress theories point out the influence of stressors which come from within, from intrapsychic stressors. Levi and Andersson (1975) talk about "psychosocial" stress. The term "strain", as in tension, was suggested in contrast to "stress". Periodic or chronic states of emotional stress (that is to say, caused by anxiety or pain) influence not only the function of the autonomous vegetative nervous system and structure of the organs, but also the functions of the ego (i.e., perception and cognition).

Another concept of stress research is the "life-stress model": life events include crises like loss, death, accidents, somatic illness, narcissistic hurts, or traumatic experiences. The important question to ask is what type of person can master this kind of stressor. Mourning is one of the most important processes to overcome loss.

Disposition for stress

Stress research supposes an increased affinity through genetic disposition. The propensity to react on a vegetative, endocrine, or immunological level is hereditary, like high blood pressure or hyperlipidaemia. But there is also an acquired disposition for pathological stress reaction to genetic causes. We call it psychogenetic disposition. Psychogenetic means acquired by experiences in early childhood, from infancy. The psychoanalytical theory of psychic and somatic development points out the importance of the intense attachment between baby and mother in the first months of life (see theories of Spitz, Mahler, Bowlby, and Winnicott), which is a precondition not only for somatic maturation, but also for the psychic and social development of the child and throughout its life. Today, it recognised that the positive experiences of emotional and somatic communication and stable and trusting relationships in childhood are of the utmost importance in protecting against pathological forms of stress.

The deficit of not having this kind of experience can be seen in neurotic and psychosomatic disorders such as general anxiety disorder, heart phobia, or hypochondria, when patients do not have the ability to calm down by themselves and reduce or stop arousal at a high level of sympathetic activity: they need another person as a maternal transference object, for example, health professionals to obtain the tranquillisers and to find a parasympathetic mode of vegetative functioning of the body.

A sufficient and satisfying early relationship leads to mentalization of the body reaction, which is the precondition necessary for dealing with this kind of danger and unpleasant feeling without the support of others (see Chapter One, subsection headed "A note on symbolisation and mentalization" (pp. 10–11) and the subsection in this chapter headed "Model of alexithymia" (p. 235)).

We can understand this theory of deficit also by means of the theory of conflict caused in an early object relationship, when a stressor leads to a psychic and somatic regression (see the subsection "Model of de- and re-somatisation" (p. 234) or the "Model of two-phasic repression", p. 235)).

There are some other, non-psychoanalytical models of stress and disposition: Zubin and Spring (1977) developed the theory of "vulnerabilty" from the behavioural point of view, when patients exhibit deficiency in coping with stressors. The concept of vulnerability postulates somatic genetic and/or acquired somatic and psychosocial aspects of personality. The "diathesis stress model" is based on the concept of vulnerability, but integrates more aspects. These concepts are used to try to understand schizophrenic disorders.

Stress and trauma

Experiments with animals and human beings show that feelings of powerlessness, hopelessness, helplessness, and loss of control are pathogenic factors of chronic stress. Resignation, the feelings of having given up and of giving up play a fundamental role (Engel, 1967).

The models of stress are close to the psychoanalytical concept of trauma: the psychodynamics of trauma contains all these emotional factors as an inundation and the inability to stop the stressor (that is, by aggressive activity, fight, or by avoidance, flight) and the breakdown of resistance against the stressor through sufficient defence mechanisms (see Chapter Eight, section headed "Traumatic neurosis: post traumatic stress disorder (PTSD)", pp. 210–214).

The traumatic influence is also caused by early experience in childhood as a pre-traumatic experience. If there is a good enough relationship, which leads to stable self-esteem and self-confidence, the traumatic situation will not have such a significant negative influence on the patient. Antonovsky (1987) stressed this aspect in his theory of "salutogenesis". He examines the reasons and preconditions for why one person can cope better with traumatic experience than another. He postulated a "sense of coherence", which can cope with stress and traumatic experiences. The concept of "resilience" is close to the model of "salutogenesis".

Final remark

The topic of stress is common in the treatment of patients and has many facets and theories. The traditional psychoanalytic theory of neuroses and psychosomatic disorders does not use the term stress explicitly, but implicitly by employing other terms such as conflict and trauma. The interdisciplinary dialogue between neuroscience, psychoanalysis, and theory of behaviour can lead to a more complete understanding of the phenomenon "stress", which exists as a psychical and somatic unit.

Somatisation and somatoform autonomous disorders

Wolfgang Merkle

Somatisation in general

According to the *ICD-10*, the characteristics of the somatoform symptoms are recurring multiple and clinically significant complaints about pain or gastrointestinal, sexual, and pseudo-neurological complaints. The patients often visit many doctors in order to obtain treatment. Somatisation disorder is a challenge for, and a burden on, medical staff and the significant others of the patients. The patients insist on further diagnostic steps even if doctors affirm a good medical condition. Even if there are somatic impairments, they cannot explain the degree of the symptoms. It is very difficult for patients and doctors to find the connection between the somatic symptoms and the psychodynamic reasons for them.

Somatisation is a very common way of coping with the serious problem of mentalization and its economic importance is increasing. In Germany, for example, the reason for early retirement developed in the past twenty-five years in the following way: in 1985, 30% of early retirement was due to cardiovascular illness and only 5% due to psychic problems. Twenty-five years later, 30% of people retire prematurely because of psychic problems and only 10% because of cardiovascular problems.

Statistics in the USA and other Western countries underline the importance of somatoform diseases: 12.9% somatoform syndromes; lifelong prevalence in German population (TACOS Study, Meyer, Rumpf, Hapke, Dilling, & John, 2000); 12.3% main symptom: pain (TACOS Study, Meyer, Rumpf, Hapke, Dilling, & John, 2000).

The reason for somatisation can be seen as a defence mechanism and the attempt to deal with overwhelming feelings, emotions, powerlessness, and stress. People who are no longer able to deal with these feelings psychically can bear these tensions physically. Usually, psychosomatic symptoms are combined with disturbances in symbolisation and mentalization caused by neglect or other negative influences on the emotional growth in childhood. Also, the body itself is often poorly developed. The hypersensitivity and the catastrophic thinking of these people are often due to narcissistic withdrawal into their own body and the growth of attention to their own body. The relationship to others is, in turn, reduced. The reduction of stimulus from outside leads to even greater attention being paid to one's own body.

One of the most important reasons for the difficulty in treating this condition is the fact that patients are deeply convinced that the illness is indeed caused by somatic change and is threatening processes in the body. Therefore, they try to discover the real reason by means of further medical investigations.

This mechanism is caused by a severe disturbance in the mental organisation in these patients: their ability to distinguish somatic sensations from emotions is severely limited. This difficulty is normally caused by neglect and often abuse during childhood.

Somatoform autonomous disorders

The symptoms appear to be due to a physical disorder of a system that is mainly under autonomic innervation and control: the cardiovascular, gastrointestinal, respiratory, and urogenital systems. There are mainly two groups of symptoms and neither indicates a somatic illness. The first group of complaints consists of objective symptoms of vegetative stimulation, such as palpitations, sweating, flushing, and tremor. These are the expression of fear of, and impairment through, a somatic disturbance. The second group contains subjective complaints of unspecific and changing character, such as fleeting pains, sensations of burning, heaviness, tightness, and a feeling of being bloated, which the patient attributes to a specific organ or system. Some of the somatoform autonomous disorders are given in Table 9.6.

Somatoform symptoms and the relationship to depression and anxiety

In the development of somatoform symptoms, we often discover that there is an affect behind these symptoms. Where the affect should or could be, there is the symptom. When we are successful in our treatment, we often discover that these affects emerge instead of the physical symptoms. Mostly, we find depression and anxiety. It is the anxiety that is important in the genesis of symptoms. There are different anxieties with different tendencies to somatic disturbances; this connection, of course, is not specific (Table 9.7).

Somatoform pain disorder

The predominant complaint is of persistent, severe, and distressing pain, which cannot be explained fully by a physiological process or a physical disorder. The pain occurs in association

Table 9.6. Examples of somatoform autonomous disorders.

Cardiac neurosis
Da Costa's syndrome
Gastric neurosis
Neurocirculatory asthenia
Psychogenic forms of:
Aerophagy
Cough
Diarrhoea
Dyspepsia
Dysuria
Flatulence
Hiccough
Hyperventilation
Increased frequency of micturition
Irritable bowel syndrome
Pylorospasm

Table 9.7. Forms of anxieties and possible symptoms (somatisation).

Reasons for anxiety		Bodily symptom
Libidinal anxieties (temptation)		Dizziness
Separation anxiety		Cardiac symptoms, headache
Anxiety about aggression (ambivalence)		Hyperventilation
Fear of flooding		Tinnitus
Anxiety about madness	→	Bizarre body feelings
Anxiety about closeness		Asthma bronchiale, obstructive asthma
Anxiety about shame		Hypochondria
Anxiety about death		Insomnia
Anxiety about loneliness and emotional hunger		Heartburn

with emotional conflict or psychosocial problems that are sufficient to allow the conclusion that they are the main causative influences. This usually results in a marked increase in support and attention, either personal or medical. Nevertheless treatment is seldom successful, which leads to the patient changing doctors frequently. The patients become convinced that they are not really understood and accepted by the medical system.

As early as 1895, Freud wrote, in the case report of Elisabeth von R, "This theory calls for closer examination. We may ask: what is it that turns into physical pain here? A cautious reply would be: something that might have become, and should have become, mental pain" (Freud, 1895d, p. 166).

The main question still remains: how can we help the patient to feel, to bear, and perhaps to solve the psychic pain that is at the root of it?

In the following, I shall describe the genesis and treatment, or approach to treatment, of patients with somatisation or somatoform autonomous disorders, using somatoform pain as an example.

Drawing 9.1 is an illustration depicting the chronic somatoform headache of a nineteen-year-old patient. One can imagine his real suffering from the pain. Several investigations, including an MRI scan, did not reveal any abnormality. He had a severe post-adolescent problem due to separation from his family and difficulty in developing his male identity. For over five years he was treated first as an inpatient, later in our day clinic, and afterwards in an outpatient psychoanalytic setting. He was able to make progress in developing his emotional capacities and in the possibilities of developing lively relationships and intimacy in heterosexual partnership. In the meantime, he has become a lawyer. The headache was strongly connected with the father's separation from the patient's family. While the son was having therapy, the father died of prostate cancer.

The pathogenetic context of somatoform pain disorder

Let us take a brief look at the theory of psychic development (Elzer, 2012). The experience of physical sensations starts at an intrauterine stage; to be aware of pain and other uncomfortable stimuli is necessary and important for life. Physical pain has the same function as psychic emotion, anxiety, and fear: both are signals triggered by perception of any kind of danger. Pain

Drawing 9.1. Drawing of a patient with strong and chronic somatoform headache.

and fear are somatic and psychic activities and reactions from outside and inside. Through the tender interaction between the mother (or the care-giver) and the baby, all aspects of the sensory nervous system will be stimulated and the self–object differentiation (inside–outside) and body self developed. By means of the experience of safe attachment to the mother during the first year of life, the baby learns to cope with fear, pain, and unpleasant feelings from inside and outside the body. A baby and a toddler need a confident, safe, and good enough relationship to cope with pain and fear and to obtain satisfaction of his needs. Pain is a communication between child and parent and other care-givers. The experience of empathy during the first years of life is necessary for coping with pain, fear, frustration, and other physical and mental problems if the primary objects are absent—in childhood and in adulthood.

Pain can be experienced in both active and passive mode: that is, if the child attacks others aggressively or is attacked or punished by others. In both situations, pain is part of an aggressive interaction. Pain also has a function that allows regulation of self-esteem by means of drive wishes in object relations. This experience, of handling aggression and pain, is important during the anal stage. The child regulates the conflict of dependency and autonomy and develops a feeling for borders between itself and others.

Chronic bodily pain can be a substitute for a painful relationship during childhood or at present. Experiences of pain will be transferred to other objects in a sense of repetition. Pain is better than loneliness, being lost by others, and losing the relationship to the self and the body.

Self-harming behaviour (cutting or burning the skin), as in borderline personality disorder, has the psychic function of feeling, of perceiving the self, of overcoming the painful feeling of being lost and neglected. As an example, after a difficult relationship with her husband, with many narcissistic hurts and sadistic interactions, a woman developed a chronic pain syndrome of the neck and lower back. Through her pain, she was in contact with her sadistic husband. The relationship was still vivid; her husband was present all the time. She had him on her back. The patient could not separate from her husband; the psychodynamic was similar to depression as a chronic mourning process. The deeper reason for this neurotic repetition was a fixation in the strong and loveless relationship to her mother, where tendencies of autonomy were suppressed and physically punished.

Coping with pain is also a question of culture and gender: boys and men are expected not show pain like girls and women. The experience of, and the coping with, pain can also be understood as a process of learning through theory of behaviour. Patients with chronic pain develop a "memory of pain"; the experience of pain is represented in the brain (cortex and amygdala), separated from the cause in the organ outside the brain, as "phantom pain".

In patients with somatoform pain, a certain pattern of development during childhood is an important factor for the subsequent illness. This development is strongly associated with lack of mentalization, described by Fonagy, Gergely, Jurist, and Target (2002). These patients have severe problems with symbolisation. Their thinking is very concrete. They have limited potential for feeling in an "as if position". The reasons for their impairments in emotional functioning are often connected with their childhood experiences (Table 9.8).

Maltreatment is often caused by psychosocial difficulties in the parents, for example, single parents, an alcohol-dependent father, or early loss of a parent.

Growing up under such difficult conditions might lead to difficult personality traits and developmental problems. Later on, these children develop immature conflict managing strategies significantly more often (Table 9.9).

Relationship between patient and doctor

The capability of having an "as if relationship" exists neither with the patient's own body nor with significant others, nor with health professionals (who are, unfortunately, often willing to

Table 9.8. Examples of early experiences in childhood.

Deprived, often hard working
Poor emotional contact
Little scope for self-development
Forced autonomy very early in life
Prematurely taking responsibility for adult functioning
Physical or psychic maltreatment
Identification with the aggressor
Passivity allowed only during physical illness
Similar physical illness in the family

Table 9.9. Examples of immature conflict managing strategies.

Defence mechanism: turning against oneself and projection
Restricted mastering of phase-specific tasks of development
Insecure self-image
Emotional feelings and signals of the body are difficult to distinguish
Emotions cannot be mastered or calmed down through adequate acting—helplessness
Emotions cause inadequate thinking (somatising phantasies, catastrophic valuation)
Emotions cannot be improved with help from others (inadequate behaviour of asking for help and support)

enter into this kind of relationship). Therefore, real support through a helpful relationship in the health system is often missing as well. Patients go "doctor shopping" or "doctor hopping" (going from one physician to the next) to get the "right" diagnosis. Generally, these patients are more interested in physical examinations than getting a somatic diagnosis that can explain the complaints (*ICD-10*, F45). They are often disappointed by the psychogenetic or psychosomatic diagnosis and the lack of somatic help. If the doctor does not understand this kind of somatisation and the patient's offer of transference (i.e., as a repetition of neglect in early childhood), he will be disappointed too, made helpless and angry by his unsatisfied and more demanding patient (countertransference). Maybe the doctor will reject this patient as a psychiatric or psychological case, or use a somatic treatment, which is not indicated and sometimes dangerous. The patient will be satisfied by this kind of somatic acting-out, but, later, he will be disappointed, because he was maltreated. The doctor is now like a disappointed and disappointing object of the patient's early childhood.

On average, it takes about five years before such patients succeed in getting psychosomatic help for the illness and additional iatrogenic damage (e.g., through unnecessary surgery). The importance of events, social aspects, and relationships for the pain experience are often denied and there is a bitter struggle against the recognition of their importance.

The outbreak of the illness in critical life situations is often triggered by particular situations.

Triggering situations for somatoform pain

Table 9.10 shows some triggering situations and reasons that lead to the symptom formation of somatoform pain. We can find these reasons in other neurotic and psychosomatic disorders. They are not significant for chronic pain disorders.

Treatment of patients with chronic pain

The treatment of patients with chronic pain syndrome is different from treatment of patients with neurotic disorders. The body language, "somatisation", of the conflict or trauma needs to overcome the strong and rigid defence mechanism, which can be understood through the "model of de- and re-somatisation" by Schur, and the "two-phasic repression" by Mitscherlich

Table 9.10. Triggering situations for somatoform pain.

Chronic conflict
Marital and partnership conflict
Disappointment at not achieving high goals—drop in performance
Long-lasting neglect of passive needs
Disappointment with one's life's work
Narcissistic disappointment at work
Loss or threatened loss
Death of a relative
Detachment of the children
Divorce or separation
Redundancy or job loss
Traumatic experience
Violence
Rape
Accident
Natural disaster

(see pp. 234–235 and 235–236, respectively). So, we need another psychodynamic attitude and technique in order to verbalise and communicate the meaning of the patient's body language.

Psychotherapeutic attitude

We need a psychosomatic attitude based on empathy and patience. Knowledge of physical connections, implications, and clinical experience is useful and necessary. Psychologists are at a disadvantage here. The countertransference traps detailed in Table 9.11 should be avoided.

Reduce your demands (less is more) and try to think of coping rather than healing. Psychoeducation is very useful: you must give the patient concrete information about somatoform connections. Improvement in the pain behaviour (for example, discontinuation of doctor shopping, investigations, surgery, and medication) and an increase in the psychosocial possibilities signify major success, even if the patient tells you that the pain did not change. The claim that pain exists lasts longer than the decrease in pain behaviour and the improvement in psychic feeling.

Table 9.11. Countertransference traps.

Impatience
Excessive expectations
Helplessness
Fury and anger
Rejection and refusal
Insecurity
Impulse to punish or to withdraw
Feeling of becoming insignificant for the patient

Initially, refrain from interpretation of connections—try to contain and listen. Develop a tolerance of your own insecurity ("Did you really not overlook a somatic illness? What is the real reason?"). Use concrete pictures in order to guide the patient to his body–mental reality.

It is always important to know that these countertransference feelings have their origin in the inner object relationships of the patient. They show something of the patient's early experiences with his parents or significant primary objects.

As an example, a patient who was neglected by his parents could give the therapist the feeling that no matter what he does his efforts are not recognised by the patient or are forgotten and erased until the next session. In this way, the rejection and loneliness is now felt by the therapist and this means relief for the patient.

Guidelines

Table 9.12 lists some recommendations from the clinical experience of treatment of patients with chronic pain disorders.

Case report

> A twenty-six-year-old male patient comes to the psychosomatic clinic after finishing his examination in administration science abroad. One month earlier, he had broken off his outpatient treatment in a special headache clinic. A neurological examination with CCT had been carried out. His complaints were diagnosed as tension headaches. The symptom has been occurring daily for the past three years. He finished his exams with a high grade and had good prospects for his job, but he felt handicapped because of the impression that he could not rely on himself and face his daily work without breaks. During his studies, he always used to take breaks when the headache set in.

Table 9.12. Guidelines for treatment of patients with chronic pain disorders.

View the physical symptoms as material for interpretation, not defence
No immediate search for the primary cause in the background of the physical symptoms
Use the thoughts of the patient concerning his body as a key to his connection to his own self (body as an object)
The obvious connection between symptoms and psychosocial problems (as seen by the physician) cannot be recognised by the patient. Therefore, they should not be interpreted by the therapist at the beginning of treatment
Begin with the body by allowing as much physical and medical therapy as is necessary to win the patient's co-operation (establishing therapy alliance). Further physical investigations can be necessary in order not to lose the patient.
Accept the paucity of psychological mindedness in the patient
Signal acceptance that the complaints are legitimate
Do not struggle with the "truth": the patient will always win because subjectivity cannot be questioned in this instance
The shame of the patient because of his poor childhood and poor self-confidence might be strong. Not to have a "real" (physical) pain often means for him that he suffers from an imaginary illness

The headache is accompanied by a strong feeling of pressure on both sides of the head. It occurs in rest periods after high levels of intellectual stress. During the night he is free from pain, but in the morning he anxiously waits for the headache to start again. The symptoms also occur when he is about to give a presentation in front of a group or during examinations. He is able to see some connection between his high expectations, ambitions, and the tendency to perfectionism. On the other hand, he feels very tense when he is bored. It is unbearable for him not to be needed.

He believes that he observes his surroundings carefully and is very strict with his colleagues, and wishes that his environment would treat him the same way. Often, he is afraid of embarrassing himself and cannot relax. During holidays and when surfing or skiing, he never suffers from headaches.

He lives with his French girlfriend, whom he met during his studies in Paris. They agree that their careers should be more important than their partnership. "Relationship yes, problems no!" is their slogan. However, in the meantime, he is a little disappointed that he has more feelings than he allows himself. On the other hand, he told me that he could not perceive feelings like happiness or sadness. He always managed to give up intimate relationships without feeling anything, even knowing that he would miss the partner later. He reported that his former girlfriend accused him of being as cold as ice!

The patient is the second of four siblings (brothers two and five years younger, and a sister one year older). His father was a businessman, his mother the manager of a fashion shop. Even as a child he had his own "head", was seen as mature for his years, very serious, and less playful. He was compared with a peculiar uncle.

In his memory, his parents did not quarrel, but they suddenly separated and divorced. He and the brother nearest in age to him went to live with the father, the other siblings with the mother. His school results deteriorated and he started to quarrel with his good-natured and likeable father.

When the patient was twelve, his father died after having been involved in a mysterious accident. Suicidal impulses could have been an issue. The mother refused to let him see his father in the intensive care unit. Following his father's death, he and his brother went to live with the mother and stepfather. Today, he is surprised that he did not mourn his father very much. Afterwards, he became very ambitious and serious, worked hard at school, and felt responsible for his siblings. He despised his stepfather and ignored him as an authority. He left home at twenty because of difficulties with the stepfather, who refused to allow his girlfriend to stay overnight. After receiving his high-school diploma and doing a gap year, he studied administration abroad. He remembers that he felt very anxious for the first two years.

With regard to therapy, at first the patient is very sceptical and refuses it. He behaves in a very competent manner and seems to have no needs. He does not allow the therapist to have an insight into his situation and biography. He looks attractive (tall, slim, and quite handsome). He will accept help only through medication. Later on, he reports that in the beginning he believed that all therapists tended to depreciate people who are ambitious, self-confident, and achievement-orientated, and he was afraid they would try to take away these capacities.

He shows a tendency to contradiction in individual therapy. Lamenting about not enough therapy, he is impatient and full of reproach. He likes to have concrete recommendations and recipes. His ideas concerning the therapy are orientated towards the passive: hypnosis, infusions. He wants to get rid of the pain without taking part in therapy, without mental pain. He increasingly connects with the therapist, talking about his father. Sadness and mental pain threaten to appear, and in this situation the headaches get worse. While, on the one hand, he is looking for an idealised father who provides him with a special narcissistic elevated place, he is, on the other hand, full of anxiety about rivalry concerning such a man. On the one hand, the guilty feelings concerning his father are crucial; on the other hand, there is anxiety concerning the revenge of the dethroned father. His father died at the time that he started to quarrel with him in adolescence. Accordingly, his dreams are full of scenes in which he belongs to criminal gangs, which are chased; he cannot progress, is paralysed. He wants to hold on to the image of his family as an ideal family without quarrels, divorce, or death of the father. He has big problems in dealing with aggression.

The further course of treatment consisted of six weeks during which the patient was treated as an inpatient with different psychoanalytically orientated therapies: individual therapy, group therapy combined with art therapy, autogenous training, and concentrative movement therapy.

In applying for a job, he experienced a tremendous up and down: from joy at the success of his application to anxiety about the possibility of losing everything and ending up as a beggar. For the first time, he mentions his uncle (his father's brother), who committed suicide some years earlier. He feels too close to his girlfriend and thinks about separation. For the first time, he has guilt feelings and cries. He can allow himself some feelings of mourning during the group treatment. He moved to another city because he obtained a position in a company there. His headaches now worried him less. We talked about the possibility of getting psychoanalytic outpatient treatment in the new city.

Six months later, he reported his success in the new position, although there were a lot of difficulties and anxieties about failure. His symptoms had changed; now he could talk more of anxiety than of pain, of tension and pressure in the head rather than of physical pain. He had great difficulty in starting psychotherapy in the new city, so he returned with some regularity to sessions with me. Following a move to another European country and a successful career as the head of a company, he phoned and did some sessions while in Germany. After ten years, I received the final report from him: he had married and, after years of trying, had had his first baby.

This case shows how long the treatment of patients with somatoform symptoms can last.

Vertigo

Somatoform vertigo is very often accompanied by anxiety, phobia, or depressive symptoms. In about 30–50% of all types of vertigo, a psychic cause is responsible. In neurology and general medicine, dizziness is a very common symptom. Interestingly, about 30% of patients with an initial somatic cause later on present secondary somatoform dizziness symptoms (Eckardt-Henn, 2011, p. 784).

Some symptoms, however, most probably exclude somatic genesis of dizziness:

- the dizziness is permanent;
- no repetitive spontaneous rotatory vertigo is observed;
- no neurological, clinical, and electro-physiological symptoms are observed (Eckhart-Henn, 2011, p. 785).

The psychodynamic reasons vary, but mostly a situation occurs where the patient feels threatened by affective stimulation because of anger or anxiety. Commonly, these affects are not conscious, but are denied by the patient. Often, the affects are not in accordance with the superego of the patient and, in consequence, he has to deny them. The patient frequently experiences some forbidden feelings, wishes, or actions he does not want to admit, so that they now must be suppressed. One has to keep in mind that anxiety and vestibular functions are closely related.

Mothers commonly soothe their children by cradling (i.e., by stimulating the vestibular organs), and, later in life, this stimulation is enjoyably experienced by riding roller-coasters and so on. If the stimulation becomes too strong, however, unpleasant symptoms, such as vomiting, accompanying the dizziness occur.

At first, the symptoms can provide relief for the patient because they allow him to escape his ambivalent and stressful feelings and to regress to the comfort of being cared for. Although this seems helpful in the short run and, in some way, he is "grateful" for the symptoms, in the long run the disadvantages of the impeding symptoms are too negative.

Normally, the symptom of dizziness occurs without psychopathological abnormalities, which means that the patient has numerous medical examinations (neurology, otolaryngology, orthopaedic) and internal medicine until he finally sees a psychosomatic doctor or psychiatrist. In psychotherapy, the conflicts need to be exposed, so we can help to overcome the high level of stress and anxiety. For some patients, hospitalisation and treatment with a multi-modal therapy may be necessary.

Case report

> A fifty-eight-year-old medical doctor (physician) came to our clinic after a long period of diagnostic examinations in internal, oto-rhinological, and neurological medicine lasting about six months. He was very anxious when it was recommended that he should seek help at our clinic because he did not consider himself to be mentally ill. He suffered from anhedonia, lack of impetus, felt empty and dead without emotional oscillation, and could not sleep. He felt exhausted. Moreover, he had very disturbing symptoms of an irritable colon.
>
> As the owner of a pathology laboratory with about thirty employees, he had a great deal of stress and work without seeing any prospect of relief. He always cared for his family: the children of his first marriage (a twenty-eight-year-old male and a twenty-six-year-old female), his children of the second marriage (an eighteen-year-old female and a fourteen-year-old male), as well as for his mother and stepfather.
>
> In the background and not obviously, he was very angry with an employee who seemed to behave irresponsibly and was often off work through being certified as sick, arrived for work late and finished early, meaning that much work remained undone.
>
> He was responsible for about 60,000 anatomical preparations every year that were crucial for the patients (i.e., benign *vs.* malignant).
>
> It was very difficult to convince this patient that he needed to take a break. He was full of anxiety that his company would falter if he were not present. Eventually, he agreed to a week's stay in the day clinic. The stay was extended for a further two weeks. An outpatient setting with concomitant concentrative movement therapy followed. Then two weeks more, and afterwards we did an outpatient setting with concomitant concentrative movement therapy. He did not have a good contact with his body.

During therapy the patient said, "Oh Doctor, with me, you must accelerate my deceleration!" It was discovered that his dizziness had started after a quarrel with the problem employee. This employee reminded him of his stepbrother. The patient's father left the family soon after the patient was born and the mother remarried. He always had the feeling that he was unwanted and tried to justify his presence by working hard, including doing housework. Yet, he still felt that he should do better. The younger brother was quite different: he was the "right" child with the "right" father and favoured. The patient had no contact with his biological father, who had died soon after leaving the family. Even with a career at university and the title of a professor, he did not receive the same recognition from his parents as his brother did. After he had married, one of his colleagues took his wife, and so the drama with the "brother" was repeated again.

Confidence in the therapist and the therapeutic setting helped the patient to lose his dizziness and to discover the connection with his existential fears, which were not caused by real difficulties but by the deep unconscious fear that a "brother" could take away everything he had built up. He began to realise that he was allowed to have his own wishes. He had a right to his own existence and he did not only have to serve others.

Tinnitus

Tinnitus is often a last warning in situations of stress overload resulting in powerlessness. It can be caused by a long period of labouring without success or at least without a hope of relief. Therefore, occurrence of tinnitus is a warning: "I cannot listen to anything any more, it is too much".

Looking at the investigation with imaging procedures, we can see the importance of neuronal nets with interactions between limbic, prefrontal, somato-sensoric, and auditory areas of the cerebral cortex (Lockwood, Salvi, & Burkard, 2002). There could be a neurobiological correlation to the reduced filter function for disturbing stimuli, the reinforced perception of noises with fixation of the attention and the substantial affective de-compensation of chronic tinnitus patients.

Jäger and Lamprecht found in a study of tinnitus that the patients with tinnitus had more burdens by the family and strains of daily life (cited by Frommer & Lagenbach, 2011, p. 791).

The extent of attention to the symptom, the degree of satisfaction with life, and the level of anxiety and fatalistic convictions seem to influence the course of the illness considerably. To be powerless and unable to influence the further development of the symptoms appear to be important factors in the course of the condition and whether it becomes chronic (Frommer & Lagenbach, 2011, p. 794).

The situation at the beginning of the illness, when the patient has to face an overwhelming situation from outside that he is unable to influence or stop, has now become an inner situation, where the patient is no longer pressed by disturbance from outside but by his inner organs and a terrifying noise instead. The main problem lies in the fact that it is necessary to detract attention from the noise and direct it to the real, pressing situation which existed at the beginning of the illness and to change the attitude concerning tasks and ambition. The main "battle" is very similar to other somatoform disturbances, as were described previously. The patients tend to force the doctor to act: medical infusion therapy, hyperbaric chambers, cortisone, stimulating the blood flow, tinnitus retraining with a sound generator, etc.

The role of the therapist is to accompany the patient on his path towards changing his attitude to outward demarcation and to finding scope for his development. In the beginning, tinnitus patients tend to be very demanding and claiming and difficult to convince that tinnitus is indeed a warning signal from the body to change one's life.

Sexual dysfunction

Dealing with sexual problems in psychoanalysis and psychodynamic therapy includes problems with pathological developments in sexual maturation (i.e., perversion), in deviation, and in sexual identification.

Moreover, sexual problems, which are dominated and influenced by neurotic developments or conflicts, can be observed in partnership. We cannot devote much space to this topic, but we can classify sexual dysfunctions into four categories, as shown in Table 9.13.

Hauch (1998, p. 71) showed that, during the past three decades, an important shift in development of sexual disturbances has taken place: in the group of males, the lack of sexual desire has grown from 4% to 20%, while erectile dysfunction has decreased from 67% to 51% (perhaps because of the use of Viagra). This percentage is from those who sought help for sexual problems.

Erectile dysfunction, or impotence, is a sexual dysfunction characterised by the inability to develop or maintain an erection of the penis. There are various underlying causes, such as damage to the nervi erigentes, which prevents or delays erection, or diabetes, which simply decreases the blood flow to the tissue in the penis. Many of these dysfunctions are medically reversible. The causes of erectile dysfunction may be psychological or physical.

Due to its embarrassing nature and the shame felt by sufferers, the subject was taboo for a long time and is the subject of many legends. In the 1990s, the introduction of the first pharmacologically effective remedy for impotence, Sildenafil (trade name, Viagra) caused a wave of public attention, propelled in part by the newsworthiness of the stories and heavy advertising.

In the past three decades, the lack of sexual desire in women has grown from 8% to 49% and vaginismus from 12% to 26%, whereas the problems in arousal and achieving orgasm have decreased from 80% to 26% (Hauch, 1998).

Sexual pain disorders affect women almost exclusively and are known as dyspareunia (painful intercourse) or vaginismus (an involuntary spasm of the muscles of the vaginal wall that interferes with intercourse).

Dyspareunia may be caused by insufficient lubrication (vaginal dryness), which may result from insufficient excitement and stimulation or from hormonal changes caused by menopause,

Table 9.13. Four categories of sexual dysfunction.

Category	What is affected by the dysfunction
1.	Sexual desire
2.	Arousal
3.	Orgasm
4.	Pain

pregnancy, or breast-feeding. Contraceptive creams and foams can also irritate and cause dryness, as can fear and anxiety about sex.

The causes of vaginismus remain unclear, but it is thought that past sexual trauma might play a role. In another female sexual pain disorder, called vulvodynia or vulvar vestibularis, women experience burning pain during sex which seems to be related to problems with the skin in the vulvar and vaginal areas. The cause is unknown.

Sexual symptoms and dysfunctions can be caused for different reasons, apart from somatic disorders (Table 9.14).

Psychodynamic aspects concerning partnership in sexual dysfunctions

Sexuality is an important drive in human life and the development of sexual maturity is crucial for the development of health. We must be aware that sometimes the knowledge about the patient's true sexual life is hidden because of shame—this applies to patients as well as therapists. Either we do not want to embarrass the patient or we are ashamed ourselves. Nevertheless, it must be pointed out that the kind of organisation of the inner world of conflicts, especially in contact with other persons of the same or the other sex, is very often expressed concretely through the type of sexual behaviour.

Psychoanalytic theory offers a deeper understanding—and many more meanings of sexual dysfunction and symptoms—than sexual medicine does. The sexual function is very sensitive and sexual problems appear if psychic conflicts come up from the unconsciousness generally: that is, depression or phobia. There are also isolated sexual dysfunctions, such as ejaculation praecox (premature ejaculation) or vaginismus. A woman with vaginismus, for example, could be conveying her wish to control the relationship and her lack of openness or fear of being hurt. Alternatively, it could be an expression of bad trust in close objects, perhaps due to

Table 9.14. Reasons for sexual symptoms (following Strauß & Becker, 1998).

Deficits of learning and experience
Sexual myths, for example, about masturbation
Insufficient sexual education
Stress, life crisis
Depressive moods (anhedonia)
Psychiatric illness
Side-effects of medication
Neurotic disorders, such as:
Inhibition
Anxiety
Primary sexual and drive anxieties
Anxiety of superego
Anxiety in relationship
Dysfunctional self-perception
Self-reinforcement mechanism and expectation anxieties
Traumatic experiences

traumatisation through having been beaten or sexually abused earlier; another hypothesis stresses the unconscious fantasies of destroying the penis. On the other hand, a man with premature ejaculation could be expressing his stinginess or his aggression against his female partner. Dependence on sex can be an expression of a disturbed development during the oral phase. So there can be a type of addiction to sexual behaviour. Disturbance in erectile function could signal a lack of closeness, castration fear, and problems in a relationship with high ambivalence.

These symptoms are caused by unconscious fantasies about the body of the patient or the partner; these fantasies produce uncomfortable feelings and fear, which destroy any sexual pleasure. In this situation, the vegetative nervous system works through the sympathicus, which is active for fight-or-flight behaviour. To permit sexual desire and pleasure, the vegetative nervous system should function through the parasympathicus, like enjoying a meal.

The sexual act is a very difficult and distinguished act for humans, including regression, dealing with aggression and libido, and, at the same time, giving up the barriers against melting and permitting symbiotic processes. This means a great effort for the whole personality organisation and presupposes much ego strength and stability. This act calls for the necessity to deal with nearness and an approach with empathy and self-confidence.

The absence of desire can also result from fatigue and depression, as well as ambivalence towards the partner. This ambivalence can be quite unconscious. The inability to achieve orgasm (anorgasm) can be traced to the individual's development: if there is early binding disturbance, where dedication and devotion is not possible, then mistrust prevents this kind of symbiosis and ego loss.

Lack of mentalization and fantasy makes it more difficult to come into contact and increases anxiety.

Sexuality can become an object controlling the relationship, where the regulation of sexual contact presents the possibility of superiority, and means a power struggle or passive aggression. Nevertheless, we should not overlook the fact that many sufferers report great anxiety about fulfilling the partner's expectations, especially if there had been previous negative experiences. These anxieties are often not consciously recognised but, nevertheless, lead to insecurity in sexual behaviour.

Diagnostic problems of sexual dysfunction

Psychotherapists and physicians show a lack of sexual–medical knowledge. Incorrect phantasies and ideas with regard to sexuality are not only a problem for patients, but also for therapists (Buddeberg, 1998). Only half of physicians considered themselves to be competent on this topic.

There are gender specific differences in the conceptualisation of sexuality: men are more often biologically orientated in their view of sexuality. They equate their male identity with the function of their penis; their sexual behaviour is more orientated towards action and performance; their emotional experience is less differentiated and contradictory. There is more power and powerlessness. The main myths about sexuality (Table 9.15) play an important role in sexual disorders.

Table 9.15. Myths about sexuality.

A man may not have "soft" feelings
In sex, only performance is important
The man takes the initiative and is responsible for the orgasm of both
Men always want to have sex and are always ready for sex
Each bodily contact will lead to sex
Sex is the same as sexual intercourse
Sex without an erection is not possible
Sexual arousal must grow steadily and culminate in (simultaneous) orgasm
Sex must be spontaneous and natural
Women's sexuality is more orientated towards the relationship
Sexual phantasies and wishes are more spontaneously inspired and biographically balanced
Women's wishes are more fleeting and not recognised by the male's perception
Myths do not influence our views about sex nowadays

Sexual disturbances are summarised in Table 9.16.

Psychoanalytic treatment of sexual dysfunctions

The therapy for sexual dysfunctions has always been, and remains, a very important task of psychodynamic and psychoanalytic treatment. However, studies have shown that somatic reasons account for 30% of sexual dysfunctions. More than in other symptoms, the couple and the real and concrete conflicts are very important as well as the role of learnt behaviour. Nevertheless, inner conflicts as well as early traumata and deficits in early development play a role in sexual dysfunctions. No genuine specific methods to treat sexual disturbances psychoanalytically are known. Of course, recognising the meaning of the symptom to make it conscious in order to identify the unconscious conflict is of predominant importance, but often in these patients we have very deep pre-oedipal conflicts and deficits. Therefore, these patients must be given more help in the structure-forming and structure-giving attitude of the analyst.

Table 9.16. Sexual disturbances in the phases of sexual intercourse.

Phase of intercourse	Disturbance in man	Disturbance in woman
Desire	Lack of desire	Lack of desire
Arousal	Disturbance in erection	Disturbance in arousal Inadequate lubrication
Penetration	Dyspareunia	Dyspareunia Vaginismus
Orgasm	Premature ejaculation Ejaculation without feeling of orgasm Retrograde ejaculation Failure to ejaculate	Inhibited orgasm Physiologic orgasm without orgasmic feeling

Psychodynamic therapy is the first choice in treating sexual disturbance, even if there is also a significant tendency to offer couple therapy an appropriate place.

Organic diseases with psychosocial components

Matthias Elzer

In the subsection headed "Definitions" (p. 228) we distinguished psychogenic, somatic, and psychosomatic disorders. Organic diseases with psychosocial components are typical psychosomatic disorders, which have somatic and psychic parts that influence each other (Table 9.17).

The organic part can exist as a result of genetic or acquired somatic causes. The psychic part acts as a trigger for the manifestation of the acute disease due to an actual psychic conflict, trauma, or emotional stress.

Earlier psychosomatic theories point out specific conflicts, which lead to particular disorders (see the concept of "organ neurosis", by Alexander (pp. 233–234)). Alexander (1950) mentions the "Holy Seven" of psychosomatic diseases: peptic ulcer, ulcerative colitis, obstructive asthma, ideopathic hypertension, atopic dermatitis, hyperthyreosis, and rheumatoid arthritis. These diseases cause dysfunctions and changes in organs of the vegetative nervous system.

Today, we know that there are no significant conflicts for particular psychosomatic disorders. The psychical reasons are unspecific and individual.

Epigenetic and psychosomatic disorders

The scientific literature on psychosomatic diseases discusses the question of why a person does not develop a manifest disease, such as rheumatic disorder, although he has the genetic or acquired disposition to do so. A further question is why a patient develops the disease at this point in time and not earlier or later in life. The timing of manifestation is determined by actualisation of latent unconscious conflicts or traumatic experiences during the person's adulthood and by insufficient psychosocial defence mechanisms.

Table 9.17. Psychosomatic disorders with psychosocial components.

	Mode	Examples
Soma and psyche influence each other	S ↔ P	Obstructive asthma Rheumatic disorders Inflammatory bowel diseases Gastric and duodenal ulcer Cardiovascular disorders Slipped disc

The relatively new theories of "psychogenetics" and "epigenetics" offer a deeper understanding of how the genetic disposition can be influenced, where special genes are triggered and started or stopped by the patient's psychosocial situation (Bauer, 2002): the genes are not like programmes of biochemical processes, which run automatically. They have a kind of switch, called a promotor or enhancer. This switch is ahead of the sequence of genes and biochemical substances of the person's environment (the so-called transcription factors), attaches to it, and switches the sequence of genes on and off. Most of the genetic dispositions for diseases need communication with transcription factors. Fewer run independently and automatically if the influence of the somatic disposition is predominant.

Psychosomatic disorders can have different components of somatic and psychic causes, like other mental disorders: depression, for example, where neurotic depression is caused by psychosocial experiences in childhood and severe depression by a high level of genetic heredity (Figure 9.8).

Table 9.18 shows some hypothetical examples of organic diseases with psychosocial components. These examples try to give an impression of how the somatic disposition can be connected with a patient's psychosocial problems. Psychosocial conflicts and traumatic experiences are unspecific and often unavoidable in life. The inhibition of the sympathetic nervous system and the inability for parasympathetic functioning of the body are common aspects in all organic diseases with psychosocial components. The genetic or acquired disposition is like the weakest link of a chain, which is broken by psychosocial conflicts. We talk about the "place of predilection", where a conflict or personality structure cannot be compensated by psychosocial defence mechanisms. It is like the process of somatisation, where only the function of the organ is working incorrectly.

Therapeutic aspects

The therapeutic principles of organic diseases with psychosocial components are a combination of somatic treatment and psychotherapy. The physician, in other words, the specialist in internal medicine, should have the psychosomatic competence to understand the disease from a patient-orientated point of view instead of a disease-orientated one. Psychoanalytically orientated psychotherapy can help in understanding the psychodynamic part of the disease. In some

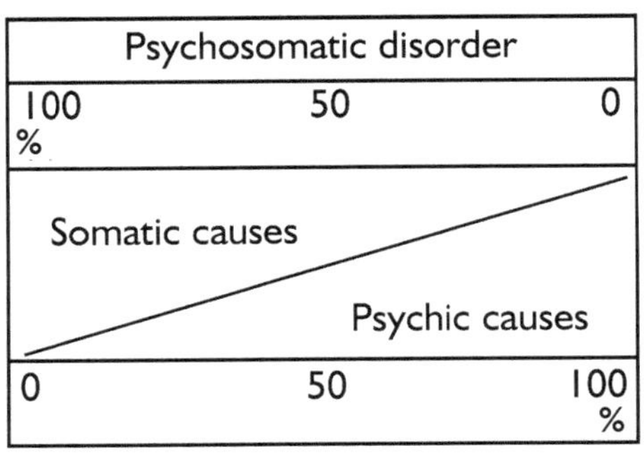

Figure 9.8. Different causes of disease.

Table 9.18. Some examples of organic diseases with psychosocial components.

Genetic somatic disposition	Acquired somatic or psychosomatic disposition and malbehaviour		Examples of psychosocial conflict, trauma, emotional stress, and insufficient defence mechanism		Organic diseases with psychosocial components
Atopy of the immune system, e.g., bronchial asthma, neurodermatitis		+	Unconscious conflict, e.g., of fear of loss, emotional stress	→	Attack of obstructive asthma or neurodermatitis
	Infect-allergic asthma or hypersensitivity of the respiratory system	+	Unconscious conflicts e.g., of separation and loss, emotional stress	→	Nervous cough, attack of obstructive asthma
Disposition to hyperlipidemia	Malnutrition, smoking	+	Chronic emotional stress, inhibition of overt aggressive feelings, depressive personality, denial	→	High blood pressure or ischaemic heart attack
	Malnutrition	+	Chronic emotional stress, inhibition of overt aggressive feelings	→	Idiopathic hypertension
Hyper secretion of gastric acid	Infection by heliobacter pylori	+	Chronic stress, oral conflict and frustration, inhibition of overt aggressive feelings	→	Gastritis or ulcus ventriculi
Antibodies against bowel tissue (mucosa)		+	Life events, high emotional stress, depressive personality structure, inhibition of handling aggressive feelings, fear of loss	→	Attack of colitis ulcerosa or Crohn's disease
Disposition to rheumatism	Negative body feelings, fear of moving	+	Life events of loss, somatisation, inhibition of overt aggressive feelings, avoidance	→	Manifest rheumatic disorders
	Negative body image, fear of moving	+	Traumatic experience, loss, inhibition of aggression narcissistic retreat to the body	→	Fibromyalgia
	Deformation of the spine/disc, hypertension of the paravertebral muscular system	+	Somatisation of aggressive inhibition through persistent emotional stress	→	Slipped disc and compression of the sciatic nerve (nervus ischiaticus) lead to pain attack and paralysis.

cases, it is necessary to treat the patient in a psychosomatic department in co-operation with other departments: internal medicine, surgery, or neurology (see the subsection "Theory and practice of inpatient psychoanalytic psychotherapy", by Wolfgang Merkle, pp. 271–278).

Some examples of treatment for outpatients

1. A young lady has been suffering from severe attacks of obstructive, genetically caused asthma since childhood. Her father died of a sudden heart attack when she was ten. The suppressed mourning for her father and the emotional dependency on her mother and, later on, her boyfriend were central topics of the analytic therapy. She was able to develop more independence and to show more emotions, such as aggressive feelings in her private and professional relationships, which she had until then suppressed. Her self-esteem improved considerably. Due to therapy, the occurrence of obstructive attacks decreased and the use of medication was significantly reduced.
2. The father of two boys who was employed as a manager had suffered from inflammatory bowel disease since he was nineteen. He started psychoanalytically orientated psychotherapy after his family doctor diagnosed him with "burnout syndrome". Incidentally, he mentioned that he suffered from colitis ulcerosa, but could not imagine that the colitis had any psychosomatic significance.
   He said that everything was perfect in his life except his colitis. During therapy, he learnt that his personality structure was to avoid conflicts. It was a revelation to him to understand the connection between his inability to say "no" to others and the dysfunction of his bowels. "Conflicts agitate me deeply," he admitted. He tried to master the increasing pressure of his job by spending more time at work; at the same time, he was more pressured at home by his wife because she felt abandoned, having to supervise the education of their teenage son alone. The patient became aware of emotions suppressed during his childhood and the relation with his father, who also suffered from colitis ulcerosa. The instances of insight and understanding for the patient were more cognitive than emotional. He could go no further into the psychodynamics of his life. He ended the therapy because his unconscious resistance increased and because he had benefited from the therapy more than he had expected to. He experienced that through therapy he could change his working conditions according to his needs. "The working conditions are ill, not me", and "Less is more" were his therapy mottos to help him cope with life.

Eating disorders

Michael Wolf and Matthias Elzer

Preliminary remarks

Nutrition (eating and drinking) is a fundamental drive of life to satisfy the biological and psychosocial needs. From the first hour of life, food intake and the interaction between the baby and the mother or care-giver play an important role for the bio-psychosocial development. The psychoanalytical theory of development points out the role of the oral stage (see Chapter Two, section "Perinatal stage and the first year of life: the oral stage", by Hanni Scheid-Gerlach, pp. 35–36) through aspects of drive, relationship, narcissism and body image. The fundamental experience of nutrition takes place in a dependent relationship between baby/child and care-givers. This is so strong as to bear comparison to addiction and dependence syndromes (see our section "The psychoanalytical theory of addiction" in Chapter Ten, p. 288) and to biochemical processes of the nervous system (i.e., reward system).

It is not surprising that nutrition and food intake is a sensitive process for psychic conflicts. The eating disorders are:

1. Anorexia nervosa.
2. Bulimia nervosa.
3. Adiposity (obesity).

In recent years, the diagnoses "bulimarexia" and "binge eating disorder (BED)" have been added: both diagnoses are combinations of the three basic eating disorders.

Some eating disorders (under- and overweight) are related to the body mass index (BMI), which was introduced by insurance companies in the USA to define unsatisfactory body weight. It is a simple index of weight-for-height. The formula is:

$$\text{BMI} = \frac{\text{Weight (kg)}}{\text{Height (m2)}}$$

The international classification of adult underweight, overweight, and obesity, according to BMI (WHO, 2004) is given in Table 9.19 and related to eating disorders.

We can recognise different eating disorders with both underweight and overweight, and also with normal weight.

In *ICD-10*, the eating disorders anorexia and bulimia nervosa are classified as mental and behavioural disorders in Chapter V. The common disorder obesity (adiposity) is classified in Chapter IV: "Endocrine, nutritional and metabolic diseases", E66.0: "Obesity due to excess calories". There is no notation about the psychological aspects of obesity.

Table 9.19. Eating disorders and BMI (close to WHO, 2004).

Body mass index (BMI)							
< 16	16–17	17–18.5	18.5–25	25–30	30–35	35–40	>40
	Underweight		Normal range	Overweight		Obese	
Eating disorders							
	Anorexia nervosa		Bulimia nervosa			Obesity (adiposity)	
	Bulimarexia			Binge eating disorder			

Psychoanalytical theories of eating disorders

Referring to our general considerations of addiction, we are focusing now on eating disorders as a kind of addiction and following the usual psychoanalytical understanding as a kind of disease unit.

Food as self-object

The "oral" aspect with eating disorders and the ambivalences of food as oral and the mother–feeding symbolising self-object is obvious.

Krueger has discussed food as self-object in eating disorder patients (1997). He reviews the literature. Kohut (1971) saw a self-object for anyone or anything as important for regulating the self-esteem, function, and cohesion of an individual. Lichtenberg (1991b) viewed self-object and self-object experiences as designators of significant developmental, as well as clinical, entities. Transmuting internalisation builds up capacities to self-regulate, self-feed, self-amuse, and self-soothe. These self-object experiences are internalised as well as the capacity to be alone (Winnicott, 1971). As Stolorow, Brandchaft, and Atwood (1987) explained, the term self-object does not refer to environmental entities or care-giving agents—that is, to real objects or people. Rather, it designates a class of psychological functions pertaining to the maintenance, restoration, and transformation of self-experience. He (as well as Lichtenberg) emphasises the dimension of the subjective experience of the function that an object serves. In narcissistically vulnerable individuals, self-objects other than people are used to supplement, substitute for, or symbolise self-object functioning. Food, the first transitional object, the bridge between mother and child, is a symbol of all that the mother is or might have been. The self-object functioning of food represents a nurturing function.

This contains three main aspects:

1. Historical use of food as a self object substitute.
2. Physiological and psychological regulatory use of food.
3. Self-object fantasy elaboration of food and eating.

Thus, food is not only food in this sense of nurturing, it is also "soul food", symbolising the nurturing and caring function of the mother or other later care-givers. Beyond all that, it becomes the function of a stabilising self-object in additional meanings. Depending on the subjective experience of the child in his early childhood, the quality of the self-object varies between more good or more bad or ambivalent or disturbing. Here, we see interconnections to the style of attachment between mother and child. As an object of fantasy, the self-object of food can attract and carry many different meanings on different levels of reality contact, more or less firm or loose.

Food intake, addiction, and compulsion

Remembering the compulsivity of addictive activities, as, for example, Wurmser (1978) has insisted on (see Chapter Ten, section "The psychoanalytical theory of addiction", p. 288), the obvious compulsive aspects of anorexia, bulimia, and obesity as the three main eating disorders are hardly astonishing. As with other addictions, they must do something to get their "pleasure", not acting directed solely by striving for satisfaction or relief.

Practically, too little or too much food will result in a change in weight over a shorter (bulimia) or longer (anorexia and obesity) period of time. The anorexic, for example, may use different methods of maintaining a low weight. This might include excessive exercise, binges followed by purging (or vomiting), or the use of laxatives, diuretics, and enemas. However, all the purging and the excessive exercise are only manifestations of a deeper problem and there are always psychological and/or developmental factors or causes that contribute to this eating disorder. A similar relation between symptoms and the underlying structure and conflicts exists in bulimia and obesity. These psychological "causes" refer to personal dynamics that contribute to how the sufferer uses food. They are based on developmental causes which refer to events and experiences in earlier life, such as the loss of a parent, the loss of home, the birth of a sibling, changes in schools, neglect, maltreatment, sexual abuse, more or less severe traumata, etc. Or family members have had a weight problem too or may have been obese at some point, have had problems with alcohol and/or drug abuse and a general lack of impulse control. There is also a higher rate of suicide. This phenomenon relates to the fact that eating disorders, especially anorexia, are very self-destructive.

Symptoms and psychodynamic aspects of eating disorders

Because of the fact that about 95% of persons with anorexia and bulimia are female, we prefer the article "she".

The following symptoms and psychodynamic causes apply to many individuals with eating disorders.

There is an obsession with weight/food and an approach to this is often extreme or all-or-nothing (narcissistic). Eating disordered persons are preoccupied constantly with food. Being obsessive as well as being all-or-nothing are both typical defence mechanisms. All-or-nothing behaviour can be assessed by the "diet mind-set". For example, "I am either on diet or off diet"; "I will be 100% compliant when I'm on the diet, but will eat as much as possible when I am not on the diet"; or "I will devour all of this food now and vomit it all immediately". This all-or-nothing thinking is also applied to other areas of the person's life because of her personality disorder.

Narcissistic conflict. There is a lack of confidence in oneself, particularly specific to the body. Sufferers can be quite high functioning in other areas of their lives, but they are not confident about their bodies. They feel particularly threatened in situations that require looking physically good (anorexia). The negative effects of dieting and the media play an important role in poor self-esteem, a deficit of self-confidence, a poor and/or distorted body image, as well as obsessions with food. One is constantly bombarded with new fad diets or emaciated-looking models. A defective or distorted body image provides fruitful ground for being prone to these influences. This is a very specific phenomenon. For anorectics, their weight is constantly overestimated, causing repeated activities to reduce, ignoring the real weight. It is a distortion, rather than merely a maladjustment. When these individuals look in the mirror, they do not see the reality. The obese person, too, seldom realises how big or fat she is.

Another aspect (also belonging to narcissistic personality disorders) is a weak self-esteem that is also centred on the body or the appearance. The entire sense of self seems to be invested in how the individual looks and how much she weighs. Her mood will depend on how she looks or feels that day. A slight increase or decrease in weight as reflected on a scale can change her whole outlook, despite how she might have felt just prior to weighing.

Defence mechanism. Eating disorders show a lack of useful (or "ripe") defence and coping mechanisms and skills. There is an inability or lack of skill to deal with an emotion, to process it, to work with it, and to cope with it. Individuals with eating disorders only know how to deal with their problems through food and exercise. They are stuck at a primitive way of dealing with the world, primarily an oral way. This means that everything in terms of how they cope with the world is done around the mouth. Besides eating, other oral fixations such as smoking and drinking are widespread. Related to this early stage of development, there is a tendency to instant gratification. This is the sense of urgency in wanting everything now. It implies an inability to wait, to postpone gratification of, or compensation for, the frustration experienced.

For example, in a stressful situation, the obese person reaches for and eats sweets before she even thinks about any other options because she was accustomed in her childhood to being "comforted" by her mother with food, sweets, etc. They cannot say "no" to themselves (their own affects, such as greed, etc.), or to anything else (food), or to anyone else, meaning that people with eating disorders also have a problem with boundaries, evident in the way of dealing with the boundaries of the body and the inability to tolerate frustration.

Affects. Essentially, problematic affects (and the skills or deficits to deal with them) contribute to, or are the effect of, the eating disorder. This means depression, anger, rage, boredom, emptiness, loneliness, feeling devalued, helpless, stressed, frightened, etc. These affects need to be controlled and "used" for human interaction and communication. However, because an individual with an eating disorder does not have suitable defence and coping skills, she resorts to the regressive eating disorder pattern. Affects that are not dealt with in a suitable manner are repressed, but do not go away. They come back (return of the repressed) when one renounces the substitute pattern of eating (or not eating, or vomiting what is eaten, etc.) so that one is urged to continue the neurotic behaviour. Food is used as a comforter that restores equilibrium, but only for a while. Food is also a tool for expressing emotions or feelings as a reward or punishment. For people with an eating disorder, food does not mean "real" food. Food is not eaten for sustenance; it is eaten as a symbol, based on a food-like substance, to provide coherence and stability and psychic equilibrium.

After referring to the psychoanalytical theories of eating disorders, we want to discuss the wide group of eating disorders in more detail. To do that, we base most of the following statements on Hoffmann and Hochapfel (2004), a textbook for medical students and physicians which reflects the clinical and scientific experience of the Psychosomatic Department at Johannes Gutenberg University, Mainz, Germany.

The three disorders (anorexia, bulimia, and adiposity) have different manifestations and specific psychodynamics, but also common causes and aspects. Some patients are suffering from one kind of eating disorder only, which, in the worst case, takes over her life completely. Some other patients switch between the three disorders, or between two of them (change of symptoms). Further, we find different levels of so-called early and mature conflicts—from the psychotic to the oedipal structure of the psychodynamic of eating disorders.

Anorexia nervosa

Definition

"Anorexia" (Ancient Greek) means "no appetite". The German terms *Magersucht* or *Pubertätsmagersucht* for anorexia nervosa (AN) express the connection to the addiction of wanting to be thin. It is like a delusion: because the patient wants to be very thin, to the point of a severe and dangerous level, normal weight is "fat" and "ugly".

Epidemiology and course of the disease

Approximately 1% of the population is suffering from AN. More than 95% are female. Male patients with AN often show a psychotic structure or deep disturbance of gender identity. Most generally, AN starts in the middle of puberty (there are two peaks, one in the fourteenth year and another in the eighteenth year), occasionally later on, in early adulthood. AN in middle adulthood is seldom seen and is closely linked with depression.

There are different forms of AN:

- short anorectic episode on a mild level, which disappears spontaneously (BMI 17–18.5);
- long phases over months, years, or lifelong, with moderate thinness, but without danger to health BMI 16–17);
- severe thinness with acute and chronic courses (BMI <16).

More than 15% of the patients suffering from AN die from complications (infection and heart disorders). It seems like a passive form of suicide. The suicide rate of depressive patients is the same.

Girls and women with special interests and professions, such as dancer or model, have a high risk for AN (18%). Some findings show that AN is a disease of the middle and higher social classes. The findings of research on twins postulate a genetic disposition (Hoffmann & Hochapfel, 2004, p. 355).

DSM-IV describes two types: the ascetic or restricting type, where the patient reduces her weight by starving only, and the hyperorective or binge-eating–purging type, where the patient uses vomiting and abuses laxatives and diuretics, together with starving.

Special case: bulimarexia. These are patients who suffer from AN and also from bulimic attacks with consecutive vomiting (see sub-section titled "Bulimia nervosa", pp. 266–268).

Symptomatology

Table 9.20 summarises the typical symptoms of AN.

Causes and psychodynamic understanding

Common to all types of AN is the first manifestation in puberty, sometimes in adulthood, and the trigger is often simple, such as comments by others about the body and sexual aspects, which are experienced with shame.

Table 9.20. Symptoms of anorexia nervosa (following Hoffman & Hochapfel, 2004).

Severe weight reduction less than 17.5 BMI until cachexia
Amenorrhoea, secondary and primary
Other hormonal dysregulation
After-effects of starving: chronic constipation, low body temperature, skin disorders, acrocyanosis, hypokalemia, polyneuropathia, osteoporosis, etc.
Disturbance of food intake: refusal to eat, compulsive behaviour, and control of nutrition ("counting calories"), restrictive or hyperorectic behaviour, abuse of medication
Motoric hyperactivity (i.e., excessive sports, use stairs instead of the lift)
No feeling or pressure of suffering and insight that the sufferer is ill
Denial of needs such as hunger, exhaustion, body symptoms
Denial of dependence and help
Independence and autonomy from biological need
Less social contact and relationship to others
Depressive mood
Disturbance of body scheme (i.e., perception of underweight and severe thinness)
Auto-aggressive behaviour (purging, sometimes cutting the skin)

The female sufferer does not want to have a feminine body; she wants to be asexual, like a pre-pubertal child. AN is the only disease where the patient can turn back biological maturation to the pre-pubertal stage (regression of mind and body).

Table 9.21 shows the typical intrapsychic conflicts of a patient with AN.

Therapeutic aspects

Young, adolescent patients with AN do not come to psychotherapy by themselves, most come at the behest of their parents. Generally, they have no feeling of suffering through AN,

Table 9.21. Psychodynamics and conflicts of anorexia nervosa.

1.	Defence against her own feminine sexuality and identity. Refusal of the social role of femininity (social, interpersonal). Refusal and avoidance of identification with her mother.
2.	High ambivalence to her mother. Refusion of relationship to father, who is instinctive and sexually motivated.
3.	Fight for autonomy: hunger is like an unbearable dependence on nature, the body, and the mother's care. Independence from relations of dependence.
4.	Narcissistic self-esteem ("splended isolation").
5.	Regression to an early level of the pre-oedipal stage.
6.	Food as self-object (see subsection with the same title, p. 261)

although they might feel this in connection with other problems. The setting of treatment is a psychosomatic clinic for inpatients or a day hospital, if the AN has manifested first on a moderate or severe level. The concept of inpatient therapy is multi-modal (see Section "Theory and practice of inpatient psychoanalytic psychotherapy", by Wolfgang Merkle, pp. 271–278). There is also an indication for family therapy and counselling. The psychodynamic psychotherapy of adolescents needs special training and qualifications that are not the topic of this textbook. However, during the history of a patient with AN, group therapy or single psychoanalytically orientated psychotherapy can be demanded for a young adult patient, if she starts to suffer from AN and is interested in understanding what is happening to her.

The therapeutic relationship, transference, and countertransference are characterised by the patient showing her needs like a sad and starving girl, but being unable to accept any therapeutic help from the therapist, because every type of close relation and help threatens the autonomy and independence that she feels by being in "splendid isolation". Unconsciously, the patient experiences help as an intrusion (feeding by mother) or penetration (pregnancy through sex) from outside. One patient said during therapy, "Everybody needs to eat, to drink and to go to the toilet, but not me!" She liked the grandiose feeling that she was "from another star".

The patient has to control every kind of object and to ignore her needs. She seems cognitive, intellectually precocious, achievement orientated, but emotionally poorly developed. Controlling the body weight leads to a fight for autonomy, in which the therapist or the nurse (in case of inpatient treatment) are cast in the role of humiliating aggressors, who will be cheated, for example, by drinking water before weighing.

The psychoanalytic therapy of patients with AN needs time and has to reflect the previously mentioned dynamic and establish a therapeutic relationship in which the patient experiences the merit and positive effects of this kind of therapy. The beginning of therapy is similar to the treatment of a patient who is suffering from addiction. A responsible setting with an arrangement of shared decision making in the case of severe instances of underweight (change to somatic therapy) is necessary. The aim of therapy should be that the patient can overcome her biological, psychic, and social stagnation and regression and can develop her self by coming out of her "splendid isolation". She should be able to soften her strong wish for autonomy (superego, ego ideal) to come into contact with defended needs (id, drive aspects, relationship, vulnerable self). The effects of psychotherapy range from minimal progress and stabilisation of moderate thinness to the complete loss of symptoms and change to the intrapersonal structure.

Bulimia nervosa

Definition and symptoms

Compared to AN, bulimia nervosa increased during the past decades in developed, industrial countries. Approximately 2–4% of young women are suffering from bulimia nervosa (BN). More than 95% are female, as with AN. The first manifestation is later than AN, in puberty and young adulthood. Fifty per cent of patients with BN have amenorrhoea.

Literally, bulimia means "hunger like an ox", because the patient devours plenty of food rapidly, with extreme greed and without any feeling of satiety, which happens daily or sometimes weekly (binge eating). After an attack, the patient tries to rid herself of the food by vomiting, because she feels very uncomfortable and fears the increase in weight. Some patients abuse laxatives and diuretics.

BN patients are of normal weight and try to avoid being overweight. Some of them are overweight and do not want to become more so. Often, they oscillate between different ranges of weight.

The patient spends a great deal of money on food. Inflammation of the mucous membrane of the mouth, damaging of the teeth by excess stomach acid, and hypokalemia are common complications.

Special case: Binge-eating disorder (BED). This term describes the behaviour of patients who do not vomit after a binge-eating attack. BED is similar to BN with relation to symptoms, situation, and psychodynamics. The difference is the increase in weight and the development of obesity.

Causes and psychodynamics

A bulimic attack happens in moments of loneliness and when the sufferer has feelings of emptiness after an inner fight between the desire to start eating and the desire to suppress the wish. Generally, the patient loses the fight. The greedy devouring and the vomiting are filled with feelings of shame and insufficiency.

BN is based on a narcissistic conflict; the patient has low self-esteem and a fixation at the oral stage. The tolerance of frustration is low. Food is a disposable object. The symptoms represent the inner conflict between suppressed oral drives and needs, which come from an unsatisfying mother–child relationship. Food is a surrogate for loving and satisfying object relations. The object (mostly sweet food) is demanded greedily and, after incorporation, the desired object changes to a dangerous object and has to be vomited out.

BN can express an early conflict in the dyadic relation of the oral stage, but also a "riper" conflict, where oedipal and sexual drive wishes are displaced to the oral stage. The oral drive wishes are strong, the ego weak, and the superego punishes the patient after the bulimic attack.

The psychodynamic affinity with addictive disorders is evident. Many patients with personality disorders, and those with borderline personality disorder, suffer from BN (co-morbidity).

Therapeutic aspects

The therapeutic principles of the treatment of patients with BN are nearly the same as for AN, but the difference is that BN is not as dangerous to the patient's life as AN. The therapeutic relationship is more vivid and can tolerate the strain of the transference and countertransference dynamic. The ego function of patients with BN is more mature than with AN.

Anorexia nervosa in comparison with bulimia nervosa

Table 9.22 shows the common aspects of, and the differences between, AN and BN.

Table 9.22. Comparison of anorexia nervosa and bulimia nervosa (Hoffmann & Hochapfel, 2004, p. 365, translated for this edition).

Anorexia nervosa	Bulimia nervosa
Symptoms	
Firm belief that one is fat	Continuous fear of putting on weight
Continuous compulsion to reduce weight	Sub-optimal weight, latent state of hunger
Refusing food, hyper-motoric, suppression of hunger (ascetic–restrictive type) self-induced vomiting, abuse of laxatives and diuretics hyperorectic type)	Time limited attacks of incorporation of plenty of food (many thousand kilocalories) with loss of control
Secondary amenorrhoea obligatory	Secondary amenorrhoea through starvation (45%)
Continuous weight reduction	Relatively constant weight +/– 5 kg and self-induced vomiting
Psychological findings	
Disturbance of the perception of one's own body and body-image:	Realistic perception of the body's situation:
• Denial of illness	• Insight into being ill and pressure of suffering
• Pride and satisfaction about weight reduction	• Contempt and shame about the symptoms
• Denial of hunger ("I don't need anything")	• Guilt feelings
• Disturbance of contact	• Anxiety about inability to stop eating
• Depressive syndrome	• Increasing isolation
• "Patients with AN are over-structured"	• Antisocial behaviour, indebtedness
	• "Patients with BN are under-structured"

Change of symptoms

Many patients experience a change in their symptoms from obesity to bulimia or anorexia, and also from bulimia to obesity.

A clinical example. A female patient (forty-seven years old, married, with a seventeen-year-old son) came to psychoanalytic psychotherapy because she had been suffering from BN for a year. She developed obesity sixteen years before, with somatisation (BMI 42.2). The patient lived in a chronic state of depressive mood and somatic pain, lost her job, and claimed disability benefit. The sexual relationship with her husband ended more than ten years before. Their relationship seemed like that of brother and sister.

A year before starting therapy, the patient had a love affair with an older married man; he was interested on her in spite of her obesity and seduced her. During her secret relationship, the patient lost over 40 kg in a period of eight months through playing sports and normal eating (BMI 24). After ending the love affair, and some more attempts at liaisons with other men, she developed bulimia nervosa and came into therapy.

The therapy reveals a narcissistic conflict of low self-esteem and an addictive structure of the personality, which leads to obesity, depression, and somatisation. The recovered sexuality acted like an antidepressant; she preferred to satisfy her partner with oral sex and was herself satisfied because the partner desired her.

This clinical example leads us to the third type of eating disorder: obesity, or adiposity.

Obesity (adiposity)

Definition and symptoms

The German word for obesity is *Fettsucht*, directly translated as "Addicted to being fat". Obesity is nearer to substance addiction (e.g., alcohol and drugs), than AN or BN.

ICD-10 classifies obesity (adiposity) under Chapter IV: "Endocrine, nutritional and metabolic diseases", not under mental and behavioural disorders (Chapter V). This is difficult to understand, because the most of the reasons for eating so much are psychological and not somatically caused. Obesity (the medical term is adiposity) is defined as the deposit of fat in different parts of the body through supplying it with more calories than it needs: the result is overweight. We use the term obesity when the BMI is more than 30.

Epidemiology

During recent decades, overweight and obesity are increasing in highly developed countries all over the world. In Germany today, 67% of men and 53% of women are overweight, and of these 23% of men and 24% of women are obese. Overweight and obesity increase over the life span. The rates for men, particularly young adult men, show the most increase. Individuals with high social status exhibit less overweight and obesity than individuals with middle or low social status (Robert Koch Institut, 2012). The reasons for these tendencies in industrial countries are incorrectly balanced nutrition and lack of exercise. The result is the rise in metabolic and vascular system diseases.

Notwithstanding these general health problems of the population, we want to focus on obesity as a psychosomatic disorder.

Symptomatology

Feelings of hunger and satiety are psycho-physical signals from the hypothalamus to regulate food intake through communication with the gastrointestinal system. However, it is easy for psychosocial factors to influence eating behaviour.

We find that there are different types of obese eater:

- binge-eater (see section headed "Bulimia nervosa", subsection "Definition and symptoms", p. 266);
- permanent eater: he or she is eating or nibbling low doses of food (mainly sweet things) over the course of the whole day during phases of inactivity and passivity—calming down;
- insatiable eater: after a rich meal, he or she does not feel sufficiently full and wants to eat more;

- night-eater: eating during the evening and night as a calming routine and to obviate the feeling of emptiness and loneliness.

Causes and psychodynamics

"Eating keeps body and soul together", "Sugar is food for the nerves", "Chocolate makes me happy" are common phrases that express the bio-psychosocial meaning of food and eating. Although the genetic and acquired biological factors play a role, mental and psychosocial causes are more important. Food intake means intrapsychic reducing of stress, strain, and unpleasurable feelings, calming, elimination of frustration, and, ultimately, represents a substitute gratification (food rather than love). In the interaction between mother and baby/child, nutrition and feeding play a central role in satisfying the basic needs. The German word for breastfeeding is *Stillen*, which means to calm down the baby.

The process of feeding is a response to stimulus. The experience of feeding can be connected with unlimited pleasure, tranquillisation, frustration, and kind of oral violence. Usually the baby regulates its demand for food. Baby and mother have to perceive and to read the signals and reaction of the body and develop a healthy body image through a safe relationship. Bowlby's theory of attachment highlights the bio-psychosocial factors which are necessary to develop a relation to others and to one's own reaction of the body.

The challenge of body maturation and psychic development is connected with the conflict between dependence and independence (autonomy). Food acts like an object and self-object that is always available to allow avoidance of feelings of separation from others and depression.

Many individuals who are overweight or obese are "communicative", often being funny and amusing with others. This is the flip side of the coin of depressive mood and low self-esteem.

Generally, patients with obesity do not like to eat and drink with others. They prefer to eat alone and in isolation, because feelings of shame and greed are dominant.

Therapeutic aspects

The dynamic of transference and countertransference is characterised by the fear of unconscious rejection by the therapist. Patients with obesity present themselves in a way that communicates, "I am fat, but I am a funny fellow." They defend against showing their depressive side and narcissistic conflicts. It is also difficult to form a close and true therapeutic relationship with such patients, because either the patient avoids the relation (he wants to stay independent from others and to have an available object—food), or else he wants a very close, symbiotic relation, to meld with the therapist or to suck him dry through his demands. The neurotic repetition of being disappointed is unavoidable and must be worked through.

As well as the psychodynamic psychotherapy for the personal structure of neurosis or personality disorder, the patient, if he really wants to change his daily life, needs the "second leg" support of counselling on nutrition by a dietician and to take part in sporting activities (mostly in groups).

Theory and practice of inpatient psychoanalytic psychotherapy

Wolfgang Merkle

Introduction

The development of inpatient psychotherapy in the past one hundred years began with modifications of psychoanalysis and has led to modern inpatient psychotherapy in the psychosomatic departments that are now common, especially in Germany. Figure 9.9 traces the history of inpatient treatment in psychosomatic hospitals. In Germany nowadays, we have more than 20,000 places for psychosomatic inpatient treatment in hospitals and rehabilitation centres, and Figure 9.9 gives an overview of this development.

There are four branches of development: psychoanalysis, internal medicine–psychosomatics, social therapy, and cognitive behaviour. These four branches overlap methodically and lead to a standardisation of what is called inpatient psychotherapy in psychosomatic medicine. We refer here to the monograph of Janssen and colleagues (1999). In summary, we notice that in

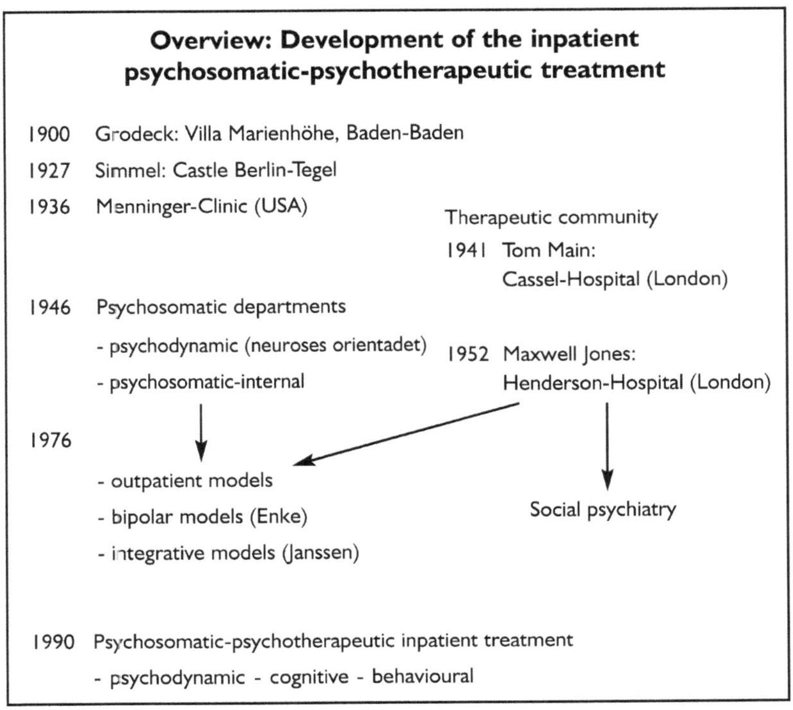

Figure 9.9. History of important psychosomatic hospitals.

Germany an autonomous psychosomatic psychotherapeutic inpatient therapy developed, of which the psychoanalytic branch represents the inpatient psychodynamic psychotherapy (Janssen Martin, Tress, & Zaudig, 1998).

Besides the specific importance for specialised treatment, the psychosomatic inpatient concept serves an important function for medicine as a whole, especially in Germany.

As at the beginning of the nineteenth century, medicine is once again at risk of being reduced to the scientifically feasible and to pandering to new ideologies and self-serving narcissistic gratuities. (See *The Lost Art of Healing*, by Lown, 1996.) Psychosomatic medicine contains an important corrective to this development, as it emphasises the experiencing subject, the interpersonal relationship, and the sociocultural influences on the subject.

This bio-psychosocial concept of disease is the paradigmatically distinguishing feature of psychosomatic medicine. In this sense, it has not only patient related tasks, but also social tasks. It could help medicine to maintain a holistic focus on the sick person.

The psychoanalytic fundamentals of inpatient psychodynamic psychotherapy

The psychoanalytic fundamentals of inpatient psychodynamic psychotherapy are positioned in the psychoanalytic paradigm of relationship and in ego psychology. From ego psychology, we derived the concept of integration, because a central function of the ego consists in the integration of different tendencies and strivings. The individual psychological understanding of the ego is also applied to groups and organisations (e.g., de Board, 1978; Rice, 1969) and was applied paradigmatically in the treatment by a team.

According to the paradigm of relationship, mental disorders are an expression of past and contemporary disturbances in the relationship with significant others. For the outpatient practice, there are treatments developed by Freud, which place the re-enactment of infantile conflicts and patterns of object relationships via transference and countertransference at the centre of treatment. In contrast to outpatient psychodynamic psychotherapy, inpatient psychotherapy provides a system of multi-personal therapeutic relationships. In the hospital, there are many opportunities for interaction with different professional groups.

The patient is included in these different systems of relationships when admitted to the hospital: for example, in the relationship with physicians, nurses, and others.

According to the psychoanalytic paradigm of relationship, these relationships with therapeutic staff are not only influenced by the specific offer of treatment (somato-therapy, nursing, and physiotherapy; in other words, by the consciously planned measures of treatment), but also by the real framework of conditions of the inpatient treatment and by unconscious aspects of interactions (transference and countertransference) that slip into these therapeutic relationships.

Furthermore, the patients communicate in a group setting among themselves in the special social situation on the ward. Many conscious and unconscious aspects also slip into these interactions (group situation).

From this, Janssen concluded, for the praxeology of inpatient psychodynamic psychotherapy (Janssen, 1994), that the relationships in the hospital towards the different professional groups are never isolated relationships. Each relationship is embedded in a conscious and an unconscious context of the group, so that the treatment is always a group treatment.

Reality of relationship and the setting in inpatient psychodynamic psychotherapy

Inpatient psychotherapy in Germany is offered in different organisations, in smaller university departments, supra-regional specialised psychosomatic hospitals, and psychosomatic departments in general hospitals, psychosomatic rehabilitation clinics, and psychotherapeutic departments in psychiatric hospitals.

The framework conditions of these institutions are not only influenced by therapeutic interests, but also by economy, law, administration, and other stakeholders. This framework is the reality of the relations within this setting. The therapist has only a limited influence in this context, but he has to take the therapeutic goals into account.

Institutional conditions, such as the size of the clinic (e.g., 12–50 beds in university departments or 100–300 beds in rehabilitation clinics), determine internal structures.

The influence of other stakeholders in such clinics and the influence of funding for this treatment, for example, through medical insurance or pension funds, are also important.

The duration of the treatment is often determined not only by therapeutic aims, but also by the influence and the limitations of insurance cover. Sometimes, the goals that can be set are limited by human resource constraints. There is a further influence from the groups of diagnoses that are defined and treated in each department.

The decisive framework for the specification of the treatment is the result of the multi-personal field of relationships in the hospital. This framework is fundamentally different in the inpatient setting and the outpatient setting.

While the treatment processes in the outpatient setting are referred to one therapist (transference–countertransference, therapeutic alliance), there are different therapists present who offer different therapies in the inpatient setting. Furthermore, usually the patient in the outpatient setting has a job that structures his day, which is not the case in the regressive status of a ward. The therapist in the outpatient setting can only be contacted during business hours; within the hospital, one of the therapists can be contacted day and night (standby duty).

The consideration of this framework has to lead to modifications of the treatment according to the paradigm of relationship. Particularly, the psychoanalytic psychotherapist has to take into account that with admission to hospital, the patients are included in different systems of relationships and, with that, in unconscious aspects of interaction: for example, reactivated infantile patterns of object relationships and unconscious fantasies in different personal relationships. Every relationship in the hospital is, therefore, not to be considered in isolation, but in a multi-personal group context.

Because of the reality of the relationship, inpatient psychotherapy is multi-methodical (individual therapy, group therapy, art therapy, music therapy, movement therapy, sociotherapy) as well as multi-personal. This means that the re-enactments lead to multi-dimensional transference processes, which have to be reintegrated into an individual transference shape. The concept that can fulfil the multi-methodical and multi-personal therapeutic field of relationship is that of group and team treatment on the ward.

Structuring of the multi-personal situation

The arrangement of this field of group and team is quite different according to the different basic orientation in the psychotherapy. This has been shown by the long history of psychoanalytical psychotherapy (cf. Janssen, 1994). The way in which the therapeutic space is structured depends on the basic orientation of the head of the ward or clinic. Much depends on what the head defines as therapeutic relationships in the respective concept.

Within the psychodynamic treatment of inpatients, Janssen distinguishes three positions (Janssen, 1994):

1. The therapeutic relationship is separated from the other therapeutic measures on the ward according to the model of the outpatient treatment and the priority of the individual relationship to the therapist. The therapeutic space of the individual therapy or of the group therapy is totally separated from the ward. The therapist should get all information about the ward but not talk to the staff of the ward about the therapy without the patient's prior knowledge (general confidentiality).
2. According to the bipolar basic concept, a space of therapy is separated from the space of reality. The latter is organised according to the principle of the therapeutic community (Main, 1946) or according to the principles of socio-therapeutic group work (e.g., Enke, 1965; Hau, 1968). The assumption of so-called bipolarity in the clinical psychotherapy forces the team on the ward to be reality orientated to the patients. On the other hand, in the therapeutic space, the transference processes should be centred and worked through.
3. The integrative concept organises the multi-personal field of relationships in the group situation in the hospital as a network of therapeutic relationships offering different methodical treatment, such as individual therapy, group therapy, or art therapy. In this field, divergent transference processes develop. The basic assumption of the integrative models is to include the multiple interactions of the different professional groups in one setting and to consider the dynamics of the relationships in the contact with the patients (cf. Janssen, 1994). This corresponds to the psychoanalytical group concept of Foulkes (1964). He, in contrast, talked about multi-lateral transferences in the group.

Integrative models want to grasp the patterns of relationships developing within the multi-personal field of relationship as completely as possible, and including infantile parts of object relation or parts of transference besides the work and the real relationship. The patients externalise their internalised object relations in interactional re-enactments even in their behaviour in the here and now of the ward, and use the whole field of relationship. The work in this multi-dimensional transference context with the corresponding countertransferences in the team represents the core of the inpatient integrative psychodynamic psychotherapy.

Transference processes within the inpatient psychodynamic therapy

The understanding of transference processes in the inpatient setting is characteristic for the chosen structure of the therapeutic space (see above). The willingness for transference is not only a product of the therapeutic setting, but can be manifested in all human relationships, especially in relationships with significant others (Gill, 1982): the hospital admission means a removal from the usual conditions of life and an immersion in the situation of the group in the hospital. Thereby, unconscious interpersonal arrangements that are stabilising the defence outside the hospital become unstable (Mentzos, 1976). Inside the hospital, patients try to re-establish the internalised patterns of object relations from working and reality relationships through multi-personal offers of relationships with hospital staff and other patients.

The team can recognise such re-establishing or re-enactments of infantile patterns of object relations in behaviour, from the selection of objects, through the interactions, and, finally, by the verbalised fantasies and wishes of patients. The team can separate them from working relationships and from real relationships and use them for specific psychotherapeutic working through.

The interactional re-enactment in the here and now, therefore, is characteristic of inpatient psychodynamic psychotherapy. The transference is, thus, largely understood according to the concept of the reactivation and externalisation of internalised object relations. They can be found in the multi-personal field of relationship of the hospital situation in different relationships and almost never show themselves only in the relationship with each therapist.

Hence, the basic rule for the team: communicate freely and openly about observations, experiences, feelings, and affects in the different fields of therapy and relationships.

Within the outpatient treatment, the therapist has to deal mostly with successive developing patterns of transference. In contrast, different shapes of transferences can show themselves simultaneously and side by side in the inpatient setting. The characteristic pattern of transference for patients in inpatient therapy is always a multi-dimensional one.

Other patients have a one-dimensional transference that shows itself as a wish for an orally giving mother in the transference to the institution or in the relationship with different therapists. Such transference can also manifest itself in the group therapy as a common fantasy of all patients. For some patients, such as those with borderline personality disorder, the splitting transference is characteristic. Each figure of multi-dimensional transference cannot be considered as split transference—only those that occur in patients with borderline personality disorder.

The splitting transference of unintegrated bad and good object representations are projected to different therapists.

Finally, there are patterns of relationships in inpatient psychodynamic therapy besides the working and real relationships that can also be called transferences: for example, with psychotic or somatically decompensated patients. These, however, cannot be interpreted, but need acting and structuring measures.

For some severely disturbed patients, the dimension of the relationship of caring nursing and the diatrophic level of the ward has the effect of supportive therapy.

Inpatient group psychotherapy

Group psychodynamic psychotherapy has a particular meaning in the spectrum of therapy offered as inpatient treatment. Clinical group therapy is therefore outlined below against the background of extensive experience with group therapy within inpatient settings.

Group psychodynamic therapy is an application of psychoanalysis in a group setting. Because the interpersonal proceedings are in the foreground within the multi-personal relationship in the group, we can grasp transference, countertransference, and resistance in group analysis only by considering the persons in the room. Furthermore, the interpersonal defence mechanism and psychosocial formations of compromises gain particular importance as unconscious group fantasies. The interactional principle in the group and the work with interpersonal conflicts or role conflicts of the participants of the group are much more intensive than in individual therapy (Heigl-Evers & Heigl, 1973).

Group psychotherapy, therefore, is an important component of inpatient psychotherapy, because it meets all the requirements of the multi-methodological, multi-personal and multi-dimensional treatment, taking the therapeutic milieu of the ward into consideration.

Whereas group psychotherapy played a central role at the beginning of inpatient psychotherapy (Janssen & Quint, 1977), it increasingly became only a component of the complex approach to inpatient therapy. This complex treatment is better adapted to the needs of patients' disorders.

Even if there are many different fields of application of group psychodynamic psychotherapy, and even if the orientation of the patients lead more and more to a specialisation of group psychotherapy, there remains a common ground to all group psychotherapies that is valid for outpatient and inpatient group psychotherapy.

During meetings with other patients in a group (eight to ten patients), patients repeat internalised experiences of interactions in a personified, interpersonal exchange within the group. These interactive actions of repeating patterns of relationships of early childhood in the group are called stagings. The common ground of all group psychodynamic psychotherapy is the interactional restaging of unconscious patterns of relationships with significant others. This staging process is the basic one, even if there are different phases within this process we cannot deal with here (Janssen, 1995).

The important difference between outpatient and inpatient group psychotherapy is in the many persons that offer relationships in the inpatient setting. As already demonstrated above, there is the possibility of development of diverging transference to different persons of the inpatient treatment team. Therefore, it is necessary that the group therapist directs his attention not only to the interaction within the small group, as in the outpatient practice, but also to all the other relationships developing in the framework of the big group on the ward.

The group therapist must also try to grasp the interactions of the other therapists and members of the team with the patient within the team sessions that are taking place and he has to use his experience and understanding in the session of group psychotherapy.

The therapist considers the transference only from the perspective of the treatment process.

Integrating teamwork

The concept of teamwork in inpatient psychodynamic therapy is derived from the basic position of the integrative model (see above). The essential rules for the teams are:

- each participant in the team has to understand himself as a part of the whole. He has to use the team to understand and treat individual patients or the group of patients adequately;
- he has to be aware of the fact that he will not be able to recognise the unconscious processes of patients without including the multi-personal field of relationships in his therapeutic considerations.

There are different ways the task is defined that each person in the team fulfils (cf. different models: Janssen, 2004). The concept of the team as a whole is very important for the atmosphere and the milieu of a department and, thereby, also very important for the treatment of the patients.

As a whole, the team in the integrative model has the following function:

1. The creation and maintenance of the framework (setting), a limiting and holding function that is essential for the therapeutic working alliance: the therapists have to care about creating a facilitating environment, even if they are not always responsible for failure. It is very important for the treatment that the team tries continuously to understand how to facilitate developments and to what extent the offerings of the setting are facilitating. The disclosure of hidden team conflicts, the detachment of the patient, or the adherence of the patient, according to the phase of treatment, springs from this understanding
2. Maintenance of the boundaries of the therapeutic space: pathological patterns of object relationships can only be re-enacted in a space that is protected and safe. Normally, the patients are in a strongly regressive state during their inpatient period. Therefore, it is the task of the teams to create this space in a way that provides the opportunity to separate the therapeutic from the non-therapeutic space.
3. Regulation of closeness and distance: the team members have to develop the capacity to be close to the patients and also to be able to keep a distance. The team has to be separated from the group of patients in order to survive attacks on them and the setting and to react appropriately.

   It has to be a perceptive and reflecting team. The perceptive team is a team that can—as in therapeutic ego-splitting in individual therapy—experience and reflect on themselves in their interaction with patients from a certain distance. This modus corresponds with the position of neutrality (abstinence) and of the reflection of the countertransference in the ambulant psychodynamic psychotherapy. However, the distance must not be so great that the empathetic recording of the patient suffers and the containing function of the team is challenged.
4. Maintenance of personal equivalence: even if there are different tasks concerning the therapeutic work, the therapeutic relationships should be considered equivalent. The value of the relationship as equivalent creates a basis of confidence and avoids narcissistic conflicts of self-esteem within the team. The head of the team especially has to assure a clear separation of the different tasks of the various professional groups to facilitate a productive exchange in a protected space for all participants of the team. In particular, the team of nurses must be protected and valued in their function because they are more frequently attacked by the patients because they have no clearly limited contact time with the patients (unlike the therapists, who have the fixed duration of the individual therapy hour, or the defined duration of a group session) and share the reality space partially with the patients. Furthermore, they have to defend the rules of living together on the ward and confront patients in the reality space.

These fundamental tasks for the whole team, the members of which have a different allocation of tasks, makes it necessary to give special attention to the structure of the team and to the kind of guidance needed. Teamwork is like a continuous affective group dynamic process, which has to be limited to the tasks. The maintenance of this "primary task" (Rice, 1969), the referentiality, is a task of leadership and must be ensured in each session.

So, it is not surprising that there is an obligatory need for external supervision to "clear the container" and to provide a good functional level of the team as a group that should always be a model of vivid communication for the patients.

The re-enactment of the pathological object relation, the transference figure, is worked out through the communication of the members of the team with regard to the relationships with the patient and by the behaviour of the patient.

The leader has an integrative function in this process. As he performs an integrative ego function for the team, he provides maintenance of the framework and maintenance for the functions of each member of the team.

Conclusion

New dynamic concepts for inpatient treatment and a new orientation of multi-methodological and multi-professional psychotherapeutic inpatient therapy developed from the application of the paradigm of relationship within inpatient psychotherapeutic treatment. Decades of experience led to a conceptualisation of an inpatient psychodynamic psychotherapy that is an autonomous procedure. The multiple experiences with such concepts also support concepts of integration and co-operation in psychotherapeutic care. The effects of such models exceed the effect in the treatment: they can be general models for institutional structures of treatment such as those practised in hospitals.

CHAPTER TEN

PSYCHOTIC DISORDERS, ADDICTION, AND SUICIDE

Ulrich Ertel, Michael Wolf, Matthias Elzer, and Hanni Scheid-Gerlach

Psychodynamics and psychotherapy of psychosis

Ulrich Ertel

Conflict and/or dilemma

In recent years, there has been an increasing tendency to use bio-psychosocial models in psychiatry. So, for many, it is business as usual to reflect on the patient's most relevant conflicts in the context of considerations on pathogenesis, diagnosis, and therapy. However, mostly, the crux of the matter is the real conflict constellations within the psychosocial field being an additional burden, or forming and complicating the process and outcome of the psychotic disease. Thus, one is dealing with conflicts as an effect or consequence of the illness.

Yet, one hardly deals with intrapsychical conflicts which might have co-determined or even caused the psychotic disease. So, in the therapeutic work and in supervisory activities, it is useful to ask what conflict (or dilemma), what quandary, should be alleviated through some sort of compromise, resolved, handled, or ignored through denial and garbling (Mentzos, 2001a,b). This and the additional question (what is the use and function for the persistent symptom with regard to the presumed intrapsychical contradiction and the resulting intrapsychical tension?) lead us to a better understanding of aberrant patterns in experience and behaviour.

The original theory of conflict became a theory of dilemma. This change became necessary to differentiate clearly psychotic from neurotic conflict: on the neurotic level, you find intrapsychically represented conflicts, whereas on the psychotic level, the conflicts are not represented but are on a presymbolic level. The polar tendencies of a conflict are not representable and that is better expressed by the concept of dilemma. Following the model of Mentzos (2001a,b) the psychotic patients are suffering from a problem of identity: the dilemma between self-related/-orientated and object-related tendencies—you might also say between self-identity and the fusion of merging, or autophile and heterophile tendencies. This allows only two rough pathological solutions: extreme narcissistic or autistic withdrawal or the dissolution of the ego boundaries and fusion with the object. With regard to affective psychoses or manic-depressives, the dilemma is between self-worth or autonomous valence and object-worth and a self-worth completely dependent on the object, allowing either a solution of absolute dominance of an archaic and draconian superego (depression) or one that involves abandoning the superego, leading to the upremacy of the grandiose self.

There have been similar concepts in the past: for example, the deed–fear dilemma (Burnham, 1969) and the antagonism between autonomy and dependency (Mahler, 1979).

The schizophrenic is entangled in projective identifications in the paranoid position (Kleinian theory); he presents a "negative intimacy" in interpersonal collusions and enmeshments, which, in relationships, does not allow him to maintain both an identity of his own and a relation to others; he oscillates between the alternative extremes of absolute isolation and fusion. What is lacking here is the mediating third, the triangulation, the thinking or self-reflecting competence, the alpha-function according to Bion (1967), an entity being in the position to appease this dyad and set it at ease. This gives rise to the symbolisation that allows a personal identity. Identity formation implies a recognition, an appreciation of the other in terms of relatedness and sameness, and, simultaneously, a recognition of difference and, thus, separation, and is bound to a symbolic representation.

The denial of the difference between self and object leads to a massive disturbance of symbolisation and triangulation. There are states of no difference between me and you, states where "me" is overwhelming "you", resulting in cosmic loneliness, or states where "me" is overpowered by "you" and the identity is lost through annihilation. There is no possibility of identification and, thus, of taking over a social role, because this is experienced as a dilemma between the horror of annihilation or that of isolation. In such situations, you may already infer the task of therapy: to enable the patient in the therapeutic process to preserve his own identity in the interpersonal exchange and in the identification.

From this theoretical perspective, the psychotic patient is revealed as a human being with the same problems as all of us, although he is affected by these unsolvable antinomies or quandaries in an extreme way. Furthermore, the psychotic is able to the claim his part in the "family novel", of which he had been deprived to a great extent through having psychoanalytic and psychiatric treatment. One reads in psychiatric case reports that such a patient's development in early childhood was unremarkable, and even psychoanalysts did not know what to look for. One managed with statements such as "weak father", or "intrusive mother", or even "schizophrenogenic mother". The problem is that the psychotic dilemma cannot be symbolised; you cannot simply ask what it is, but it is made accessible by the externalisation of unbearable affects and their inevitable effect on the therapist.

In the meantime, there as been a growing insight into the impact of trauma and experiences of severe deprivation on the development of psychoses in the sense of the fixed rigidity of the polar conflict between self-identity and autonomous self-worth and the ability to exist depending on an object.

There is a lack of meta-perspective in reporting on relations in which the problem of identity is a matter of negotiation. Taking a look at the relation to the primary care-givers, where there were no clear connections and demarcations, one regularly finds the difficulty "of staying yourself" when entering a relation to another person: that is, the antagonism between self-directed and object-directed tendencies, which is also visible in the transference. The lack of empathy of the primary care-giver drives the patient to escape into a dissociated world. Pathological parental intrusions into the child's mind might cause confusion and false identities and boost the child's psychic retreat and his compulsive need to get rid of these unbearable states of mind by using others as a dumping ground.

Mostly, the first manifestations of schizophrenic disorders occur at the end of adolescence and the beginning of early adulthood, when the young man or woman is pushed into an object relation by the development of sexual identity and the sexual body (Elzer, 1992, 2005).

It is reasonable to view the fear of loss of identity as a central problem in the schizophrenic's sexuality. The experience of orgasmic feeling is one danger, the other the constituent of relation or attachment. One way of dealing with this is to suppress, devalue, or control the relational issue: schizophrenics often talk about sex as a secret act. Sometimes sexuality is utterly avoided, and sometimes hypersexual behaviour is used to eliminate object-related tendencies to evade the dilemma.

There is an analogous dilemmatic constellation of relation in the manic-depressive patients leading to the antagonism between dismantling the self-worth of all others but then losing ground in the manic state, and sacrificing one's own self-worth in the depressive state, which means devaluing oneself completely just to maintain the relation to the other.

The existence of a primary autistic phase can be seen to have been refuted by infant research: the baby is primarily attached and the path of development does not only consist in emerging out of an initial chaos or fragmentation, but also in separating or even in dissolving something, more precisely to establish a balance between dissolution and attachment or connection on ever-changing levels of development.

In some agreement with Bion, unhinging the paranoid–schizoid and depressive positions from their theoretical connection, you may say that it is essential to strike a balance between tendencies to dissolution and those which favour unification. You might create unities and completions too fast and you might integrate insufficiently, causing excessive fragmenting. Peciccia and Benedetti (1997) speak of a split between the symbiotic self and the separated self in schizophrenics. Self-related tendencies are dissociating and result in distancing, object-related tendencies are unifying and integrating.

The role of anxiety

Freud (1911c) spoke of the experience of apocalypse in schizophrenia. In his work *Inhibitions, Symptoms and Anxiety* (1926d), in which he assigned the conditions of anxiety to libidinal stages, the most primitive anxiety is that of the loss of the object. In schizophrenia, the point is more the panic about completely losing the sense of reality, a kind of apocalypse provoking dramatic countermeasures. It is a matter of reality at any cost, even if the psychosis leads to the loss of social reality shared with others.

Putzke (2004) describes three different modes of coping with psychotic anxiety, summarising Heinzmann (2003), who refers to the ideas in *The Primitive Edge of Experience*, by Ogden (2004):

- the autistic–contiguous mode;
- the paranoid–schizoid mode;
- the depressive mode.

In the autistic–contiguous mode, which is the basic mode of experience, the sensory perceptions, the experience of rhythm and one's own motility, and the finiteness of one's own surface are predominant. In this phase, a feeling of continuity of being, which became fragmented by birth, is established. Since complete continuity cannot be redressed completely on the sensory level, the task in this mode is to compensate on a psychic level for the shortcomings experienced on the sensory level. This process is unstable: the drives, the intense affects, threaten the continuity of being. This process is presymbolic, meaning that it cannot be recognised by becoming aware of unconscious fantasies. Psychotic anxieties at this level lead to annihilation anxiety, catastrophic feelings, a sense of dissolution, against which the child might defend through the complete detachment of exchange processes with the environment, resulting in an autistic defensive manoeuvre.

The paranoid–schizoid mode is characterised by the self being experienced as a container with a border having a content. If this structure is exposed to deprivation, the child is placed in a dependency relationship, at first perceived physically: that is, the quality of the affects and thoughts is tied more closely to the physical reality. The psychotic fear in this mode manifests itself as fear of absolute dependence, of being stuffed with evil and being destroyed by the evil inside. The major defence mechanisms consist of splitting and projective identification. The more fierce and catastrophic are the separation and frustration that the patient experiences, the more destructive are the defences, and the more pronounced are the consequent psychotic anxieties that are expressed mainly in a fear of retaliation and persecution. In this mode, there is a splitting-off of the perceptual functions: the feeling of being watched and listened to. The danger lies in the destruction of the ability to symbolise and, thus, of a clear subject–object differentiation, leading to a fading out of reality.

The depressive mode provides sufficient inner security that the gap arising from the absence need not be filled immediately. The capacity to think and symbolic language is created, further comprising an external "objective object". Since the object contains both good and bad parts, which are perceived as such, this leads to ambivalence; everything can assume an uncertain character. The subject is the author of his feelings and thoughts, which creates new autonomies and new dependencies: on the one hand, empathy, concern, compassion, and the ability to freely decide, on the other, the perception of feelings of loss, grief, guilt, remorse, and loneliness. Everything becomes relative and ambiguous; the gaining of thought and language is accompanied by the loss of immediacy and sensual–affective experience. The psychotic fear in this mode is of not being able to establish relations any more, and that one has killed, injured, or displaced the good inner object through one's own culpable activity. A primitive superego is formed; the outwardly directed wishes are abandoned, thus leading to a state of immobility associated with painful inner isolation.

The role of aggression

One could ask if there is a fear of loss of identity, or whether aggression plays an important role. Every therapist working with psychotic patients knows the massive anxiety connected with accepting or receiving something and digesting it. You experience different kinds of expelling or ejection (attacks on linking, Bion, 1959): that is, a defence against acknowledging experiences as psychic reality. You meet with frosty contempt and sometimes open fury, hate, and violent attacks. Does this happen because the schizophrenic is mobilising murderous hatred from an innate or acquired programme of excessive aggression? Is he afraid of your revenge, because he wants to destroy you so greedily? Or have you to do here with mechanisms of protection? Is he afraid of his love, his passive–clingy tendencies that cause him to lose the basis of his reality?

Freud (1911c) expressed the logic of paranoia as follows: I love him—no, he loves me—No, he hates, persecutes me! Following Freud, it is a matter of the feelings of attraction and love becoming so frightening that they threaten the self and become persecutory. The hatred discharged protects the self-related tendencies to catastrophe by re-establishing ego boundaries and the feeling of threatened reality. At the same time, relations become possible again, albeit to objects kept at bay because of their persecutory qualities.

A short example: a patient of mine came as usual to the psychotherapeutic practice and after having been registered and having paid his fee he took his place in the waiting room. When I opened the door to my treatment room to invite him in, he suddenly started screaming in a very loud and hostile manner, "Leave me alone, don't bother me!", and left the practice. Thus, the patient clearly demonstrated both his wish for attachment and, at the same time, his anxiety about losing his identity, which leads him to project his need for a relation on to me.

Lempa (2001a) also gives a good example:

> A patient, having already benefited considerably from therapy, called him one day full of hatred after not having come to the session. "You are a pig, a damned pig", she cried, "You have made me have feelings; your wife has screamed at me in a dream!" Her schizophrenia started after having fallen in love with a man. He soon changed—as I had now—to a persecutor. Subsequently, after having restarted the therapy, the patient would speak gently and in a well-modulated manner, alternating with furious and psychotic attacks on me, but she preferred to sit in her chair at a distance of 4 m. without looking at me. After a new outburst, she said quickly and in a concerned way, "I am sorry, I have to be this way!" (p. 59, translated for this edition)

The question always arises as to what is defended against/repelled by the patient's aggression. The patients in the above examples demonstrate that if they were not angry with the therapist, thus demarcating themselves from their object-related tendencies, they would lose their identity. Racamier (1982) put it this way, in more drive-orientated language:

> For a psychotic, the object is the enemy. It is hostile, because it exists: the risk for the psychotic is to be aspirated, to be sucked dry and completely devoured by the object. We know that the object becomes dangerous through the projections sent to it, but an even more pressing danger is lurking . . .: the object is to be hated solely because it is cathected. Why is it hateful and hated? Because it is loved! (p. 79, translated for this edition)

The role of narcissism

In psychotics, you can often observe a strong bonding to paradisiacal states. Racamier (1995) is talking about the *incestuel* as a disguised substitute for an act of incestuous nature. It is a matter of the refusal to leave forbidden zones of unity.

Narcissism in schizophrenia is not so such made up of trespassing on bounds and taboos and providing oneself with all the forbidden bonuses that would be typical for a manic constitution. The schizophrenic tries to elevate himself to a hyper-existence and hyper-individuality, above all shortcomings and dependencies, to the point of an idea of self-procreation. This narcissism of "standing above all" runs the risk of changing into its opposite, a kind of wiping out and vanishing in terms of a loss of any difference experienced as a curse.

In summary, the schizophrenic dilemma provides the framework by which requirements coming from the drives, narcissistic needs and relocation of attachments, become manageable. The basis of the dilemma is a dysfunction of integration of the polar tendencies in the relation to the primary care-givers; you may think here of a lack of triangulation. Sometimes, if a schizophrenic is ruling over the whole family, dictating the rhythm of every day activities, but without generating any objections or constraints from the family, this is quite fundamental. So, the point is often the real confusion of identity, the disregarding of boundaries of generation or incestuous entanglements. The theory seems open enough to relate these phenomena, besides their fantasmatic processing, to quite real interactions. Racamier (1982) speaks of *engrenage*, meaning the interlocking of the patient with his environment. This allows omnipotence without fantasy: relations and the social reality become manipulable, so that the patient may experience himself as a ruler over reality. The defence mechanisms of psychotics are not only operative intrapsychically, but also interpsychologically or interpersonally. To a large extent, psychotic people need to shape their environment according to their inner needs and desires. To that end, they develop very impressive skills and strength, and even violence. The environment being implied, changed, affected, and manipulated is often unable to identify the origin of this impact.

The development of psychoanalytic treatment of psychotics

For a long time, the mainstream of the psychoanalytic community—apart from the occasional hypercritical attitude of psychiatry—was very sceptical about the possibility of a psychoanalytic understanding and treatment of psychoses. Initially, Freud considered that the "narcissistic neuroses", which is what he called the psychoses, do not establish a sustainable transference, so that the condition for analytic work is missing. Many who came after him agreed, considering psychosis as a sign of a defect or a weakness of the ego and recommending supportive measures.

Following Lempa (2001b), there were some pioneers whose contributions led to polarisation: some insisted on the classical method and tried to find the appropriate and effective interpretations (e.g., Rosen, 1962), some made the attempt with affection and appreciation, trying to make good the damage in early childhood through therapeutic measures. As Lempa (2001b, p. 113) put it: "In these eventualities there were 'hard fathers' and 'soft mothers', but in no way a combined pair of parents" (translated for this edition). In retrospect, you might link this polarisation to the anxiety provoked by the schizophrenic, linked to his questioning the fundamentals of identity. So, as a therapist, either you are pushed into insisting on your concept of reality, using the psychoanalytic method (or the psychiatric position) as a protective shield against the patient and trying to convert him to seeing it in that way, or you let yourself be seduced by the patient, thus running the risk of sharing his concept of reality and changing the therapy into a coalition against established reality and society. On the one hand, the patient is the victim of the unkindness of his environment and the psychosis a deficiency disease, on the other hand, he is someone with constitutionally excessive aggression and vigorous projection. You can consider both as reactions to the threat of the sense of reality, as countertransference reactions.

Soon it was realised that neither method of proceeding worked. The point was not to make good the damage, but to help the patient to develop inner structures. The unmodified technique of interpretation (Rosen, 1962) failed with the experiment in applying interpretations like injections.

Sechehaye (1955), with her "symbolic wish-fulfilment" (instead of the breast, she offered an apple to the patient), tried to facilitate new and healthier cognitive and emotional coping mechanisms, using the psychoanalytic theories of development to provide an orientation and to transform naïve mothering into professional support to overcome the developmental crisis.

Following the Kleinian school, the image of the aggressive patient attacking the therapist through his projections changed to that of a patient communicating with the projective process, such as a message about his object relations. The therapist adopts maternal functions in carrying out the containment, transforming the unbearable affects into digestible elements for the patient.

Winnicott (1965) emphasised the importance of regression to a state of dependency, at first induced by only very spare use of interpretations and allowing the patient to go back to the time before his psychic catastrophe, then followed by a phase of working through the frustration experienced by the patient who, after this encounter with the necessary but never experienced illusion, again has to face reality.

So, one could say that those therapists who viewed the patient as a person lacking devotion tried to maintain distance by introducing "third" elements, others preferring classical interpretations had to acknowledge the significance of regression and containment in order to facilitate the processing of the patients' experiences.

Searles (1976) described the schizophrenic's attempts to drive the analyst crazy and thus staging experiences out of the patient's own history. He also described his efforts to approach inaccessible patients by introducing a kind of reciprocity, recommending that the analyst should approve the patient's effort to be his therapist and test his delusions for their reality content. Hence, the merit of Searles was the intuition that the point in the treatment of psychotics was the overcoming of the countertransference resistance against the threat of the analyst's identity, and that one should face this danger resulting from the clash of two realities.

Benedetti (1992) recommended the construction of spaces between the psychosis and the reality ("transitional subject") and he showed how the communication of his dreams and ideas, in terms of amplification and therapeutic counter-responses, could be helpful as a kind of progressive psychopathology, enabling the building of bridges between two initially incompatible realities. He differentiated between delusion-external and delusion-internal interpretations. The delusion-external interpretation implies the confrontation of the delusion with our reality, trying to address an unconscious demand expressed by the delusion. Sometimes, this might be a reasonable way of proceeding, but often it is not sufficient because the patient feels assaulted and mentally increases his defence. In the delusion-internal interpretation, there is no debate about the delusion itself, but the therapist aims at a phantasmatic communication within the borders set by the delusion. He gives an example of a psychotic child thinking that he is obliged to kill his father on the orders given by God's voice. The therapist reacts by reading the Bible story of Abraham, who was ordered to kill his son. The interpretation lay in the message for the patient that God might command him to kill, but is not willing to turn him into a killer. The delusion is modified by an "antipsychotic intention"—amplifying the delusion by therapeutic counter-imaginations—from an idiosyncratic and autistic entity into a zone between delusion and reality where a dialogue could happen. This could mean a rather unusual activity on the part of the therapist, bringing in his ideas or even dreams containing an overcoming of the difficulty.

Benedetti (1992) gave an example of where he reacted to the patient's ideas of death with a description of his own dream: in this dream, he sees the patient jumping out of the window and himself running to the window, but getting there too late to grab hold of the patient. He is looking down, seeing the patient resting in his glance and levitating in space. When this dream was communicated to the patient, she responded by saying that she could not now take her own life.

Volkan (1995) thinks of the interpretative work as beneficial, giving the patient trust and confidence even when initially there are no proper processes of insight. He proposes "linking interpretations", establishing a reference from inner to outer experiences to facilitate the contact with reality, particularly at the beginning of treatment. He gives an example of a schizophrenic patient suffering stomach pain when, on the way to the therapist, he saw a policeman. Volkan interpreted the connection between the sight of the policeman and the pain by saying that the patient had perceived the policeman as too bad to digest him. Volkan suggests aiming the interpretations at the introjection (depressive side) and not to the externalisation (paranoid side).

Steiner (1998) dealt with the difficulties arising when one tries to help patients with a psychotic personality organisation, being in a psychic retreat, to psychic growth. He differentiated between patient-orientated and analyst-orientated interpretations. According to him, patients who are not willing to understand themselves still want the analyst to understand them. Therefore, it might be helpful if the analyst describes how he feels experienced by the patient by using phrases such as, "You think I might do this or that . . .", "You experience me as . . .", or "You fear that I might . . ." and not—as in the patient-orientated interpretation—how he, the analyst, experiences the patient. Thus, the analyst is responsive to the patient's threat of being negated in his basis of reality and creates a less threatening transitional zone.

Lempa (2001b) suggests a further way, consisting of negotiating the therapeutic relation: the analyst will not interpret the perception he receives from the patient, but raise it as a topic in the dialogue. As an example, one may think of a patient who, after having made up his mind to undertake therapy, comes to the first session with a book about a certain country, declaring that he seriously thinks of emigrating there. In this case, one would not take the position of interpreting the patient's fear of engaging in therapy and his protective measures against it, but would discuss the pros and cons of emigration while also making it clear that one is pleased with the decision to accept therapy and the agreed frequency of sessions.

So, the point is to escape the pitfall of taking psychical possession of the other, of quarrelling about the concepts of reality, "the power struggle of 'objective reality' against 'erring delusion'" (Lempa, 2001b, p. 114). Psychotic symptoms are seen as a desperate attempt to maintain belief in the reliability of the subjective reality, as an attempt to stabilise the reality through concretions. The optimal therapeutic answer consists in not allowing yourself to be bedazzled by the concrete literal meaning of the delusional formation, but to assert and acknowledge its real basis.

One could roughly classify schizophrenic patients according to their degree of disturbance of symbolisation, meaning the patient's capability to reflect on himself and to link his difficulties to his inner situation. However, it is rare for these patients to have that ability from the beginning. Thus, the classic setting and technique are applicable only to a tiny minority of patients, if at all. Someone who cannot take a social role, such as the one of an analytic patient, because he experiences identification as annihilation, will consider the couch or even the therapist's seat as anything but a professional tool. Other patients, however well they may benefit from an analytic approach, need a modification of the setting to prepare the necessary effective process of insight, owing to their massive disturbance of symbolisation. Therefore, the therapist tries—in a similar way to that of negotiations between hostile ethnic groups—to make basic processes of mutual exchange possible again.

An example: a patient, after having undergone a severe catatonia, had a tendency to deliver endless monomaniac lectures. His face almost completely obscured by his hair and his impressive beard, he did not look at me, but at once began to talk continuously, as if I were not present, about his master thesis on a philosophical topic; it seemed to me to be a weapon he used to avoid contact, or, in other words, this was his only way of committing himself to me and the situation. Nothing remained to be done by me other than accepting his protection against my concept of reality and trying to get involved in sometimes exhausting work of translation as I attempted to translate his theories into mine and vice versa; thus we managed to escape a quarrel about our concepts of reality. After a long period, he was able to tolerate "linking" interventions concerning his biography and transference, but this would not have worked if I had insisted on my concept too early, without giving him a chance as a partner to take up diplomatic relations with the reality that was shareable with others.

So, the aim is to create a space that will allow the patient to become interested in his own productions, thus preventing him from experiencing them as sensations and ideas emanating from a pursuing outside world. The analyst will address the patient's mental processing and digestion and offer thoughts and hypotheses to it, which the patient can pick up and use in his own way.

The different hypotheses, offered to the patient rather than being imposed, have the function of returning to psychic reality its character of ambivalence, doubt, and uncertainty, while in contrast the psychotic defence mechanisms tend to deny the ambivalence conflict and to embed the subject in a world of absolute certainty and predictability (Gibeault, 2004). In individual therapy, strong countertransference reactions are dealing with the fear of losing your own reality. Thus, as has been shown above, you run the risk of using psychoanalytic theories as a protective shield or becoming involved in a coalition with madness by fighting with the patient against an enemy, for example, his intrusive mother, or a "bad" psychiatric treatment. Or you will be inclined to impose your concept of normality by applying huge doses of medication and to try to convince the patient of his irrational and insane perception.

These powerful affects and impact on action certainly give a clue to the reason why colleagues keep away from an intensive encounter with such patients. It also makes it more comprehensible why we sometimes have to take refuge in a more psychiatric, scientifically objectifying position, trying to treat the patient from the seemingly safe grounds of scientifically assured knowledge. The difficult and tense relation between psychiatry and psychoanalysis is another issue, however, although the allusion that psychoanalysis clearly has shown advances in the treatment of psychoses is necessary to prevent it being withheld from patients, as it has been in the past.

The psychoanalytical theory of addiction

Michael Wolf and Matthias Elzer

Preliminary remarks

In 1964, the WHO introduced the term "dependence" to replace the terms "addiction" and "habituation". The *ICD-10* defines the "dependence syndrome" as a

> cluster of physiological, behavioural, and cognitive phenomena in which the use of a substance or a class of substances takes on a much higher priority for a given individual than other behaviours that once had greater value. A central descriptive characteristic of the dependence syndrome is the desire (often strong, sometimes overpowering) to take the psychoactive drugs (which may or not have been medically prescribed), alcohol, or tobacco. There may be evidence that return to substance use after a period of abstinence leads to a more rapid reappearance of other features of the syndrome than occurs with nondependent individuals. (WHO, 2012)

Addiction is a process of use, abuse, and dependence. The accumulation of the dosage, the loss of control, and the inability for abstinence are important criteria of the addiction and dependence syndrome. We quote the definition of the "dependence syndrome" from the *ICD-10* diagnostic guidelines:

> A definite diagnosis of dependence should usually be made only if three or more of the following have been present together at some time during the previous year:
>
> - A strong desire or sense of compulsion to take the substance;
> - Difficulties in controlling substance-taking behaviour in terms of its onset, termination, or levels of use;
> - A physiological withdrawal state when substance use has ceased or has been reduced, as evidenced by: the characteristic withdrawal syndrome for the substance; or use of the same (or closely related) substance with the intention of relieving or avoiding withdrawal symptoms;
> - Evidence of tolerance, such that increased doses of the psychoactive substance are required in order to achieve effects originally produced by lower doses (clear examples of this are found in alcohol- and opiate-dependent individuals who may take daily doses sufficient to incapacitate or kill non-tolerant users);
> - Progressive neglect of alternative pleasures or interests because of psychoactive substance use, increased amount of time necessary to obtain or take the substance or to recover from its effects;
> - Persisting with substance use despite clear evidence of overtly harmful consequences, such as harm to the liver through excessive drinking, depressive mood states consequent to periods of heavy substance use, or drug-related impairment of cognitive functioning; efforts should be

> made to determine that the user was actually, or could be expected to be, aware of the nature and extent of the harm. (WHO, 2012)

In this chapter, we prefer the term "addiction" and not the narrow, substance-related term "dependence syndrome", because there are many different types of addiction: addiction to substances, for example, drugs such as alcohol, nicotine, cannabis, cocaine, amphetamines, benzodiazepines, opiates, or to so-called consciousness widening drugs such as LSD, Ecstasy, and psychotropic drugs such as benzodiazepines and hypnotics etc. In Chapter Nine, we discussed mental disorders related to addiction to eating, such as anorexia nervosa, bulimia nervosa, and obesity. There are also other addictions that are not substance related, such as to gambling, shopping, work, use of the Internet, sex, and love.

The German translation of addiction is *Sucht*. Etymologically, *Sucht* comes from the German *Siechtum* (English: infirmity). This meaning reflects the human experience, that addiction or dependence can lead to severe somatic and mental diseases, social problems, and to death. Addiction is one method of auto-destruction.

Addiction is a disease with many causes: biological, psychical, and social. But addiction is also a symptom of other mental disorders, such as personality disorder, neurosis (anxiety, depression), trauma, psychosis, pain disorder (co-morbidity), etc.

The existence of so many different types of addiction raises the questions of what is typical for addiction, what the mode of addiction is, and how the addiction works.

In accordance with most of the research (Leshner, 2007; Lürssen, 1976), we suppose there are three different dimensions related to addiction: first, the personality, its structure and behaviour, second, the drug, its representation in the mind, and its effects on the body, and third, the environment—culture, family, etc.—and its contributions to addictive behaviour (Table 10.1).

Psychoanalytical theories

For a psychodynamic perspective, we concentrate here on the first dimension of addiction, while not forgetting the relevance of the other two.

As we know, the main teachings of psychoanalysis can be differentiated into drive, ego, self, and object psychology.

Table 10.1. Three dimensions of addiction.

Individual	Personality Psychic structure Behaviour Genetic disposition
Drug	Neuro-physiological processes in brain such as reward system, desire/pleasure system by dopamine
Environment	Culture, society, family

At the beginning of psychoanalysis, both Freud (1898a) and Abraham (1908) understood the abuse of alcohol and other drugs as insufficient means for the solution of drive conflict, representing a regression to the oral stage of psychic development, a substitute for masturbation, comparable with mania, all based on the drive psychology. The main reason given for this understanding is the dominance of the pleasure principle over the reality principle in ignoring inhibitions and defence, determined by the immediate realisation of wishes and drives and the closeness to fantasies or daydreams, mental activities that are divorced from reality. An element of this understanding was the concept proposed by Rado (1926) of the (oral) "alimentary orgasm" instead of genital orgasm.

It was also Rado who later (1934) conceptualised the (ego-psychological) idea of addiction as protection against overwhelming inner tensions or other stressing affects. He saw addiction as a kind of artificial stimulus protection against pain and depression. In this ego-psychological perspective, the focus shifted from pleasure-seeking to avoidance of unpleasant feelings. The ego of the addict is too weak, its defence mechanisms are insufficient to deal with the inner tensions and the drug helps to (re-)establish an adequate defence organisation. The drug is functioning as a means of self-healing, helping the ego to protect itself against unbearable affects and defective control of affects. This is particularly important for dealing with the so-called basis affect (Krystal & Raskin, 1970), which—reaching back to the earliest overwhelming and/or traumatic affect-related experiences in life—can only be controlled with the help of the addictive substance. This interpretation recalls the concept of the protective shield provided by the mother against overwhelming and potential traumatic experiences of the baby (as Winnicott stated in the 1950s). This explanation was given also for many different types of pharmacological effects of addictive substances, as well as those of stimulating, damping down, exciting, etc. The ego-psychological perspective referred also to the reality-testing function of the ego, the function of judgement, which was particularly related to one's own behaviour, tolerance of frustration, and impulse control.

There are two important ego-psychological models that pursue the ideas of Rado: that of Krystal and Raskin (1970) and that of Wurmser (1978).

Krystal and Raskin emphasise that there are three dimensions important for the development of addiction: the ego and the affects, particularly fear and depression, the representations of objects and self, and the changes of the state of consciousness.

The first dimension that we have just discussed above under the title of self-medication will be dealt with later on. The second refers to the fact that at the earliest stages of development, object and self were quite undifferentiated and existed in a state of fusion. The same holds true for the affects, which were not precisely differentiated between good and bad and also not precisely connected with the respective object- and self-representations. So, by means of the workings of ego regression through addictive behaviour (taking drugs, etc.), which is aimed at relief from the overwhelming affective tensions, the individual gets into a state of confusion between these object representations and the feelings related with them. We shall return to this topic later by discussing the object-psychological conceptualisation of addiction. Now to the third dimension: the change of consciousness. The most important factor here is the relief of the tensions that result from being conscious of the conflicts in the outer world as well as in the inner world—tensions that are overwhelming the capacity of the ego or the self. Thus, such altered states of consciousness (damped down, ecstatic, delusional, etc.) are experienced as helpful, although they are often particularly dangerous (because of the regression of important ego functions).

Wurmser again draws attention to the compulsivity of addictive behavior. The addict must find a solution for the problems he cannot solve with his defective ego organisation. That means a defective defence organisation, defective self-esteem, under-symbolisation (inability to express suffering and other affects), seeking a substitute for the (lost, desired) object, self-destruction, and regressive gratification. Wurmser interprets the process of compulsive drug abuse/addiction as having seven steps (Table 10.2)

These seven steps are called the "heptade of specifity" (from *hepta*, Greek for seven) of compulsive drug abuse. All these steps are compromises of affects or impulses, defences, and, perhaps, also defects. The most specific ones seem to be three and four, the splitting and externalisation by concrete activities such as taking drugs and comparable behaviour.

The self-psychological perspective of addiction interprets it as narcissistic substitutive satisfaction and compensation for a structural deficit. These are regressions to a primary state, denial of the painful reality (supported by grandiose fantasies) and identification with the idealised (self-) objects (Mentzos, 2000). The use or abuse of an addictive substance facilitates all of these: the easing and widening of the ego borders enables a more diffuse mode of experience remembering to the primary state of the pleasure principle. The exciting or dampening effect of the drug or the drug-like activity leads to a shrinking of reality testing through denial of the harmful reality with the help of grandiose fantasies and feelings. These changes of the mind are all originated by an incorporation of the "miracle drug" that symbolically becomes a self-object to satisfy all needs of the self. This incorporation resembles, through its "oral" mode, an early satisfaction in life, whether by the incorporation of the concrete substance or by the symbolic incorporation of "good" experiences. (To this understanding of substances of abuse as oral self-objects see p. 259 and the topic of eating disorders.) So, the addiction is understood as a mode (defence/coping strategy) of severe narcissistically disordered personalities. The addiction provides a narcissistic supply that the individual is unable to provide from his own capacities.

But the drug or the addictive behaviour is experienced as very ambivalent as well, both subjective and objective. It provides ecstasy or deep relief, but, at the same time, entails severe self-destruction. The role of habituation is important. The character of the addictive substance or activity as a substitute is important for the dynamics of addiction. It becomes more and more a part of everyday behaviour, a way to achieve physiological and psychological satisfaction through gaining pleasure and avoiding qualms, a part of the otherwise defective personality

Table 10.2. "Heptade of specifity" (Wurmser, 1978).

1.	The acute narcissistic crisis.
2.	Regression of affects.
3.	Searching for affect defence, applying mainly denial and splitting.
4.	Externalisation as defence by magic power.
5.	Aggression, mobilised and applied.
6.	Splitting of superego.
7.	Pleasure.

structure and a needed, desired, and highly appreciated object as a substitute for real, that is, human, objects.

This aspect of being a substitute and compensation is particularly important for the relationship of the addict with reality. Related to the inner reality, we have just discussed many aspects. Related to the outer reality, many addictions divert the addict from continuous reality testing towards entertaining mental activities that are led by mostly grandiose wishes and fantasies or (by suitable drugs) to similar grandiose activities, a kind of mental or real mania, coming back to one of Freud's first hypotheses about this topic.

The object quality of addictive objects and behaviour is the core topic of many theories of addiction. Following Klein's differentiation between the good and the bad breast of the mother, they present a model of both the satisfying and the destructive effects and functions of addiction. The splitting between them (related to the so-called paranoid–schizoid position), connected with the denial of this operation instead of integrating them to a holistic object experience in the depressive position, is seen as characteristic for severe personality disorders. Kernberg (1975) describes several object-related dynamics of addiction: it might replace the parental imago of the oral and all-good mother in borderline personality, or refuel a grandiose self in narcissism. Wurmser describes the terror of being separated and sees the intense shame and rage manifested in the addictive behaviour as an attempt to maintain a connection with objects.

Johnson (1993) has presented an object model that employs a unique definition of addiction: an addiction is an ostensibly pleasurable activity which causes repeated harm because the person involuntarily and unintentionally acquires the inability to regulate the activity and has a persistent urge to engage in the activity. A psychological system referred to as "denial" is created around the harmful behaviour and allows the addictive individual to continue this activity despite its detrimental effects. The function of the united system of an addiction is to protect the relationship with the addiction. This definition is used to link the number of pleasurable activities that are addictive only if they become compulsive behaviour, such as drinking, gambling, use of stimulants, opiates, eating, shopping, working, etc. These activities are required to be compulsive for reasons of the personality structure, because they provide a constant sense of being accompanied. Addicted individuals are unable to have their dependency needs effectively met in human relationships because of a lack of good and stable inner object representations and therefore are unable to tolerate being alone and being always driven by the need or "craving" to the object, the drug or drug-like activity. So, these seem to have or to obtain the quality of self-objects, stabilising the coping-defective individual by mirroring and/or by providing the affects and neurobiological activities related with this experience.

One is the actualisation of the earlier psychodynamic concept of addiction as stabilisation of the ego: defence and coping. This self-medication hypothesis (SMH), recently articulated by Khantzian (1997), states that drugs relieve psychological suffering and that preference for a particular drug imposes some degree of psychopharmacologic and specific effect. Khantzian believes that opiates attenuate feedings of rage or violence, that central nervous system depressants such as alcohol relieve feelings of isolation, emptiness, and anxiety, and that stimulants can augment hypomania, relieve depression, or counteract hyperactivity and attention deficit. He sees his work as expanding the work of self psychologists, especially Kohut. He traces the origins of the inability to regulate affects to early life, and to a failure to internalise sufficient self-care from parents. Because they lack these internalisations, addicted persons cannot regulate self-esteem or relationships or provide themselves with caring. This emphasis on affect intolerance related to early developmental failure is similar to that of Krystal and Raskin. The difference is that Khantzian views a lack of self-care as an ego defect and a function that never developed, whereas Krystal and Raskin view a lack of self-care as having been prohibited by an over-controlling parent. In any case, the self-medication hypothesis is confirmed by many patients who report their drug use or abuse as being aimed at obtaining control over otherwise unbearable affective states.

The other is the hypothesis of addiction as a brain disease (Leshner, 2001, 2007). Leshner first gives a definition of addiction. In his understanding, the essence of addiction is uncontrollable, compulsive drug seeking and use, even in the face of negative health and social consequences. Leshner (2007) also sees an interaction between psychological factors (personality, behaviour) for the beginning of addiction development and the process of rehabilitation and therapy and physiological factors, especially persistent changes in brain structure and function. We should mention here, diverging for a moment from our predominantly psychodynamic context, that Leshner does not cling to the theory of the "hijacked brain" now being under the control of the drug or the addictive behaviour, but he does emphasise the relevance of biochemical factors to the effect of the drugs and on the bodily structures they are aimed at.

Psychotherapeutic aspects

We mentioned the different causes of addiction and the different theoretical concepts. Psychoanalytic and psychodynamic psychotherapy is useful in cases of co-morbidity, for instance, if the patient is suffering from a neurotic, traumatic, or personality disorder too. Many patients try to treat their mental problems themselves by using addictive substances (e.g., alcohol or medication) and develop a dependence syndrome. An important primary, but difficult, aim is abstinence from the addictive substance (e.g., alcohol) or behaviour (e.g., gambling). Relapses are unavoidable. The patient has to abstain from the reward and pleasure system of his or her brain, and this is very hard.

Psychoanalytical psychotherapy makes it possible to look behind the symptom of addiction, but the technique has to be modified to include more activity by the therapist and a strict setting. The therapist should not ignore or avoid the quantity and quality of chronic abuse and addiction. The therapist becomes a superego transference object and representation of the reality. He or she is like the third object that disturbs the dyad relationship. Sometimes, it is necessary for the patient to use a special addiction related therapy, for example, a self-help group that runs parallel to psychotherapy.

Psychodynamics and psychotherapy of suicide

Hanni Scheid-Gerlach

Every physician and every psychotherapist will experience patients who want to commit suicide. Suicidal tendencies (death wish, thoughts of committing suicide, suicidal behaviour, and suicide attempts) and executed suicides are difficult to handle, because they arouse complicated countertransference feelings such as fear, aggressive impulses, and rage.

Suicidal tendencies, suicide attempts, and suicide are not diseases. They are a symptom of a mental disorder. The reasons for such symptoms are very different. For example, patients who suffer from depression are often in danger of committing suicide. These patients suffer from low self-esteem and auto-aggression. Fifteen per cent of the severely depressed commit suicide; up to 60% attempt suicide, and 80% of depressed patients have suicidal thoughts. Paradoxically, the risk of committing suicide is high when the patients feel better. This is because, if a patient is severely depressed, he is passive with a low level of activity. In this condition, he is not motivated enough to take action. When the activity level rises, the risk of suicide is also higher. Very often, there is a risk of suicide when there are occurrences of special circumstances in daily life which are very hard to bear and which devalue the person and trigger difficult feelings of narcissistic hurt and feelings of hopelessness (Elzer, 2004)

Epidemiology of suicide and suicide attempts

Suicide rates by countries, age, and gender: The global rate of suicide increased between 1950 and 1995 from ten to sixteen suicides per 100,000 people (WHO, 1999). Suicide rates in countries all over the word differ and the data do not correspond. The rate of suicide is higher among men than among women (Table 10.3).

Table 10.3. Selected rates of suicide in different countries (WHO, 1999).

	Suicide rates Year	Total no. per 100,000	Male %	Female %
Global	1950	10	16.6	5.2
Global	1995	16	24.7	6.9
Brazil	1995	3.5	5.6	1.6
China (mainland)	1994	16.1	14.3	7.9
Germany	1997	17.9	22.1	8.1
Japan	1996	24.3	24.3	11.5
Russian Federation	1995	37.6	72.9	13.7
England and Wales	1997	6.6	10.3	2.9
USA	1996	11.8	19.3	4.4

All statistical data show that three to five times more men than women commit suicide. Only China shows opposite rates: the suicide rate in rural China is higher among women than men, but suicide of males has increased during recent years.

Four times more women make suicide attempts than men. During puberty and adolescence, the risk of suicide attempts is high, but seldom lead to death. Suicides increase and attempts are more successful the older one becomes. The suicide rate by age is variable. In some countries the highest suicide rate is during mid-life, in others there is an increase from the age of sixty.

In Germany, two trends in suicide have become evident during the past thirty years:

1. The suicide rate per 100,000 inhabitants halved from 1980 (23.6) to 2010 (11.8) (Table 10.4).
2. The suicide rate among adolescents and young adults decreased, but the suicide of older inhabitants, men in particular, increased strongly (*Statistical Yearbook of the Federal Republic of Germany*, 2011) (Figure 10.1).

In phases of economic depression and changes in the political system, suicide rates also increase significantly.

Table 10.4. Rates of suicide per 100,000 inhabitants in Germany (Rübenach, 2007; *Statistical Yearbook of the Federal Republic of Germany*, 2011).

	1950	1960	1970	1980	1990	2000	2010
All	22.0	22.7	23.5	23.6	17.5	13.5	11.8
Male	30.0	30.1	31.1	31.7	24.7	20.6	16.5
Female	15.1	16.2	16.7	16.3	10.6	7.0	5.6

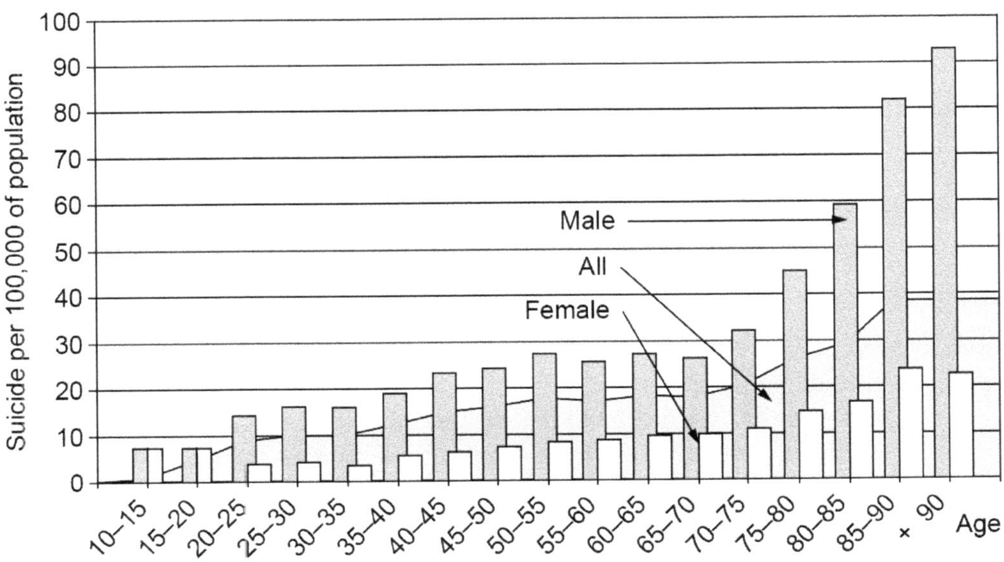

Figure 10.1. Suicide rates per age and gender in Germany 2004 (following *Statistical Yearbook of the Federal Republic of Germany*, 2006).

Forms of suicide

We differentiate between two forms of suicide: hard and soft forms. Most forms of suicide are death by hanging, taking pills, or jumping from great heights or in front of a train. Men mostly choose the more cruel and hard ways (shooting, hanging, jumping), whereas women generally choose medication or drowning.

Some kinds of suicide can also be understood to be culture bound; for example, "hara-kiri" in Japan, when someone feels ashamed or is "losing face".

The form of suicide expresses its aggressive and destructive power. Suicide is a shock and a trauma for relatives, friends, and especially children. The picture of the damaged body is deeply burnt into the memory and mind of others. Very often suicide traumatizes others.

Hidden suicide is a phrase used to describe the damaging effects of abuse of drugs or alcohol: for example, people who take drugs all the time harm their bodies and their souls. We could call this suicide by instalments. Many traffic accidents might be hidden suicide in the sense of acting out.

Triggers for suicide: according to some overviews in the literature, everybody has suicidal thoughts at some time. In special situations and circumstances, it seems that many people think about suicide when facing a hopeless crisis.

All humans have to solve certain crises during their lives, but particularly difficult situations and experiences may overwhelm the inner world and are hard to bear and to suffer.

Traumatic situations, such as the loss (death) of a loved one, severe illness, loss of work and money, robbery, accidents, or natural catastrophes (earthquakes, etc.) may trigger the wish to die. Following uncontainable "inner stress", some humans react with suicidal thoughts and impulses.

The psychoanalytical theory of suicide

Suicide is mostly a symptom of an acute or chronic psychic disease. There can be psychological or physical components of suicide.

The biological theory states that genetic causes trigger depression when there is a lack of serotonin metabolites.

The classical psychoanalytical view

In this theory, according to Freud, we first have to state the difference between conscious and unconscious determinants of depression.

Both Freud (1917e) and Abraham stated in their theory of suicide that suicidal patients turn their aggression on themselves. That often means that these patients have a very rigid, persuasive superego, which is harming a weak ego, and the dominant effect is aggression that emerges from the id and is directed to the superego.

Thus, the suicidal impulse is an aggression that is directed at the inner world and belongs to the "death drive". Freud also stated that the aggression is directed at an inner object—an introject—which has entered the inner structure through identification. Hence, someone could kill the inner mother (introject) by killing themselves. In this case, suicide is an instance of acting out and is dealt with as a substitute for remembering traumatic childhood experiences. The acting out should overcome the trauma, which was originally suffered in a passive way.

In this sense, suicide is the final state of melancholy or severe depression.

In these depressive developments, we mostly find real and fantasised object losses: many disappointments, narcissistic hurts, and rejections of important "other" objects. These feelings are difficult to bear, especially when a child is still very young and not yet able to bear such negative feelings. This will lead to a feeling of being insecure, with accompanying ambivalent feelings of love and hate. Then the lost object, together with the defended aggression, is fixed inside the inner structure of the patient by incorporation. Suicide, in this case, is aimed against the self and is a murder of the hated object that is in the inner unconscious structure.

Patients in a suicidal state often have no other way of escaping from their inner conflict. Even when they try to get out of the repletion compulsion, they are not able to find a way out by themselves. "In suicide, the unconscious fantasy often revolves around settling old scores from unfinished and unacknowledged battles of childhood" (Briggs, Lemma, & Crouch, 2010, p. 15).

Suicide as a reaction to severe narcissistic hurts

In further theories (Kohut, Sandler, Balint, Kernberg, Argelander), the concept of narcissism was more clearly formulated: the theory of narcissism points out the different states of the development of the feeling towards oneself, which is differentiated according to the development of the drives.

In this sense, it is important that a healthy narcissism is developed in the interaction with the objects of childhood. The opposite, that is, the development of a negative or weak narcissism, would harm children. Narcissism in this context means that besides the drive regulations we have a regulation of affects from being secure, being seen and being loved by others. The negative feelings should not overcome the positive feelings; they should be in balance (pleasure principle–unpleasure principle). To feel well, we need an emotional balance of inner security, coherence, and continuity, a feeling of comfort, a feeling of self-confidence. In short, we should feel all right.

Regarding suicide, it is fruitful to clarify if the patient has a drive conflict: for example, a sadistic impulse against the father, or if the patient suffered from a narcissistic hurt, which means that the patient had to deal with unbearable feelings of disappointment. Both conflicts may appear simultaneously.

To understand how the hurts of narcissism are established, I briefly outline the development of the narcissistic system below.

1. The harmonising primary state: in this theory model, we state that the intrauterine unit of the baby with the mother is the model for harmony; there is no suffering and always a feeling of being safe.
2. Feeling insecure and the separation of self and object: with birth, the baby's feelings will change to another modus of "what the world feels like". On the one hand, the

development of the different stages (oral, anal, etc.) continues. During this development the baby will feel that something is outside of him, which is not with him. Cognitive and emotional development slowly leads to representations of the self (self-representations) and others. Parents, siblings, and other important persons are then represented in the inner world (object representations).

In the interactions with others, the baby has to deal with unpleasant feelings, such as fear and rage. Satisfaction with others is not the same as it used to be in the harmonising state. The baby has no way to get rid of frustrating feelings from the objects' reactions; the child has to use his defence mechanisms, which are in the genetic programme, which allows him to hide these bad feeling from himself.

3. Defence mechanism: as I pointed out, the baby/child has to bear certain unpleasant feelings during his development which are then removed by compensation mechanisms to balance the feelings of being disappointed.

There are four defences which can be used in childhood and which could last throughout life.

- *Regression to the primary state.* This is the first possibility that might solve the inner problem. In the early stage of development, a baby does not yet have the capacity to differentiate between fantasy and reality. Accordingly, the baby would rather withdraw to the primary state when there are too many negative feelings. To be fixed in this mechanism means that we will always depend on another person being constantly present.
- *Denial and idealisation.* Another way to balance out negative feelings that make a baby feel bad is to deny that there is something wrong. With this defence, we turn the negative around into its opposite: I am an ideal person, and no one sees what a genius I am. Normally, as parents, we transmit the feeling to our child that we are all ideal together. We stress that our child is wonderful, lovely, strong, etc. Also, we give the child the feeling that we are omniscient and the best of parents. It seems, therefore, that parents feel that a baby needs some time of idealisation, but while the child is going through different development stages, we should reduce the idealisations that we impart to the child. That means we should try to start to give the child a realistic answer, mirroring how he is acting and what he is doing, without being destructive or too negative. We should handle our relationship with a hopeful attitude that the child will grow up "good enough".
- *Adaptation to reality.* A child has to adapt to reality. That means that in the development of a child up to adolescence and adulthood, we have to realise that certain ideals of one's own person or one's parents are not real. In certain circumstances, we have to realise that we ourselves are not ideal, and that parents behave in a way that does not satisfy our ideal thinking.
- Internalisation of ideal aspects. While no human being is ideal, we still keep some aspects of being ideal in our inner life; because we cannot always bear unpleasant feelings. So, with this ideal internalisation we can also balance out our narcissistic feeling, and be able to say, "Most of the time I am good, but sometimes I am not so good".

If we go back to the theme of suicide, we now understand that patients who are tempted by suicide are not in a state of having a well-balanced inner life. They have been confronted by many disappointments in their early life. Thus, narcissistic needs have not been satisfied and the baby, later the child, could develop the compensations or defence mechanisms mentioned earlier.

Within people drawn to suicide, we can point out three kinds of personality constellations.

1. Narcissistic personalities with an inner ideal of perfectionism and the inability to tolerate failure and imperfection, combined with a schizoid structure: this kind of personality can also ask someone for help and deny his wish to have intimacy. The other object for this kind of patient is not really accepted as a separate object; instead, it is seen as a component that cancels out the inadequacies of the patient's structure.
2. Personalities with impulsive and aggressive characteristics, combined with an over-sensitivity to life events. It is mostly the "little things" of life to which these people react with anxiety or anger. These patients usually employ defences such as regression, splitting, dissociation, and displacement. In these cases, we often find sexual abuse and physical suffering in childhood; often we also find alcohol or other substance abuse. In adult life, we can see these patients as impulsive and aggressive, with a low tolerance of frustration, which ends up being diagnosed as a borderline personality.
3. Personalities who are driven by hopelessness and who are depressed for a long time in their development. In this case, we have an affective disorder, such as schizophrenia or anxiety disorder. The depressive state of such patients is connected with inner negative representations, which were built up in childhood through incorporation and identification. The "good object" identifications are not installed, so we have a structural problem of missing good objects.

In conclusion, we can say that the patient with suicidal tendencies is a personality with very weak self-esteem. That means that the patient deals with pathological reactions by using the compensation mechanisms on a very low level, such as denial of the reality or idealisation. To cope with future disappointments, this person uses his low-level compensations again, thus increasing denial or idealisation. In denying reality, the patient rejects the fact that there is a gap between what he is doing and what he is thinking about his ideal self.

It must be said that people with suicidal tendencies have very weak and insecure personalities. In trying to deal with future disappointments, they react with regressive mechanisms, such as denying the reality or idealisation. This explains the strange behaviour of a suicidal person. We can see that because of this inner solution, the patients are free from aggressive conflicts. We have to point out again that these patients cover their weak inner structure by means of megalomaniac fantasies and denying reality. If denial and idealisation break down, the patients regress to more a primitive defence; this means regression to the primary harmonising state.

In many studies, it is pointed out that the thinking of a suicidal patient is closely connected with harmonising primary-state fantasies such as quietness, warmth, liberation, triumph, balance of mind, fusion, feeling safe. Through these fantasies, death can be denied and the cruel part of killing themselves is obviated. With this inner process, the suicidal person is active and is rescuing his low self-esteem.

Suicide driven by fantasies

In this type of suicide, the body takes up an important role with the suicidal fantasies. The fantasies of these patients centre on the wish to gratify pre-genital impulses, which are often sadomasochistic or oral-incorporative.

First, the *revenge fantasy* is one of the most universal fantasies; often the patients think that the others "will feel sorry when I am dead". In this case, the patient is hurting his parents or other people of his childhood who did not love him enough in his early days.

Second, the *fantasy of self-punishment* mostly demonstrates guilt, which is often associated with masturbation to satisfy incestuous wishes. Thus, there is a connection with the eroticisation of pain and death. Generally, it is perverse personalities that have this kind of dynamic.

Third, the *assassination fantasy*, in which the body assumes the role of being the "bad one". That means the body is responsible for the madness and is confusing the person. Also, the body is a kind of alien to the person, which has to be killed to save the "self". In this case, therefore, suicide is self-defence.

The fourth fantasy is the *dicing with death fantasy*. Here, the person plays with death. In trying to commit suicide, the thought of being dead is not really in the person's mind.

The fifth fantasy is the *merging fantasy*. The suicide expresses in this case, ". . . the wish to fuse with an omnipotent mother: By becoming one with her, the suicidal patient hopes to taste again the omnipotent, timeless, mindless peace of his baby origins, far from the wearisome, hostile inner presence of the miserable adulthood" (Briggs, Lemma, Crouch, 2011, p. 20).

Treatment of suicidal patients

According to the theories, we have to help these patients to deal with their disappointing and aggressive feelings, which trigger hate and hostility. They should try to be aware of their feelings and also talk about them. The aggressive feelings should become conscious; otherwise they will cause internal harm.

Kernberg stated that the risk of suicide with infantile or borderline personalities is high. The risk is mainly a factor during fits of rage following disappointments that are blamed on others; or else there is a risk of suicide because of failure to achieve success (guilt feelings), or even the failure of the therapeutic work (negative therapeutic reaction).

Within this theory, I would like to remind you of the theory of depression, which you will also find in the book. In that section, we traced the different spectrums of depressive symptoms. Besides somatisation disorders, where the depression is underlying, we find depressive reactions among alcoholics and those with eating disorders. Chronic unhappiness, anhedonia, low self-esteem, and inferiority are the main causes.

In Table 10.5, we list the different motives that might trigger the suicidal act. These acts are often connected with suicidal fantasies, mentioned above.

In treating suicidal patients, some interventions for the technique should be pointed out. These are listed in Table 10.6.

In the treatment, the relationship between the suicidal patient and his therapist is of greatest importance. When treating a suicidal patient, it is of utmost importance to uncover the hostility, rage, and vengefulness relatively quickly. This should be spoken about quite openly

Table 10.5. Examples of suicidal fantasies.

The wish to find inner peace because conflicts, narcissistic hurts, mental or somatic disorders are unbearable
The wish to be free of high demands
To send an appeal to someone
Rage to induce guilt feelings in somebody
To try to force someone to love them
To try to balance out feelings of disappointment
Auto-aggression, because someone cannot deal with certain parts of his personality (for example, homosexuality)
The wish to be together with a beloved person
To stop severe pain due to shame caused by sexual abuse or severe disease

Table 10.6. Some examples of intervention.

Ask about suicidal wishes and fantasies empathically; talking about this taboo eases the burden of the patient and the therapist
According to the theory mentioned above, we should find out what the trigger point is for the disappointments that are denied.
We should show emotional understanding for the patient's feelings of disappointment
If we are idealised, we should be understanding about it, but also point out that each human being has his own force with which to help himself.
Watch out for megalomaniac fantasies which can be projected to you
Give interpretations that connect the disappointment with the unconscious conflict
Talk about the problem of looking for further disappointments in their life
Ask for conflict solving ideas, such as "How do you manage your wishes?"

in a confronting way, because the patient will try to hide himself and his rage and hostility behind high-minded and noble-sounding sentiments. In suicidal depression, such open confrontation of his rage, revenge motives, and hostility against those he pretends to love makes it very difficult for the patient to maintain the illusion that his pretended high and noble motives will be believed by the therapist. In the face of this confrontation, the patient can no longer be sure that he will be able to uphold the idealised self-image.

The following example should illustrate this. When a patient talks of his huge love for his girlfriend, he tells us that he cannot live without her but it would be much better for her to be free of him. In this, we can see that the patient is leaving out the aggression which he feels towards his beloved partner (it would be much better when she is free of me). So we can be aware that these kind of patients omit their aggressions, which are transferred to the partner. The same could happen in the transference, that the patient may think that the therapist would be happier when he is free of the patient. In this case, we can see that it is not love to contemplate doing such harm (suicide) to a partner.

Often, we find out that the patient is preoccupied with self-critical thoughts. Either he is no good, or the criticism is limited to a specific part of the self-representation: for example, a harmful emotional part or a homosexual impulse. So, in the suicidal act, the patients want to get rid of either this part or of the whole criticism.

Other psychotic patients have fusing fantasies, which might even be conscious, such as becoming a part of God, or entering a secret kingdom.

The suicide's aim is always to resolve an intrapsychic conflict. For example, we can follow the inner quarrels of a patient by using his own writings about his inner condition. I will present the following as an example.

> "These last few days were a death-like existence. I am so tired I just want to sleep. My mind, oh, my mind, it's sick. I feel as if I am sinking and I cannot call for any help but to death. I don't seem to feel as though I want to die. It's like another person telling me what to do. I feel as though my mind isn't connected to my body and it seems to refer to me as "you" as in "Die you fool, die". I feel as though there are two of me, and the killer is winning.
>
> "When my death comes, it won't be suicide. It's that someone who will have murdered me. While I am writing this letter, it's like the other part is laughing at me and calling me a fool for writing this nonsense, but it's how I feel, I know I must sound confusing to you, but this is the only way I can express myself. I wish I could have told you many of my confused feelings, but I feel as though you won't understand and believe me and then the other part takes over and goes in therapy to do it, while it's trying to kill me; I'll kill myself and take it with me. You have done your best to help me, but I just couldn't help myself. I'm so tired I can't fight any more. I wish I could tell someone now, but they can't help me, even worse is they won't understand, oh—if they only would understand, it would mean so much, but nobody has ever understood me so how could I expect someone to understand me now? I took those pills before, it was to kill the other part of me, but I really won't die. I'll just wake up and things will be different. That's how I feel tonight, that I'm not really going to die, and the other one is and I don't know how to explain that to you. I seem to be contradicting myself, but I am writing as I feel. So if you are confused, just think of how I must feel. I have used the term robot to you; it's like someone is hurt up in my head and is using my eyes as windows and controlling me and my actions. Last week during ward meeting when the people were talking, it was like the voices weren't coming from them and I had to keep looking at their mouths to be sure. I can't even explain that one, it's too hard and you wouldn't understand anyway. I don't know why the hell I'm telling you this anyway, it sounds like a bunch of shit all thrown in together. If you think I'm looking for pity through this, you're crazy, because it won't do me any good, for where I'm going I need pity like I need another problem. Well, that's it, so have a good laugh. It's on me."

What we can see from this case is that the patient's self-representations are divided into two parts, where one is called "me" and there is another "person" who seems to be rude and destructive, a killer. The killer orders the patient to die, and is controlling the body of the patient.

This kind of model is congruent with the Freudian explanation of melancholic suicide: the hostile inner presence, the "killer", represents the hated yet loved object, which has become identified with the self (ego).

REFERENCES

Abraham, K. (1908). Die psychologischen Beziehungen zwischen Sexualität und Alkoholismus. In: *Psychoanalytische Studien II*. Frankfurt: Fischer, 1971.

Abraham, K. (1924). A short study of the development of the libido in the light of mental disorders. I. Melancholia and obsessional neurosis. In: *Selected Papers* (pp. 422–433). New York: Basic Books, 1953.

Alexander, F. (1935). Über den Einfluß psychischer Faktoren auf gastrointestinale Störungen. *Internationale Zeitschrift für Psychoanalyse, 21*: 189–219.

Alexander, F. (1950). *Psychosomatic Medicine. Its Principles and Applications*. New York: Norton.

American Psychiatric Association (2000). *Diagnostic and Statistical Manual of Mental Disorders*. Arlington, VA: American Psychiatric Association.

Antonovsky, A. (1987). *Unraveling the Mystery of Health: How People Manage Stress and Stay Well*. San Francisco, CA: Jossey-Bass.

APsaA (2007). Ethics code of the American Psychoanalytical Association. Accessed on 12 October 2012 at: http://apsa.org/ABOUTAPSAA/ETHICSCODE/tabid/200/Default.aspx

Argelander, H. (1970). *Das Erstinterview in der Psychotherapie*. Darmstadt: Wissenschaftliche Buchgesellschaft.

Argelander, H. (1971). Ein Versuch zur Neuformulierung des primären Narzissmus. *Psyche, 25*: 358–373.

Aserinsky, E., & Kleitman, N. (1953). Regularly ocurring periods of eye motility and concomitant phenomena during sleep. *Science, 118*: 273–274.

Balint, M. (1959). *Thrills and Regressions*. New York: International Universities Press.

Balint, M. (1965). The doctor's therapeutic function. *Lancet, 285*: 1177–1180.

Balint, M. (1968). *The Basic Fault: Therapeutic Aspects of Regression*. London: Tavistock.

Baranger, M., Baranger, W., & Mom, J. M. (1988). The infantile psychic trauma from us to Freud: pure trauma, retroactivity and reconstruction. *International Journal of Psychoanalysis, 69*: 113–128.

Barnett, J. (1966). On cognitive disorders in the obsessional. *Contemporary Psychoanalysis, 2*: 122–133.

Barnett, J. (1969). On aggression in the obsessional neuroses. *Contemporary Psychoanalysis, 6*: 48–57.

Barwinski, R. (2005). *Traumabearbeitung in analytischen Langzeitbehandlungen*. Köning: Asanger.

Bateman, A., & Holmes, J. (1995). *Introduction to Psychoanalysis: Contemporary Theory and Practice*. London: Routledge.

Bauer, J. (2002). *Das Gedächtnis des Körpers. Wie Beziehungen und Lebensstile unsere Gene steuern*. Munich: Piper.

Baxter, L. (1992). Neuroimaging studies of obsessive-compulsive disorder. *Psychiatric Clinics of North America, 15*: 87–844.

Beauchamp, T. L., & Childress, J. F. (2001). *Principles of Biomedical Ethics* (5th edn). Oxford: Oxford University Press.

Benedetti, G. (1992). *Psychotherapie als existentielle Herausforderung*. Göttingen: Vandenhoeck & Ruprecht.

Bion, W. R. (1959). Attacks on linking. *International Journal of Psycho-Analysis, 40*: 308–315.

Bion, W. R. (1962). *Learning from Experience*. London: Heinemann.

Bion, W. R. (1967). *Second Thoughts*. London: William Heinemann [reprinted London: Karnac, 1984].

Blass, R. B. (2001). The teaching of the Oedipus complex. *International Journal of Psychoanalysis, 82*: 1105–1121.

Blos, P. (1962). *On Adolescence*. Glencoe: Free Press.

Blos, P. (1963). The concept of acting out in relation to the adolescent process. *Journal of the American Academy of Child Psychiatry, 2*: 118–143.

Bohleber, W. (2000). Die Entwicklung der Traumatheorie in der Psychoanalyse [The development of trauma theory in psychoanalysis]. *Psyche, 54*: 797–839.

Brette, F. (2005). Trauma. In: A. De Mijolla (Ed.), *International Dictionary of Psychoanalysis* (pp. 1800–1802). Farmington Hills, MI: Thomson Gale.

Briggs, S., Lemma, A., & Crouch, W. (2010). *Relating to Self-harm and Suicide*. London: Routledge.

Britton, R., Feldman, M., & O'Shaughnessy, E. (1989). *The Oedipus Complex Today: Clinical Implications*. London: Karnac.

Buchholz, M. B. (2008). Psycho-News-Letter no. 68: Klassifikation oder Kontext?

Buddeberg, C. (1998). Praktische Probleme bei der Diagnostik sexueller Störungen. In: B. Strauß & N. Becker (Eds.), *Psychotherapie der Sexualstörungen* (pp. 34–41). Stuttgart: Thieme.

Burnham, D. L. (1969). *Schizophrenia and the Need–Fear Dilemma*. New York: International Universities Press.

Bushra, A. L. (1998). Mutual regression: altered states in the psychoanalytic situation. *Journal of the American Psychoanalytic Association, 46*(2): 389–412.

Cannon, W. B. (1939). *The Wisdom of the Body* (2nd edn). New York: Norton.

Cierpka, M., Grande, T., Stasch, M., Oberbracht, C., Schneider, W., Schüssler, G., Heuft, G., Dahlbender, R., Schauenburg, H., & Schneider, G. (2001). Zur Validität der Operationalisierten Psychodynamischen Diagnostik (OPD). *Psychotherapeut, 46*: 122–133.

Costa, Jr, P. T., & McCrae, R. R. (1992). *Revised NEO Personality Inventory (NEO-PI-R) and NEO Five-Factor Inventory (NEO-FFI) Manual*. Odessa, FL: Psychological Assessment Resources.

Cremerius, J. (1984). Die psychoanalytische Abstinenzregel. Vom regelhaften zum operativen Gebrauch. *Psyche, 38*: 769–800.

De Board, R. (1978). *The Psychoanalysis of Organizations*. London: Tavistock.

De Mijolla, A. (Ed.) (2005). *International Dictionary of Psychoanalysis*. Farmington Hills, MI: Thomson Gale.

Digman, J. M. (1990). Personality structure: emergence of the five-factor model. *Annual Review of Psychology, 41*: 417–440.

Dilling, H., Weyerer, S., & Castell, R. (1984). *Psychische Erkrankungen in der Bevölkerung*. Stuttgart: Enke.

Eckardt-Henn, A. (2011). Schwindel. In: R. H. Adler, W. Herzog, P. Joraschky, K. Köhle, W. Langewitz, W. Söllner, & W. Wesiack (Eds.), *Uexküll, Psychosomatische Medizin* (pp. 1088–1090). Munich: Urban & Fischer.

Eissler, K. (1966). Bemerkungen zur Technik der psychoanalytischen Behandlung Pubertierender nebst einigen Überlegungen zum Problem der Perversion. *Psyche, 20*: 837–872.

Elzer, M. (1992). Psychose und Adoleszenz. Zur Bedeutung von Triebkonflikten für die Manifestation psychotischer Störungen. In: S. Mentzos (Ed.), *Psychose und Konflikt* (pp. 103–126). Göttingen: Vandenhoeck & Ruprecht.

Elzer, M. (2004). *Krankheitslehre Psychiatrie*. Skript. Hochschule Fulda.

Elzer, M. (2005). Psychoanalytical concepts of the schizophrenic psychosis. Unpublished Paper. Lecture at the Pan-Asia-Pacific Congress on Mental Health, Shanghai, November.

Elzer, M. (2009a). Einführung in die Entwicklungspsychologie. Skript, Hochschule Fulda.

Elzer, M. (Ed.) (2009b). *Kommunikative Kompetenzen in der Physiotherapie*. Bern: Huber.

Elzer, M. (2012). *Psychosomatik und Neurosenlehre*. Skript. Hochschule Fulda.

Engel, G. F. (1967). A psychological setting of somatic disease: the 'giving up–given up' complex. *Proceedings of the Royal Society of Medicine, 60*(6): 553–555.

Enke, H. (1965). Bipolare Gruppenpsychotherapie als Möglichkeit psychoanalytischer Arbeit in der stationären Psychotherapie. *Zeitschrift für Psychotherapie und medizinische Psychologie, 15*: 116–121.

Erdheim, M. (1984). *Die gesellschaftliche Produktion von Unbewußtheit*. Frankfurt: Suhrkamp.

Erikson, E. H. (1950). *Childhood and Society*. New York: W. W. Norton.

Erikson, E. H. (1954). The dream specimen of psychoanalysis. *Journal of the American Psychoanalytic Association, 2*: 5–56.

Erikson, E. H. (1959). *Identity and the Life Cycle*. New York: International Universities Press.

Feldman, M. (2008). Grievance: the underlying oedipal configuration. *International Journal of Psychoanalysis, 89*: 743–758.

Fenichel, O. (1945). *The Psychoanalytic Theory of the Neuroses*. New York: W. W. Norton.

Fischer, G., & Riedesser, P. (1998). *Lehrbuch der Psychotraumatologie*. Munich: Reinhardt.

Flader, D., & Grodzicki, W. D. (1978). Hypothesen zur Wirkungsweise der psychoanalytischen Grundregel. *Psyche, 32*: 545–594.

Fonagy, P., Gergely, G., Jurist, E. L., & Target, M. (2002). *Affect Regulation, Mentalization, and the Development of the Self*. London: Karnac [new edition 2005].

Foulkes, D. (1999). *Children's Dreaming and the Development of Consciousness*. Cambridge, MA: Harvard University Press.

Foulkes, S. H. (1964). *Therapeutic Group Analysis*. London: Maresfield Library.

Foulkes, S. H. (1992). *Gruppenanalytische Psychotherapie*. Munich: Pfeiffer.

Franz, M., Lieberz, K., & Schepank, H. (Eds.) (2000). *Seelische Gesundheit und neurotisches Elend. Der Langzeitverlauf in der Bevölkerung*. Wien: Springer.

Freud, A. (1937). *The Ego and the Mechanisms of Defence*. London: Hogarth.

Freud, S. (1894a). The neuro-psychoses of defence. *S.E., 3*: 43–68. London: Hogarth.

Freud, S. (1895d). *Studies on Hysteria. S.E., 2*: 1–223. London: Hogarth.

Freud, S. (1898a). Sexuality in the aetiology of the neuroses. *S.E.*, 3: 259–285. London: Hogarth.

Freud, S. (1900a). *The Interpretation of Dreams. S.E., 4–5*. London: Hogarth.

Freud, S. (1905d). *Three Essays on the Theory of Sexuality. S.E., 7*: 125–245. London: Hogarth.

Freud, S. (1905e). *Fragment of an Analysis of a Case of Hysteria*. S.E., 7: 1–122. London: Hogarth.

Freud, S. (1909b). *Analysis of a Phobia in a Five-year-old Boy. S.E., 10*: 3–149. London: Hogarth.

Freud, S. (1909d). *Notes Upon a Case of Obsessional Neurosis*. *S.E., 10*: 153–249. London: Hogarth.
Freud, S. (1910a). Five lectures on psycho-analysis. *S.E., 11*: 1–55. London: Hogarth.
Freud, S. (1911b). *Formulations on the Two Principles of Mental Functioning*. *S.E., 12*: 213–226.
Freud, S. (1911c). *Psycho-analytic Notes on an Autobiographical Account of a Case of Paranoia*. *S.E., 12*: 3–82. London: Hogarth.
Freud, S. (1912b). The dynamics of transference. *S.E., 11*: 97–108. London: Hogarth.
Freud, S. (1912e). Recommendations to physicians practising psycho-analysis. *S.E., 12*: 109–120. London: Hogarth.
Freud, S. (1913c). On beginning the treatment. *S.E., 12*: 121–144. London: Hogarth.
Freud, S. (1913i). The disposition to obsessional neurosis. *S.E., 12*: 311–326. London: Hogarth.
Freud, S. (1914c). On narcissism: an introduction. *S.E., 14*: 73–102. London: Hogarth.
Freud, S. (1914g). Remembering, repeating, and working-through. *S.E., 12*: 145–156. London: Hogarth.
Freud, S. (1915a). Observations on transference love. *S.E., 12*: 157–171. London: Hogarth.
Freud, S. (1915c). Instincts and their vicissitudes. *S.E., 14*: 111–140. London: Hogarth.
Freud, S. (1915e). The unconscious. *S.E., 14*: 161–245. London: Hogarth.
Freud, S. (1916–1917). *Introductory Lectures on Psycho-analysis*. *S.E., 16*: 243–463. London: Hogarth.
Freud, S. (1917d). A metapsychological supplement to the theory of dreams. *S.E., 14*: 222–236. London: Hogarth.
Freud, S. (1917e). Mourning and melancholia. *S.E., 14*: 239–258. London: Hogarth.
Freud, S. (1923b). *The Ego and the Id*. *S.E., 19*: 3–66. London: Hogarth.
Freud, S. (1926d). *Inhibitions, Symptoms and Anxiety*. *S.E., 20*: 77–174. London: Hogarth.
Freud, S. (1933a). *New Introductory Lectures on Psycho-Analysis*. *S.E., 22*: 7–182. London: Hogarth.
Freud, S. (1940a). *An Outline of Psycho-analysis*. *S.E., 23*: 141–207. London: Hogarth.
Freud, S. (1950[1895]). Project for a scientific psychology. *S.E., 1*: 283–397. London: Hogarth.
Friedman, R. C., & Downey, J. I. (2008). Sexual differentiation of behavior: the foundation of a developmental model of psychosexuality. *Journal of the American Psychoanalytic Association, 56*: 147–175.
Frommer, J., & Langenbach, M. (2011). Tinnitus. In: R. H. Adler, W. Herzog, P. Joraschky, K. Köhle, W. Langewitz, W. Söllner, & W. Wesiack (Eds.), *Uexküll, Psychosomatische Medizin* (pp. 790–795). Munich: Urban & Fischer.
Fürstenau, P. (1977). Die beiden Dimensionen des psychoanalytischen Umgangs mit strukturell ichgestörten Patienten. *Psyche, 31*(3): 197–207.
Gabbard, G. (2000). Disguise or consent. Problems and recommendations concerning the publication and presentation of clinical material. *International Journal of Psychoanalysis, 81*: 1071–1086.
Gabbard, G. (2001). Psychoanalytically informed approaches to the treatment of obsessive–compulsive disorder. *Psychoanalytic Inquiry, 21*: 208–221.
Gibeault, A. (2004). Travailler avec les psychotiques: stratégie thérapeutique et tactique interprétative dans la psychose, 3ème Conférence Annuelle de la F.E.P., Helsinki, 15–18 avril.
Gill, M. (1982). *Analysis of Transference, Vol. 1*. New York: International Universities Press.
Gill, M. M., Newman, R., & Redlich, F. C. (1954). *The Initial Interview in Psychiatric Practice*. New York: International Universities Press.
Gu, M. D. (2006). The filial piety complex: variations on the Oedipus theme in Chinese literature and culture. *Psychoanalytic Quarterly, 75*: 163–195.
Hartmann, E. (1995). Making connections in a safe place: is dreaming psychotherapy? *Dreaming, 5*: 213–228.
Hartmann, E. (1998). *Dreams and Nightmares*. New York: Plenum.

Hau, S. (2004). Psychoanalytic dream theories: new developments and clinical implications. Paper presented at the 2004 China Annual Meeting for Psychoanalysis, Shanghai, 1–3 September.

Hau, S. (2009). *Unsichtbares sichtbar machen. Forschungsprobleme in der Psychoanalyse. 2. veränderte Auflage*. Göttingen: Vandenhoeck & Ruprecht.

Hau, T. F. (1968). Stationäre Psychotherapie: Ihre Indikation und ihre Anforderungen an die psychoanalytische Technik. *Zeitschrift für Psychosomatische Medizin und Psychoanalyse, 14*: 25–37.

Hauch, M. (1998). Paartherapie bei sexuellen Funktionsstörungen und so genannter sexueller Lustlosigkeit. In: B. Strauß & N. Becker (Eds.), *Psychotherapie der Sexualstörungen* (pp. 70–88). Stuttgart: Thieme.

Heigl-Evers, A., & Heigl, F. (1973). Gruppentherapie: interaktionell – tiefenpsychologisch fundiert – psychoanalytisch orientiert – psychoanalytisch. *Gruppenpsychotherapie und Gruppendynamik, 7*: 132–157.

Heimann, P. (1950). On counter-transference. *International Journal of Psycho-Analysis, 31*: 81–84.

Heinzmann, B. (2003). Psychotische Angst zwischen Auflösung und Abdichtung. In: *Verein für Psychoanalytische Sozialarbeit*. Rottenburg & Tübingen.

Henseler, H. (1975). Suizidhandlung und Narzißmustheorie. *Psyche, 3*: 191–207.

Hobson, A. (2009). REM sleep and dreaming: towards a theory of protoconsciousness. *Nature Reviews, 10*: 803–813.

Hobson, J., & McCarley, R. (1977). The brain as a dream-state generator. *American Journal of Psychiatry, 134*: 1335–1348.

Hoffmann, S. O., & Hochapfel, G. (1999). *Neurosenlehre, Psychotherapeutische und Psychosomatische Medizin* (6th edn). Stuttgart: Schattauer.

Hoffmann, S. O., & Hochapfel, G. (2004). *Neurotische Störungen und Psychosomatische Medizin* (7th edn). Stuttgart: Schattauer.

Holderegger, H. (2012). Trauma und Übertragung. *Psyche, 66*: 1102–1117.

Holt, R. (1989a). The development of the primary process: a structural view. In: R. Holt (Ed.), *Freud Reappraised. A Fresh Look at Psychoanalytic Theory* (pp. 253–279). New York: Guilford Press.

Holt, R. (1989b). The present status of Freud's theory of the primary process. In: R. Holt (Ed.), *Freud Reappraised. A Fresh Look at Psychoanalytic Theory* (pp. 280–301). New York: Guilford Press.

Horowitz, M. (1976). *Stress Response Syndromes*. New York: Jason Aronson.

Huang, Y., Kotov, R., de Girolamo, G., Preti, A., Angermeyer, M., Benjet, C., Demyttenaere, K., de Graaf, R., Gureje, O., Karam, A. N., Lee, S., Lepine, J. P., Matschinger, H., Posada-Villa, J., Suliman, S., Vilagut, G., & Kessler, R. C. (2009). DSM-IV personality disorders in the WHO World Mental Health Surveys. *British Journal of Psychiatry, 195*(1): 46–53.

International Classification of Diseases (*ICD-10*) (2010). Geneva: World Health Organization.

Jacobs, T. (1986). On countertransference enactments. *Journal of the American Psychoanalytic Association, 34*: 289–307.

Janssen, P. L. (1994). *Psychoanalytic Therapy in the Hospital Setting* (International Library of Group Psychotherapy and Group Process). London: Routledge.

Janssen, P. L. (1995). Erfahrungen mit analytischer Gruppenpsychotherapie bei strukturellen Ich-Störungen. *Jahrbuch der Gruppenanalyse, 1*: 150–170.

Janssen, P. L. (2004). Berufsgruppen- und methodenintegrierende Teamarbeit in der stationären psychodynamischen Psychotherapie. *Psychotherapeuten, 49*: 217–226.

Janssen, P. L., & Quint, H. (1977). Stationäre analytische Gruppenpsychotherapie im Rahmen einer neuropsychiatrischen Klinik. *Gruppenpsychotherapie und Gruppendynamik, 11*: 211–243.

Janssen, P. L., Franz, M., Herzog, T., Heuft, G., Paar, G., & Schneider, W. (1999). *Psychotherapeutische Medizin - Standortbestimmung in Differenzierung der Versorgung psychisch und psychosomatisch Kranker*. Stuttgart: Schattauer.

Janssen, P. L., Martin, K., Tress, W., & Zaudig, M. (1998). Struktur und Methodik der stationären Psychotherapie aus psychoanalytischer und verhaltenstherapeutischer Sicht. *Psychotherapeuten*, *43*: 265–276.

Joffe, W. G., & Sandler, J. (1968). Comments on the psychoanalytic psychology of adaptation, with special reference to the role of affects and the representational world. *International Journal of Psychoanalysis*, *49*: 445–454.

Johnson, B. (1993). *Three Perspectives on Addiction*. New York: Basic Books.

Josephs, L. (2006). The impulse to infidelity and oedipal splitting. *International Journal of Psycho-Analysis*, *87*: 423–437.

Keilson, H. (1979). *Sequentielle Traumatisierung*. Stuttgart: F. Enke

Kernberg, O. F. (1965). Notes on countertransference. *Journal of the American Psychoanalytic Association*, *13*: 38–56.

Kernberg, O. F. (1975). *Borderline Conditions and Pathological Narcissism*. New York: Jason Aronson.

Kernberg, O. F. (1981). Structural interviewing. *Psychiatric Clinics of North America*, *4*: 169–195.

Kernberg, O. F. (1995). *Object Relations Theory and Clinical Psychoanalysis*. New York: Jason Aronson.

Kernberg, O. F., & Caligor, E. (1996). A psychoanalytic theory of personality disorders. In: M. F. Lenzenweger & J. F. Clarkin (Eds.), *Major Thories of Personality Disorders* (pp. 114–156). New York: Guilford Press.

Khan, M. R. (1963). The concept of cumulative trauma. *Psychoanalytic Study of the Child*, *18*: 286–306.

Khantzian, E. J. (1997). The self-medication hypothesis of drug use disorders: a reconsideration and recent applications. *Harvard Review of Psychiatry*, *4*: 231–244.

Klüwer, R. (1983). Agieren und Mitagieren. *Psyche*, *37*: 828–840.

Kocher, K. (2011). Transgenerational aspects of trauma (unpublished manuscript).

Kohut, H. (1966). Forms and transformations of narcissism. *Journal of the American Psychoanalytic Association*, *14*: 243–272.

Kohut, H. (1971). *The Analysis of the Self. A Systematic Approach to the Psychoanalytic Treatment of Narcissistic Personality Disorder*. New York: International Universities Press.

Kohut, H. (1972). Thoughts on narcissism and narcissistic rage. *Psychoanalytic Study of the Child*, *27*: 360–400.

Körner, J. (2000). Regression–progression. In: W. Mertens & B. Waldvogel (Eds.), *Handbuch Psychoanalytischer Grundbegriffe* (pp. 603–609). Stuttgart: Kohlhammer.

Kramer, M. (1993). The selective mood regulatory function of dreaming: an update and revision. In: A. Moffit, M. Kramer, & R. Hoffman (Ed.), *The Functions of Dreaming* (pp. 139–164). Albany, NY: State University of New York Press.

Kramer, M. (2007). *The Dream Experience*. New York: Routledge.

Kris, E. (1934). Zur Psychologie der Karikatur. *Imago*, *20*: 450–466.

Krueger, D. (1997). Food as selfobject in eating disorder patients. *Psychoanalytic Review*, *84*(4): 617–624

Krystal, H., & Raskin, H. A. (1970). *Drug Dependence*. Detroit, MI: Wayne State University Press.

Lang, H. (1997). Obsessive–compulsive disorders in neurosis and psychosis. *Journal of the American Academy of Psychoanalysis*, *25*: 143–150.

Langs, R. (1976). *The Therapeutic Interaction, Vol. II*. New York: Jason Aronson.

Langs, R. (1999). *The Evolution of the Emotion-Processing Mind*. London: Karnac.

Laplanche, J. (1997). The theory of seduction and the problem of the other. *International Journal of Psychoanalysis*, *78*: 653–666.

Laplanche, J., & Pontalis, J.-B. (1973). *The Language of Psychoanalysis*. London: Hogarth.

Laub, D. (2000). Eros oder Thanatos? Der Kampf um die Erzählbarkeit des Traumas. *Psyche*, *54*: 860–894.

Laufer, M., & Laufer, M. E. (2002). *Adolescence and Developmental Breakdown: A Psychoanalytic View*. New Haven, CT: Yale University Press [reprinted London: Karnac, 1995].

Lax, R. F. (2003). Boy's envy of mother and the consequences of this narcissistic mortification. In: A. M. Alizade (Ed.), *Masculine Scenarios* (pp. 125–136). London: Karnac.

Lecours, S., & Bouchard, M. A. (1997). Dimensions of mentalization: outlining levels of psychic transformation. *International Journal of Psychoanalysis*, *78*: 855–875.

Lempa, G. (2001a). Der psychotische Konflikt. In: M. Wolf (Ed.), *Selbst, Objekt und der Grundkonflikt*. Frankfurt: Brandes & Apsel.

Lempa, G. (2001b). Einzeltherapie. Desymbolisierung, Versprachlichung – Modifikation der Behandlungstechnik auf Grund des schizophrenen Dilemmas. In: F. Schwarz & C. Maier (Eds.), *Psychotherapie der Psychosen* (pp. 11–48). Stuttgart: Thieme.

Lenzenweger, M. (2008). Epidemiology of personality disorders. *Psychiatric Clinics of North America*, *31*(3): 395–403.

Leshner, A. I. (2001). Addiction is a brain disease. Issues Online: www.issues.org/17.3/leshner.html

Leshner, A. I. (2007). The essence of drug addiction. www.nida.nih.gov/publishedarticles/essence.html

Levi, L., & Andersson, L. (1975). *Psychosocial Stress: Population, Environment, and Quality of Life*. New York: Halsted Press.

Lichtenberg, J. D. (1991a). Fear, phobia and panic. *Psychoanalytic Inquiry*, *11*: 395–415.

Lichtenberg, J. D. (1991b). *Psychoanalysis and Infant Research*. Hillsdale, NJ: Analytic Press.

Loch, W. (1999). *Die Krankheitslehre der Psychoanalyse*. Leipzig: S. Hirzel.

Lockwood, A. H., Salvi, R. J., & Burkard, R. F. (2002). Tinnitus. *New England Journal of Medicine*, *347*: 904–910.

Lown, B. (1996). *The Lost Art of Healing*. New York: Houghton Miffin.

Luborsky, L. & Crits-Christoph, P. (1998). *Understanding Transference: The Core Conflictual Relationship Theme Method*. Washington DC: APA Books.

Lürssen, E. (1976). Das Suchtproblem in neuerer psychoanalytischer Sicht. In: *Psychologie des 20. Jhdts., Bd II* (pp. 838 ff). Munich: Kindler.

Mahler, M. (1979). *Symbiose und Individuation*. Stuttgart: Klett-Cotta.

Mahler, M. S., Pine, F., & Bergman, A. (1975). *The Psychological Birth of the Human Infant*. New York: Basic Books.

Main, T. F. (1946). The hospital as a therapeutic institution. *Bulletin of the Menninger Clinic*, *10*: 66–70.

Marty, P., & de M'Uzan, M. (1957). Das operative Denken (pensée opératoire). *Psyche*, *32*: 974–984.

McGlashan, T. H., & Miller, G. H. (1982). The goals of psychoanalysis, psychoanalytic psychotherapy. *Archives of General Psychiatry*, *39*: 377–388.

Meltzer, D. (1984). *Dreamlife. A Re-examination of the Psycho-analytical Theory and Technique*. Strathtay, Perthshire: Clunie Press.

Mentzos, S. (1976). *Interpersonale und institutionalisierte Abwehr*. Frankfurt: Suhrkamp.

Mentzos, S. (1980). *Hysterie. Zur Psychodynamik unbewusster Inszenierungen*. Munich: Kindler.

Mentzos, S. (1982). *Neurotische Konfliktverarbeitung*. Munich: Kindler.

Mentzos, S. (Ed.) (1984). *Angstneurose. Psychodynamische und psychotherapeutische Aspekte*. Frankfurt: Fischer Taschenbuch.

Mentzos, S. (1995). *Depression und Manie. Psychodynamik und Therapie affektiver Störungen [Depression and Mania. Psychodyanmics and Psychotherapy of Affective Disorders*]. Goettingen: Vandenhoeck & Ruprecht.

Mentzos, S. (2001a). Psychodynamik im psychiatrischen Alltag. In: F. Schwarz & C. Maier (Eds.), *Psychotherapie der Psychosen* (pp. 212–223). Stuttgart: Thieme.

Mentzos, S. (2001b). Der bipolare Mensch und sein Dilemma. In: M. Wolf (Ed.), *Selbst, Objekt und der Grundkonflikt* (pp. 101–113). Frankfurt: Brandes & Apsel.

Mertens, W. (1981). *Psychoanalyse*. Stuttgart: W. Kohlhammer.

Mertens, W. (1992). *Einführung in die psychoanalytische Psychotherapie, Bd. 1*. Stuttgart: Kohlhammer.

Meyer, C., Rumpf, H.-J., Hapke, U., Dilling, H., & John, U. (2000). Lebenszeitprävalenz psychischer Störungen in der erwachsenen Allgemeinbevölkerung. *Der Nervenarzt, 71*: 535–542.

Meyer, O. (2005). *Leib-Seele-Problem und Medizin*. Würzburg: Königshausen und Neumann.

Milton, J., Polmear, C., & Fabricius, J. (2004). *A Short Introduction to Psychoanalysis*. London: Sage.

Mitscherlich, A. (1974). *Krankheit als Konflikt. Studien zur psychosomatischen Medizin*, Bd. 1 und 2. Frankfurt: Suhrkamp.

Müller-Pozzi, H. (1991). *Psychoanalytisches Denken*. Bern: Huber.

Myqel, M. (2005). Regression. In: A. de Mijolla (Ed.), *International Dictionary of Psychoanalysis* (pp. 1459–1460). Farmington Hills, MI: Thomson Gale.

Oevermann, U. (1996). Theoretische Skizze einer revidierten Theorie professionalisierten Handelns. In: A. W. Combe & W. Helsper (Eds.), *Pädagogische Professionalität*. Frankfurt: Suhrkamp.

Ogden, T. H. (2004). *The Primitive Edge of Experience*. Lanham, MD: Jason Aronson.

Ogden, T. H. (2005). *This Art of Psychoanalysis: Dreaming Undreamt Dreams and Interrupted Cries*. London: Routledge.

Operationalized Psychodynamic Diagnosis (*OPD*) (2008). *OPD-2: Manual of Diagnosis and Treatment Planning*. Göttingen www.opd-online.net 2011.

Oppenheim, H. (1889). *Die traumatischen Neurosen*. Berlin: A. Hirschwald.

Peciccia, M., & Benedetti, G. (1997). The integration of the separate and symbiotic states of the self in the psychotherapy of schizophrenia. 12th International Symposium for the Psychotherapy of Schizophrenia, International Conference, London.

Piaget, J. (1952). *The Origins of Intelligence in Children*. New York: International University Press.

Pine, F. (1988). The four psychologies of psychoanalysis and their place in clinical work. *Journal of the American Psychoanalytic Association, 36*: 571–596.

Pollak, T. (2006). The setting: an essential of clinical psychoanalysis? On the history and topicality of a concept. Lecture given in October 2006 at Shanghai Mental Health Center, German–Chinese Training Course on Psychodynamic Psychotherapy.

Pollak, T. (2008). Träume in der klinischen Arbeit- ein Werkstattbericht, M. Walker (Trans.). *Texte, 2*: 22–35.

Putzke, M. (2004). Angst und Psychose: Psychoanalyse im psychiatrischen Alltag. In: A. U. Dreher, M. Juszczak, & M. Schmidt (Eds.), Theorie und Klinik der Angst, Arbeitstagung der Deutschen Psychoanalytischen Vereinigung in Bad Homburg, 17–20 November 2004.

Racamier, P. C. (1982). *Die Schizophrenen*. Berlin: Springer.

Racamier, P. C. (1995). *Le génie des origines: psychanalyse et psychoses*. Paris: Payot.

Rado, S. (1926). The psychic effects of intoxicants. *International Journal of Psychoanalysis, 7*: 396–413.

Rado, S. (1934). Psychoanalyse der Pharmakothymie. *Int. Z .Psa., 20*: 16–32

Rado, S. (1959). Obsessive behavior (so-called obsessive–compulsive neurosis). In: S. Arieti (Ed.), *American Handbook of Psychiatry, Vol. I*. New York: Basic Books.

Reich, A. (1960). Pathologic forms of self-esteem regulation. *Psychoanalytic Study of the Child, 15*: 215–232.

Reik, T. (1949). *The Inner Experience of a Psychoanalyst*. London: Allen and Unwin.

Reinecker, H. (2007). Zwangserkrankungen im verhaltenstherapeutischen Kontext. In: W. Senf & M. Broda (Eds.), *Praxis der Psychotherapie* (4th edn) (pp. 412–426). Stuttgart: Georg Thieme.

Ricaud, M. M. (2005). Benign/malignant regression. In: A. de Mijolla (Ed.), *International Dictionary of Psychoanalysis, Vol. 1*. Farmington Hills, MI: Thomson Gale.

Rice, A. K. (1969). Individual, group and inter-group processes. *Human Relations, 22*: 565–584.

Robert Koch Institut (2012). Studie zur Gesundheit Erwachsener in Deutschland (DEGS). Accessed on 29 August 2012 at: www.rki.de/DE/Content/Gesundheitsmonitoring/Studien/Degs/degs_w1/Symposium/degs_uebergewicht_adipositas.html

Robertson, J. (1976). Young children in brief separation, series of five. London: Robertson Centre and Ipswich, Concord Films Council

Robertson, J., & Bowlby, J. (1989). *Separation and the Very Young*. London: Free Association Books.

Rosen, J. N. (1962). *Direct Psychoanalytic Psychiatry*. London: Grune & Stratton.

Roth, G. (2001). *Denken, Fühlen, Handeln. Wie das Gehirn unser Verhalten steuert*. Frankfurt: Suhrkamp.

Rübenach, S. P. (2007). *Todesursache Suizid*. Statistisches Bundesamt. Wirtschaft und Statistik. Wiesbaden: Destatis.

Rupprecht-Schampera, U. (1995). The concept of early triangulation as a key to a unified model of hysteria. *International Journal of Psychoanalysis, 76*: 457–473.

Sandler, J. (1960). The background of safety. *International Journal of Psychoanalysis, 41*: 352–356.

Sandler, J. (1976). Countertransference and role-responsiveness. *International Review of Psycho-Analysis, 3*: 43–47.

Sandler, J., & Sandler, A.-M. (1993). Regression und Antiregression. *Forum der Psychoanalyse, 9*: 283–292.

Sandler, J., Dare, C., & Holder, A. (2004). *The Patient and the Analyst*. London: Karnac.

Schultz, H. (2008). On premature termination (drop out, forced termination). Chinese–Norway Training Program for Psychodynamic Psychotherapy Seminar in Beijing, June, 2008.

Schur, M. (1955). Comments on the metapsychology of somatization. *Psychoanalytic Study of the Child, 10*: 119–164.

Searles, H. F. (1976). Psychoanalytic therapy with schizophrenic patients in a private-practice context. *Contemporary Psychoanalysis, 12*: 387–406.

Sechehaye, M. (1955). *Die symbolische Wunscherfüllung. Darstellung einer neuen psychotherapeutischen Methode und Tagebuch der Kranken*. Huber: Bern.

Seiffge-Krenke, I. (1994). *Gesundheitspsychologie des Jugendalters*. Göttingen: Hogrefe.

Selye, H. (1950). *The Physiology and Pathology of Exposure of Stress*. Montreal: Acta, Inc. Medical Publishers.

Selye, H. (1974). *Streß*. Munich: Piper.

Senf, W., & Broda, M. (2005). *Praxis der Psychotherapie*. Stuttgart: Thieme.

Siegel, J. M. (2005). Functional implications of sleep development. *PLoS Biol., 3*(5): e178.

Solms, M. (2000). *Clinical Studies in Neuro-psychoanalysis – Introduction to a Depth Neuropsychology*. London: Karnac.

Spitz, R. (1965). *The First Year of Life*. New York: International Universities Press.

Spurling, S. L. (2008). Is there still a place for the concept of 'therapeutic regression' in psychoanalysis? *International Journal of Psychoanalysis, 89*(3): 523–540.
Statistical Yearbook of the Federal Republic of Germany (2006). Wiesbaden: Destatis.
Statistical Yearbook of the Federal Republic of Germany (2011). Wiesbaden: Destatis.
Steiner, J. (1998). *Psychic Retreats*. London: Routledge.
Sterba, R. (1934). The fate of the ego in analytic therapy. *International Journal of Psycho-Analysis, 15*: 117–126.
Stolorow, R. D., Brandchaft, B., & Atwood, G. E. (1987). *Psychoanalytic Treatment. An Intersubjective Approach*. Hillsdale, NJ: Analytic Press.
Strauch, I., & Meier, B. (1996). *In Search of Dreams. Results of Experimental Dream Research*. New York: State University of New York Press.
Strauß, B., & Becker, N. (1998). *Psychotherapie der Sexualstörungen*. Stuttgart: Thieme.
Sullivan, H. S. (1956). *Clinical Studies in Psychiatry*. New York: W. W. Norton.
Thomä, H., & Kächele, H. (1987). *Psychoanalytic Practice 1: Principles*. New York: Springer.
Thomä, H., & Kächele, H. (1992). *Psychoanalytic Practice 2: Clinical Studies*. New York: Springer.
Ticho, E. A. (1972). Termination of psychoanalysis: treatment goals, life goals. *Psychoanalytic Quarterly, 41*: 315–333.
Ursano, R. J., Sonnenberg, S. M., & Lazar, S. G. (1998). *Concise Guide to Psychodynamic Psychotherapy* (2nd edn). Washington DC: American Psychiatric Press.
Vaillant, G. (1971). Theoretical hierarchy of adaptive ego mechanisms. *Archives of General Psychiatry, 25*: 107–111.
Vaillant, G. (1995). *Adaptation to Life*. Cambridge, MA: Harvard University Press.
Volkan, V. D. (1988). *The Need to Have Enemies and Allies*. Northvale, NJ/London: Jason Aronson.
Volkan, V. D. (1995). *The Infantile Self and its Fates: Understanding and Treating Schizophrenics and Other Difficult Patients*. London: Jason Aronson.
Von Uexküll, T. (Ed.) (2003). *Psychosomatische Medizin* (6th edn). Munich: Urban & Fischer.
Weiss, J., & Sampson, H. (1984). *The Psychotherapeutic Process*. New York: Guilford Press.
Will, H., Grabenstedt, Y., & Völkl, G. (2000). *Depression: Psychodynamik und Therapie* (2nd edn). Goettingen: Vandenhoeck & Ruprecht.
Willi, J. (1975). *Die Zweierbeziehung. Spannungsursachen – Störungsmuster – Klärungsprozesse – Lösungsmodelle*. Rowohlt: Reinbek bei Hamburg.
Winnicott, D. W. (1965). *The Maturational Processes and the Facilitating Environment: Studies in the Theory of Emotional Development*. New York: International Universities Press.
Winnicott, D. W. (1971). *Playing and Reality*. London: Tavistock.
World Health Organization (WHO) (1999). *Figures and Facts About Suicide*. WHO/MNH/MBD/99.1, Geneva.
World Health Organization (WHO) (2004). Global database on body mass index. Accessed on 26 August 2012 at: http://apps.who.int/bmi/index.jsp
World Health Organization (WHO) (2012). Dependence syndrome. Accessed on 20 August 2012 at: www.who.int/substance_abuse/terminology/definition1/en/
Wurmser, L. (1978). *The Hidden Dimension: Psychodynamics in Compulsive Drug Abuse*. New York: Jason Aronson.
Zubin, J., & Spring, B. (1977). Vulnerability – a new view of schizophrenia. *Journal of Abnormal Psychology, 86*(2): 103–124.

INDEX

For Product Safety Concerns and Information please contact our EU representative GPSR@taylorandfrancis.com
Taylor & Francis Verlag GmbH, Kaufingerstraße 24, 80331 München, Germany

www.ingramcontent.com/pod-product-compliance
Ingram Content Group UK Ltd.
Pitfield, Milton Keynes, MK11 3LW, UK
UKHW050800180926
475701UK00008B/1157
9781780491196